THE PROPHECIES OF
NOSTRADAMUS

and the WORLD'S GREATEST
SEERS and MYSTICS

THE PROPHECIES OF
NOSTRADAMUS

and the WORLD'S GREATEST SEERS and MYSTICS

Prophecies and predictions for the millennium and beyond

FRANCIS KING *and* STEPHEN SKINNER

CARLTON
BOOKS

THIS IS A CARLTON BOOK

This edition published by Carlton Books Limited 2000
20 Mortimer Street
London
W1N 7RD

ISBN 1 85868 545 4

Printed in Great Britain

CONTENTS

INTRODUCTION

We live in a world of high technology, a world in which our everyday realities – from television to transplant surgery and space travel – are what were a century or less ago merely the fantasies of such imaginative writers as Jules Verne and H.G. Wells.

Yet we also live in a pervading atmosphere of mystery and magic, for today many men and women consult professional clairvoyants, astrologers and tarot-card readers in an attempt to find guidance about their emotional lives, financial affairs and the future destiny of humanity as a whole.

The methods adopted by those who interest themselves in the latter are many and various. They range from consulting that ancient Chinese oracle book the *I Ching* (Book of Changes) to attempting to attain an altered state of consciousness in which the spirit is liberated from the body and is free to roam throughout all time and space.

None of these techniques is new. One of the most popular of them has been practised, with varying degrees of success, since the middle of the 16th century: the interpretation of the predictive four-line verses (quatrains) composed over 400 years ago by the French prophet Nostradamus – the one seer and astrologer of whom almost everyone has heard. The quatrains, collectively entitled the *Centuries*, were written in a largely coded terminology, the full understanding of which requires much time and effort. Are those who engage in it and similar pursuits no more than the human relics of a superstitious past, their beliefs outmoded by the development of modern science and technology, their activities utterly futile? Or is it genuinely possible to see the pattern of the future, and did Nostradamus in reality travel through time and discern events that still lie before us?

A recent example of an ancient divinatory art successfully predicting future events is illustrated by the gyrations of prices in 1992 on the high-tech Hong-Kong Stock Exchange and their link with the 'Wind and Water (Feng Shui) Index'.

This Index was compiled in the early part of 1992 by Credit Lyonnais Securities (Asia), on the basis of consultations with three adepts of the ancient Chinese predictive art known as Feng Shui. It successfully forecast the large price rise of March to May 1992, the Hong Kong market's peak in November, and its heavy fall to its low point for the year in early December. However, Credit Lyonnais Securities (Asia) advised its clients on the basis of more orthodox forecasting than that derived from Feng Shui and, while such advice was as excellent as always, it was not nearly as good as that given by the Feng Shui adepts. Maybe ancient arts are not as outmoded by modern technology as some think.

RENAISSANCE TRAVELLER IN TIME

There are and always have been a multitude of alleged prophecies which indicate that the immediate future is likely to be grim. Few are worth taking seriously – but those of Nostradamus are truly impressive.

It is prophesied that in the seventh month (July) of 1999, or perhaps in early August, just after the end of that seventh month, the 'King of Terror' will descend upon the Earth.

Who – or what – is the King of Terror? Almost certainly an individual who will unleash nuclear war upon our planet or, perhaps, an exceptionally large and destructive fusion bomb.

Before and after the coming of the King of Terror 'Mars rules happily' – but not happily for humanity. As Mars is both the name of the Roman god of war and the planet that, in ancient astrological tradition, is the ruler of battle, slaughter and human rage, this phrase means only one thing: that in the months or years before and after the descent of the King of Terror the world will be ravaged by conflict of a previously unknown ferocity.

At the time of the Olympic Games of 2008 a world leader who will be the head of a sinister necromantic cult and may well be the 'King of Terror' will carry out an action of major importance connected with 'setting the East aflame'.

These are not the only events that threaten us in the years that are now imminent. The Four Horsemen of the Apocalypse – plague, famine, war and death – are destined to ride the winds, spreading bloodshed and misery amongst us.

However, not all that lies ahead of us is as gloomy as this; beyond the dark ravine of history through which the human race is destined to travel lie sunlit uplands upon which men and women shall stand, their heads amidst the stars.

All these predictions are derived from the works of the French writer Nostradamus (1503-66), a man often referred to as 'the Seer of Salon' – Salon being the place where he finally settled down after a wandering life during which he had acquired much strange knowledge.

What sort of man was Nostradamus? What is known of the adventures he underwent during his wanderings? And, most importantly, does he have a record of fulfilled prophecy that might induce us to take seriously his predictions for the future of the human race? The first section of this book attempts to answer these questions.

MAGICIAN, SEER OR CHARLATAN?

Nostradamus was born in the Provençal city of St Rémy on 14 December 1503 to a family of Jewish origin, albeit Catholic converts. According to one tradition his father's ancestors were eminent physicians, renowned for their learning, although there is hard evidence that many of the seer's direct forebears were Jewish traders in the papal enclave of Avignon. This fact does not entirely disprove the tradition, however, for there were plenty of quite humble Jewish trading families in 16th-century Europe who were collaterally or directly descended from learned rabbis, physicians and philosophers and the family of the prophet may have been one of these.

What is certain is that whatever his ancestry may have been, Nostradamus was an intelligent child who by the time he had reached puberty had mastered the rudiments of Greek, Latin and mathematics and had been sent away to study in Avignon.

In 1522, when he was 18 years old, Nostradamus left Avignon and was sent to Montpellier to study medicine. After three years, at the age of only 21, he received a licence to practise the healing art and for some years was a wanderer, specializing in the treatment of what was termed le charbon, a disease which was probably a variant of either bubonic or pneumonic plague.

He would seem to have been much more successful in treating victims of le charbon than most of his medical contemporaries. This was probably not because of any great virtue in the remedies he used in therapy, the formulae of some of which have survived. One of them, for instance, was compounded of rose petals, cloves, lignum aloes and the dried and powdered roots of iris and sweet flag. It could not have harmed his patients but it is unlikely that it did them any good; he more probably owed his success to the fact that he was opposed to the use of most of the violent treatments then in vogue – bloodletting and the use of violent purgatives, for instance – all of which tended to reduce rather than increase the patient's chances of survival.

It was almost certainly during his years as a wandering physician that Nostradamus began to acquire a knowledge of some of the ancient techniques of prediction that he was later to use in order to tear aside the veils of time and look into the future. However, there is no need to assume, as some have done, that because of his abilities as a prophet Nostradamus was years ahead of his time as a medical practitioner. As far as one can tell, most of the mixtures he prescribed for his patients were quite as odd as any of the remedies commonly practised at the time.

Take, for example, the ointment with which he claimed to have cured the Bishop of Carcassonne of a number of maladies. Its ingredients included powdered coral, lapis lazuli and gold beaten to sheets of such thinness that they were translucent; it could have done no great harm but it is difficult to believe that such a mixture did, as Nostradamus subsequently claimed, 'rejuvenate the person ... preserve from headaches and constipation ... and will augment the sperm in such abundance that a man can do as he will without damaging his health.' There was a distinct element of charlatanry in this claim but, as will be shown in this book, while Nostradamus may sometimes have aped the charlatan he was also an authentic prophet and a practising magician.

NOSTRADAMUS AND THE VIRGIN

After his death, Nostradamus seems to have acquired a reputation as a man who had a sense of humour as well as the ability to perceive what was happening in places separated from him in time and space. Within just a few years of his death, for instance, it was asserted that one day he saw a demure young girl walking towards a locality where the adolescents of Salon were accustomed to meet one another. 'Bonjour pucelle (Good morning, maiden),' said the seer; 'Bonjour, Monsieur Nostredame,' replied the girl with a polite curtsey.

An hour later he encountered her once more, still looking as demure as ever. She curtseyed again and repeated: 'Bonjour, Monsieur Nostredame' – to which the seer responded with a smile and the words 'Bonjour petite femme (Good morning, grown up little woman).'

This and similar stories can safely be dismissed as fiction, but their very existence is an indication of the prophet's reputation for being a man capable of freeing himself from the bonds of everyday existence and discerning the hidden realities that lurk beneath outward appearances. This reputation would appear to have been well justified for, as will be demonstrated on numerous subsequent pages, many of his predictions – some of them including both names and implied or actual dates for specific events – have been fulfilled to the very letter.

NOSTRADAMUS
THE ASTROLOGER

For a time Nostradamus abandoned his wandering life, married and settled down in the town of Agen, but he soon began to encounter both ill fortune and personal tragedies. His wife and two children died of plague, his dead wife's family sued him for the return of her dowry and, worst of all, in 1538 he fell under suspicion of heresy because of an observation he had made to someone engaged in casting a bronze image of the Blessed Virgin Mary. He had remarked that the man was 'casting the statue of a devil' – an unfortunate statement, but one which, he insisted, was only intended as a judgement on the artistic merit of the work.

These events led to Nostradamus resuming the life of a wandering physician. Little definite is known of his activities over the next few years until 1544, by which date he was in Marseilles, although there is some evidence that he had previously travelled in Lombardy, in the territories under Venetian rule, and in Sicily.

In 1546 he was invited to Aix, where the plague had broken out in such a virulent form that, so it was said, women attacked by the first symptoms of the disease sewed themselves into shrouds so that their naked corpses would not be on public view when they were carted through the city on their way to the communal burial pits. It would seem that a surprisingly high proportion of Nostradamus's patients recovered and that the grateful citizens of Aix voted him a pension. Nevertheless, he soon moved to Salon de Craux – hence the frequent literary references to him as 'the seer of Salon' – where he married a second wife who bore him a number of children.

Soon after his move to Salon he was summoned to Lyons to help treat the victims of what has been described as an outbreak of a particularly virulent form of whooping cough but was more likely to have been an epidemic of bubonic plague. For some reason his good reputation as a physician declined amongst the citizens of Salon during his absence and it was this, according to one 19th-century source, that induced him to commence a serious study of astrology and other of the occult sciences.

I am somewhat sceptical of this claim, and, as will be made clear in later pages of this book, think that it is likely that Nostradamus's concern with matters esoteric commenced at a much earlier period of his life. In relation to this it is interesting to note that Théophile de Garencières, a 17th-century student of the life and prophecies of Nostradamus, asserted that the seer took up the serious study of astrology because he was convinced that a truly competent physician had need of some knowledge of it – in which case his practical acquaintance with ancient predictive and other occult techniques may have begun when he was not much more than 18 years old.

Whatever the truth of the matter may have been, it is certain that from 1550 Nostradamus was issuing annual almanacs containing a considerable amount of astrological material and that these enjoyed a surprisingly wide circulation; one of them seems to have been published in English translation as the Almanacke For 1559 almost as soon as its French original.

In 1555 Nostradamus published the first edition of the Centuries, which contained less than 400 quatrains. It attracted wide attention, though some thought its author must be either an impostor or a madman. However, it really made its mark four years later with what was widely regarded as an accurate prediction of the accidental death of King Henri II of France – an event that took place in the summer of 1559.

From that time onward the seer's reputation as a true prophet steadily grew, and by 1566, when he died (probably of kidney failure resulting from a diseased heart), his fame fully justified the inscription carved upon his memorial:

Here lie the bones of the illustrious Michael Nostradamus, whose near divine
pen was alone, in the judgement of all mortals, worthy to record under the
inspiration of the stars, the future events of the whole world ...
Posterity, invade not his rest ...

Nostradamus certainly did practise astrology and his memorialist claimed that he recorded the future 'under the inspiration of the stars'. However, there is no doubt at all that most of the predictions made in the Centuries – both those that have already been fulfilled and those that appear to prophesy a bloody age of force and fire which is close upon us – were arrived at by methods other than astrology. More is said of these powerful (and perhaps perilous) techniques later in this book.

FULFILLED PREDICTIONS

The forty-second quatrain of Nostradamus's Century I is of major importance in relation to the nature of the methods used by the seer in order to look down the long vistas of time. In that context its content is examined in more detail later.

One line of the same quatrain is significant in quite another way: it is evidence that Nostradamus knew of coming events long before they happened. In translation, this line reads, 'The tenth day of the Gothic Calends of April'.

This dating seems simple enough – yet it demonstrates beyond any doubt that the seer was aware of a coming reform of the Christian calendar which did not even begin until 16 years after his death and is still not quite completed.

Nostradamus's use of the word 'Calends' was derived from antiquity. In the

Roman calendar the 'Calends of April' was the first of April, 'Calends' simply meaning the first day of any month. So by the phrase 'the tenth day of the ... Calends of April' Nostradamus meant 10 April, but by qualifying the words with the adjective 'Gothic' he was stating that the date he had in mind was one which 'Goths' called the tenth day of April but was not the true 10 April.

But whom did Nostradamus mean to indicate by his reference to 'Goths', and what was so peculiar about their calendar that they got the days of the month wrong?

What seems certain to be the right answer to this question was given more than 300 years ago by Théophile de Garencières in The True Prophecies or Prognostications of Michel Nostradamus (1672). De Garencières pointed out that the Julian calendar, which was in general use throughout Christendom during the lifetime of Nostradamus, ran slightly fast – it contained the occasional leap year too many. Over the centuries the cumulative error had steadily grown until by the 16th century the calendar that was used by all Christians was 10 days behind the true, solar calendar. For instance, what the Julian calendar called midsummer day (i.e. the longest day of the year) was actually 10 days after what was in reality the longest day.

In 1582, Pope Gregory XIII reformed the calendar by the simple expedient of adding 10 days to the nominal date and arranging that in future an occasional leap year should be omitted. The reform was quickly adopted by the Catholic states of Europe, but the largely Protestant peoples of northern Europe, the 'Goths', meaning non-Latins, retained the old and incorrect Julian calendar until much later. Indeed, at the time that de Garencières published his book England had not yet accepted the Gregorian calendar, which the English seem to have thought of as an unpleasant Papistical innovation, and was not to do so until 80 years later.

The 'Goths' who ruled Czarist Russia (in the 16th century the word Goth was often used as a term for any Christian barbarian) were even more conservative than the English, and Russia did not abandon the Julian calendar until after the 1917 revolution. (The Orthodox and monophysite churches of the world still cling to the inaccurate Julian calendar, which the passage of time has now made no less than 13 days slow.)

A lucky guess on Nostradamus's part? Perhaps. After all, the quatrain contained no names (such as that of Pope Gregory) relevant to the reform nor any indication of the date at which it might begin to be put into action. In any case, at the time when Nostradamus penned his prediction, suggestions for the reform of the Julian calendar had been around for some time and some of the seer's fellow-seekers after hidden knowledge (such as England's John Dee) were keen supporters of the idea.

Yet no hypotheses concerning chance or lucky guesses would seem to explain other of the predictive hits to be found in quatrains of the Centuries, such as those which do contain specific names – sometimes in anagrammatic or slightly distorted form – or dates. Take, for instance, the sixteenth quatrain of Century IX, which reads:

> *From Castel* [i.e. Castille, Spain] *Franco will bring out the Assembly,*
> *The Ambassadors will not agree and cause splitting,*
> *The people of Ribiere will be in the crowd,*
> *And the great man will be denied entry to the Gulf.*

This quatrain contains references to two names, Franco and Ribiere, which are relevant to its content. It seems to refer to the diplomatic differences which arose in 1940 between Adolf Hitler and the Spanish dictator, General Franco, and denied 'the great man', Hitler, entry to the Gulf – in this context, control of the Straits of Gibraltar.

What of the mysterious person whom Nostradamus referred to as 'Ribiere'? He cannot be identified with complete certainty, but his name bears a resemblance to that of the murdered founder of Spanish fascism, Jose Primo de Rivera – whose 'people', leading officials of the Falange Party, were certainly 'amongst the crowd' at the time of the unsuccessful negotiations held between Hitler and Franco.

These are only two of the fulfilled predictions to be found in the Centuries. In the pages which follow readers will learn of many others.

DEATH OF THE LION

While the first edition of the Centuries attracted widespread attention, some readers of it considered its contents to indicate that its author was quite mad. Still others believed him to be nothing but a prophetic charlatan – that is to say, someone who wrote allegedly predictive verses that were in reality no more than obscure and almost meaningless nonsense.

In the summer of 1559 at least some of these sceptics changed their minds and concluded that the man they had denounced as either a fraud or a lunatic was truly possessed of authentic prophetic gifts. This reversal of belief was a direct consequence of the accidental death of King Henri II of France as the result of an injury received in a joust.

The fatal accident occurred when the 40-year-old King, who sometimes used a lion as his personal emblem (although for him to do so was not in accordance with the laws of heraldry) was taking part in a three-day tournament which was being held in honour of the joint betrothals of his sister Elizabeth and his daughter Marguerite to, respectively, Philip II of Spain and the Duke of Savoy.

On the third day of the tourney the King jousted with the 33-year-old commander of his Scottish guards, a man known as Coryes, or, more commonly, Montgomery. Although the commander bore a Norman name and seems to have been born in France, his ancestors were reputed to have been natives of Scotland, a country of which the heraldic symbol was (and still is) a lion rampant. Montgomery's lance splintered: one portion inflicted a slight wound in the King's throat, while the main part of the head of the lance slipped through the gilded bars of the cage-like visor that covered the King's face and entered one of his eyes. The unhappy monarch's eye festered and, in addition, at least part of his opponent's lance seems to have penetrated his brain. After 10 days of the most excruciating suffering, the King's agonized screams were ended by a merciful death.

It was almost immediately pointed out that the event seemed to have been predicted by Nostradamus in Century I Quatrain 35, which had been published some four years earlier but at the time of its publication had appeared to be meaningless. It reads:

> *The young Lion shall overcome the old*
> *On a warlike field in single combat,*
> *He will pierce his eyes in a cage of gold,*
> *One of two breakings, then he shall die a cruel death.*

The quatrain was widely regarded as being astonishingly apposite to the circumstances of the King's terrible end. The 'young Lion' was obviously Montgomery, the commander of the Scottish guards. The 'old Lion' who was defeated by him 'on a warlike field in single combat' (that is, a joust at a tournament) was, equally obviously, King Henri II, whose eye was pierced even though it was protected by a 'cage of gold' – his gilded visor – and who did indeed 'die a cruel death' as the consequence of 'one of two breakings' of his opponent's lance.

A PREDICTIVE JOKE

The immediate results of Nostradamus's successful prediction of the death of Henri II included his appointment as one of the physicians-in-ordinary to King Charles IX of France and an increase in his reputation as a seer among the nobility, many of whom consulted him in relation to both their physical health and their personal affairs. This reputation was to prove an abiding and increasing one, both during and after the seer's death, not only among the nobility but also among peasants, tradesmen and even, it would seem, treasure-hunters and tomb-robbers.

It may have been the case that Nostradamus even predicted his posthumous fame, for, according to a story first printed in the early 18th century, he engaged in a practical joke that would not be fully effective until he had been long dead and tales had begun to be spread concerning manuscripts or treasures allegedly interred within his tomb.

Tales such as this were very common in relation to the graves of holy men, seers and wizards and they were widely circulated regarding the sepulchre of Nostradamus by, at the latest, the 1690s. So strong was the belief in these legends that in 1700 the grave was opened by a gang of daring tomb-robbers.

The robbers found neither treasure nor documents containing hitherto unknown Nostradamian revelations – but the tomb contained, as well as the bones of the seer, a thin, gilded medallion. On it were the letters MDCC – the Latin equivalent of 1700, the year in which the thieves committed their act of sacrilege. Nostradamus seems to have had a sense of humour!

THE SERPENT AND HER BROOD

After the death of Henri II, Francis II, one of Henri's seven children by Catherine de' Medici, succeeded to the throne.

Catherine was a cultured and intelligent woman but one who seems to have had no real principles, her only true desire being to maintain the power of her children and, more especially, herself. In pursuit of these ends she was both ruthless and treacherous, displaying all the merciless cunning that is traditionally attributed (although most unfairly) to snakes.

Oddly enough – and with exquisite suitability – after the death of her husband she changed her heraldic emblem to a serpent with its tail in its mouth. Nostradamus predicted this in the first two lines of Century I Quatrain 19, which read:

> *When the snakes encircle the altar,*
> *And the Trojan blood is troubled …*

The second line offers a good example of how Nostradamus often saw fit to convey his meanings by obscure allusions rather than direct statements. Here and elsewhere in the Centuries he used the phrase 'Trojan blood' as a coded term for the French royal family, alluding to a medieval legend that the family were descendants of a mythical Francus, supposedly a son of Priam of Troy.

The period of 30 years or so during which the doings of the serpent and her brood – Catherine de' Medici and her children – were of major importance in French history seems to have been the focus of many of Nostradamus's visions. Except for the period of the French Revolution and the First Empire which was its culmination, no other epoch had so many quatrains devoted to it by the seer. This may have been because he was fascinated by the character of Catherine de' Medici, to whom he made factual but prejudiced references in more than one of his verses – for instance, in Century VI Quatrain 63, which reads:

The great lady left alone in the Kingdom,
Her only [husband] first dead on the bed of honour:
For seven years she will be crying with grief,
Then a long life for the happiness of the Kingdom.

Catherine did indeed never remarry after the death of Henri II, and, as the seer predicted, she formally mourned his passing for a full seven years, subsequently living a long life. However, few historians would share the opinion of Nostradamus that the rest of her life was devoted to the pursuit of 'the happiness of the Kingdom'. It would seem that either the seer was extremely partisan in his views or, more probably, that as the quatrain was obviously applicable to Catherine, and was published during the lifetimes of both its subject and its author, he considered it more politic to present her motives in a flattering, if inaccurate, light.

Francis II, the eldest of Catherine's five sons and the first husband of Mary Queen of Scots remained on the throne for only two years, and there are only two references – one of them notably vague – in the Centuries which have been applied directly to him. Although he was officially held to have reached his majority he was considered too young to govern and for his brief reign the real rulers of France were Mary's uncles, the Guise brothers. An elaborate plot known as the conspiracy of Amboise, which was largely Protestant in its instigation, was hatched against the influence of the brothers, but it miscarried and was vigorously suppressed – as may have been predicted by Nostradamus in Century I Quatrain 13, in which he wrote in very general terms of a conspiracy involving (Protestant) exiles who were consumed by anger and 'gut hatred'.

The death of Francis II in 1560 seemed to offer no threat to the continuation of the Valois dynasty as the kings of France, for although his two sisters were barred by the sixth-century Salic law from inheriting the throne he had four younger brothers. However, Nostradamus knew that all were fated to die without legitimate issue. This he made clear in Century I Quatrain 10, which reads:

A coffin is put into the iron vault
Which holds the seven children of the King,
Their forefathers will emerge from the depths of hell,
Lamenting the death of the fruit of their line.

In spite of the gnomic terminology in which Nostradamus couched this quatrain (as so many other of his verses) there seems no doubt that it was prophetic of both the end of the Valois dynasty and one specific event that took place in 1610 – the removal of the body of the last Valois monarch (Henri III, d. 1589) from its temporary resting place to the family mausoleum at Saint Denis.

Francis II was succeeded to the throne of France by his younger brother, Charles IX, who reigned 1560-74. However, much of the real power was wielded by his mother, the serpent-queen Catherine de' Medici, who seems to have been the instigator of certain excesses which took place during his reign. More than one of these was predicted by Nostradamus.

ALL HER LINE WILL DIE

According to common report, Catherine de' Medici, although largely without any genuine religious feelings, was deeply concerned with the impact of the supernatural upon the lives of herself and her family, and as time went on her interest in the uncanny became more and more noticeable. While this shocked some of her subjects it was hardly surprising for, one by one, she saw the fulfilment of predictions Nostradamus had made which were of direct personal relevance – for example, Century VI Quatrain 11, which reads:

The seven branches will be reduced to three,
The older ones will be surprised [i.e. taken unawares] *by death,*
The two will be seduced towards fratricide,
The conspirators will die while asleep.

By December 1588 those who were familiar with this quatrain looked upon it as an accurate prediction – yet another piece of evidence that Nostradamus had truly seen into the future. For 'the seven branches' of line one were the seven children of Catherine, of whom only three – Henri III, François and Marguerite – were left alive by the beginning of 1576. There was fratricidal strife between the two brothers, with François, who hoped to put himself on the throne, allying himself with the Guise brothers and conspiring with them against the King.

The conspirators – the two Guise brothers – did indeed die, murdered at the King's orders, albeit not 'while asleep' as foretold in the quatrain's last line. There can be little doubt, however, that it was indeed the death of these two to which the seer was referring, for he made a fairly detailed prediction of the murders and their circumstances in Century III Quatrain 51, which reads:

Paris conspires [literally, 'swears together'] *to commit great murder,*
Blois will ensure that it is carried out,
The people of Orléans will want to replace their leader,
Angers, Troyes and Langres will do them a disservice.

The murders of the Duc de Guise and his brother Louis, the Cardinal of Guise, had been planned in Paris; the first of them took place at Blois on 23 December 1588, the other a day later. At around the same time the bourgeoisie of Orléans revolted against their governor and replaced him with an ardently Catholic relation of the Guises. In view of the accuracy of this and other predictions in the

Centuries which appeared to relate to the murders it is not surprising that stories which had been told in Nostradamus's lifetime concerning his miraculous gifts became more widely circulated.

Eight months after the callous murders had been carried out at the King's orders, he himself was assassinated by a monk who had been a partisan of the Guise cause. This event was again prophesied by Nostradamus, who wrote of it in Century I Quatrain 97. The quatrain reads:

That which neither fire nor iron could achieve,
By a sweet tongue in counsel will be performed:
Sleeping, in dream, the King will see An enemy, not in
fire or military blood.

And so it happened. Three nights prior to his murder Henri III had a dream which disturbed him, as it seemed premonitory of an imminent death at the hands of either a monk or one of the common people. In his dream, Henri saw his crown, sceptre, sword and royal robe being trodden into the mud by a large gathering of monks and poor laymen.

Three days later the dream and Nostradamus's prophecy were alike fulfilled. At St Cloud the King was approached by a monk who said he had counsel to give concerning a secret letter. As Henri bent forward to hear him, he was stabbed in the stomach by the false counsellor. It took almost a day for him to die.

The monk's surname was Clement, which means sweet; it seems that the seer hinted at this when he described the murderer as 'sweet tongued'.

NOSTRADAMUS AND THE PIGS

Because Nostradamus attached specific dates to some of his predictions it is not surprising that even in his own lifetime he began to acquire a reputation for invariably being right and that tales were told concerning his virtual omniscience.

According to one of these tales, a nobleman enquired of the seer which of two piglets, one black and one white, he would eat first. Nostradamus said, 'The white one.' The nobleman then tried to prove the prophet wrong by ordering that the black piglet should be immediately killed and served at dinner.

Roast pork was on the table within the space of an hour or so – but the cook had to apologize to his master; a wolf had stolen the black piglet, so it was the white one that was being served.

HENRI OF NAVARRE

Even before the death of Henri III it was obvious to most that the end of the Valois dynasty was nigh and, as a consequence of this recognition, there were various claimants to the rightful heirship to the throne of France.

Prominent amongst these claimants were various members of the Guise family. These men were leading opponents of Protestantism and active in the doings of the militant Catholic League. Some of them had even gone so far as to have procured the fabrication of a completely bogus genealogy purporting to demonstrate that they were entitled to the throne because of their (imagined) descent from the Emperor Charlemagne.

In truth, however, on genealogical grounds the real heir to the throne was undoubtedly King Henri of Navarre – a man whose domain was small, who had spent most of his adult life as a soldier, and who was a Protestant. In view of the latter he was unacceptable as the future King of France to Spain, to the Pope, to the French bishops, who made it clear that they would not anoint and crown a 'heretic king', and to a majority of the French people.

Nevertheless, Henri of Navarre was to triumph – as had been prophesied by Nostradamus in the anagrammatically loaded Century IX Quatrain 50, which reads:

> *Mendosus will soon come to his great reign,*
> *Leaving Nolaris in the rear,*
> *The pale red one, the one of the time between kingdoms,*
> *The timid youth and the fear of Barbaris.*

'Mendosus' is one of the many partial anagrams that Nostradamus employed; it stands for 'Vendosme' – that is, Henri of Navarre, who had inherited the dukedom of Vendosme from his father. 'Nolaris' was the word, based on another partial anagram, which the seer often employed to mean Lorraine, the traditional home of the Guise family. Consequently, the first two lines of the verse can be paraphrased as:

> *Henri of Navarre will soon come to his great reign,*
> *Leaving the Guises in the rear ...*

The opening words of the third line, 'the pale red one, the one of the time between kingdoms', is equally easily interpreted. In December 1585, almost four years before the death of Henri III, an agreement had been made at Joinville between King Philip of Spain, the Pope and the Guises with the object of preventing Henri of Navarre from ascending to the throne. It had been arranged that upon the death of Henri III one of the Guises, Charles, the aged Cardinal of Bourbon, should be proclaimed King of France and that he should then make a will recognizing Henri of Guise as his successor.

It was the Cardinal of Bourbon who was termed 'the pale red one' by Nostradamus. This was because red is the colour of a cardinal's hat and the old man was pallid with age – and, perhaps, also with approaching death. While the aged cleric was indeed proclaimed as King Charles X towards the end of 1589, he was never to rule, for all throughout his phantom reign he was the prisoner of Henri of Navarre and he died soon afterwards.

As for 'the one of the time between kingdoms', the 'timid youth' and 'Barbaris', these were all coded Nostradamian references to other rivals who challenged Henri of Navarre's right to the throne – the first one being the Duc de Mayenne, the second the younger Duc de Guise, and the last King Philip of Spain, whose personal claim was never taken very seriously, not even by himself.

Henri of Navarre not only had to fight hard to gain the throne of France but was also forced to change his religion. Nevertheless, he eventually attained his goal, destroying the pretensions of his only serious rivals, the Duc de Mayenne and the timid young Duc de Guise, as had been prophesied by Nostradamus in Century X Quatrain 18:

> *The House of Lorraine will make way for Vendosme,*
> *The great will be abased and the humble exalted,*
> *The son of Mamon* [or Hamon – in either case a heretic
> is in dicated] *will be chosen in Rome,*
> *And the two great ones will be defeated.*

The significance of the seer's use of the words 'Lorraine' and 'Vendosme' has already been explained, so it will be seen that the quatrain's first line means 'The Guises will have to give way to Henri of Navarre'. The content of the second line is apparent; the third means that the Pope would eventually recognize Henri as the rightful king; and the two defeated great ones of the verse's last line were the two Pretenders, the dukes of Mayenne and Guise.

Nostradamus made at least one other specific reference to King Henri IV (albeit one of some obscurity). In the forty-fifth quatrain of Century X, he predicted:

> *The shadow of the King of Navarre is false,*
> *It will make a strong man a bastard* [or unlawful]
> *The vague promise made at Cambrai,*
> *The king at Orléans will give a lawful wall* [boundary].

It seems likely that in this quatrain Nostradamus was referring to irregularities in Henri's personal life rather than to political events of major importance, for Henri certainly had numerous mistresses, including the wife of the Governor of Cambrai, and was reputed to have fathered a number of illegitimate children. However, the second line of the verse could have been a reference to one of the Pretenders to the throne having been made 'unlawful' by Henri.

THE SPANISH YOKE

The Europe of Nostradamus's time was a continent dominated by theological disputes over such matters as free will and predestination, the nature of the presence of Christ in the bread and wine of the Eucharist, and the Papal supremacy. Such disputes were almost inextricably entangled with the dynastic ambitions of some and the economic designs of others. For example, the struggle of the Calvinists and other Protestants of the Netherlands to practise their religion freely was entwined with both the first stirrings of a sense of national identity which led to a resentment of 'the Spanish yoke' – the Low Countries' subjugation to the King of Spain – and economic tensions derived from the increasing mercantile importance of the northern areas (roughly speaking, modern Holland) and the relative decline of Antwerp.

Nevertheless, while purely political and economic factors were of real importance, it was religious differences that were at the root of the whole series of conflicts, uprisings and wars which inflicted enormous damage upon Europe and its peoples over a period extending from the third decade of Nostradamus's own century until the middle years of the succeeding one.

Being both a man of his own times and a devoted Catholic (see panel opposite), Nostradamus tended not only to interpret his visions of the conflicts of the near future in purely religious terms but to do so with a markedly pro-Catholic bias. This bias is apparent in almost all the quatrains that in any way relate, even marginally, to the Church and those who rebelled against it, but nowhere is it more blatant than in Century III Quatrain 67, which reads:

> *A new sect of philosophers*
> *Despising death, honours, gold and other riches*
> *Will not be limited by the borders* [literally, mountains] *of Germany*
> [in this context all German speaking areas]
> *Their supporters will be multitudinous.*

This is a somewhat vaguely worded prediction to almost anyone who reads it at the present day. However, to those Catholics who came across it in the three or four decades after its first publication it was a grimly fulfilled prophecy of the way in which the doctrines of Calvin (Calvinus – literally 'the bald man') had spread right throughout Europe from their German-speaking stronghold of Geneva. One of the places in which these doctrines took root was Lausanne, whence, as Nostradamus had somewhat inelegantly predicted in the first line of Century VIII Quatrain 10, 'a great stink will come' as the consequence of the activities of Calvin's disciple Theodore Beza.

Nostradamus's Catholic bias was such that he had no hesitation in publishing prophecies relating to Protestantism that could be described as libellous – that is to say, predictions in which he falsely attributed to all Protestants the intemperate opinions of only a small proportion of them. The second line of the quatrain quoted above provides an example of this, with Nostradamus implying that all Protestants shared the communistic opinions of such violent extremists as Jan of Leyden. Some Nostradamian commentators have even alleged that the seer quite deliberately published false prophecies of mass conversions from Protestantism to the Church. As an example of this mendacity they point to Century III Quatrain 76, which reads:

> *In Germany will arise various sects*
> *Which will resemble a happy paganism,*
> *The heart enslaved and little received,*
> *They will return to pay the true tithe.*

To the present writer, however, it seems likely that Nostradamus was innocent of the imputation of falsehood and that the above quatrain refers to Nordic neo-pagan sects which came into existence in the period 1890-1945.

CATHOLICISM AND REINCARNATION

While at one brief period Nostradamus came under suspicion of heresy, it is certain that throughout his life he regularly attended Mass and performed the other religious duties of a loyal son of the Church.

Some have suggested that the seer's Catholicism was feigned, simply a device to ensure freedom from unwelcome ecclesiastical attention, and that Nostradamus's religious views were in reality extremely unorthodox, extending to a belief in reincarnation. As evidence for these assertions they have instanced Century II Quatrain 13, which reads:

> *The soulless body no longer at the sacrifice,*
> *At the day of death it is brought to rebirth.*
> *The Divine Spirit will make the soul rejoice,*
> *Seeing the eternity of the Word.*

The first line of this quatrain, so it has been argued, means that Nostradamus privately rejected the Christian doctrine of the resurrection of the body while the second line demonstrates that he believed in reincarnation.

In the opinion of the present writer, all such arguments are based upon a misunderstanding of the content of Century II Quatrain 13, for, while the verse undoubtedly did carry a personal religious significance for its author, its content is impeccably orthodox. All that the seer was expressing in this quatrain was his assurance of salvation and his doggerel can be paraphrased thus:

After my death my body will no longer be present at the Sacrifice of the Mass, my soul will be reborn into heaven, where I shall view eternity with the Holy Spirit [i.e. the Logos, literally 'Word', of St John's Gospel].

There seems to be no good reason to doubt Nostradamus's Catholicism – although, like a number of other occultists throughout the centuries, he appears to have found his faith quite compatible with the practice of ritual magic and other of the forbidden arts.

PARIS WAS WORTH A MASS

Henri of Navarre's accession to the throne of France had been predicted in the Centuries of Nostradamus. So were at least some of the military and diplomatic struggles he had to undertake before he was secure upon the throne that rightfully belonged to him – for example, in Century III Quatrain 25, which reads:

He who holds [or inherits] *the Kingdom of Navarre*
When Naples and Sicily are joined,
He will hold [or grasp] *Bigore and Landes through Foix and Oloron,*
From one too strictly conjoined with Spain.

The prophecy is somewhat vague but, read in conjunction with one another, its first and second lines enable one to date the events to which Nostradamus was referring with a reasonable degree of accuracy – for while the kingdoms of Naples and Sicily were, in practice, conjoined with one another for centuries there were only three historical occasions on which their unity was formally proclaimed.

The last two of these occasions were in the 19th century, by which time the tiny kingdom of Navarre had long since ceased to exist as an independent state. Consequently, the quatrain could not possibly relate to either of them. This leaves only the first occasion – in 1554, when Philip of Spain asserted the unity of the two kingdoms. And it was in 1562, during the reign of Philip, that the future Henri IV of France inherited the throne of Navarre. We can be sure, then, that it was him rather than some other ruler of Navarre whom Nostradamus had in mind when he wrote the words of Century III Quatrain 25.

The names in line three are all those of places in Navarre, but one of them, Bigore, is of significance in a different context – that of the battles between the Protestant soldiers of Henri IV and their Catholic opponents, for 'Bigorro' was a word that was chanted in conflict by Henri's Protestant infantrymen.

The meaning of the last line of the quatrain is vague – many of Henri's enemies were too closely allied with Spain for his comfort – but from the verse one thing seems to be definitely established: Nostradamus knew a great deal about the struggles between Henri and his opponents long before they began!

Although Henri was a soldier of genius his military successes were not enough to secure his throne fully. To do that he had to change his religion, adopting the Catholic faith because, as he himself cynically put it, 'Paris is worth a Mass'. However, while he abandoned Protestantism Henri did not abandon the Protestants who had fought for him, and by the Edict of Nantes in 1598 the French followers of Calvinism were granted an almost complete religious toleration and exactly the same civil rights as the King's Catholic subjects.

Predictably, the Edict of Nantes was not looked upon with favour by the more extreme, and largely pro-Spanish, Catholics; it was one of these who, in 1610, murdered Henri IV – yet another future event of which Nostradamus obviously knew a great deal (see below).

LOPPING OF THE SACRED BRANCH

In the spring of 1610, as the consequence of a complex dispute which involved the succession to the throne of the small state of Julich-Cleves, Henri IV was making preparations to go to war against the Hapsburgs.

It was a serious and dangerous course for the French king to consider embarking upon and, had it been proceeded with, it would have meant France was at loggerheads with half of Europe – for one branch of the Hapsburg dynasty ruled still-mighty Spain while another ruled the sprawling Holy Roman Empire, which included within its boundaries Bohemia, Moravia, and all the German-speaking lands of Middle Europe with the exception of Switzerland.

The war did not take place, for on 14 May 1610 Henri IV was stabbed to death by a pro-Spanish assassin named François Ravaillac, to be succeeded by his youthful son, Louis XIII. The new King's mother, appointed as Regent, gave in to the pro-Spanish party – men who were 'more Catholic than the Pope' – and arrived at a rapprochement with the Hapsburgs.

Henri's murder was predicted by Nostradamus in Century III Quatrain 11:

> *For a long season the weapons fight in the sky,*
> *The tree fell in the midst of the city,*
> *The sacred branch lopped by a sword opposite Tison,*
> *Then the monarch Hadrie succumbs [falls].*

The first line of the verse, with its reference to a 'fight in the sky', makes it sound as though the quatrain applied to the 20th century or later. However, the last line shows that this is not the case, for Nostradamus's various mentions of the code name 'Hadrie' all seem to apply to Henri IV. In fact, the first line refers to the fact that at the time of the assassination of Henri there were reports, very similar to those circulating at the outbreak of the English Civil War, of spectral armies seen in the heavens.

The sacred branch lopped off in the midst of the city was Henri himself – as an anointed king his person was considered sacred – and his murder took place not far from the Rue Tison (see line three of the quatrain).

Yet again, a strangely worded quatrain was destined to be fulfilled by the course of history.

THE TWO QUEENS

The first husband of Mary Stuart, perhaps more often referred to as Mary Queen of Scots, was the Valois monarch Francis II, son of Henri II and his queen, Catherine de' Medici.

The marriage of Francis and Mary and its brief duration, which ended with her widowhood, was accurately predicted in Century X Quatrain 39, which reads:

> *The first son, a widow, an unlucky marriage,*
> *Childless, two islands [kingdoms?] in discord.*
> *Before eighteen years of age, a minor,*
> *Of the other the [age of] betrothal will be even less.*

In spite of its curious wording and odd syntax the predictive significance of this quatrain was immediately apparent to the French court at the time the events to which it pertained took place; it was rightly regarded as a notable prophetic hit and helped to make Nostradamus's reputation as a seer.

Francis was the eldest son of the French monarchs, and his wife Mary – spelt in this English/Scots manner, not in the French form of 'Marie', by Nostradamus in Century X Quatrain 55 (see below) – was left a childless widow by his death. Furthermore, Francis had still been a minor of less than 18 years of age at the date of his betrothal, and the consequences of Mary's return to Scotland after the early death of her husband were to be the cause of much discord in both England and Scotland.

The last line of the quatrain was also of significance to Nostradamus's contemporaries; they took it as a direct reference to the betrothal at the age of 11 of Francis's brother Charles to Elizabeth of Austria.

Nostradamus made a second reference to Mary's unlucky first marriage in Century X Quatrain 55:

> *The unlucky marriage will be celebrated*
> *With great joy, but the end will be unhappy.*
> *The mother* [of the husband] *will despise Mary,*
> *The Phybe dead and the daughter-in-law most piteous.*

The predictive meaning of the first two lines was easily apparent and rapidly fulfilled. The third line would also appear to have had an obvious meaning and to have proved accurate, for Catherine and Mary disliked one another – indeed, Mary was reported to have dared to go so far as to make a rude allusion to the (distant) bourgeois origins of the Medici family, referring to her mother-in-law as 'the merchant's daughter'.

The first three words of the fourth line of the quatrain seem meaningless on a first reading, but are explicable by two of the many tricks involving word games with classical languages in which Nostradamus indulged. 'Phybe' is a compound of two letters of the Greek alphabet, the first being phi, pronounced 'F', and the second being Beta, which was used in ancient Greece to represent the number two. So 'Phybe' meant no more than 'FII' – in other words, Francis II.

MARRIAGE, MURDER AND CASKET LETTERS

The second and third marriages of Mary Queen of Scots were even more unfortunate, both for her and for others, than the first. Her second husband was Henry Stewart, Lord Darnley, whom she married in the chapel at Holyrood in the summer of 1565. At the time of the marriage Darnley was a good-looking young man – after their first meeting Mary described him as 'the best proportioned lang [i.e. tall] man I have ever seen' – and, while the Queen probably chose her husband largely on political grounds, she also seems to have looked upon him with real affection. Certainly the relationship between them was close enough for her to become pregnant by him with the child who was in the course of time to become James I of England and James VI of Scotland.

However, by the time of the child's birth the Queen already looked upon his father with utter loathing and contempt. He had been responsible for the murder of Rizzio, Mary's Italian secretary; he had lost his youthful good looks; he was suffering from the ravages of tertiary syphilis; and Mary was in the process of falling in love. The object of her affections was the Earl of Bothwell who, most probably with the connivance of Mary, murdered Darnley and married his widow a few weeks later.

The discovery of some letters and other documents in a casket led to Mary's alleged involvement in the murder of her second husband becoming generally accepted as fact. The result of this was a rebellion against her in Scotland, whereupon she took flight to England in order to take refuge with Queen Elizabeth I, her first cousin once removed.

This refuge proved to be only a temporary one. Mary had a genealogical claim to the English throne and she now began to conspire against her cousin. Her plots were ingenious but they always failed, and she became a prisoner, rather than a guest, of Queen Elizabeth who, in 1587, had her beheaded.

Nostradamus made no prediction of this, but seems to have accurately prophesied the finding of the 'Casket Letters' in the mysterious Century VIII Quatrain 23, which reads:

> *Letters are found in the Queen's caskets,*
> *Without signature and the writer nameless,*
> *The trick* [or the government] *will hide the offers,*
> *So that they do not know who is the lover.*

THE ENGLISH
REVOLUTION

A surprisingly large number of the quatrains of the Centuries have been taken as referring to the English Revolutionary period – that is, to the years of the struggles between Crown and Parliament, the first and second Civil Wars, the personal rule of Oliver Cromwell as Lord Protector, and the events resulting in the Stuart Restoration of 1660.

To the present writer some of these referrals seem somewhat far-fetched, based upon a twisting of the meanings of the prophet's obscurely worded predictions rather than on scholarly attempts at unravelling their often coded content. Take, for example, Century III Quatrain 81:

> *The bold and shameless great talker,*
> *Will be chosen as head of the army,*
> *The audacity of his contention,*
> *The broken bridge, the city faint with dread.*

It has often been argued that the person described in the first two lines of this quatrain as an audacious and unabashed orator who becomes head of the army was Oliver Cromwell. And 'the city faint with dread'? That, it is said, was the Royalist stronghold of Pontefract – the name of the town being derived from two Latin words meaning 'bridge' and 'broken' – which underwent two major sieges during the Civil Wars.

Perhaps – but the verse could equally well be interpreted as referring to the Kronstadt revolt of 1921 against the Bolshevik government led by Lenin, in which case the bold orator would be Trotsky, the head of the Red Army, the fearful city would be Kronstadt itself, and the 'broken bridge' would be the shell-shattered ice-link with the mainland over which Trotsky's troops advanced when storming the rebel stronghold.

Another dubiously interpreted 'Cromwellian' quatrain (Century VIII Quatrain 56) is alleged to have been predictive of Cromwell's victory over the Scots at the Battle of Dunbar. However, this verse, which contains a typically Nostradamian partial anagram of Edinburgh, seems to be more applicable to the battle of Culloden (1746) than to Dunbar.

In spite of the existence of such over-enthusiastic Cromwellian interpretations of particular verses of the Centuries there seems little doubt that Nostradamus knew a good deal about the English Civil War almost 100 years before it took place. Indeed, he specifically predicted that 'the Senate [i.e. Parliament] of London will put their King to death' in Century IX Quatrain 49. The numbering of this quatrain may be significant, for it suggests that the seer may have even known the year in which this event, the execution of Charles I, was destined to take place — 1649.

In reading the quatrains that certainly, probably, or possibly refer to the men and events that dominated English history in the period 1641-1660 one is conscious of an intense anti-Parliamentarian bias that was responsible, for instance, for the seer's unflatteringly negative view of the character of Oliver Cromwell (see below). A similar bias is apparent in quatrains pertaining to other epochs of revolution and social turmoil. When he looked in psychic vision down the years Nostradamus was always on the side of the rulers, never the ruled; it was as if a haze of blood distorted his clairvoyant perceptions. He always saw the sufferings of royalty and the nobility, and rarely those of the common people; in viewing the cycles of change and revolution he tended to pity the plumage and forget the dying bird.

That pity was expressed in several of the quatrains in relation to Charles I, whom he saw as an innocent man whose blood was shed for no good reason.

CROMWELL AS BUTCHER

Nostradamus would seem to have disapproved of Cromwell almost as much as he did the leaders of the French Revolution, referring to him as a 'meat basket' (butcher) and a 'bastard'. The latter term, found in Century III Quatrain 80, which is largely concerned with the character of Charles I, would appear to have been applied metaphorically, in the sense of 'ignoble', rather than literally. The former is to be found in Century VIII Quatrain 76, which reads:

> *More a basket of meat than a king in England,*
> *Born in obscurity he will gain his rank through force,*
> *Coward without [the Catholic] faith he will bleed the land;*
> *His time approaches so near that I sigh.*

The reference to Cromwell as a butcher has a double application of the sort to which Nostradamus was inclined. On the one hand it referred to the butchery of camp followers which invariably followed upon Cromwell's victories; on the other to a legend that in the 15th century his ancestors had been butchers and blacksmiths. In reality Cromwell's origins were obscure (see line two of the quatrain) only in the sense that he was not of noble blood and that prior to the outbreak of the Civil War he lived the life of a quiet country gentleman.

The 'nearness' of the approach of Cromwell referred to in the quatrain's final line was about 40 years – that is to say, the period between the first publication of the quatrain and the year of Cromwell's birth (1597).

THE BLOOD
OF THE JUST MAN

Nostradamus was a conservative in the primary sense of the word – that is to say, he was a man who was attached to tradition and disapproved of all change unless it seemed quite certain to him that such change would be for the better.

This conservatism, combined with a typically 16th-century reverence for the principle of hereditary monarchy, was reflected in many of the quatrains predictive of events involving social upheaval. Thus, for instance, those many verses of the Centuries which would appear to refer to the French Revolution are often notable not only for their accuracy but for their disapproval – implicit and explicit – of the revolutionaries and all their doings. Such a note of censure is particularly marked in those quatrains that are thought to relate to the execution of Louis XVI and his Queen; it is clear that Nostradamus believed in the sacredness of the Blood Royal.

His attitude towards an earlier act of regicide, the beheading of King Charles I by his English subjects on 30 January 1649, was equally condemnatory. Indeed, the seer's predictions concerning the two major disasters that were to take place in the London of the 1660s make it obvious that he regarded them as being in the nature of divine retribution. London, he predicted, was going to receive punishment for its sinful part in the King's execution.

The quatrains in which these disasters were foretold by the seer – Century II Quatrain 51 and Century II Quatrain 53 – are examined in relation to London's 'punishments' and to one another later in this book. Here we are concerned with those parts of them that were predictive references to the execution of King Charles – namely the first line of Century II Quatrain 51, which reads 'The blood of the just shall be required of London', and the third line of Quatrain 53: 'The blood of the just [man] condemned for no crime'. In the latter quatrain Nostradamus made no specific mention of London, but he did refer to the place where the unjust condemnation took place as being 'a maritime city'. No major port other than London experienced similar disasters to those which are dealt with later at the date indicated by the seer, so we can be quite sure that England's capital was the location where he foretold that the just man's blood was destined to be shed.

It is fairly obvious that the two lines quoted in the preceding paragraph were intended, like the two relevant quatrains in their entirety, to be read in conjunction with one another – in which case the 'blood of the just man' who was described by Nostradamus as being destined to be condemned for no crime could only have been that of King Charles the Martyr, executed at the orders of those who had illegally tried him and sentenced him to death. In both quatrains the French word Dame was used to mean Saint Paul's Cathedral – described as 'outraged' in the last line of Century II Quatrain 53 because at the time of the King's judicial murder its lawful occupants, clerics loyal to the Church of England, had been expelled and replaced by sectaries of one sort or another.

Surely, it might be asked by the sceptic, there were 'just men' other than Charles I who were executed in London prior to the disasters which Nostradamus foretold? Why should 'the just man' of the quatrains be identified with the martyred King?

There are three good reasons for making the identification. First, the reference to St Paul's Cathedral as being occupied by 'pretenders', by which term Nostradamus was indicating ministers of religion who were sectaries rather than mere schismatics. The latter term, not the former, was the one normally applied by Catholics to Anglican priests and bishops in the lifetime of Nostradamus – Anglican orders were not formally condemned by the Holy Office until 1896. As schismatics, Anglican clerics were considered to be in a state of mortal sin but not as pretenders to a priesthood they did not possess. The only period between the publication of the Centuries and our own lifetimes when the Cathedral was wholly or partially occupied by those whom Nostradamus called 'pretenders' was between 1641 and 1662, so it must have been during those years that the blood of the just man was shed.

Secondly, the phrase 'the just man' was used by English royalists to refer to their former monarch – the form of words had a textual significance derived from the King James translation of the Bible and was, in any case, a safer phrase to use than its alternative, 'the Royal Martyr'.

And thirdly, in the third line of Century IX Quatrain 49 Nostradamus specifically predicted that 'the Senate of London will put their King to death'.

Read together, the two quatrains suggest that Nostradamus certainly had visions of events that were to take place in London in the years 1649-66. The first two of his clairvoyant glimpses of London's future were, in chronological order, one of 'pretenders' in Saint Paul's Cathedral and one of the execution of King Charles I.

The second two were of the disasters described later. Being a man of his own time, when it was accepted that heaven was constantly intervening in the affairs of earth, the seer drew the conclusion that the latter two of the four events were inflicted upon London as punishments for the part that its citizens had played in the first two of them.

PLAGUE AND FIRE

Both the outbreak of bubonic plague that swept London in 1665 and the Great Fire that succeeded it in the following year are believed to have been prophesied by Nostradamus. For the latter event he went so far as to give the relevant date, for Century II Quatrain 51 reads:

> *The blood of the just shall be required of London,*
> *Burned by fire in thrice twenty and six,*
> *The ancient Dame shall fall from her high place,*
> *And many of the same sect shall fall.*

The coded significance of the first line of this verse was dealt with above; the literal meaning of the second is apparent – much of London burned to ashes. The only dates on which great fires took place in London were 1941, the result of German bombing, and 1666, when a conflagration which began in a bakery raged for many days, destroying huge areas of the City. Clearly the fire to which Nostradamus referred, the one predicted to break out in 'thrice twenty and six', was the latter.

The 'ancient Dame' would seem to have been Saint Paul's Cathedral – the word 'Dame' was frequently employed by the seer in the sense of 'church' – and the 'many of the same sect' predicted to fall were, it can be presumed, the more than 80 London churches that were destroyed in the Great Fire.

Like so many other of the seer's prophecies, this prediction could not have been made on the basis of astrology. While there were, and are, predictive methods which supposedly enable astrologers to make tentative prognostications such as 'at such-and-such a date the opposition between Mars in such-and-such a degree of Aries to Jupiter combined with the square of the sun in Gemini to Saturn indicate a risk of serious fires breaking out in London', there never has been an astrological technique capable of making such a detailed forecast as that contained in Century II Quatrain 51.

The plague which preceded the Fire would seem to be referred to in Century II Quatrain 53, which reads:

> *The Great Plague of the maritime city*
> *Shall not lessen until death has taken vengeance,*
> *For the blood of the just [man] condemned for no crime,*
> *The great Dame is outraged by pretenders.*

For reasons that were explained later it is likely that the maritime city referred to in this quatrain was London, and it seems to be relevant to the plague outbreak of 1665, which temporarily reduced the City of London to something like a ghost town with grass growing in the streets and all those of its inhabitants who could afford to do so taking refuge in the countryside. It is thought virtually certain that the two quatrains were intended to be read in conjunction with one another as referring to events close in time to one another.

To the present writer, it seems that the two quatrains were likely to have been based upon a vision or a series of visions experienced by the seer in which he saw, in the mind's 'psychic eye', four separate events taking place in a city which it was apparent to him was London in the years 1649–66. The first two of these were dealt with above. The third (judging from the order in which the quatrains were first printed) was the Great Fire of 1666; and the fourth was the outbreak of bubonic plague in 1665.

BURIED TREASURE

Nostradamus was not the only seer who seems to have successfully foretold both London's outbreak of bubonic plague and the Great Fire that succeeded it in the following year. Another was the Englishman William Lilly (1602–81), a man who was, like Nostradamus, best known as an astrologer and physician but also practised a number of other occult arts and took an interest in every aspect of the supernatural – on one occasion going so far as to express the opinion that a creature reported to have vanished 'with a most melodious twang' was a fairy.

His mystic pursuits were typified by an adventure which he undertook one night in the early 1660s. In company with other occult experimenters, he used 'the Mosaicall Rods' – which seem to have pertained to ritual dowsing – in order to seek buried treasure in London's Old St Paul's Cathedral. The attempt was unsuccessful; the treasure seekers only managed to annoy some guardian spirits who raised such a tempest that they feared the Cathedral roof might crash upon their heads.

Similar storms were encountered by other seekers of buried treasure. Dr John Dee, mathematician and geographer to Queen Elizabeth I, used his divining rod 'to find things that might be missing and with his rod did bring back to many persons silver and such objects which had been missing sometimes over years'. On one such occasion, Dee discovered gold in a pool in Breconshire in Wales. His activities, noticed by the local village folk, were followed by such a severe storm at the critical harvest time that it was said 'people had not known the like.' Dee and his colleagues were arrested as conjurors and suspected of worse by the irate villagers.

THE SUN KING

Charles II, the Stuart king who was restored to the thrones of England, Scotland and Ireland in 1660, and his younger brother, James, had endured unhappy early lives. As children they had experienced the alarms and upheavals of the Civil War; as adolescents they had known the agony of learning of the trial and execution of their father, Charles I – the 'just man' of the Centuries; as young men they had lived with those loyal to them in poverty-stricken exile, utterly dependent on meagre financial help supplied by French and Dutch sources.

The early years of the Stuart Restoration were happy enough; the compliant Cavalier Parliament was more obliging than any with which their father had had to deal and they were popular among all sections of the community save those that were firmly attached to the 'Good Old Cause' – Protestant Republicanism.

It was all too good to last. London was devastated by plague and fire, Parliament grew critical – the royal family seemed to have an insatiable appetite for money and was also suspected of Catholic sympathies – and an unpopular war against the Netherlands saw defeats at sea and a humiliating Dutch incursion into the Thames, in the course of which many English ships were destroyed or towed away captive.

By 1670 the Treasury was empty and both Charles II and his brother James, the Duke of York, began to look to the example set them from across the Channel. It was a decision that was eventually to prove disastrous: it led to James, who inherited the throne from his brother in 1685, losing his crown and then, in 1714, the replacement of the Stuart dynasty by the stolid Hanoverian line. All of these events had been predicted by Nostradamus, but in 1670 they still lay in the future and it seemed to make good sense for the Stuarts to ally themselves with France. This Charles did by signing the Treaty of Dover, an agreement which had appended to it secret protocols, not revealed until over a century later, under which Charles was to receive large subsidies in return for converting to Catholicism and making Britain's policies, both foreign and domestic, subservient to French interests.

In France itself, Louis XIV, the 'Sun King' who was destined to dominate the political life of Europe for half a century, had begun his personal rule in 1661 and had already greatly increased the power and reputation of his country. France had left behind the internal conflicts of the preceding 20 years and had embarked upon a period of material prosperity and physical transformation which had been prophesied by Nostradamus in Century X Quatrain 89:

> *The walls will be transformed from brick to marble,*
> *Fifty-seven* [or seventy-five] *peaceful years.*
> *Joy to all people, the aqueduct renovated,*
> *Health, the joy of abundant harvests, honey-sweet times.*

The first line of this quatrain is of particular interest as it makes a similar allusion to Louis XIV as was made by the Roman historian Suetonius to the Emperor Augustus (63bc–ad14), whom he claimed had described himself as 'finding Rome brick and leaving it marble'. The semi-identification of the two rulers was particularly significant as Louis was referred to as the 'Sun King' and Augustus was posthumously deified as an avatar (an incarnation) of the 'Invincible Sun'.

However, while the quatrain was accurate enough in essence it displayed the Nostradamian bias in favour of powerful French monarchs which is apparent throughout the Centuries, for while the years of Louis XIV's rule were peaceful enough at home (save for those of his subjects who clung to the Protestant faith) his foreign policy was belligerent in the extreme. In fairness to Louis it has to be admitted that his warlike policies were, in the early years of his personal rule at any rate, a natural reaction to the environment of foreign and civil war into which he had been born and in which he had spent his childhood.

This period of turmoil in France had been foreseen by Nostradamus, who described it in Century X Quatrain 58:

> *At a time of mourning the feline monarch,*
> *Will go to war with the youthful Aemathien,*
> *Gaul shivers, the barque [of Peter] in danger,*
> *Marseilles tested and talks in the West.*

The phrase 'youthful Aemathien' in the second line of the quatrain is obviously a reference to Louis' transmutation into the Sun King, for in classical mythology Aemathien was the child of dawn and can therefore be identified with the sun. The 'feline monarch' of the preceding line was the cunning Philip IV of Spain, who actively waged war against France during the period of mourning which followed the death of Louis XIII in 1643. And 'Gaul shivered' (see line three) because of the Fronde (the rebellions against excessive tax demands and the administration of Cardinal Mazarin) and the other civil struggles and upheavals that marked the years of the minority of Louis XIV.

The phrase 'the barque [of Peter] in danger' in the third line has a dual meaning of the type that is often met with in the Centuries. First, it applies to the difficult position of the Gallican Church during the years 1643–61; secondly, to the later disputes between Rome and Louis XIV. The former was the consequence of the fact that during the years in question the Church was hampered in its often difficult relations with the state because Louis XIV's chief minister, Cardinal Mazarin, was himself a prince of the Church.

THE GLORY OF EUROPE

In Century X Quatrain 58, Nostradamus predicted that the policies of Louis XIV, the Sun King, would place the Catholic Church – 'the barque [of Peter]' – in danger. As Louis XIV was a fanatical Catholic (albeit not always a devout one) this might be dismissed as one of Nostradamus's predictive misses. In reality the forecast was surprisingly accurate, for at the very moment that Louis reached a pinnacle of both diplomatic and military success that led sycophants to hail him as 'the Glory of Europe' a long-festering dispute between the King and the papacy finally erupted.

The quarrel was about the ownership of the material benefits and the spiritual rights of vacant bishoprics, which the King asserted belonged to him. The French Assembly of the Clergy agreed, and by the four Articles of 1682 Louis and the Assembly proclaimed that the papacy had power over spiritual matters only and that the rules of the French church were inviolable. The Pope responded by refusing to authorize the consecration of bishops who had been nominated by Louis, and the complicated in-fighting which ensued weakened both church and state.

Louis had persuaded the Assembly of the Clergy on to his side in this matter by going along with the rigid approach of the French clergy towards native Protestantism. French Protestants, men and women who were devoted to the rigidly logical theology of Calvinism, had been granted full toleration by the Edict of Nantes in 1598. From 1651 onwards, however, the Catholic clergy of France in general, and a group called the 'Company of the Holy Sacrament' in particular, had done all that was within their power to nullify the effects of the Edict by the use of a narrowly legalistic interpretation of its articles.

Desirous of having the Gallican Church on his side in his approaching struggles with Rome, Louis supported this policy of religious confrontation from the commencement of his personal rule in 1661. Between then and 1685 the Huguenots (French Calvinists) were subjected to a process of attrition which successively deprived them of their schools, colleges and hospitals. Large fines were imposed upon them and, when these proved ineffective in producing conversions to Catholicism, violent and brutal soldiers were billeted upon them. Finally, in 1685, Louis simply revoked the Edict of Nantes and embarked upon a policy of outright persecution that was ultimately to result in an eight-year guerrilla war which had been successfully predicted by Nostradamus almost 150 years earlier (see panel below).

Three years after the Revocation, the efforts that Louis had been making since 1670 to ensure Catholic rule in England collapsed into utter ruin. That collapse, and the identity of the man whose doing it was – William, Prince of Orange – had both been discerned in advance by Nostradamus, who spoke of them in

Century II Quatrains 67, 68 and 69.

William of Orange was the son-in-law of James II of England – the former Duke of York and younger brother of Charles II. At the invitation of a large number of eminent Protestants he invaded England and, with his wife, Mary, seized the English throne. It was a major blow to Louis, which had been accurately predicted by Nostradamus:

> *A Gallic king from the Celtic right* [i.e. Holland],
> *Seeing the discord of the Great Monarchy,*
> *Will flourish his sceptre over the three leopards,*
> *Against the Cappe* [Capet, i.e. French king] *of the great Hierarchy.*

GUERRILLA WARFARE

When Louis revoked the Edict of Nantes in 1685, he thought that he was putting an end to French Calvinism; in reality, while his action ensured both mass conversions and a mass emigration, Huguenot organization managed to survive, most notably in the mountainous area of the Cevennes.

In 1703, driven to desperation by brutality and bloodshed, the Protestant mountaineers rose in revolt and for eight years waged a brave but ultimately unsuccessful guerrilla war against the royal armies. This courageous struggle and its unhappy ending were foretold by Nostradamus in Century III Quatrain 63 and Century II Quatrain 64. The relevant lines of the former read:

> *The Celtic* [in this context Gallic, i.e. French] *Army*
> *against the mountaineers,*
> *Who will become known, and trapped,*
> *Will perish by the sword ...*

This is a somewhat vague prediction, and it could be argued that it is easily applicable to a French army defeating mountaineers. However, Century II Quatrain 64, with its references to the followers of Calvin and the Cevennes, is specific:

> *The people of Geneva* [i.e. the Calvinists] *will dry up with thirst and hunger,*
> *Their hopes will fail;*
> *The law of the Cevennes will be at breaking point,*
> *The fleet cannot enter the great port.*

The only line that requires any explanation is the last, which seems to be a reference to the failure of international Calvinism to deliver effective help to the Camisards, the Protestant guerrillas.

REVOLUTION BLOODSHED & THE ATOM

Nostradamus lived in an age when monarchs ruled the world and a galloping horse was the fastest means of locomotion – yet, travelling through time, he foresaw space travel, republican revolutions and the conquests of modern technology.

Revolutions, the rise and fall of the Napoleonic Empire, the evil politics of Adolf Hitler, famine, bloodshed and modern technology are the predominating themes of this section. Before beginning upon these themes, however, readers should keep in mind some important points.

The initial reaction of most people on reading the Centuries in either its original form or in translation is usually one of bewilderment, for, as readers of this book will by now have appreciated, the quatrains were largely written in an oblique and coded language in which anagrams and classical neologisms (invented words derived from Greek and Latin) abound and individuals are referred to by allusive names – Henri of Navarre as 'Vendosme', for instance. Even the title is misleading, for the word 'Centuries' suggests that Nostradamus wrote his prophecies in accordance with some sort of chronological structure – that is to say, that the predictive quatrains at the commencement of the book would deal with events close to the seer's own times and those at its end with the far-distant future. Alas, it is not so. The Centuries seems to be the record of a series of visions which were not entirely under the control of the seer and gave him a random selection of glimpses into the future – and of the past, for there are a few quatrains which seem to be 'retrospective predictions'.

There are other explanations for the apparently random nature of the quatrains. The most plausible of these, which is concerned with theories concerning 'alternate realities' that are accepted by some mathematical physicists, is examined later. However, whatever the explanation may be for the fact that the quatrains are neither in chronological order nor, as far as can be seen, arranged in any structured pattern, Nostradamian interpreters have to accept it as fact and endeavour to cope with it as best they can.

Nowhere is the problem greater than in interpreting the predictions dealt with in this section. Quatrains which pertain to Napoleon, for instance, are to be found in almost all of the 10 sections of the Centuries and yet there seems to be no doubt that these scattered verses do refer to the same man.

TEMPEST, FIRE AND BLOODY SLICING

How much the greatest event it is that ever happened in the world! and how much the best!' wrote Charles James Fox (1749–1806), leader of the radical wing of the Whig Party in the British House of Commons and perhaps the greatest English parliamentary orator of all time, when news of the outbreak of the French Revolution reached England.

Nostradamus, who died more than 200 years before the event on which Fox was commenting in a letter to his friend Richard Fitzpatrick, took a very different point of view of the matter. As far as he was concerned the French Revolution was one of the worst events in human history, not the best; almost all of the references to the Jacobins and other revolutionaries that appear in the quatrains of the Centuries are uncomplimentary in the extreme.

But, it might be asked, did Nostradamus really make specific references to the Revolution more than 200 years before it occurred? There is very strong evidence that he did. Take, for instance, the content of Century IX Quatrain 20:

At night will come through the forest of Reines
Two partners, by a roundabout way, the Queen, the white stone,
The monk-king in grey at Varennes,
The elect Capet, resulting in tempest, fire, bloody slicing.

At the time it was first published the meaning of this quatrain was not known, but by the early years of the 1790s its significance became apparent and what had looked like near gibberish had been transformed by history into something important and evidential of Nostradamus's ability to see into the future.

The most remarkable thing about this quatrain is that it should actually mention the name of Varennes, for this somewhat insignificant commune has only one association of any historical importance whatsoever – the fact that it was there, in 1791, that the attempt to escape the Revolution made by Louis XVI and his Queen, Marie Antoinette, was foiled.

The two did indeed make their way to Varennes by a somewhat roundabout way through the forest of Reines, Louis does seem to have been clad in quiet grey rather than the scarlet and gold more usually associated with 18th-century monarchs, and the capture of the royal pair certainly resulted in tempest (in the sense of social turmoil), the blazing up of the fire of revolution, and 'bloody slicing' in the most literal sense – both Louis and his Queen were sent to the guillotine.

Two phrases used in the quatrain – 'the elect Capet' and 'the white stone' – require explanation.

By using the term 'elect' or 'chosen' Capet, Nostradamus was almost certainly referring to Louis XVI himself. Strictly speaking, the name 'Capet' should only have been used in reference to monarchs of an earlier French dynasty than the Bourbon family of which Louis XVI was the head. However, the word was often employed in a looser sense, meaning any reigning king of France.

The 'white stone' of the quatrain is not quite so easy to explain, although many commentators have attempted to do so. It has been suggested, for instance, that these words refer to a curious scandal of the 1780s termed 'The Affair of the Diamond Necklace' which did much to bring the monarchy into disrepute, and involved a diamond necklace, a senile and gullible cardinal, Marie Antoinette and the occult adventurer who called himself Cagliostro – a man who had a large element of the charlatan in his character but may also have had certain predictive abilities.

It is possible that those who have identified the 'white stone' of Nostradamus with the diamond necklace of the scandal are right, although to the present writer such an interpretation seems strained. In a sense, however, the question is of no great moment. The real significance of Century IX Quatrain 20 is that it would appear to provide hard evidence that in the 1550s Nostradamus was aware of obscure details of an event that did not take place until 1791.

PROPHETIC OBSCURITIES

The task of interpreting the predictive quatrains of Nostradamus is made even more difficult than would otherwise be the case by the seer's deliberate use of crabbed and obscure phrases, neologisms (invented words) derived from Greek and Latin, and anagrams, sometimes complete (such as substituting the word 'Rapis' for Paris, for example), but more often only partial.

The original French of the quatrain predicting the flight of Louis XVI and his consort contains two typical partial anagrams. One of these is 'Herne', a partial anagram of Reine (Queen) with a transmutation of the letter 'i' into an 'h', the preceding letter of the alphabet, while the other is 'noir' (black), a distortion used more than once in the Centuries to convey the French word for a king – roi.

THE EVIL
SCYTHE-BEARER

Nostradamus's fulfilled prophecy of the attempted escape of Louis XVI and Marie Antoinette from France was by no means the only prediction in the Centuries and other writings of the seer that pertained to the French Revolution of 1789 and the events that succeeded it in the years from 1790 to 1815. Indeed, if any one theme is dominant in the Centuries it is the Revolution. Of the fewer than 1000 quatrains which made up the final version of that strange work, at least 40 seem to be relevant to French history during the period of the First Republic and the Napoleonic Empire which succeeded it.

This is only just over four per cent, of course – but as the years in question only amounted to around a quarter of a century and the Centuries dealt with events forecast to take place between the seer's own lifetime and a date subsequent to the year AD 3000, it is an astonishingly high proportion.

Not all of these 40 'revolutionary quatrains' are as specific as Century IX Quatrain 20 or other predictions considered on later pages. Some of them are fairly general in nature – that is, while they seem in every respect to be applicable to the Revolution it is just possible that they relate instead (or also – Nostradamus had a trick of writing prophecies relating to more than one event) to events in French history that still lie in the future. Typical of such a verse is Century VI Quatrain 23, which reads:

> *Defences* [of the realm] *undermined by the spirit of the Kingdom,*
> *The people will be stirred up against their King,*
> *Peace made newly, Holy Laws degenerate,*
> *Never was Rapis* [Paris] *in such great tribulation.*

The verse fits the early years of the Revolution better than any other time, but it could be a double or even a treble prediction, one applicable not only to the early years of the Revolution but also to events that took place during the minority of Louis XIV and to things destined to happen in our future.

Another double prediction is to be found in Century I Quatrain 53, which would appear to be predictive of very similar events that took place as consequences of the French and Russian revolutions. In loose translation this double prophecy reads:

> *We will see a great people tormented,*
> *And the Holy Law in utter ruin,*
> *Christendom under other laws* [than Christian ones],
> *When a new source of gold and silver* [i.e. money] *is found.*

The quatrain seems to refer to both the suppression of Catholicism in the France of the early 1790s (see below) and the even more savage suppression of Russian Orthodoxy following the Bolshevik Revolution of 1917. The last line is also of significance in that the French and Russian revolutionaries found 'a new source of money' by printing quantities of paper money which rapidly depreciated and eventually became almost worthless.

Was the double meaning of this quatrain – the reference to similar events in two different revolutions – intended by Nostradamus? Or does it show that Nostradamian commentators twist the meaning of the verses to make them fit specific events?

The answer to the first question would appear to be 'yes', that to the second an equally decisive 'no', for Nostradamus made it clear in the two lines that follow immediately upon Century I Quatrain 53 that he had been making reference to two revolutions:

Two revolutions will be caused by the evil scythe-bearer,
Making a change of kingdoms and centuries ...

By 'the evil scythe bearer' the seer meant the planet Saturn – the 'Great Malefic' of 16th-century astrology – whose symbols are the hour-glass and the scythe. In these two lines he was claiming that, in the final analysis, Saturnian influences caused both the French and Russian revolutions.

BEESWAX AND HONEY

Nostradamus made a further prediction relating to the persecution of the Catholic clergy of France during the early 1790s in Century I Quatrain 44. This reads:

In a short time [non-Christian] sacrifices will be revived,
Those opposed will be martyred.
There will no longer be monks, abbots or novices,
Honey will cost more than beeswax.

Traditionally, the price of beeswax had exceeded that of the honey it contained, so by the last line of the verse Nostradamus was implying that the price of beeswax would fall during a period of religious persecution because it would no longer be in such demand for the manufacture of votive and altar candles. The previous line pertains to the suppression of the monastic and other religious orders as a consequence of the adoption of the Constitution of 1790 and other legislative innovations. Those who opposed these changes were indeed martyred, as predicted.

The mention of pagan sacrifices being reinstituted with which the quatrain opens is a reference to the pseudo-religious rites that were temporarily introduced into France by the more extreme of the revolutionaries. The most notable of such ceremonies were the honouring of the 'goddess of Reason' (10 November 1793) and the absurd 'Festival of the Supreme Being' that was orchestrated by Robespierre.

FIGHTING AT THE TUILERIES

While many quatrains of the Centuries may have seemed obscure to earlier interpreters, they were subsequently to be clarified by the passage of historical events. One such is Century IX Quatrain 34, which reads:

> *The solitary marriage partner will be mitred*
> *On return, fighting will proceed at the thuille,*
> *By five hundred one dignified will be betrayed,*
> *Narbone and Saulce, we shall have oil for knives.*

While 'Narbone' might mean the city of Narbonne, to early Nostradamians 'thuille' seemed to be either one of the seer's neologisms or an unusual version of a word meaning tiles – or, alternatively, tile kilns. In either case, no commentator on the quatrains could possibly make sense of this prediction until some 250 years or so after its first publication.

One 17th-century student of Nostradamus made a brave attempt at interpretation. Taking thuille as a slightly distorted version of a French word meaning roof tiles, he translated the verse as:

> *The separated husband shall wear a mitre,*
> *Returning battle, he shall go over the tyle,*
> *By five hundred one dignified shall be betrayed,*
> *Narbon and Salces shall have oil by the quintal.*

His interpretation of this was as follows: 'The verse signifieth, that some certain man who was married shall be parted from his wife, and shall attain to some ecclesiastical dignity ... coming back from some place or enterprise, he shall be met and fought with, and compelled to escape over the tiles of a house ... a man of great account shall be betrayed by 500 of his men ... when these things shall come to pass, Narbon and Salces ... shall reap [i.e. harvest] and make a great deal of oil.'

Ingenious, of course – but pretty unlikely. Odd as the church may have been in some respects in the 17th century, it was improbable that a man, subsequent to separating from his wife, would attain to high office in it and then 'be met and fought with', retreating from his assailants by cavorting about on the rooftops.

However, the seemingly meaningless obscurities of this quatrain ceased to be meaningless in 1791 and 1792. In the June of the former year, the King of France, Louis XVI, and his consort, Marie Antoinette, made their attempted escape from revolutionary France. The venture was bungled right from the start, with the entire royal party, including the King and Queen, travelling together in an enormous lumbering coach that was almost bound to draw attention to its occupants en route.

At the small municipality of Ste Menehould a man named Drouet noticed that one of the men in the coach had a face reminiscent of the appearance of the King as portrayed on a 50-livre assignat (paper money secured on seized church lands). At Varennes the entire party was stopped and arrested, largely as the result of the activities of a man named Saulce, a chandler, grocer and oil merchant – whose name and occupation suggest the Salces mentioned in the last line of the quatrain in association with oil.

The rest of the quatrain also applies very neatly to the flight of Louis XVI and the events following close upon it. The first line reads 'The solitary marriage partner will be mitred', and after his return to Paris from Varennes the King was both 'mitred' and a 'solitary marriage partner' – the latter because he was politically more and more isolated from his own advisers and, increasingly, from Marie Antoinette, who was herself the puppet of her reactionary Swedish adviser Count Hans Axel von Fersen, a man whose political influence was disastrous. He was enmitred in a literal way on 20 June 1792, when a mob invaded the Tuileries palace and compelled their monarch to don the bonnet rouge, the red cap of Liberty, modelled on the Phrygian mitre of antiquity.

What, then, of the meaning of next lines of the quatrain, 'On return, fighting will proceed at the thuille' and 'By five hundred one dignified will be betrayed'?

As described later, the scene of the fighting that took place on 10 August 1792 and resulted in the overthrow of the King shortly afterwards was the palace of the Tuileries. This palace, not under construction or even, as far as is known, planned at the time of the first publication of the Centuries, was erected on a site that had formerly been occupied by at least one tile-firing kiln – the thuille of the quatrain.

So fighting did proceed at the tile kiln following the return of Louis XVI to Paris after his failed escape. At what had been, two centuries earlier, a place where mounds of clay had been fired into coverings for the rooftops of Paris, a new ideology which had been moulded by Jacobin theorists was fired in the heat of battle into a French Republic.

And the 'five hundred' who were predicted to betray 'one dignified'?

The one dignified was the King; the 'five hundred' who betrayed him were probably the Marseillais 'federals' who took part in the fighting at the Tuileries.

For, according to the 19th-century historian Louis Thiers (1797-1877), 'ils étaient cinq cents' – there were five hundred.

THE BEGINNING
OF A NEW ERA

Nostradamus prefaced the first edition of the Centuries with an apocalyptically worded Epistle to Henri II. Such is the tone of the language in which much of this is couched that sceptics assert that it is nothing more than a vague, even meaningless, catalogue of disaster, whole sections of which can be distorted by ingenious interpreters so that they can be applied to any unpleasant event which has taken place within the last 400 years or so.

However, there are significant and absolutely specific prophecies in the Epistle that have definitely been verified by the course of history. One in particular is of enormous interest because it gives a specific year – 1792 – for a predicted major event. The relevant passage reads as follows:

Then will be the beginning [of an era] *that will include within itself* [patterns of behaviour and thought, the way in which people look at the world] *which will last long, and in its first year there shall be a great persecution of the Christian Church, fiercer than that in Africa* [almost certainly a historical reference to the savage Vandal persecution of the church that took place in North Africa in the fifth century], *and this will burst out during the year One Thousand, Seven Hundred and Ninety Two.*

It cannot really be denied that Nostradamus's prediction that the events taking place in the course of 1792 would inaugurate a new era was correct. If any one year can be regarded as marking the beginning of the age in which we live at the present day it was 1792 – far more so than other candidates for that doubtful honour, such as 1776, when Britain's North American colonies declared their independence from the Motherland, or 1789, when Louis XVI of France summoned the Estates General. The event which, above all else, marks 1792 off from all other years took place on 10 August, when the so-called mob attacked the Tuileries, which had become the French royal family's home after they had been removed from Versailles. In actuality the attack was a carefully organized affair, brilliantly planned by an insurrectionary committee, largely under the control of Jacobins, the extreme left of the revolutionary movement, which worked in close collaboration with extremist groups from Brest and Marseilles.

The immediate consequences of the attack included the deaths in hand-to-hand fighting of 400 insurrectionaries and 800 royal troops; the King being first suspended from the throne, then deposed, and eventually executed; the ghastly

September massacres in which many hundreds of imprisoned ecclesiastics, men and women of the aristocracy, rank and file royalists – even prostitutes and minor criminals – were butchered by the sans-culottes allies of the middle-class Jacobins; and the Paris commune becoming, in all but name, the central government of France.

The eventual consequences of the successful insurrection which took place on that hot afternoon in August 1792 have affected, and are still affecting, the lives of each and every one of us. To make any sort of attempt to recount them in full would be quite outside the scope of a book such as this. It suffices to say that those events that took place in Paris in 1792 – events of which Nostradamus seems to have had psychic intimations some 250 years earlier – directly led to the emergence of the ideologies that have largely dominated world politics for over two centuries: secularism, nationalism, revolutionary democracy and socialism.

There is a further point worth making in relation to the prediction that 1792 would mark the beginning of a new era.

In that year France's Jacobin revolutionaries introduced a new calendar. The traditional names of the 12 months of the year, their names derived from classical mythology and history and thus looked upon by the more radical revolutionaries as outmoded relics of the past, were abandoned and the number of the year was changed so that it could no longer be regarded as based upon a Christian chronology.

At midnight on 21-22 September 1792 'Year I of the Republic' began. It ran for a full 365 days and was made up of 12 months, each of 30 days plus 5 additional days. The new months were given what were considered to be 'rational' names; thus, for instance, the month thought likely to be usually the hottest – the one that began on what most people still thought of as July 22 – was called 'Thermidor' (heat).

Thus, in September 1792, the prognostication made by Nostradamus was fulfilled to the very letter. Or was it? After all, the seer predicted that the new era would 'last long', and one does not meet people complaining of 'a very cold Thermidor' or 'a wet Prairal'. However, anyone who reads the theoretical literature of contemporary Marxism continually comes across references to that calendar in the use of such hackneyed phrases as 'a Thermidorean reaction'. In one sense at least the revolutionary calendar, like the new social era inaugurated in 1792, is still with us.

NAPOLEON – EMPEROR AND SOLDIER

The European turmoil that was begun by the outbreak of the French Revolution was no passing phase, and the First Republic that succeeded the reign of Louis XVI existed in a state of perpetual change. Robespierre and his allies replaced the more moderate Republicans, only to be themselves supplanted by the corrupt Directory, which was in turn succeeded by the Consulate and the Empire of Napoleon Bonaparte.

The rise and fall of Napoleon was predicted by Nostradamus; indeed, there are so many quatrains which would seem to refer to Napoleon, the obscure Corsican artillery officer who became a great emperor, that it is impossible to give a detailed interpretation of more than a few of them. Perhaps the best-known is Century VIII Quatrain 57, which reads:

> *From a simple soldier he will attain to Empire,*
> *He will exchange the short robe for the long,*
> *Brave in arms, much worse towards the Church,*
> *He vexes the priests as water soaks a sponge.*

The phrase 'short robe' was one of the seer's double allusions, for by it he signified both the cloak that the future emperor wore when he was a mere military cadet and the robe he wore on formal occasions when he held the office of First Consul. The 'long robe' for which he exchanged the latter was the Coronation robe he donned when crowned emperor by Pope Pius VII in 1804. The meaning of the third line is apparent, and the way in which Napoleon 'vexed the priests' as prognosticated in line four is described below with reference to two other quatrains.

Not only was Nostradamus aware that a 'simple soldier' would 'attain to Empire', he may even have had a fair idea of that soldier's name – or so it has been argued on an ingenious interpretation of Century VIII Quatrain 1, which reads:

> *PAU, NAY, LORON, will be more of fire than blood.*
> *To swim in praise the great man will swim to the confluence.*
> *He will deny the magpies entrance.*
> *Pampon and the Durance will keep them confined.*

The three names with which line one begins are all those of small and historically insignificant towns in the west of France. However, Nostradamus thought fit to have these names printed in capitals, which is almost always an indication that the words capitalized were used by the seer in a secondary sense – usually one involving an anagram or some other variety of wordplay.

An anagram found in these names by one usually reliable French interpreter of the Centuries is NAPAULON ROY – that is, 'King Napoleon'. As the same commentator pointed out over a century ago, in Napoleon's own lifetime the spelling of his unusual name with an 'au' instead of an 'o' was common – and, in any case, Nostradamus may have been hinting at the way in which the Emperor changed the spelling of his surname from the Corsican 'Buonaparte' to the more Gallic 'Bonaparte'.

That this was perhaps the case is suggested by the fact that in Century I Quatrain 76, one of those strange dual quatrains in which Nostradamus would appear to have been making a prophecy applicable to two different men, he gibed at the 'barbaric' surnames of both Napoleon and Adolf Hitler.

Nostradamus may or may not have known Napoleon's surname – but it seems a certainty that, as described on the next two pages, he knew of the Emperor's final destiny.

THE EAGLE, MILAN AND PAVIA

Napoleon's rising military reputation was thoroughly established by the victorious whirlwind of his Italian campaign of 1796-7. Two of the outstanding episodes in this, the first and in some ways the greatest of Napoleon's military triumphs, were referred to by Nostradamus in Century III Quatrain 37, which reads:

> *Before the assault a speech* [or prayer] *is orated,*
> *Milan, deceived by the ambuscade, is captured by the Eagle,*
> *The ancient walls are breached by artillery,*
> *In fire and blood only a few are granted mercy.*

The 'Eagle' of line two who captures Milan is Napoleon – referred to as the Eagle in several of the quatrains – but to which of the two Napoleonic captures of Milan (1796 and 1800) does the verse refer?

Clearly the first, for the speech to which the quatrain refers was that all-important one made by the future Emperor to his troops at the beginning of the Italian campaign of 1796-97: 'Soldiers, you are starving and almost naked ... I will lead you into the most fertile plains in the world ... There you will find honour, glory and riches ... will you be wanting in courage?'

With the occupation of Milan and other nearby cities the soldiers of the French army found the riches that their General had promised them. Alas, their exactions were on such a scale that the citizens of Milan, Pavia and Binasco broke into an open revolt in which they allied themselves with the peasantry of the surrounding countryside. The insurrection was suppressed with the utmost brutality, most notably in Pavia, and, as predicted in the last line of the quatrain, little mercy was given by Napoleon's men to those captured in arms against them.

THE END OF EMPIRE

By the time that Napoleon was crowned Emperor of the French he dominated the whole of continental Europe west of the Russian border. Not since the time of the Emperor Charles V had any one man wielded such power in the western world.

Britain was the only dangerous and powerful enemy still threatening him; its fleet still dominated the seas, and its commercial wealth was employed to subsidize any European state bold enough to oppose his seemingly unstoppable armies. Napoleon felt that Britain was the one remaining major obstacle which must be removed from his path; he had to destroy its naval supremacy and, if possible, invade its territory.

He attempted to do both, and failed – as Nostradamus had accurately predicted would be the case in, respectively, Century I Quatrain 77 and Century VIII Quatrain 53. The former reads:

> *Between two seas stands a promontory,*
> *A man who will die later by a horse's bridle* [or bit],
> *Neptune unfurls a black sail for his man,*
> *The fleet near Calpre* [Gibraltar?] *and Rocheval* [Cape Roche].

While this verse was obviously intended to prophesy some sort of naval battle in which one of the opposing fleets would have a 'black sail' unfurled for it (i.e. be decisively defeated) it seems, on first reading, to be as obscurely worded as almost any quatrain in the Centuries.

However, its second line, 'a man who will die later by a horse's bridle', gives a clue which enables the event to be identified with some certainty as the Battle of Trafalgar – the decisive naval battle in which the English destroyed the combined French and Spanish fleets and finally thwarted Napoleon's ambition to be as supreme at sea as he was on land. For while few naval commanders of any historical importance can have been killed by a horse's bridle, Villeneuve, the admiral who commanded the French fleet at Trafalgar, does seem to have died in this curious fashion. Taken prisoner at the battle, he was released and returned to France in the following year – only to be strangled in mysterious circumstances at an inn in Rennes. According to contemporary reports, the assassin had used a horse's bridle as his chosen weapon.

The rest of the quatrain is easily understandable – the 'promontory between two seas' being Gibraltar, which stands between the Atlantic and the Mediterranean.

Napoleon's failure to invade England and the way in which he used his untested army of invasion after he withdrew it from its lines near Boulogne some two months before his navy was smashed at Trafalgar was predicted by Nostradamus in Century VIII Quatrain 53, which reads:

> *Within Bolongne* [Boulogne] *he will want to wash away his faults,*
> *He cannot do so at the Temple of the Sun,*
> *He will haste away to do great things,*
> *In the hierarchy he was never equalled.*

The 'faults' which Napoleon wished to wash away were not moral failings; they were his successive misjudgements of the importance of Britain's naval supremacy and economic strength which had largely negated his military successes ever since his Egyptian campaign of 1798. But what was the 'Temple of the Sun' in which Nostradamus said that Napoleon would, metaphorically speaking, be unable to wash away his faults?

The phrase simply meant Britain, for by employing the words 'Temple of the Sun' the seer was making two of the classical allusions of which he was so fond. First, he was referring to the writings of a pre-Christian Greek geographer who described what was almost certainly Stonehenge as a temple of the sun god Apollo; secondly, he was alluding to a traditionally held belief that Westminster Abbey, where English monarchs have been crowned since Norman times, was built on the site of a Romano-British sun temple.

After Napoleon abandoned his invasion barges on the Channel coast in the summer of 1804 he marched his army eastwards, occupying Vienna and smashing the combined Austrian and Russian armies at Austerlitz. In other words, he hastened away from Boulogne to do 'great things' – just as Nostradamus had foretold. But Britain continued to forge against him coalitions of which it was the paymaster.

After his invasion of Russia ended in disaster and he was defeated at the Battle of Leipzig Napoleon was forced to abdicate as Emperor in 1814. He was exiled to the mini-state of Elba, of which he was given sovereignty. Inevitably the tiny island was too small for him; he escaped and returned to France, where he was proclaimed Emperor. However, after a rule of only 100 days he was defeated by the British and Prussians at Waterloo and exiled to the windswept island of St Helena in the south Atlantic Ocean, where he died in 1821.

These latter events seem to have been the subjects of more than one of Nostradamus's visions, for they are described, under the usual veils of allegory and symbol, in several quatrains. For instance, both Century II Quatrain 66 and Century X Quatrain 25 describe in symbolized yet easily interpreted outline some events of the brief restoration of the Napoleonic Empire, and Century I

49

Quatrains 23 and 38 were both prophetic of the Battle of Waterloo. The last two quatrains were written in the symbolic quasi-heraldic terminology so beloved of the seer – but both are meaningful and the first gave a clear prediction that the heraldic Leopard of England would triumph over the Eagles of Napoleon's Grand Army.

THE THRONE OF PETER

In the Centuries there are to be found numerous references to the papacy and to individual Popes. It would seem that, as might have been expected of a man of his times – when the Pope was a temporal as well as a spiritual ruler, generally considered by western Christians to be the most important man in the world – Nostradamus sought many visions pertaining to the papacy and particular persons destined to occupy the 'Throne of Peter'.

Some of the 'papal quatrains' relate to events that have not as yet taken place, and it is to be presumed that in these either Nostradamus prophesied falsely or, more likely, that they will take place at some time in the future – probably the very near future. Others are so specific and fit the facts of history so neatly that one can take it as reasonably certain that they are notable examples of Nostradamian predictive hits – for instance, the prognostication of the circumstances in which that rarest of post-medieval ecclesiastical creatures, an exiled Pope, would meet his end (see panel opposite).

Another very specific Nostradamian prediction concerning the papacy is to be found in Century V Quatrain 29, which reads:

> *Liberty will not be recovered,*
> *It will be occupied by a* [man who is] *black, proud, fierce and evil,*
> *When the matter of the Pope is opened*
> *By Hister, the Republic of Venice will be vexed.*

Taking the last line of this verse in its literal sense, it would appear that the prediction must relate to the 18th century or earlier, for the patrician Venetian Republic ceased to exist as an independent state as a consequence of the conquests made by the armies of revolutionary France. However, it has long been the consensus of opinion among Nostradamian interpreters that in this quatrain the seer was using the phrase 'Republic of Venice' in a semi-allegorical fashion, implying by it something like 'popular liberties in the Italian peninsula and the Pope's freedom of action'.

If this interpretation is accepted – and the arguments for it are varied and ingenious – its relevance seems to be to the period 1939-45 and the predicted 'Hister' is none other than Adolf Hitler. Under this interpretation, the unrecovered liberty of line one had a double meaning for Nostradamus. On the one hand it was the political freedom of the Italian people which had been lost as a result of the seizure of power by Mussolini – who was the black [shirted] evil man of line two. On the other, it was the temporal freedom of the Popes which had been lost in 1870, when Rome was forcibly incorporated into the Kingdom of Italy; it was not really regained as a consequence of the concordat between Mussolini and the Vatican, and the burdens inflicted upon the papacy as a consequence of its loss of temporal power were made even more onerous by the interference of Hitler in the affairs of both Italy and the Vatican.

All very ingenious, but in the opinion of the present writer it may be just too ingenious an interpretation of prophecy – one of those occasions in which legitimate speculation has crossed the boundaries of common sense. It has to be admitted, however, that several quatrains in the Centuries mention 'Hister', and that what is said of him seems generally compatible with events in the life of Adolf Hitler.

THE VEXED PRIESTS

As mentioned earlier, in the fourth line of Century VIII Quatrain 57 Nostradamus prophesied that Napoleon Bonaparte would 'vex the priests as water soaks a sponge'.

The seer's prophecy was accurate, for in one way or another Napoleon vexed a very large number of the Catholic clergy, both before and after he became Emperor. They included not only humble parish priests, but also bishops (and at least one former bishop, the aristocratic Talleyrand), cardinals and two Popes, Pius VI and Pius VII.

As one of the consequences of the French successes that followed upon Napoleon's Italian triumphs, Pope Pius VI was taken to France as a prisoner of the French and subsequently died at Valence, vomiting and spitting blood, in the late summer of 1799. Nostradamus may have rather vaguely prophesied this death on foreign soil in the last line of Century I Quatrain 37, which mentions 'Pope and ... sepulchre both in foreign lands'. A much more specific prediction was given in Century II Quatrain 97, which reads:

> *Roman Pontiff, beware of approaching*
> *The city with two rivers.*
> *You will spit your blood in that place,*
> *You and yours, when the roses bloom.*

The successor of the Pope who died spitting blood when the roses of both summer and the Revolution were in full bloom was Pope Pius VII, who entered into a concordat with France in 1814 but was, nevertheless, held captive by Napoleon for almost four years. Nostradamus allusively predicted this captivity in both line three of Century I Quatrain 4 – 'At this time the barque of the Papacy will be lost' – and in the first two lines of Century V Quatrain 15, which read as follows:

> *While travelling* [literally 'navigating' or 'sailing']
> *the Great Pontiff will be captured,*
> *The efforts of the troubled clergy fail ...*

MISTAKEN PROPHECIES

Nostradamus is perhaps the best-known prophet of the future in the world – certainly the Western world – but he was not always correct in every detail of his predictions. Thus, for instance, his prophecy of the murder of the Guise brothers in Century III Quatrain 51 was right in almost every particular save those relating to the last line.

In this line, which reads 'Angers, Troyes and Langres will do them a disservice', he was clearly predicting that the cities mentioned would be hostile to the cause with which the Guise brothers were associated – the supremacy of the Catholic faith in France. In reality none of those who governed these places displayed any notable sympathy for the Protestant cause in the French Wars of Religion – one of them stayed more or less neutral and the other two supported the Catholic League.

There are several such largely, but not entirely, correct predictions relating to events that took place in the 19th century. These may be examples of Nostradamian errors – but the present writer suspects that in at least some of them the errors have arisen from mistaken interpretations rather than from psychic clouds obscuring Nostradamus's visions of the future.

One outstanding example of a probably misinterpreted prophecy is provided by Century X Quatrain 8. The first two lines of this have been applied to the baptism of the son of Napoleon III in the summer of 1856 and its third line to Napoleon III's wife, the Empress Eugenie; the fourth line of the verse has been assumed either to have not been fulfilled at all or to be so obscure in meaning that no one can appreciate just how it has been fulfilled. The quatrain reads:

> *With first finger and thumb he will sprinkle the forehead,*
> *The Count of Senegalia to his own* [god]*son,*
> *Venus through several in short order,*
> *In a week three are mortally wounded.*

There is no difficulty at all in arriving at a Napoleonic interpretation of the first two lines – clearly a baptism was being described at which a 'Count of Senegalia' would be the foremost godfather of the child. As the godfather of

Napoleon III's son was Pio Nono (Pope Pius IX), who was the son of Count Mastoi Feretti of Senigallia, the quatrain fits well enough. However, there seems to be no good reason to assume that the quatrain is predictively associated in any fashion whatsoever with either Napoleon III or his family. Pope Pius IX stood as godfather to a great many children both before and after his elevation to the 'Throne of Peter' and the verse's prophetic significance may be relevant to the lives of individuals whom history has forgotten.

The Napoleonic misinterpretation (if misinterpretation it be) of Century X Quatrain 8 arose as a result of the overeagerness of 19th-century French students of the prophecies of Nostradamus to interpret obscure quatrains to fit events with which they were familiar or which they were hoping would happen in their own lifetimes – for example, a Bourbon Restoration after the fall of the Second Empire and the proclamation of the Third Republic (1870).

Not all the 19th-century applications of Nostradamian predictions to incidents in the life of Napoleon III have been based on such dubious reasoning as that of Century X Quatrain 8. Century IV Quatrain 100 and Century V Quatrain 32 both seem to have been predictive of the Franco-Prussian War which resulted in the abdication of Napoleon III, the end of his empire, the proclamation of the Third Republic and a bitter internecine struggle between its army and the forces of the Paris Commune. The former quatrain is especially applicable to these events. It reads:

> *Fire will fall from the sky on the royal building*
> *When the fire of Mars is weakened:*
> *For seven months a mighty war, the populace dying through evil,*
> *Rouen and Evreux will not fail the King.*

During the 1870 siege of Paris, when the seven-month-long Franco-Prussian war was drawing towards its close ('the fire of Mars ... weakened') that 'royal building' the Tuileries was destroyed by heavy, and high-elevation, artillery fire. During the siege the evil of famine and resulting disease killed even more Parisians than did the military activities of the Prussians. And after the proclamation Rouen, Evreux and other cities of Normandy did not 'fail the King', for they were centres of legitimism, the cause of those who wanted the Second Empire to give way to a Bourbon, not a Republican, restoration.

In the case of this particular 19th-century interpretation there seems to have been no ingenious deformation of the meaning of the relevant quatrain. However, it has to be borne in mind that in every century, not just the last, there has been an understandable and almost inevitable tendency among commentators on the Centuries of Nostradamus to unconsciously tailor quatrains to fit recent events. Those who interpret Nostradamus at the present day cannot entirely escape following the same pattern, however hard they may try to do so.

Readers of some of the pages that follow should, therefore, always be conscious of the possibility that sometimes the present writer may have fallen into the same trap as did the 19th-century commentator who first applied Century X Quatrain 8 to the baptism of the son of Napoleon III.

NOSTRADAMUS
AND THE NAZIS

O ne evening in the winter of 1939–40, during the period of military inactivity preceding the German blitzkrieg that resulted in the fall of France, Magda Goebbels, wife of Hitler's brilliant but totally amoral Minister of Propaganda and Enlightenment, was reading in bed. Suddenly she called out to her husband in great excitement, 'Did you know that over 400 years ago it was prophesied that in 1939 Germany would go to war with France and Britain over Poland?'

It is likely that Goebbels already knew something of this prediction, for it would seem that four different members of the Nazi Party had already sent him copies of the book that had so excited his wife. Nevertheless, he looked at the passage to which she had drawn his attention and was immediately struck by its potential value as propaganda, for it did seem to accurately foretell both the date and the cause of the war that had broken out some three months or so previously. Perhaps, he thought, the author of the book knew of other prophecies which might serve to convince the enemies of the Reich of the inevitability of a German victory.

The book was entitled Mysterien von Sonne und Seele (Mysteries of the Sun and Spirit). It had been written by a certain Doktor H. H. Kritzinger, and had been published in 1922, 17 years before the outbreak of war. The prediction which so excited Magda Goebbels and the four other Nazis who had drawn her husband's attention to it was based upon a particular, and extremely ingenious, interpretation of Century III Quatrain 57. This interpretation was not originated by Doktor Kritzinger – indeed, some elements of this particular piece of prophetic exegesis can be dated back to at least 1715, when an English interpreter of Nostradamus, a man who wrote under the pseudonym of 'D.D.', turned his attention to this quatrain, which reads:

> *Seven times you will see the British nation change,*
> *Tinged with blood for two hundred and ninety years:*
> *Not at all free through German support,*
> *Aries fears for his 'pole' Bastarnien.*

D.D. gave it as his opinion that the phrase 'tinged with blood for two hundred and ninety years' referred to a period beginning with the shedding of the Blood Royal by the execution of King Charles I in 1649. This gave D.D. the date 1939 as the year of some notable event in British history. The first line of the quatrain was interpreted by D.D. as seven dynastic or quasi-dynastic changes – such as, for instance, the Restoration of the Stuart monarchy in 1660.

Between 1715 and 1921 other students of Nostradamus extended D.D.'s theories. The last of these, a Herr Loog, combined all these interpretations into one and added to them his own explanation of the last line of the quatrain, 'Aries fears for his "pole" Bastarnien'. This he took to mean 'France doubts (or fears for) her subordinate ally, the land of the Bastarnae (Poland)'.

Why should Herr Loog have taken Aries to mean France? Was he just making a wild guess? No, he was not – for as long ago as the 17th century Théophile de Garencières had written in relation to this particular quatrain that Aries signified France because 'the sign of Aries doth govern France'.

Loog followed earlier commentators in interpreting 1939 as the year to be 'tinged with blood' and, on this basis, forecast for it war involving Poland, France, Germany, and Britain – the prediction which was inserted by Doktor Kritzinger into his book.

Was this fulfilled prediction of Nostradamus just a lucky hit, as sceptics have claimed? To this question the unbiased observer can only reply that if the prediction that seems to have been fulfilled by Hitler's invasion of Poland and the outbreak of World War II in September 1939 was just a lucky hit, then it has to be admitted that the seer had an extraordinary capacity for making lucky hits. For, as readers of this book will appreciate, there are numerous examples of the same sort of fulfilled predictions to be found in the Centuries and other writings of Nostradamus.

HITLER, HIMMLER AND THE NAZIS

As was pointed out earlier, Nostradamus sometimes wrote prophetic verses of a double nature – that is, predictions which, without being exceptionally vague, do seem to fit more than one person or event. The sceptic's explanation for the aptness of such quatrains is that the seer never made a genuinely fulfilled prophecy, that interpreters have simply twisted the meanings of the components of the Centuries to fit their own preconceived ideas, and that the existence of quatrains with more than one supposed meaning does no more than illustrate the fact that two or more Nostradamian commentators have arrived at different interpretations.

It is an ingenious and, in some ways, a persuasive argument – but it is based on the premise that none of Nostradamus's predictions were ever genuinely fulfilled. To the present writer and many others this position seems quite untenable in view of various prognostications which were explicitly or implicitly dated by the seer. A more likely explanation for the double-meaning quatrains is that in vision Nostradamus discerned two separate individuals whose lives were separated in time, who may well have been very different from one another in character, but who had certain things in common that enabled him to write a prophetic verse that pertained to both.

A good example of such an ingeniously worded double prediction is provided by Century I Quatrain 76, which seems to apply to both Napoleon Bonaparte and the equally – to any German of the 1920s not born on the borderlands of Slavdom – 'barbarically named' Hitler. The meaning of this quatrain is apparent. It reads:

> *This man will be called by a barbaric name*
> *Which the three sisters will have received,*
> *He will speak to a great people in words and actions,*
> *He will have fame and renown beyond any other man* [of his time].

It seems likely, however, that some quatrains that have been applied to more than one person have been misinterpreted by over-credulous interpreters. One such is Century II Quatrain 70, applied to Napoleon by some, but very probably prophetic of the character and death of Heinrich Himmler, leader of Hitler's SS, who ended his life while talking – just as did the 'human monster' in the verse in question, which reads:

> *The dart from heaven will make its journey,*
> *Death while speaking, a great execution;*
> *The stone in the tree, a proud race abased,*
> *Talk of a human monster, purge and expiation.*

Another quatrain which has been applied to Napoleon but seems far more apposite in the context of Nazism is Century III Quatrain 35, which reads:

> *In the farthest depths of Western Europe,*
> *A child will be born of a poor people,*
> *Who by his speeches will seduce great numbers,*
> *His reputation will grow even greater in the eastern domain.*

This seems to be another reference to Adolf Hitler, for his parents were a good deal poorer than those of Napoleon, he was born on the eastern boundaries of western Europe, his rise to power came about as a consequence of his oratory 'seducing many', and his drive for Lebensraum was primarily directed towards the 'eastern domain' of the Soviet Union.

Of the numerous quatrains that have been applied to the Nazis over the last 50 years or so, some seem dubious in the extreme – but it is hard to doubt many of them. For instance, Century IX Quatrain 90 accurately predicts the disastrous effects upon Hungary of that country's ruler, Admiral Horthy, accepting the 'help' offered by Hitler:

> *A captain of Greater Germany* [i.e. Hitler]
> *Will deliver counterfeit help,*
> *A King of Kings to support Hungary,*
> *His war will cause great bloodshed.*

Similarly, Century V Quatrain 29 obviously applies to Hitler, Mussolini and the Papacy, Century V Quatrain 51 to the activities of the two dictators at the time of the Spanish Civil War, and Century VI Quatrain 51 to the unsuccessful attempt that was made upon Hitler's life in November 1939.

The conquests made by Hitler the following spring also seem to have been perceived by Nostradamus who, in Century V Quatrain 94, wrote:

> *He* [presumably Hitler] *will transform into Greater Germany,*
> *Brabant, Flanders, Ghent, Bruges and Boulogne …*

THE SIGN OF THE SWASTIKA

The swastika, or hakenkreuz (literally, 'hooked cross'), is now forever associated in the minds of most of us with the Nazis and the terrible crimes that they committed in World War II. Originally, however, the symbol had a purely spiritual significance in both the eastern and western hemispheres of our planet; indeed, at the present day the swastika symbol is still to be found in many Hindu temples.

Prior to the outbreak of World War I, the swastika was regarded in Germany as a symbol of the god Thor (or Thunor) and for this reason the Freikorps – the armed groups who defended Germany after the war – adopted it. In the early 1920s Hitler reversed the position of the arms of the swastika and made it the badge of his movement.

Nostradamus seems to have predicted the future notoriety of both the swastika and the Nazi leader in Century VI Quatrain 49, which reads:

> *The great Priest of the Party of Mars* [i.e. Hitler]
> *Who will subjugate the Danube, The cross*
> *harried by the crook …*

FRANCE, SPAIN
AND WORLD WAR II

Describing the Nazi leader as a 'bird of prey flying on the left', Nostradamus wrote prophetically of European perceptions of Adolf Hitler in the period 1933–39 in Century I Quatrain 34, which reads:

The bird of prey flying to the left
Makes [warlike] preparations before combating the French:
Some will regard him as good, some as evil, some as ambiguous,
The weaker party will regard him as a good augury.

The first line's description of Hitler as 'flying to the left' was a typical piece of Nostradamian wordplay. His primary reference was to the fact that the word 'sinister' is derived from the Latin word for left; his secondary one was that Hitler, as he explained in his book Mein Kampf, deliberately modelled his propaganda methods on those used by Marxists and that many members of his storm troops, the SA, had been recruited from the ranks of former communists.

The second line of the quatrain requires little clarification – Hitler's war preparations against France were such that in the summer of 1940 hundreds of thousands of refugees were to jam that country's roads – but the third does need some explanation .

To us, with all the advantages of hindsight, it seems obvious that Hitler was a megalomaniac warmonger with a desire to dominate the world and to destroy any individuals or peoples who either stood directly in his way or were considered by him to be racially undesirable. In the 1930s, however, none of this was quite so apparent. On the right, Soviet Communism was seen as the major threat to European stability and peace and it was generally thought that the Nazis had 'saved Germany from Bolshevism'. And on both the liberal left and the right it was quite widely believed that for all his fire-breathing oratory Hitler did not really desire war, but that he was prepared to use the threat of it in order to remedy the injustices that Germany had suffered under the provisions of the 1919 Treaty of Versailles.

So attitudes towards the Führer were, as Nostradamus had predicted, very mixed. Some, like British Liberal leader Lloyd George, for a time regarded him with admiration; others discerned his evil nature at an early stage of his career; others were unsure. The 'weaker party' of the quatrain's fourth line who the seer foretold would regard the coming to power of Hitler as a 'good augury' was, rather surprisingly, the KPD, the German Communist Party, whose Stalinist leaders argued that a phase of Nazi rule would precede the German proletarian revolution.

There are several quatrains in the Centuries referring to somebody or something named 'Hister', almost all of which bear the double predictive meanings in which Nostradamus, so to speak, specialized; that is to say they all refer to both the river Ister, a classical name for the Danube, and to Adolf Hitler. One of them is Century II Quatrain 24. This would appear to relate to both the imprisonment of Hungary's leader, Admiral Horthy, by 'Hister' in its Hitlerian sense and to the eventual defeat of the Wehrmacht in Hungary and its panic-stricken retreat across the 'Hister' in its Danubian sense. It reads:

> Beasts mad with hunger will swim across the rivers,
> The most part of the battlefield will be against Hister.
> In an iron cage the leader will be dragged [by him?],
> When the child of Germany follows no law.

Nostradamus was responsible for prophecies on Hitler's defeats in western Europe as well as those on the Danube and Century II Quatrain 16 is clearly a reference to the 'new tyranny' of Italian fascists and their German patrons, the Allied invasion of Sicily in 1943, and the intense air and naval bombardment ('great noise and fire in the heavens') which preceded it. The quatrain reads:

> In Naples, Palermo, Syracuse and throughout Sicily
> New tyrants [rule], great noise and fire in the heavens,
>
> A force from London, Ghent, Brussels and Suse,
> A great slaughter, then triumph and festivities.

The final line was a foretelling of Allied victory – but elsewhere, in Century I Quatrain 31, the seer made it apparent that he knew that this victory would be to some extent a hollow one for the Allies, with Spanish fascism still in power, new threats from the Soviet Union, and an awareness by the 'three great ones, the Eagle [the USA], the Cock [France] ... the Lion [Britain]' that they had enjoyed at best 'an uncertain victory'.

THE FEAST OF THE CARRION

The flight of the unhappy French refugees who, bombed by Stukas and raked by fire from fighter aircraft, made their way along the roads leading south as the Wehrmacht advanced upon Paris in the early summer of 1940 was predicted by Nostradamus in Century III Quatrain 7, which reads:

> The refugees [literally, fugitives], fire from the sky on their weapons,

The next battle will be that of the carrion crows,
They [the refugees] call on earth and heaven for relief
When the warriors draw near the walls.

The 'fire from the sky' was that which came from Luftwaffe aeroplanes and was so effective that men, women and children were killed and – as the seer had foretold – carrion crows battled with one another for their share of the human flesh upon which they were able to feast.

WAR IN THE AIR

For a period of more than 400 years students of prophecy and the predictive arts have brooded upon the tortuous and often obscure verses which collectively make up the Centuries of Nostradamus. Some of them, such as the late James Laver, have merely wanted to discover examples of fulfilled prophecy; others have also wanted to interpret the quatrains with the object of finding out what the future holds in store both for them and for their descendants. Still others have studied the Centuries with quite a different end in view: they wish, for reasons which can only be surmised, to discredit prophecies in general and those of Nostradamus in particular.

Most of these professional sceptics have rejected all examples of fulfilled Nostradamian predictions – even including those in which specific dates were given by the seer – as either coincidental or as the product of what could be termed 'delusional hindsight', by which is meant the ingenious twisting of the content and import of particular quatrains in order to make them fit a past event. There is no doubt at all that this has sometimes been done, both by over-enthusiastic Nostradamians and by those wanting to carry out an amusing hoax.

Thus, for instance, one American commentator (who it is to be hoped was a hoaxer rather than a man who wished to contribute towards a serious commentary upon the Centuries) went to considerable trouble to reinterpret a quatrain usually held to be a fairly clear prediction of the 18th-century invention of balloon flight by the Montgolfier brothers. According to him, the quatrain in question had been misunderstood; it was in reality a revelation of the result of a US Open golf championship that took place in the 1920s.

Amusing as it is that such a ludicrous interpretation can be made, it is usually by no means easy to twist the quatrains of the Centuries to a particular purpose. In relation to this it is interesting to note a circumstance connected with the German army's advance into France in the early part of the summer of 1940.

The 'black propaganda' section of either the Wehrmacht or the Propaganda Ministry was anxious to find a Nostradamus quatrain of which the meaning could be perverted in order that it could be used to encourage French civilian refugees to take to, and thus block, the roads leading towards the south-west of

France. The idea was that leaflets containing a suitably interpreted quatrain should be dropped by the Luftwaffe over areas in which there were known to be refugee concentrations.

However, in spite of the 'black propaganda' experts calling on the assistance of various Nostradamian experts – at least one of whom, Karl Krafft, was a committed Nazi – they totally failed to find a quatrain that would suit their purpose. There was, of course, the quatrain described below, but as it suggested that those who took to the roads might well end up being eaten by birds of prey it hardly suited German intentions. Instead, the Nazis were forced to rely on dropping crude forgeries from the air. These were attributed to Nostradamus, but they in no way resembled genuine quatrains in either style or content.

It is likely that Nostradamus would not have been particularly surprised if he had known that almost 400 years after his death verses attributed to him were destined to be dropped from the air from flying machines – for, although he lived in an age in which the fastest mode of transportation was a galloping horse, he seems to have experienced visions of aerial combat. One such vision would appear to be described in Century I Quatrain 64, which reads:

> *At night they will think that they have seen the sun,*
> *When they see the pig-like half-man,*
> *Noise, shouts, battles seen in the heavens:*
> *Brute beasts will be heard speaking.*

This suggests a description of an air battle such as might have taken place at any time between the beginning of World War I and the Gulf War of 1991. If such an interpretation is to be accepted, the sun at night would be the glare of exploding anti-aircraft shells or missiles, the 'pig-like half-man' would be a pilot or navigator wearing flying helmet and oxygen mask, these in appearance vaguely resembling a porcine snout. And the 'brute beasts' heard speaking would be the 'half-men', i.e. the airmen, communicating by radio with their bases and one another.

MODERN TECHNOLOGY

Many of the quatrains which seemed to be no more than a string of incomprehensible phrases to those who read them in the 1690s, the 1790s and the 1890s appear to have a fairly clear meaning to those of us who attempt to interpret them in the 1990s. Much of the Nostradamian verse which in, say, the 1890s seemed to be meaninglessly symbolic, vaguely mystical stuff now makes sense as a record of a vision interpreted by a man living in the 16th century – a man who was trying to describe a technology of which he knew nothing.

Century I Quatrain 64 provides an excellent example of such a Nostradamian attempt at a description of a technology of a future century.

THE ENERGY
OF THE ATOM

If we accept that, as was explained earlier, Nostradamus saw visions of modern aerial combat and found the task of describing it so difficult that he was forced to use terms such as 'pig-like men', we can appreciate that if he had clairvoyant glimpses of even more recent technologies he would have found it even more of an effort to convey in words the nature of what he had seen.

Yet there are a number of quatrains in the Centuries in which it seems likely that the prophet was attempting to describe both atomic explosions and space flight.

For instance, Century II Quatrain 6 looks as though it could well have been a prediction of the events that brought about the Japanese surrender in August 1945 – the dropping of atomic bombs upon the cities of Hiroshima and Nagasaki. This quatrain reads:

Near the harbour and in two cities
Will be two scourges never previously witnessed.
Hunger and plague, those thrown down by the weapon [literally 'iron']
Will cry to Immortal God for succour.

It is possible, of course, that in this verse the seer was prognosticating twin disasters that still lie in our future – but it has to be admitted that they very aptly fit the events of August 1945. Both cities are contiguous to harbours; their inhabitants were subjected to 'scourges never previously witnessed' – that is, the deliberate release of atomic energy in order to kill human beings; and many of those who survived the immediate effects of the bombs suffered never previously witnessed types of plague and hunger, the plague being radiation sickness and the hunger a consequence of one of its symptoms – continuous vomiting of such severity that the body of the victim is incapable of absorbing any nourishment.

Nostradamus also seems to have been aware of the possibilities of space travel and to have done his best to describe it. In the first two lines of Century VI Quatrain 34 he probably referred to the military uses of space vehicles when he wrote of 'the machine of flying fire' and the last two lines of Century VI Quatrain 5 are completely meaningless except in the context of a manned space station. They read:

Samarobin one hundred leagues from the hemisphere [i.e. the earth],
They will live without law, exempt from politics.

The word 'politics' was probably used here in its primary 16th-century senses – roughly speaking, moderation, balance, reasoned calculation – so Nostradamus was predicting that a group of people would live lawlessly and immoderately one hundred leagues above the earth's surface in some structure he termed 'Samarobin'.

It seems likely that Nostradamus discerned the nature of some modern epidemics as well as 20th-century technology, for the first three lines of Century IX Quatrain 55 can reasonably be interpreted as a double prediction of the influenza epidemic that swept Europe in 1917-18 (and resulted in even more deaths than World War I itself) and of the current epidemic of AIDS. The relevant lines of this quatrain read:

> *The dreadful war which is prepared in the west,*
> *The following year the pestilence will come,*
> *So horrible that neither young nor old* [will survive].

Both of these epidemics were caused by mutated viruses; the influenza outbreak followed upon the slaughters of the Western front in World War I, and the AIDS epidemic, although its causative virus may have been in existence for centuries, did not really get into its terrible stride until the time when Iraq invaded Iran from the west and began a war that has been described as more productive of casualties than anything since the great infantry advances of World War I.

COMPUTER VIRUSES?

As was explained earlier, in relation to a quatrain referring to a 'mitred husband', on occasion old, ingenious, but improbable interpretations of a Nostradamian prediction have to be abandoned in the clarifying light of actual historical events.

Another such old interpretation is that of the first two lines of Century I Quatrain 22, which read:

> *A thing existing without any senses*
> *Will cause its own death to happen through artifice ...*

Since 1672, when Théophile de Garencières commented on these lines, some Nostradamians have tried to apply them to an event that took place in 1613 – the surgical removal of a petrified embryo from the womb of a woman named Colomba Chantry.

To some, this interpretation has always appeared unlikely – apart from it being a somewhat insignificant event to be the subject of prophecy it has been hard to understand how the embryo could be considered to have caused 'its own death to happen through artifice'. An up-to-date alternative suggestion is that the thing (or things) which paradoxically exists, is capable of causing its own demise and yet has no senses is a modern computer. A 'senseless savant' of this sort can destroy itself as a result of the artifice being loaded with a program carrying a hidden virus that instructs the machine to progressively eradicate its own memory.

Fantastic? Perhaps – but no more so than some of the accurate predictions that are made elsewhere in the Centuries.

THE FALL OF THE SOVIET UNION

Twenty years ago, many Sovietologists – supposed experts on the economic, social and political affairs of the Soviet Union and the bloc of allegedly socialist countries which it led – were gloomily or joyfully (depending upon their political orientation) forecasting the decline of the market economies of western capitalism and the 'inevitable' triumph of the socialist bloc. Even five years ago, when the structure of Soviet bureaucracy was already crumbling, there were not only those who talked ceaselessly of 'coming to terms with the Soviet actuality' but some who still clung to the opinion that in some mysterious fashion the Soviet tyranny was morally superior to modern capitalism.

Nostradamus was wiser than all the self-appointed experts. More than four centuries before they were born he was prophesying not only the Russian Bolshevik triumph of 1917 and the persecution of the Orthodox Church which was its consequence, but the eventual downfall of both the Berlin Wall and the empire which had built it.

He predicted the first two of these events in Century VIII Quatrain 80, which reads:

> *The blood of the innocents, of widow and virgin.*
> *So many evils committed by the Great Red,*
> *Holy icons placed over burning candles,*
> *Terrified by fright every one will be afraid to move.*

This was an excellent description, not only of what actually happened during the era of Lenin and Stalin but also of the psychological state of fearful immobility that it induced among Russia's Christians.

The eventual downfall of communism in Russia and the other Soviet Republics was predicted in Century III Quatrain 95, which reads:

> *The Moorish law* [way of life] *will be seen to fail,*
> *Followed by another that is more attractive:*
> *The Boristhenes will be the first to give way*
> *To another more pleasing* [way of life]
> *as a consequence of gifts and tongues.*

The verse as a whole made very little sense until quite recently, although some years ago at least one commentator on the quatrain suggested that it prophesied the downfall of Russia as a Marxist state. His interpretation was based on a piece of Nostradamian wordplay to be discerned in the first line – an ingenious use of the phrase 'Moorish law' to signify something not immediately apparent from its literal meaning. Karl Marx, the theoretician whose writings inspired Lenin, Trotsky, Bukharin and the other leaders of the Russian Revolution, had a nickname which was used only by his family and by such close associates as Friedrich Engels. It was 'the Moor' – and by his use of the term 'the Moorish law' Nostradamus meant 'a society based on the teachings of Karl Marx'.

'The Boristhenes will be the first to give way to another more pleasing [way of life] as a consequence of gifts and tongues,' said Nostradamus in his third and fourth lines. Boristhenes was the classical name for the Dnieper, Russia's great river, while in all probability the phrase 'gifts and tongues' referred to Western influences, the former being smuggled consumer goods, the latter the effect of the siren voices of capitalism heard on Radio Free Europe and other Western radio stations. The quatrain can now be paraphrased:

> *The Marxist way of life will be seen to fail*
> *And will be succeeded by one that is more pleasing.*
> *Russia will be the first* [i.e. before China]
> *to abandon communism*
> *As a consequence of outside influences upon it.*

While, in the last analysis, all these outside influences emanated from the Western world, some of them made their way into Russia as a consequence of the events witnessed by soldiers of the Red Army at the time of the fall of the Berlin Wall – yet another largely unexpected happening which had been foretold by Nostradamus, for he appears to have predicted it in Century V Quatrain 81, which reads:

> *The Royal bird over the city of the sun,*
> *Will give its nightly augury* [prophecy] *for seven months,*
> *Thunder and lightning, the Eastern wall will fall,*
> *In seven days the enemy directly at the gates.*

The 'Royal bird' is the eagle, a symbol of the old monarchy of Prussia whose capital was Berlin, thought to have been termed 'city of the sun' by the seer for two reasons – the more likely one being that according to at least one 16th-century astrologer, Brandenburg – the state that evolved into Prussia – was 'ruled' by Leo, the sun's own sign.

The events that immediately precipitated the downfall of both the East German state and the wall that it had built with the object of keeping its citizens at home had been preceded by roughly seven months of steadily increasing civil unrest; all in all, the quatrain fits in very neatly with what actually happened and can fairly be considered to rank as yet another of Nostradamus's predictive successes.

It is only right to say, however, that in the past the verse in question has been applied to at least two other events – namely the defeats suffered by France in 1870 and 1940. As against this it has to be admitted that as long ago as 1972, almost 20 years before the Wall came down, the Nostradamian commentator Erika Cheetham published her opinion that the quatrain was likely to refer to that possible and much hoped-for event.

THE GULF WAR

As was pointed out earlier, Nostradamus sometimes wrote predictive verses which, until very recently, were seemingly jumbles of confused nonsense but which now make sense in terms of the technology of modern warfare.

A 'nonsense' prophecy of this sort is provided by Century I Quatrain 29, which is now thought likely to refer either to some future nuclear war which will soon be upon us or, more probably and more to be hoped, the Gulf War fought against Iraq and that country's occupation of Kuwait. The quatrain reads:

When the [travelling] earthly and watery fish
Is thrown upon the shore by a great wave,
Its strange form wild and horrifying,
From the sea its enemies soon reach the walls.

In the last line 'the walls' would appear to mean, in the terminology of our own era, 'static defences' – fortified walls were the only important form of stationary defence in the 16th century – and 'its enemies' clearly refer to armed forces trying to break through those defences.

Once again, we have a quatrain that would have been utterly obscure in meaning to someone who read it in, say, the 1840s or even the 1940s. With its wall-threatening fish travelling over land and sea it could be interpreted only by straining its supposed symbolism in a manner hardly convincing to any but the most enthusiastic Nostradamus devotee. In the 1990s, however, it seems probable that, like the 'pig-like half-man', it pertains to the weapon systems of advanced military technology. It could be a reference to an atomic missile being launched from a submarine against an enemy, an event that has not yet taken place. However, to the present writer it sounds much more like a description of the 1991 Gulf War as clairvoyantly seen by a Renaissance psychic and/or practitioner of ceremonial divination.

If so, the fish travelling over land and sea would be one of the ship-launched Cruise missiles that smashed the command structure of the Iraqi military machine and the supply system which kept it in operation. The 'great wave' that threw it up upon the land would be the sustained roar of the missile's rocket motor, a sound so unlike any noise known to a man of the 16th century that it would probably be suggestive to him of the sound of large waves breaking upon the shore in a storm.

Finally, the 'enemy from the sea' which was enabled to smash the 'walls' – defensive lines constructed by Iraq's soldiers – as a consequence of the havoc wreaked by the 'fish' (ship-based Cruise missiles) would be the American, British and other allied troops who travelled over the oceans of the world to liberate Kuwait.

As has been remarked earlier, Nostradamus was a man of his own time, one who had to interpret the confusing visions he experienced in terms of what he was familiar with. One can compare his position in this respect with that of the early 19th-century European settlers in Tasmania, who encountered forms of wildlife quite new to them and interpreted what they saw in terms of the fauna of which they did know something. So, for instance, they considered the largest and most ferocious Tasmanian carnivore they encountered to be a tiger – although the 'Tasmanian tiger' was not even a member of the cat family. In the same way, the seer Nostradamus interpreted any streamlined object (such as a missile) he clairvoyantly perceived in terms of the only streamlined creature familiar to him, that is, a fish.

A similar 'fish', in this case a submarine, is referred to in Century II Quatrain 5, which reads:

> *When iron* [i.e. weapons] *and letters are enclosed in a fish,*
> *From it will come a man who will make war:*
> *His fleet will have journeyed across the sea,*
> *To appear near the Latin shore.*

Perhaps this is a description of the leader of a band of saboteurs making a surreptitious landing behind the enemy lines during the Gulf War or some other recent conflict – or perhaps, more alarmingly, Nostradamus was making a prediction of a war that is destined to break out in 1996.

CONJUNCTION IN PISCES

There is an alternative and alarming interpretation of the first line of Century I Quatrain 29 ('When iron [i.e. weapons] and letters are enclosed in a fish') that is derived from the traditional astrological symbolism with which Nostradamus would have been extremely familiar. On this reading of the verse, 'fish' indicates the zodiacal sign of Pisces, 'iron' means the planet Mars, astrological ruler of that metal, war and its weapons, and 'letters' means Mercury, the innermost planet of the solar system and the ruler of all means of communication. The whole line would thus mean something like 'When Mars and Mercury are in conjunction in Pisces', and the quatrain as a whole could be taken as predicting that at the time of such an event there would be war in the Mediterranean – 'near the Latin shore' – involving a fleet which had travelled from afar.

The next conjunction of Mercury and Mars in Pisces is due in the spring of 1996. Will this date be marked by the outbreak of some major conflict that involves the US fleet?

THE KENNEDYS IN THE QUATRAINS

In every age there has been an understandable tendency among those who have commented upon the Centuries of Nostradamus to seek for references to events that have taken place in their own lifetimes. Thus French Nostradamians of the last two decades of the 19th century sought for quatrains applicable to the Franco-Prussian War; English students of the Centuries in the late 1930s believed that they had detected in Century X Quatrain 40 a prognostication of the abdication of Edward VIII; and some contemporary seekers after hidden prophetic knowledge have found – so they assert – an astonishingly large number of quatrains relating to the murdered brothers President John F. Kennedy and Robert Kennedy.

The present writer thinks it likely that many of these Kennedy attributions are mistaken. They are sufficiently vague for it to be impossible to say truthfully of any of them 'this must refer to the Kennedys' in the same way that one can say of, for instance, Century IX Quatrain 20 'this must refer to the flight of Louis XVI', or of the last two lines of Century VI Quatrain 5 'this must be descriptive of a manned space station'.

One cannot be sure, for instance, that Century II Quatrain 57 really does apply, as has been claimed, to the Cuban missile crisis and the death of President Kennedy. Certainly it does not read very appositely in translation:

Before the conflict the great man will fall,
The lamented great one [will fall] to sudden death,
Born imperfect, he will go the greater part of the way,
Near the river of blood the ground is stained.

President Kennedy, although suffering throughout his presidency from a crippling spinal condition and the after-effects of a chronic gonorrhoeal infection, could hardly be said to have been born imperfect, save perhaps in a moral sense. The rest of the quatrain appears to be even less relevant, for while the second line clearly implies an unexpected and probably violent death the murder of the President took place after, not before, the diplomatic conflicts associated with the Cuban missile crisis.

Still vague, but a little more justifiably applicable to John F. Kennedy and Robert Kennedy in that both of these brothers were murdered, are the first three lines of Century X Quatrain 26, which read:

The successor will avenge his handsome brother,
And occupy the realm under the shadow of revenge,
He, killed, the obstacle of the guilty dead, his blood …

The problems with accepting, as many have done, that this was even a fairly general Kennedy prophecy are a) that Robert Kennedy neither avenged his brother nor succeeded him as President, either immediately or subsequently, and b) that the last line of the quatrain – 'For a long period Britain will hold with France' – seems to have predicted that whatever the nature of the foretold event or events involving two brothers it was, or they were, destined to be in some way important in the context of Franco-British relations. This could hardly be said of the Kennedy deaths.

Yet another quatrain that has been applied to the Kennedy family is Century IX Quatrain 36, the last two lines of which read:

Everlasting captives, a time when the lightning is above,
When three brothers will be mortally wounded.

The present writer is sceptical about the supposed prophetic import of this quatrain. If he is wrong the outlook for the third brother, presumably Edward Kennedy, is poor and the last murder predicted in the final line will take place at some Eastertide – for, according to the quatrain's second line, 'Not far from Easter there will be confusion, a stroke of the knife'.

NUMBERS OF MORTALITY

One reason for doubting the existence of any particular Nostradamian quatrain that can be taken as a definite prediction of the assassination of President John F. Kennedy is that no interpreter of the Centuries identified such a verse prior to the event. This is particularly surprising as a number of occultists specializing in numerology – the study of the supposedly mystic attributes of numbers – had, upon Kennedy's election to office in 1960, predicted that he would certainly die in office and would probably do so as the victim of an assassin.

The idea that whoever was to be elected president in 1960 was destined to die in office had been, as it were, 'in the air' ever since President Roosevelt's death in office in the spring of 1944. This was because, as those interested in numerology had noted at the time of Roosevelt's death, since 1840 every US president who had been elected to office in a year ending with a zero had died in office, and three of them – presidents Lincoln, Garfield and McKinley, first elected to office in, respectively, the years 1860, 1880, and 1900 – had been murdered.

The so-called 'presidential curse of the zeros' was probably no more than an unusual series of coincidences. If it ever really existed it was either limited to a duration of 120 years (in itself a significant period, according to some numerologists) or was, in a sense, lifted by Ronald Reagan, first elected to the presidency in 1980, who managed to survive assassination attempts as well as life-threatening illnesses.

END OF THE COLD WAR

The tendency of most of us to wish to be told that our own country (or continent) and its leaders are central to world history is perhaps largely to blame for Nostradamian misinterpretations and dubious predictive attributions of the types described previously in relation to the Kennedy brothers. If, for instance, someone believes both that a) presidents Lincoln and Kennedy were figures of outstanding world importance and b) that Nostradamus was able to clairvoyantly discern the main outlines of history from his own times into the far-distant future, it is difficult to accept the possibility that these men were not mentioned somewhere in the Centuries.

Alas, as far as the events that were close to him in time were concerned, Nostradamus appears to have had the thoroughly Eurocentric attitude which, as a 16th-century Frenchman, might well have been expected of him. Apart from some vague references to the 'Hesperides' and their wealth, there are really no Nostradamian predictions that can reasonably be applied to events in American history prior to the present century.

As he looked further into the future, however, the seer's field of vision seems to have enlarged and, as readers of this book will discover, there are a large number of quatrains relating to events that still lie in the future and that are likely to relate, wholly or in part, to the USA. As far as the present century is concerned, there are a number of predictions in the Centuries that can be interpreted as pertaining to the USA and some that seem to fit events with a certain exactitude.

As always, the most interesting of the latter are those which not only fit events that have actually happened but were interpreted as being predictive of these events before they took place – which invalidates suspicions of interpretive ingenuity based on hindsight. Good examples are those quatrains that were interpreted at a time when the Cold War was at its height as prophecies of a short-lived future friendship between the USA and the Soviet Union.

Such a friendship – of short duration only because of the disintegration of the USSR into its component parts – came into existence in the years of the Reagan/Bush/Gorbachev presidencies and without it the world would have become a very different place. One of the quatrains interpreted as predicting it long before it happened is Century II Quatrain 89, which reads:

> One day the two great leaders [leaders of the superpowers] *will be friends,*
> *Their great power will be seen to grow:*
> *The New Land* [America] *will be at the height of its power,*
> *To the man of blood the number is reported.*

With its mentions of two great leaders and 'the New Land', a common enough 16th-century term for America, this quatrain was taken as indicative of future American-Soviet friendship as long ago as the 1960s. Commentators, however, were puzzled by the meaning of the last line. Was the USA, they asked themselves, to become a virtual ally of a country ruled by a person whose character was such that the seer referred to him as 'a man of blood'?

With the presidency of Gorbachev, however, the meaning of the last line seemed to become clear – Nostradamus had been referring to the most obvious distinguishing mark of the Soviet leader, the large naevus (a discoloured area of skin caused by hypertrophied blood vessels) resembling the appearance of dried blood upon his head.

This seems very clear and apposite, but some contemporary Nostradamians take an altogether gloomier viewpoint, identifying the 'man of blood' with the Antichrist, an evil ruler whose hour may be close at hand.

The brevity of the endurance of Soviet-American friendship was predicted by Nostradamus in the first two lines of Century V Quatrain 78 ('the two will not remain allied for long [the Soviet Union] giving way to barbarian satrapies').

BALLOONS, BATTLE, BALONEY

One of the oddest attempts at giving an American slant to a Nostradamian prediction involved Century V Quatrain 57, which reads in partial translation – for reasons which will be made apparent some words have been left in their original form – as follows:

> *There will go forth from Mont Gaulfier*
> *and the Aventine one*
> *Who through a whole will give information*
> *to the army . . .*

It is generally accepted among interpreters of the Centuries that these lines refer to the first use of hot-air balloons for military observational purposes. This was at the Battle of Fleurus (1794), and at the time balloons of this variety were known as Montgolfiers, their name having been derived from that of the two Montgolfier brothers who had invented them in 1783.

However, in the 1930s one determined American, who seems to have been convinced that almost any Nostradamian prediction could be twisted to give it some relevance to the USA, decided that the phrase Mont Gaulfier referred to the game of golf and that the whole verse prophesied the result of a particular US Open championship. If one indulges in a single interpretation of this sort one is a comedian; two or more and the comedy becomes eccentricity!

FALSE PREDICTIONS

In the preceding pages details have been given of some of the astonishing predictive hits contained in the Centuries of Nostradamus: of how, for instance, he prophesied the exact years in which the Great Fire of London would take place and World War II would begin; of how he displayed a detailed knowledge of events that took place in the French Revolution, which broke out more than two centuries after his death; and of how he described the guided missiles used in modern high-tech warfare.

In the next section of the book Nostradamian predictions which are, as yet, unfulfilled will be examined – those prophecies which relate to the near future of our planet and are likely to affect the lives of each and every one of us. The study of such predictions is an exciting one, for those who engage in it are, in a sense, endeavouring to emulate Nostradamus by tearing apart the very fabric of time. However, excitement must be tempered by a realization that there are two major factors that must always be borne in mind by those Nostradamians who desire to know what the future holds in store both for them and for the world.

The first is this: the exact meanings of Nostradamus's predictions relating to our collective futures are derived from the interpretations made by individual students of the Centuries from the crabbed and obscure language often employed by Nostradamus – and some such assessments of the seer's exact meanings may be partially or wholly incorrect. The second is that some prophecies supposedly made by Nostradamus are probably or certainly forgeries. Some of the latter were originated by the Nazi propaganda machine during World War II, others would seem likely to have come into existence as the result of self-delusion or a desire to hoax the gullible.

In this connection the story of a curious event that was reported to have taken place in the early 1970s is relevant. According to this tale, Nostradamus reappeared as 'a living, breathing human' in a dressing room off a television studio in America. He uttered various new prophecies that were in French but were 'understandable as in English', and gave an exposition of something called the 'Druid Tarot'.

The sole witness to this remarkable event was a well-known American psychic going by the name of 'Criswell', who told of his experience in his book Criswell's Forbidden Predictions Based on Nostradamus and the Tarot. Criswell, a man who seems to disdain forenames, was sitting in his dressing room removing his make-up when there was a sharp tap at the door, followed by the entry of a man wearing 16th-century dress. With admirable brevity the unexpected visitor proceeded to introduce himself by saying 'I am Nostradamus.'

Suddenly Criswell found himself whisked away to an enormous grotto furnished with only an oaken table and two chairs. Nostradamus seated himself on one and directed Criswell to the other, whereupon Criswell – clearly a man more able to cope with odd situations than the present writer – calmly listened to his visitor from the 16th century while he made a large number of completely new predictions. Criswell was so impressed by these predictions that he remembered them sufficiently well to be able to include their text in his book. Almost all were startling. And all of them – or rather all of them that pertain to any dates prior to the publication of this book – have in the event proved to be totally and utterly wrong!

GIANT MOTHS AND TOPPLING PYRAMIDS

While the present writer has no confidence in those predictions relating to the years immediately before AD 2000 that were given by Nostradamus to Criswell it seems worth summarizing a few of them as a warning to the unwary.

1 There will be a temporary phase of total sexual licence in which a world orgy will continue until 'even animals are pressed into service'.

2 Bacteria will grow to the size of moths which will then bite people and animals and render them beyond all help. Texas and Mexico will be hardest hit and 'will piteously plead for aid'. Fortunately the bacterial threat will be nullfied

by the air becoming solid with electricity'.

3 An immense occult revival will result in men, women and children casting spells 'on everybody and everything'. Five thousand of such spell-casters will gather at the Niagara Falls and collectively reverse the flow of the river. Another such group will 'topple the pyramids' while one million psychics will gather at Prairie, South Dakota, in order to hold an enormous seance. At this the spirits of such individuals as Adolf Hitler, Mussolini and Stalin will manifest themselves.

4 All television sets, telephones, typewriters, pens and pencils will be confiscated by the rulers of the world, who will also make a law forbidding three or more people to gather together.

It all sounds very nasty indeed!

NECROMANCY & THE MARK OF THE BEAST

The strange coded language employed by Nostradamus in many of his quatrains was of such a nature that we can be confident that he had knowledge of an ancient mystical lore – to most of us living in a sceptical age, an enigma to which we are unlikely to find the key.

To interpret the predictions of Nostradamus in relation to events that have already happened is not at all easy save, perhaps, for those prophecies in which a specific date such as 1666 or 1792 was explicitly or implicitly expressed by the seer. Yet that task is simplicity itself compared with the difficulties of interpreting the exact meanings of prophetic quatrains which have not as yet been fulfilled – those, for example, which seem to pertain to vast social and political upheavals throughout the world, to wars fought with new and terrifying weapons capable of mass destruction, to the emergence of a sinister cult led by one whom Nostradamus identified with the long-prophesied Antichrist, and to travel between the stars.

The majority of the quatrains fall into this category of unfulfilled prophecies – that is, their content seems to relate to the future or else they employ terminology that will only become comprehensible in the light of future events.

Another possibility is that some refer to secret matters pertaining to mystic arts of which the majority of us know little or nothing. The latter verses, sometimes referred to as 'occult quatrains', are rightly attracting the attention of some present-day Nostradamian researchers.

Nevertheless, it has to be remembered by the Nostradamian interpreter that at least some of the 'occult quatrains' may not – in spite of the mystic language they employ – truly refer to ritual magic, alchemy and other esoteric disciplines. It is possible that in them the seer was using occult symbolism to describe events and concepts which he could not express in the language of his own time because the words needed had not yet been invented.

Even those quatrains relating to the year 2000 and beyond, which are more easily comprehensible than those couched in the language of occultism, are often obscure or capable of more than one interpretation. Consequently, some of the interpretations of Nostradamian predictions analysed in the pages that follow are going to be wrong; others are more than likely to be correct.

NOSTRADAMUS AND NECROMANCY

For more than 400 years there have been those who have sought to find some key which would unlock the (hypothetical) concealed structural framework which they have believed underlies theCenturies.

Those who have sought to find this key have been driven by a belief that no seer whose predictions have proved as strikingly accurate as some of those made by Nostradamus could have recorded his visions of things to come in a totally unplanned way; there must, they have felt, have been a hidden inner logic behind the seemingly random order in which the quatrains were written. And, if so, Nostradamus must have intended that those who, like himself, had devoted years of study to the mystic arts of divination should be able to discern the nature of that secret structural logic and, by applying it, be enabled to read the Centuries in a manner which will make complete sense of both their chronology and their content.

As was said earlier, the Centuries contain a number of verses of which the content and terminology is such that they have been labelled 'occult quatrains' – that is, they seem to be concerned with the magical arts. Of course, in the original sense of the word 'occult' – that is to say, 'secret' – there are a substantial number of quatrains in the Centuries of which the significance is occult in that they are certainly prophecies but their exact meaning is not likely to become apparent until either they are fulfilled or the long-sought-after predictive key to the Centuries is discovered. If indeed that key is ever found it may well be through the analysis of quatrains which, according to some, link Nostradamus with cabbalism, alchemy, numerology, and even the black art of necromancy.

The present writer does not feel competent to make any attempt to discern the innermost secrets of the Centuries; but to any readers of this book who may wish to try for themselves he suggests that Century IV Quatrains 28–31 may be of particular significance in this context – for the numbering of these verses may not have been haphazard but have had a numerological import. This is particularly the case with the last two of them, Century IV Quatrains 30 and 31, which read, respectively:

> *More than eleven times the moon will not want the sun,*
> *All raised and lessened in degree:*
> *Put so low that one will sew little gold*
> *After famine and plague the secret will be discovered.*

> *The moon in the middle of the high mountain,*
> *The new wise man has discerned it:*
> *By his disciples invited to become immortal,*
> *Eyes southward, hands on breast, body aflame.*

Whether or not these two quatrains do indeed provide a secret key to the complex structural framework of the Centuries is a matter of opinion; what they do reveal, however, is that Nostradamus was aware of curious developments of secret cultism which are already in train and may, if some commentators are correct, dominate many aspects of our everyday lives in the near future.

THE SPLENDID LIGHTS

One approach to the finding of a secret key to the interpretation of the Centuries which is being pursued by some students of western esotericism at the present day is based upon the virtual certainty that Nostradamus was well acquainted with the outlines of the Christian cabbala.

The cabbala is an ancient Jewish mystical system which by the 16th century also existed in a Christianized form almost inextricably associated with magic and alchemy. That Nostradamus had at one time possessed books on such subjects is made apparent by a passage in a letter he published:

> *… I caution you against the seduction of … execrable magic …*
> *Although many volumes have come before me which have long lain concealed*
> *I have felt no desire to divulge their contents …*
> *after reading them … I reduced them to ashes.*

It is likely that this passage was written by the seer with the intention of averting suspicion that he practised cabbalistic magic; it is improbable that the scholarly Nostradamus, an avid book collector, would have deliberately destroyed rare magical texts.

Those present-day students of Christian cabbalism who have endeavoured to use it in order to understand the innermost structure of the Centuries have been struck by the fact that there are 10 Centuries (not all of them complete) and that cabbalistic theory is based on a system of 10 emanations – the sephiroth or 'splendid lights' – from 'the Unmanifest'. According to the doctrines of contemporary cabbalists, everything in the universe, from ideas and emotions to material objects, can be classified in terms of the 10 sephiroth. Thus, for example, everything connected with conflict can be taken as mystically corresponding with the fifth of the sephiroth, everything to do with love to the seventh, and everything to do with money to the tenth.

It would be agreeable if the 10 individual Centuries had some obvious correspondences with the 10 sephiroth – if, for instance, Century X was clearly relevant to money, property and so on. Alas, they don't; but it may be that there is a concealed but genuine relationship between the structure of the Centuries and the patterns of the sephiroth and that the discovery of the exact nature of this relationship will provide a complete solution to all the problems of Nostradamian interpretation.

A few decades ago the idea would have seemed fantastic beyond belief – but recent historical research has shown that a number of 16th-century books do have a hidden structure derived from cabbalistic teachings, and the Centuries may be another of them.

THE END OF THE PAPACY?

A number of dedicated students of the writings of Nostradamus, among them the late James Laver, have been fascinated by the so-called 'prophecy of Saint Malachy' – for they have come to the conclusion that they have discerned a concordance between it and certain of the predictive verses of Nostradamus which pertain to the papacy – for instance, Century V Quatrain 56, which reads:

> *Because of the death of the very old Pope,*
> *Will be elected a Roman of very good [i.e. young] age,*
> *It will be said of him that he weakens the Seat [i.e. the Throne of Peter],*
> *But he will hold it long with stinging labour.*

The meaning of this quatrain is clear. Nostradamus was saying that a young Pope is destined to be elected in succession to an elderly one and to be attacked by some on the grounds that he is weakening the Church. Nevertheless, with great effort ('stinging labour') he will occupy the papal throne for a long time.

This prophecy has clearly not as yet been fulfilled, for the only Pope elected at what could reasonably be called a 'young age' between the publication of the Centuries and our own times was Gregory XIV who, far from enjoying a long occupation of the papacy, had an unusually short reign.

If, like James Laver and others, one does accept that there is a concordance between the 'prophecy of Saint Malachy' and the Centuries it seems likely, for reasons which will be made apparent, that the young Pope whose election Nostradamus predicted in Century V Quatrain 56 is fated to be the successor of the present Pontiff, Pope John Paul II.

The 'prophecy of Saint Malachy' has been put in inverted commas here because the general consensus of scholarly opinion is that whoever may in truth have been its author it was not the Irish monastic Saint Malachy (c. 1095–1148). Indeed, there are those who say it is not a genuine prophecy at all but a forgery, probably dating from no earlier than 1590. On the other hand, many pious men and women have believed the attribution of the prophecy to Malachy to be justified: a 19th-century French priest, Father Cucherat, specifically stated that the prophecies were written by Malachy, that the vision or visions on which they were based were experienced in Rome in 1140, and that Malachy wrote down his prophetic mottoes on a parchment which he handed to Pope Innocent II, who deposited it in the Vatican Library – where no one looked at it for the next four centuries or so.

It all sounds a bit improbable – but the office of the Breviary for the Feast of Saint Malachy refers to him as having been blessed with the gift of prophecy and, more importantly, Saint Bernard of Clairvaux stated that Malachy accurately foretold to him the day and the very hour at which he, Malachy, would die.

The prophecy attributed to Malachy is only short. It consists of 108 Latin mottoes, each of which is supposedly appropriate to a particular Pope, beginning with Celestine II (Pope 1143–4) and ending with 'Peter the Roman', supposedly fated to be the final Pope. The Latin mottoes are often of only two or three words; for instance, that given to Celestine II was Ex Castro Tiberis ('From a Castle on the Tiber'), an allusion to his family name, Guido de Castello. To the present Pope, John Paul II, is attributed the 107th motto contained in the prophecy – so there would seem to be only one more Pope to come. Of him Malachy (or whoever wrote what became attributed to him) chillingly said:

In the final persecution of the Holy Roman Church there will reign Peter the Roman, who will feed his flock amongst many tribulations; after which the seven-hilled City will be destroyed and the dreadful Judge will judge the people.

The expression 'dreadful Judge' is usually taken as a reference to the Last Judgment, when the living and the resurrected dead are to be sentenced to either eternal damnation or given the reward of eternal bliss. But it could mean a judgment of a quite different sort – some world-shattering event, or series of events, which destroys the Church. In either case, if Nostradamus and Malachy are in concordance, then the next Pope is going to be the last.

THE EX-SWINEHERD

Pope Sixtus V, who occupied the Throne of Peter from 1585 to 1590, was a man of extremely humble origins. In this he was quite unlike the majority of other Popes of his time, who tended to be closely related to the great families of Italy.

Born in 1521 as Felice Peretti, the son of a gardener, the future Sixtus V was sent to labour as a swineherd when he was only eight years old. He was, however, an exceptionally intelligent child and after a year with the pigs was taken away to begin his education in a convent. He was ordained as a priest in 1547, consecrated a bishop in 1566, and made a cardinal four years later.

His eventual elevation to the papacy was foreseen by Nostradamus almost 40 years before that event took place. On a visit to Italy the seer fell on his knees before Peretti, then only a newly ordained priest, and addressed him as 'Your Holiness'.

ISLAM RESURGENT

In recent years, fundamentalist Islam – the belief that the Koran is the inspired word of God, dictated to his messenger Mahomet by an angel, which lays down rules for the conduct of human affairs that are valid for all time – has made more than something of a come-back. For, as has been shown by events that have taken place over the last 15 years in such countries as Iran, Afghanistan and the central Asian republics of the former Soviet Union, the faith of the Prophet Mahomet is once more a considerable force in the world and is likely to play an increasingly important part in international affairs during the first years and decades of the 21st century.

The origins of the current Islamic renaissance can be traced back to at least the 1920s, though the movement really began to gather momentum with the decline of communism in the 1970s. It was then that there began to be a feeling among the peoples of Iran, Afghanistan and Soviet Asia that the solutions to their social and economic problems might be found in a return to Islamic law rather than in the adoption of the materialist atheism of Marxist ideology.

The decline and fall of communism was foretold by Nostradamus in more than one quatrain, and one such prediction that appears highly relevant to Islamic resurgence is Century IV Quatrain 32, in which the third and fourth lines refer to 'the old order [Islam] being renewed' and 'Panta chiona philon' (a late classical Greek phrase meaning 'all things in common', i.e. communism) being abandoned.

From the point of view of those who see fundamentalist religion of any variety as being in opposition to the values associated with the dominant western ideologies of both left and right, this Islamic resurgence is an unmitigated evil. Nevertheless, whether the march of Islam be for better or worse we are going to have to learn to live with it – or, at least, such is the case if the predictions of Nostradamus are to be fulfilled in the future as they have been in the past. Live with it and perhaps, for some of us, die with it – for it would appear that Nostradamus predicted that one of the features of the decades close at hand to us would be mighty and enormously destructive wars between Islamic and non-Islamic countries.

The course of these wars, as predicted in the Centuries, will include some Islamic set-backs – including the possible capture of a Caliph (see below) – but it will also be marked by disasters such as the total destruction of Monte Carlo, some of which are described later.

PROPHETIC OBSCURITIES

One of the problems that faces all commentators upon the Centuries is the existence of quatrains of which the content is such that some have termed them 'retroactive predictions' – that is to say, they seem to relate to events which took place before Nostradamus wrote concerning them. Examples of such retroactive predictions are Century VIII Quatrains 51 and 83, the former of which would appear to pertain to events that took place prior to the expulsion of the Moors from Spain in 1492 and the latter to Venetian atrocities at the time of the Fourth Crusade, some 350 years before Nostradamus 'prophesied' them.

Obviously there is something very odd about any seer going to the bother of writing obscurely worded descriptions of events that had taken place long before his own time. Consequently, the seeming existence of such pseudo-predictions in the Centuries has always been something of a puzzle to Nostradamian students, and various rationalizations for their appearance have been offered. Among them are ideas connected with alternate realities, worlds which exist in a discrete space time parallel to our own in which history has followed a different course, and a suggestion that sometimes the visions of Nostradamus were outside his control and that he clairvoyantly discerned events that had transpired long previously. Both these hypotheses may well be wholly or partially true – but it may equally be the case that some of the 'retroactive' predictions are not retroactive at all, but relate to a future time when an Islamic superpower has come into existence. One such prophecy is made in Century VI Quatrain 78, which reads:

To shout aloud the victory of the growing crescent moon,
The Eagle will be proclaimed by the Romans,
Ticcan, Milan and the Genoese will not agree to it,
And the great Basil [a Nostradamian term derived from Greek and
meaning King or Emperor] *will be claimed by them.*

For complex interpretive reasons this quatrain has been generally assumed to describe the capture by Western forces of a Muslim Sultan who also laid claim to the Caliphate, the spiritual leadership of the Islamic world. As the last such Sultan/Caliph ceased to rule when the Ottoman Empire collapsed at the end of World War I the prediction is now held to have been retroactive, probably pertaining to the capture of Sultan Jemm in the 15th century. However, there seems to be no good reason to assume that there will never again be a powerful Caliph who is made prisoner by Westerners whom Nostradamus would, employing the terminology of his own century, describe as 'Romans'. It thus seems likely that Century VI Quatrain 78 pertains to our world or that of our descendants, not to that of our ancestors.

ISLAM'S HOLY WARS

The idea of a jihad – a holy war against those who dwell outside the 'House of Islam' – is one of great antiquity and enormous potency throughout the Muslim world. Between AD 622 and 732, Arabs inspired by the concept conquered almost the whole of North Africa and invaded France; in the 15th century the jihad waged by the Ottoman Turks against Byzantium resulted in the fall of Constantinople, and as late as the 1680s Muslim warriors were unsuccessfully besieging Vienna.

In the 300 years that followed, however, the ideology of the jihad was to lose a good deal of its practical impact, albeit none of its mystical appeal. Such few attempts as were made to use the jihad as a political and diplomatic weapon – by, for instance, the Sultan of Turkey in World War I – were on the whole ineffectual.

For the last 10 years or so there have been signs that this is no longer the case; in Afghanistan the Red Army was defeated by the guerrilla warfare waged against it by devotees of the jihad concept and in Bosnia the idea has inspired some of the most fanatical Muslim fighters against the Orthodox Serbs and the Catholic Croats. If Nostradamus is to be believed, this is only the beginning and we are destined to witness one or more Muslim holy wars.

The seer predicted that the effects of these wars, fought with weapons of mass destruction of such a nature that he was forced to use strange analogies in his attempts to describe them, will be devastating. In Century IV Quatrain 23, which for complex reasons is believed to pertain to a conflict between Islam and the West, he prophesied that the use of such weapons would result in the complete destruction of Monte Carlo, today the 'pleasure capital' of the world. This verse reads:

> *The Legion in the sea fleet*
> *Will burn – lime, magnetic ore, sulphur and tar:*
> *The long rest in a safe place,*
> *Port Selyn and Hercle will be consumed by the fire.*

The phrase 'sea fleet' (*marine classe* – the latter word, derived from Latin, was invariably used by the seer to mean armada, flotilla or fleet) in line one appeared tautological to Nostradamian students of the last century. It seemed akin to referring to a three-sided triangle or a four-sided square; how could there possibly be any fleet other than a marine one? Today we know the answer to this question – there are also air fleets and, in the not too distant future, there may well be space fleets. So it would seem that by qualifying the word fleet Nostradamus was intending to convey to us that he was aware of humanity's future conquest of the air and outer space.

The second line of the quatrain lists some of the ingredients of the Byzantine incendiary material known as Greek Fire and is presumably a metaphor intended to describe a fire-storm – in this context the mention of a 'long rest' in line three is of sinister import – but it is the specific prediction of the fiery fate of 'Port Selyn and Hercle' in line four which is of primary interest. 'Port Selyn' means 'the Port of the Crescent', the crescent being the symbol of Islam, while 'Hercle' is an abbreviation of Herculeis Monacei, a Latin name for Monaco and its capital Monte Carlo. It would appear that in this quatrain Nostradamus was prophesying the simultaneous destruction by fire of a fleet, an important Islamic port and Monte Carlo. Obviously such conflagrations would result in enormous casualties and these would not be confined just to 'Port Selyn' and Monte Carlo – indeed, if one Nostradamian student is correct in his interpretations there would be nearly one million casualties in France alone (see panel right).

Clearly, a world war or perhaps a series of wars is foretold in Century IV Quatrain 23. As is explained on the next two pages, other Nostradamian quatrains seem to predict that this titanic struggle will involve the use of bacteriological and nuclear weapons.

A MILLION FRENCH DEAD

At least one contemporary student of the Centuries known to the present writer – a member of that small band of Nostradamian interpreters who endeavour to analyse the seer's predictions in the light of the cabbala – contests on numerological as well as other grounds that Nostradamus's prophecy of the total destruction of Monte Carlo contained in Century IV Quatrain 23 is structurally linked with Century I Quatrains 71 and 72, which read respectively:

Three times the marine tower will be captured and recaptured,
By the Spaniards, Barbarians [perhaps Berbers, i.e. North Africans] and Italians:
Marseilles and Aix, Arles by Pisans,
Laid waste by fire and sword, Avignon pillaged by the Turinese.

The dwellers in Marseilles changed utterly,
In flight, pursued as far as Lyons,
Narbonne and Toulouse outraged by Bordeaux,
Dead and imprisoned, almost a million.

While the exact meanings of the above quatrains cannot yet be established with certainty, their general import is definite enough. If indeed they were truly intended to be read in conjunction with Century IV Quatrain 23, then the world faces even bloodier battles than those associated with any previous wars in history. As is explained later, there are reasons to believe that these terrifying conflicts may be close to us in time.

ATOMIC AND GERM WARFARE

For reasons that are explained below and later, it is likely that many of the most dismal predictions to be found in the Centuries pertain to times which are very close indeed – particularly to the early decades of the 21st century and possibly to the late 1990s.

One of the most bloodcurdling of these gloomy prognostications is to be found in Century VIII Quatrain 77, which is concerned with a war lasting for no less than 27 years. Its final line reads: 'Red hail, water, blood and corpses cover the earth.' This line is agreed by the majority of present-day Nostradamian students to refer to a coming conflict involving nuclear and/or biological weapons.

Obviously, the use of weapons such as these would have the effect of strewing the earth with corpses. As for the red hail and water discerned by Nostradamus, that would be either an aerosol used deliberately to spread bacterial infections or atmospheric water contaminated by the radioactive fall-out associated with any nuclear explosion (or both). At its worst the latter could even be the product of deliberate radioactive 'dusting' of an entire area by means of an exceptionally dirty weapon – a nuclear device fitted with a cobalt jacket.

That the predicted fall of the red hail of death upon our planet is nigh is suggested by the content of Century I Quatrain 16, which predicts 'plague, famine and death from military hands' at a time when the centuries 'approach their renewal'. This latter phrase is strongly suggestive of a deliberate reference by Nostradamus to esoteric theories concerning astrological and chronological cycles with which he was almost certainly acquainted – notably with the Neo-platonic concept of a 'Great Year' consisting of 12 'months', each of around 2000 years of time as ordinarily measured.

If 'the renewal of the centuries' referred to in Century I Quatrain 16 does apply to the 'Great Year' of the Platonists it is likely that it indicates a date for the fulfilment of the 'plague, famine and death from military hands' prediction coinciding exactly with what some modern occultists term 'the transition from the Age of Pisces to that of Aquarius' – that is, a few years shortly before or after AD 2000, the precise date for that event being a little uncertain as it is dependent upon whichever particular fixed star is taken as the marking point for the beginning of the zodiac. This latter is a technical point, a subject for debate among those who have delved deeply into esoteric theory, but the essence of the matter is quite clear; the fulfilment of Nostradamus's predictions of universal plague and famine is near at hand.

Other quatrains in the Centuries would seem to confirm this interpretation – for example, Century I Quatrain 91, which reads:

> *The gods will make it apparent to humanity*
> *That they are the devisers of a great war:*
> *Prior to this the heavens were free of espée et lance*
> *The greatest damage will be imposed upon the left.*

The words left in their original form in line three would literally imply that the sky would, most improbably, become darkened by swords and spears in the seer's predicted great war. It is therefore likely that the phrase was intended to be taken figuratively by those who read it when the foretold event drew near and that by espée et lance the present-day student of prophecy can understand 'weapons and missiles'. The likely significance of the phrase 'the left' used by Nostradamus in line four of the quatrain is examined later; it suffices here to say that it is possible but improbable that the seer used it in its modern political sense, which dates from only the late 18th century.

THE GREAT STAR BURNS

Century II Quatrain 41 is of much interest in relation to Nostradamian predictions of great world conflicts involving the use of nuclear and biological weapons breaking out shortly before or after the end of the present century. This quatrain reads:

The Great Star will boil for seven days,
Its cloud making the sun appear to have a double image:
The great dog will howl throughout the night
When the Pope changes his habitation.

In an attempt to date the time at which the predicted event will take place, the 'Great Star' of line one has been identified with the return of Halley's comet. However, as the last two appearances of this comet have been so unspectacular that it has been almost invisible to the naked eye, this interpretation is difficult to believe. It seems far more likely that the 'star' will be the explosion of an extremely large fusion weapon. Such weapons produce their energy by exactly the same process as that which takes place in the interiors of most stars – the transmutation of hydrogen into helium. In a man-made fusion bomb, however, the actual explosion does not 'boil' for a week, and nor does it produce a double solar image.

Possibly the reference is to a whole series of nuclear attacks, but a more likely explanation is that the boiling metaphor used by Nostradamus implies an enormous dust cloud thrown up by fusion bombs and taking a very long time to fall even partially back to earth.

THE COMING
OF THE ANTICHRIST

As suggested by the interpretation of the last line of Century VIII Quatrain 77 given earlier, Nostradamus predicted that the early years of the new millennium would be marked by the strewing of the earth with corpses as a consequence of bacteriological or atomic warfare. But how is the remainder of the same quatrain to be interpreted?

To consider it in its entirety, Century VIII Quatrain 77 reads:

The Antichrist very soon annihilates the three,
Seven and twenty years his war will endure,
The heretics are dead, imprisoned, exiled,
Red hail, water, blood and corpses cover the earth.

The identity of 'the three' whom the Antichrist is described as annihilating is a mystery to all students of the Centuries; it has been suggested they are three major world powers or three great world leaders, either spiritual or temporal. But whatever or whoever 'the three' may be, who are the heretics mentioned in line three, and what is the meaning of the word 'Antichrist' as used in the opening line?

It is best to try to answer the last question first. According to traditional Christian beliefs (see panel opposite), the Antichrist is destined to be a false saviour who will serve the great Princes of Hell, wreak havoc in the world, and lead much of humanity into spiritually destructive paths which will, quite literally, result in damn-ation. While such a belief is of great antiquity it is still held by some at the present day and it is worth remembering that in the comparatively recent past as learned and pious a man as Cardinal Manning (1808-92) delivered a series of lectures concerning the Antichrist and expressed his conviction that some of the stranger events associated with the emergence of modern spiritualism might indicate that the infernal Advent – the birth of the Antichrist – was imminent.

Whether or not the Cardinal was right in his beliefs, there seems no doubt that Nostradamus adhered to theological concepts which were, in essence, identical to them. Of central relevance, to be held constantly in mind when endeavouring to interpret those quatrains of the Centuries in which Nostradamus mentioned the Antichrist, is that ideas about the coming of the counter-Christ, the 'son of perdition', were as much part of the 'world picture' of Nostradamus as they were of every learned Christian of his time. It must consequently be assumed that if Nostradamus could see into the future he would interpret his vision of unpleasant persons and events in terms of a concept familiar to him – that is, the advent of the Antichrist, the manifestation of a miracle-working false Saviour whose disciples would be the servants of the Powers and Principalities of Hell.

In other words, just as Nostradamus seems to have endeavoured to describe 20th-century warfare in terms of the material things and the military technology familiar to him, so he would have tried to describe those moral attitudes and the actions resulting from them which most of us would characterize as absolutely inhuman and pertaining to the principle of eternal evil in terms of 16th-century eschatology – that is, religious beliefs and teachings concerning the end of the world. On the following pages we shall see how such beliefs tie in with what appear to be Nostradamus's predictions concerning the coming of a terrifying 'Supreme Antichrist' at a date shortly after the year 2000.

THE MESSIAH OF EVIL

Ever since Christianity was in its infancy, the word 'Antichrist' has been used to describe any extraordinarily wicked person. While Nostradamus and other 16th-century Christians employed the word in this sense, for them the Supreme Antichrist would be a Messiah of evil – a prophet of truly hellish wickedness.

The views of Saint Roberto Bellarmine (1542-1651) regarding the origins of the Antichrist were typical of those held by theologians living at much the same time as Nostradamus. Bellarmine believed that the father of the Antichrist would be an incubus – that is, a demon who has sexual congress with human females – and that his mother would be a practitioner of black magic.

A Dominican friar of the 17th century asserted that the coming Antichrist would not only be fathered by a devil but would be:

> ... *as malicious as a madman, with such wickedness as was never seen on earth ... he will treat Christians as condemned souls are treated in hell. He will have a multitude of Synagogue names, and he will be able to fly when he wishes. Beelzebub will be his father, Lucifer his grandfather.*

THE MARK OF THE BEAST

In the time of Nostradamus, eschatological beliefs concerning world experiences supposedly destined to happen before the Last Judgment were almost inextricably entwined with traditional lore concerning events which it was held would precede and follow the coming of the Antichrist. This means that if Nostradamus clairvoyantly perceived, far in the future, the teachings and the actions of a Hitler, a Stalin, or some absolute ruler who has yet to come to power, he would almost certainly have interpreted them as manifestations of one or more Antichrists.

In this context it is worth taking a look at a particular passage in the Epistle to Henri II which was printed with the first edition of the Centuries and which, as described earlier, gave a specific and completely accurate date for events which took place during the French Revolution. This passage gives a chilling account of the events which would, according to Nostradamus, precede the rule of the one he termed 'the third [i.e. the Supreme] Antichrist'.

Writing of a 'King' (which in this context means an absolute ruler of any sort) who would commit great crimes against the Church, the seer asserted that this man-monster:

> ... *will have shed the blood of more Churchmen than any could do* [i.e. pour out] *with wine ... Human blood will flow in the churches and streets, as does water after heavy rain, and will crimson with blood the neighbouring rivers ... then in the same year and those following there will ensue the most horrible plague, all the more virulent because of the famine that will precede it, and such suffering that there will have been nothing like it since the foundation of Christianity .... The great Vicar of the Cope* [the Pope] *shall be ... desolated and abandoned by all .... After that Antichrist will be the hellish prince ... all the ... world will be shaken for twenty five years ... and the wars and battles will be grievous ... and so many evils will be committed by Satan ... that nearly all the world will be undone and desolated.*

Save for the mention of the Antichrist as 'the hellish prince' and the reference to the world being desolated as the result of many evils committed by Satan, there is nothing at all in this prose prophecy that could not be taken as a description of a future series of political events. Once it is accepted that there is a genuine possibility that Nostradamus and other seers and prophets could discern the pattern of future events, the passage contains nothing to unduly strain the credulity of its readers. It could well be a prophetic description of some future and monstrously evil dictator – a later and more successful version of Hitler or Pol Pot – who will manage to dominate world events for a period of a quarter of a century. It would not be surprising if a man like Nostradamus, acquainted with only the technology and physics of the 16th century, were to assume that such a dictator, with all the gifts of a perverted science from nuclear weapons to anthrax-loaded bombs at his command, was not a man but a devil – either the Antichrist or a forerunner of the Antichrist.

Some students of prophecy in general, and the writings of Nostradamus in particular, assert – for interpretative reasons that are too complex to be even briefly outlined in these pages – that the advent of the monstrous ruler described by the seer in his Epistle to Henri II is close upon us. Furthermore, they identify this 'King' as the third and great Antichrist. They believe, as did Nostradamus, that this vile creature is destined to pour out 'the blood of more Churchmen than any could do with wine'. His horrible activities, which will result in the outbreak of 'the most horrible plague, all the more virulent because of the famine that will precede it', are held to pertain to bacteriological warfare.

The coming third Antichrist, it is argued, is almost certain to be the very same individual who will be responsible for the descent of the King of Terror from the sky in July or perhaps August 1999. If this is indeed the case, the imminent prospects for the future of us all are very grim indeed.

THE SON OF PERDITION

The third Antichrist, the being that Nostradamus prophesied would cause blood to 'flow in the churches and streets as does water after heavy rain', has been identified by many Nostradamian interpreters with a 'son of perdition' referred to in the New Testament as one who would deceive many with 'lying wonders'.

The relevant text is in the thirteenth chapter of the Bible's last book, The Revelation of Saint John the Divine. It describes a 'second Beast', held by traditionalist New Testament commentators to be the same infernal entity as the Antichrist. The passage reads:

… And I beheld another beast … and he spake as a dragon. And he …
causeth the earth and them which dwell therein to worship the first beast …
And he doeth great wonders, so that he maketh fire from heaven on the earth

*...And deceiveth them that dwell on the earth by the means of those miracles
which he had power to do ...*

RESURGENCE
OF TRADITIONALISM

As has been recounted already, Nostradamus foretold that the opening decades
of the third millennium, now only six years or so away from us in time, would
be characterized by wars, plague, famine, an upsurge of militant Islam and the
appearance of a religio-political leader of such malignancy that the seer identified
him with the Antichrist.

Inevitably, an epoch foretold by Nostradamus in such doom-laden detail will
not leave traditional Christianity unscathed, but that religion will, it is predicted
in more than one quatrain of the Centuries, retain a capacity to fight back – to
be exalted in the sight of some even if it is humbled in that of others. In this
context Century I Quatrain 15 is relevant. It reads:

> *Mars threatens us with warlike force,*
> *Seventy times this will cause the spilling of blood:*
> *The clergy will be both exalted and dragged down,*
> *By those who wish to learn nothing from them.*

In other words, following a series of wars there will be a partially successful
dragging down of Christianity and its leaders by those who are ideologically
opposed to the traditional faith of the West ('who wish to learn nothing') but
there will be a reaction in favour of historic Christianity which will exalt, or
raise on high, the leadership of the Church Militant.

Nostradamus may have given an interesting clue to the nature of the wars he
predicted would bring about such religious conflicts by his use of the phrase
'seventy times this will cause the spilling of blood' in line two. He is unlikely to
have been employing the number 70 in a literal sense and, while he may have
meant no more than that he was foretelling a very large number of conflicts, it may
well be that he was making a reference to the significance of 70 in terms of the
Christian cabbalistic numerology with which he would have been acquainted.

The number 70 supposedly has a mystical connection with Hebrew and
Chaldee words meaning 'night', 'wine' and 'secret'; this suggests the possibility
that Nostradamus was implying that those responsible for many of the prognosticated conflicts would be devotees of a faith which taught what Christians
would regard as 'dark, nocturnal secrets' and practised rites involving the use of
wine and, perhaps, strange drugs.

There is an enigmatic description of one of those destined to lead or inspire the traditionalist resurgence in Century I Quatrain 96, which reads:

A man will be given the task of destroying
Temples and sects changed by [strange] fantasies:
He will harm rocks rather than the living,
By filling ears with eloquence.

Whether the destructive task prophesied to be given to somebody in lines one and two is predicted to be laid upon him by other human beings or by some supernatural power is unclear. But the nature of the work is apparent – to destroy, wholly or partially, fantastic pseudo-religions which will have deceived many. On this interpretation it is to be presumed that the cult led by the evil one the seer termed the 'third Antichrist' is fated to be the most notable of these 'temples changed by fantasy'.

THE MAN IN THE IRON MASK

It has been suggested to the present writer by one contemporary Nostradamian interpreter (the esoteric numerologist who is referred to earlier) that apart from mere propinquity there is a hidden link between Century I Quatrain 96 (see above) and Century I Quatrain 95. This link, derived from cabbalistic doctrines concerning a relationship between the letter combinations of the Hebrew alphabet and particular number manipulations of an ancient occult instrument termed 'the cabbala of Nine Chambers', has led this esotericist to suggest that the religious leader forecast in Century I Quatrain 96 to destroy 'temples and sects changed by fantasy' and to 'fill ears with eloquence' must be identified with a mysterious child referred to by Nostradamus in Century I Quatrain 95, which reads:

Before a monastery will be found a twin infant,
Descended from an ancient monastic bloodline:
His fame and power through sects and eloquence
Is such that they will say the living twin is rightly the elect [the chosen one].

Most commentators of the last century – and some of the present day also – have based their interpretations of this quatrain on the legend that Louis XIV of France was both the illegitimate son of Cardinal Mazarin and one of a pair of identical twins, and that to avoid any disputes over the succession to the throne his brother was imprisoned from infancy until his death as the silent, aged and unidentified prisoner known to history as 'the man in the Iron Mask'. However, modern research has shown that this ancient interpretation of Century I Quatrain 95 was erroneous, for while the man in the Iron Mask did indeed exist he was not the twin brother of Louis XIV. Consequently, there is no good reason why the subject of this quatrain should not be the same man as the traditionalist Christian leader of the succeeding verse. If this does in the course of time prove to be the case it is likely that his descent 'from an ancient monastic bloodline' will prove to be a symbolic reference to his beliefs rather than a literal description of his ancestry.

THE GREAT CHYREN

In the last century, in a period following the fall of the Empire of Napoleon III in 1870, a number of French Nostradamians were also dedicated Legitimists – advocates of a restoration of the representative of the senior Bourbon line to the throne of France. Their royalism induced them to make an intense study of a number of quatrains in the Centuries containing references to a man whom Nostradamus called 'the Great Chyren' and whom these interpreters employed much ingenious argument to identify with the Comte de Chambord, the then Bourbon Pretender of the elder line.

We can be sure that these interpretations were wrong, for the older Bourbon line became extinct in the 1880s – the present Pretender to the French throne is a member of the Orléans branch of the family – but there can be no doubt that under the code name of Chyren Nostradamus predicted the advent of a particular Frenchman who would exert an immense influence for good upon both his own country and the entire world. According to some Nostradamians of the present day, this Frenchman may well be the same person as the traditionalist destroyer of false religion and a Pope whose future election was predicted in Century V Quatrain 49, which reads:

> Not from Spain but from ancient France
> Will be chosen [elected] one to guide the shaking ship
> [the barque of the Papacy],
> He will make an assurance to the enemy,
> Who will cause a vile pestilence during his reign.

There has been no French Pope since before the birth of Nostradamus, so we know that this prophecy is not yet fulfilled. The content of the quatrain's first line is very curious, for while it made sense for Nostradamus to give the nationality of the predicted Pope there seems to have been no good reason why he should have thought fit to state that he would not be Spanish. The most likely explanation is that the quatrain foretells an imminent schism and that there will shortly be two claimants to the papacy – the one considered legitimate by Nostradamus being of French origin.

The last line, with its suggestion of chemical or biological weapons being used against the true Pope's partisans, is disagreeably concordant with another quatrain which prophesies that such weapons will be used by the third Antichrist.

PROPHETIC OBSCURITIES

Whether or not the man prophesied by Nostradamus in Century I Quatrain 96 to be destined to destroy what the seer, looking far into the future, regarded as being temples dedicated to a false and fantastic faith can be identified with either or both the 'Great Chyren' and the French Pope who will guide the shaking ship of the Papacy (see below) is a matter for debate amongst students of the Centuries. However, unless the seer's many predictions relating to the third Antichrist are completely in error there can be no doubt that the main opponents of the Christian traditionalist 'destroyer' whose advent was foretold in Century I Quatrain 96 will be the threatened Messiah of evil, his disciples, and those who ally themselves with him.

Various Nostradamian verses make it apparent that the seer believed that the third Antichrist would be an Asian by birth and either the site of this event or, alternatively, the place at which the power of the Antichrist will be centred is probably predicted in Century IX Quatrain 62, which for complex numerological reasons is linked to the concept of the Antichrist. It reads:

> *To the great one of Cheramon agora*
> *Will all the crosses be attached by rank,*
> *The pertinacious* [probably meaning 'perpetual in effect']
> *opium and mandragora,*
> *Rougon will be released on October the third.*

This quatrain, as obscurely worded as any in the Centuries, has often been interpreted by modern commentators as referring to secret magical techniques involving the use of hallucinogenic drugs ('opium and mandragora') and what the magicians of the ancient world termed 'barbarous words of evocation' – of which Cheramon agora have been claimed to be two.

This interpretation is likely to be in error on two counts. The seer's use of the phrase 'pertinacious opium and mandragora' implies that he was not employing the names of these consciousness-altering drugs in a literal sense; rather was he trying to convey, in words current in his own time, that the subject of the quatrain would use substances productive of frenzy, coma and death as weapons – in other words he would employ exactly the same types of chemical warfare as those associated with the Antichrist in other quatrains. Secondly, Cheramon agora is not an occult 'Word of Power'; it was the classical name for an obscure town in what is now Turkey and the 'crosses' predicted by Nostradamus to be 'attached to it by rank' are likely to be the hierarchy of the sect led by the pseudo-Messiah.

The last line of the quatrain seems to foretell that the third Antichrist will launch an attack by chemical poisons ('Rougon') on a precisely dated 3 October. It is a pity that Nostradamus was not equally precise about the predicted year of the event!

THE RAVAGING
OF FORT KNOX

As readers of this book will by now be well aware, from the content of some of his quatrains it seems that Nostradamus prophesied that the years immediately before and/or after AD 2000 will be a time of continued and unprecedented crises. We are doomed, so the seer predicted, to endure an epoch of political and social turmoil, schism and wars – largely religiously motivated – fought with chemical and bacteriological weapons. It is quite certain that if these predicted events do indeed take place they will directly or indirectly result in a disastrous decline in all the world's economies and in misery, starvation, disease and death for hundreds of millions of men and women. Not surprisingly, the seer predicted exactly such happenings – plague, famine, the debauching of currencies and consequent riots and civil disturbance.

It is likely that in every decade of every century since the very beginnings of humanity, people have been starving to death in some part or parts of the earth – and any seer who has made an undated prophecy of future starvation in a particular country must have been sure that it would eventually be fulfilled. The Centuries do, indeed, contain some prophecies of this sort – for instance, an Iranian famine is predicted in Century I Quatrain 70, which reads:

> Rain, famine and war will be ceaseless in Persia,
> Too great trustfulness will betray the monarch,
> The matters begun in Gaul will also end there,
> A secret augury for one to be sparing.

Interesting, and possibly connected with future developments in the Islamic Republic of Iran – but its precise significance is much too vague to be even largely, let alone completely, interpreted with a reasonable prospect of success prior to the occurrence of the actual events. On the other hand there is a Nostradamian prediction of a worldwide famine of unique severity which would seem to pertain to the epoch of political, religious and social upheaval which the seer foretold for the years around the turn of the present century. This depressing prophecy is made in Century I Quatrain 67, which reads:

The great famine which I feel approaching
Will often recur [in particular countries] *and then become universal:*
So great will it be, and so long will it last
That they [the starving] *will eat*
woodland roots and drag children from the breast.

This last line may mean that the starving will drag children from the breast to suckle the milk themselves – or it may be that Nostradamus was prophesying a famine of such severity that cannibalism will be practised on a considerable scale throughout the entire world!

This famine is destined to be accompanied by an equally ubiquitous inflation in which all paper money loses its entire value – or so it would appear from Century VIII Quatrain 28. This verse reads:

The simulacra [images or reproductions] *of gold and silver inflated,*
Which after the theft [of real value] *were chucked into the lake,*
At the discovery that all is destroyed by debt.
All bonds and scrip will be cancelled.

As paper money, 'the simulacra of gold and silver', was unknown in Europe at the time when Nostradamus was writing the Centuries the first line of the verse is remarkable in itself; if the entire prophecy is destined to prove accurate this approaching inflation will be the most complete and devastating that the world has known, for not only will paper money become worthless but 'all bonds and scrip' – in other words all wealth save real property and other material riches – will be wiped out.

In such a situation it would be likely that there would be a universal desire to get hold of some form of the only easily portable medium of exchange – gold and other precious metals. Such a desire, accompanied by rage against the bankers who would be blamed for the economic situation which had resulted in mass pauperism, could undoubtedly result in civil disturbance, riots and the looting of buildings associated with financial institutions.

Such an eruption of burning fury from an angry people against a system which they believe has robbed them of everything is apparently predicted in Century X Quatrain 81, which reads:

Treasure is placed in a temple by citizens of the Hesperides [America] .
Withdrawn within it to a secret hiding place,
The temple to be thrown open by famished liens [meaning uncertain],
Recaptured, ravished, a terrible prey in the midst [of it?].

Bank vaults and similar modern constructs for the storage of precious metals were, of course, unknown to Nostradamus, who might well have used the word 'temple' in reference to one – in classical times it was quite usual for citizens to store their wealth in temples of the gods. As the 'temple' of this quatrain is in America the whole verse is probably a prophetic description of a violent attack on Fort Knox, the vaults of which contain the bulk of the USA's gold reserves.

THE POISONING OF NEW YORK

There is, and perhaps always has been, a tendency among Nostradamian commentators to fit particular predictions to events which have been in the news in comparatively recent times. While this tendency has been responsible for identifying some remarkable predictive hits, such as the Great Fire of London quatrain, it is one which is not without its dangers. First, the interpreter is likely to begin to twist the already convoluted verse of the seer to make it fit events which have taken place in the interpreter's own lifetime. Secondly, it sometimes results in the interpreter abandoning all common sense and coming to the conclusion that Nostradamus made a large number of prophecies about events that took place hundreds of years after his death which are, except on the shortest of timescales and in the most parochial of perspectives, almost triflingly insignificant.

This tendency has resulted in more than one contemporary student of the Centuries hailing Century X Quatrain 49 as a prediction of the American nuclear accident which took place some years ago at the Three Mile Island power station – an accident which was, until the Chernobyl disaster, the most serious to have happened anywhere in the world. The quatrain in question reads:

Garden of the world near to the new city,
In the road of the hollow mountains,
It will be seized and run into the tank,
Forced to drink water poisoned with sulphur.

Those who have claimed that this prediction relates to the Three Mile Island emergency assert that the 'new city' of line one is New York (which is, in fact, almost certainly the case – see below), that the 'hollow mountains' of line two was Nostradamus's way of describing skyscrapers seen by him in vision, and that lines three and four refer to the threat that the accident could have posed to New York's water supply as a consequence of radioactive fall-out.

Perhaps, but even if one accepts the suggestion made by one interpreter that the 'sulphur' of line four is to be taken as meaning the alchemical principle of that name – the essence of the fiery 'element' of destruction, of which uncontrolled radioactivity is a particular manifestation – rather than some compound of the chemical element of sulphur, the prediction can hardly apply to the effects of the Three Mile Island incident. The plain fact of the matter is that while the accidental events which took place at Three Mile Island threatened disaster to a large area of the north-east of the USA they were brought under control in such a way that no catastrophe actually took place and the water supply of neither New York nor anywhere else was poisoned.

Nevertheless, with its mentions of the 'new city' (which, according to general consensus of opinion, was Nostradamus's way of describing New York) the quatrain would seem to be applicable to the (literal) poisoning of the water supply of either New York or some other population centre fairly close to it. Unless the prediction that Nostradamus made in Century X Quatrain 49 was completely in error – and it must be remembered that a few of the seer's prognostications do seem to have been quite erroneous – this event must still lie in the future, for it certainly hasn't happened yet.

The content of this prophecy is not obviously such as to give any indication of the likely date for its fulfilment, but numerological and other considerations seem to link it to a number of other predictive quatrains which pertain to events foretold for the closing years of this century and the opening ones of the next. In other words, this prophecy of New Yorkers or other Americans being in a position where they have no choice save to 'drink water poisoned with sulphur' relates to the epoch of Nostradamian predictions concerning militant Islamic holy wars, the third Antichrist, world conflicts and famines.

It is therefore likely that if the poisoned water prophecy is to be fulfilled it will happen a) at some time in the near future, probably between the years 1995 and 2005 and b) as a consequence of a military attack upon the United States. It is also likely, because of the content of the first line of the verse – 'Garden of the world near to the new city' – that the poisoning will make its main impact on New York's neighbour, New Jersey, 'the Garden State', rather than New York itself.

If water purification plants were knocked out by bombing as happened in Baghdad during the Gulf War, water supplies could be polluted in such a way that they were dangerous to drink. However, this could be easily countered by boiling the water before use, so Nostradamus's use of the phrase 'forced to drink' suggests a poisoning of an altogether more serious nature than mere pollution – most likely the use of chemical or nuclear weapons. The former would be the more likely if the seer's use of the word 'sulphur' was intended to be taken literally – there are a number of sulphur compounds of the utmost virulence. If, however, the word was intended to be understood symbolically it is more likely that the prophecy relates to radioactive poisons and a nuclear assault upon the USA. In relation to the possibility of a nuclear assault, the content of Century VI Quatrain 97, examined in detail on the next pages, is of major and frightening relevance.

WARPLANES
OVER THE AMERICAS

No part of the land area of the continental United States has ever suffered the direct effects of modern warfare – that is to say, of warfare involving the use of airpower and surface-to-surface missiles. While from 1917 to the present day countless American families and whole communities have suffered from the effects of foreign wars – from economic hardships to the grief suffered as a consequence of the deaths of neighbours, friends, and relations – the only damage directly inflicted on the American mainland by foreign military forces since 1814 was the trifling inconveniences inflicted on the West Coast in World War II by shells from Japanese submarines and, even more trifling, incendiary balloon devices launched from the other side of the Pacific.

It is predicted in the Centuries that such comparative immunity to the ravages of modern war as they affect the civilian population is not scheduled to last much longer, for Nostradamus prophesied that the series of worldwide conflicts he saw beginning at about the turn of the present century – at some time between 1995 and 2004 if one accepts the Nostradamian chronology that is adhered to by most contemporary students of the Centuries – would directly inflict an immense amount of damage upon the Americas and their peoples. Take, for example, the prediction of global conflict contained in Century I Quatrain 91, the whole of which is to be found earlier. The last line of this quatrain reads: 'The greatest damage will be imposed upon the left'.

The word 'left' is most unlikely to have been used in its modern political sense by the seer – although one cannot completely rule this out, for in some of his fulfilled predictions he seems to have used the word 'Reds' in its modern sense of 'social revolutionaries' instead of one of its more normal sixteenth-century senses, such as 'the Roman Cardinals'. It is also just possible that by 'the left' Nostradamus simply meant the more sinisterly motivated of the antagonists, for the word sinister derives from a Latin word meaning 'left'.

It seems most likely, however, that the seer was making a reference to the most common type of map of the world that was used in his own times and indeed still is at the present day. In such essentially Eurocentric productions the northern hemisphere is shown at the top of the map and the western hemisphere – the Americas – on the left. If the prophet was, as seems virtually certain, making a geographical reference of this sort the last line of Century I Quatrain 91 can then be paraphrased, in the context of its first three lines, to mean 'In the predicted World War fought with missiles and other weapons of aerial warfare the greatest damage will be suffered by the Americas'.

Such an interpretation of the meaning of this verse's last line is made more likely by the content of a surprisingly large number of other predictions made in the Centuries – for example, Century VI Quatrain 97, which also contains what is clearly a geographical reference:

> *The heaven will broil at forty-five degrees,*
> *Fire approaches the great new city,*
> *An enormous, widespread flame leaps high*
> *When they want to have proof* [or evidence] *of the Normans.*

It is often difficult to be sure exactly what is being said in Nostradamian verses relating to our futures, but in the case of this quatrain only the meaning of the last line seems to be in any real doubt (see panel below). The reference to 'forty-five degrees' in line one must relate to the approximate latitude and/or longitude (perhaps extending between 40° and 50°) of some particular area of the earth's surface; it cannot reasonably be taken as an astronomical reference relating to, for instance, elevation or a particular zodiacal degree, as in this case the rest of the quatrain would be meaningless.

As a geographical reference to latitude and/or longitude of between 40° and 50°, 45° could apply to a number of regions, among them oil-producing areas of the Middle East and a huge segment of the continental USA including the whole of New England and New York. It could be that this was one of Nostradamus's double predictions, applying to both these parts of the world, but the mention of the 'great new city' in line two of the quatrain makes it clear that the primary import of the prophecy is to the USA, for every other mention of a 'new city' in the quatrains seems to bear an American interpretation, referring to Washington, San Francisco or, most usually, New York.

It would appear, then, that lines two and three are a prophecy of a widespread nuclear attack on the USA (which may possibly coincide with a similar event in the Middle East), in which New York is damaged – and perhaps utterly destroyed – by the 'approaching flame'.

NORMANS AND NORTHMEN

Century VI Quatrain 97 would appear to contain a specific prediction of a nuclear attack on New York and other areas of the United States. Only the significance of the quatrain's last line, 'when they want to have proof [or evidence] of the Normans' seems to be a matter for much debate.

Some distinguished Nostradamians, Erika Cheetham among them, have taken the line as a possible reference to the military and diplomatic involvement of France in events associated with the bombing of New York. Possibly – but the word 'Normans' derives from an Old Norse word meaning no more than 'Northmen', so it may well be that the line pertains not to France but to a northern Asian alliance – perhaps one led by Nostradamus's 'third Antichrist'.

NOSTRADAMUS & THE AGE OF TERROR

The film Jurassic Park *takes for its theme the re-creation of ancient monsters extinct for millions of years. Nostradamus believed that long-dead monsters in human form – such as Genghis Khan – would return to stalk the Earth in our near future.*

As has been demonstrated in the preceding pages, the prophecies made by Nostradamus which are believed to relate to the approaching decades – from roughly the middle of the 1990s until well into the next century – are grim indeed. We are threatened with worldwide famine of such profundity that many of us will find ourselves eating forest roots and others will practise cannibalism; with wars fought with chemical, bacteriological and nuclear weapons; with the worst inflation that humanity has ever known; and with all the economic and social consequences of fanatical religious excess. In short, an age of monstrous terror and almost unmitigated horror is close upon us.

Such is the dreadful nature of what Nostradamus prophesied for us and our children – or, at least, what the majority of contemporary Nostradamians believe that the seer prophesied for us – that even the most dedicated admirer of the Centuries and the track record of its author must hope that as far as the next 10 or 15 years are concerned he was in hopeless error; or, better still, that interpreters of the obscure language of what seem to be the chronologically relevant quatrains have misunderstood their import or will prove to be several centuries out in their calculations of the timescale appropriate to them. This is all the more to be hoped because of the doom-laden nature of many of the predictions commented upon in the following pages.

Such predictions include: a major disaster, probably involving the use of fusion weapons, taking place at the same time as an imminent Olympic Games; the intervention in the affairs of the world of some horror – which may be either an individual or a material thing – upon which Nostradamus bestowed the enigmatic code name 'King Reb'; sinister religious movements; more wars and famine; and a grim future for Russia.

Not all is quite as dismal as this, for while Nostradamus seems to have predicted many miseries for the years which lie immediately before us he also seems to have believed that one day, long after all this suffering, human beings will live in happiness and will travel amidst the stars.

THE GAMES OF DEATH

An amazing assertion is made by some present-day students of the strange prophetic quatrains of Nostradamus. They claim that in two of them – Century X Quatrain 74 and Century I Quatrain 50 – the seer predicted that at the time of the Olympic Games in the year 2008 ancient secret cults long thought to be extinct or the preserve of a handful of occult cranks will demonstrate their hidden power to the world. These weird sects are of a pagan nature, pertain to necromancy (the cult of the dead), will be bloody in nature, and by 2008 may be headed by the individual who is destined to be responsible for the coming of the 'King of Terror' in the summer of 1999.

So here, for what it is worth, is a paraphrase of this interpretation of Century X Quatrain 74 and Century I Quatrain 50, from which are drawn the sensational and alarming predictive conclusions outlined on the first page of this section. Century X quatrain 74 reads:

> *The year of the great seventh number revolved*
> *It will appear at the time of the games of the Hecatomb,*
> *Not distant from the great Millennium,*
> *When the dead will leave their graves.*

'Not distant from the great Millennium' is taken as meaning 'not far from (i.e. not many years in time from) the year 2000'. This could mean either before or after the millennium year. However, as the exact year intended to be indicated by Nostradamus is after a year date ending with a seven ('The year of the great seventh number revolved', that is, completed) a date subsequent to either 1997 or 2007 is applicable to this prediction. As it is the great seventh number of which Nostradamus wrote it is obviously 2007 rather than 1997 to which he was making reference, so the predicted event, the time when, metaphorically or literally, the dead will leave their graves, will take place shortly after 2007, probably in the year 2008.

That 2008 is the year strongly indicated for the fulfilment of the prophecy is confirmed by the second line of the quatrain, 'It will appear at the time of the games of the Hecatomb'. A hecatomb – the word is derived from a classical Greek word literally meaning 'a hundred oxen' – is a large public blood sacrifice involving the ritual slaughter of many victims. In early classical Greece such a public blood sacrifice was held at the beginning of the regularly held athletic Games which took place at Corinth and other cities. These Games, of which the best known were those held at Olympus, were far more than mere 'games' in the modern sense of the word; they were solemn pagan festivals frequented by athletes from all over the Greek-speaking areas of the eastern Mediterranean. The original Olympic Games were connected with the cults of the underworld goddess Demeter (the only women allowed at the Olympics were her priestesses) and of the moon goddess Selene, which probably derived from a primitive fertility cult.

Towards the end of the fourth century AD all the Games, including those held at Olympus, were suppressed by the Emperor Theodosius, who was, like all the emperors of the latter half of that century save Julian the Apostate, a Christian. This was done because of the pagan nature of all the Games and the fact that the convention that athletes taking part in them should compete in the nude was deeply offensive to Christian prudery. This brought an end to all of what were, in name at least, still the 'games of the Hecatomb' although the actual sacrifices would seem to have ceased to be performed many years earlier.

Is there anything at the present day to which Nostradamus's phrase 'the games of the Hecatomb' could apply? Well, there are certainly no public games at which animals are sacrificed to the ancient gods, but the modern Olympics were established in 1896 as a deliberate revival, after 1500 years of near oblivion, of the greatest of all the 'games of the Hecatomb' – those held at Olympus and associated with the cults of Demeter and Selene.

The first of the revived Olympic Games scheduled to take place after the year 2007 – 'the year of the great seventh number' of the first line of Century X Quatrain 74 – will be those due to be held in 2008. It is in that year that 'it' – whatever or whoever that may be – will appear and that, actually and/or symbolically, 'the dead will arise from their graves'. For complex reasons, 'it' is identified as a person referred to in Century I Quatrain 50, which is to be found later.

EASTERN TEMPESTS

The three great religious faiths with which Nostradamus and his contemporaries were familiar were Islam, Judaism and Christianity, of which Friday, Saturday and Sunday respectively are the holy days. But in Century I Quatrain 50 Nostradamus refers to someone who is a follower of none of these three faiths, for the quatrain reads:

> *From the Watery Triplicity will be born,*
> *One who will celebrate Thursday as his holy day,*
> *His fame, acclamation and power will grow*
> *On land and sea, causing Eastern tempests.*

The first line of this strange prophetic verse merely tells us something about the astrological influences fated to be prominent in the horoscope of the person to whom the prediction pertains (see panel opposite). But what of the second line of the quatrain, describing the person concerned as 'one who will celebrate Thursday as his holy day'? The exact form of paganism to which this individual will adhere is uncertain, but because of the reference in the last line of Century X Quatrain 74 to the dead leaving their graves it is likely that it will involve the revival of an ancient cult of the dead – perhaps, in view of the reference to 'Eastern tempests', some degenerated form of left hand tantrism or a Bon cult.

The interpretations of the two quatrains in relation to both one another and other Nostradamian predictions are apparent and can be summarized thus: by the early years of the new millennium a new and powerful influence will be at work in the world – a malignant political leader who will also be a religious leader or, at any rate, a quasi-religious leader. It is to be presumed that his followers will look upon him as a spiritual genius, and it is quite evident that he will not even claim to be a Christian, a Muslim or a Jew – for he is described as one 'who will celebrate Thursday as his holy day'.

In the year 2008 this ruler will engage in an action, or actions, of a major and unpleasant significance. There is good reason to tentatively identify the 1999 'King of Terror' discussed later (or, alternatively, the individual who sets whatever reality is symbolized by that phrase into motion) with the one whose fame grows to such an extent that 'Eastern tempests' ensue – unless and until the course of future history demonstrates that they relate to two completely different people. However, this seems improbable; it is far more likely that the one who raises 'Eastern tempests' – which in this context must be presumed to be religious, social and political upheavals rather than meteorological turmoils – will prove to be the same person as the one who will be, or be associated with, the 'King of Terror'. It is also very likely that he is identical with the 'Antichrist' referred to as being associated with 'King Reb' in Century X Quatrain 66.

THE WATERY TRIPLICITY

According to traditional astrology, the 12 signs of the zodiac are divided into four triplicities, each made up of three signs. Each triplicity is attributed to one of the 'elements' of ancient esoteric lore – Earth, Air, Fire and Water. The zodiacal signs of the Water triplicity are Cancer, Scorpio and Pisces, so Nostradamus was indicating in the first line of Century I Quatrain 50 that these signs would be significant in his subject's horoscope. Perhaps, for instance, the person concerned would be born with a Scorpio ascendant, with the sun and Mercury in Pisces, and with the moon in Cancer. In other words, Nostradamus was predicting that a future ruler will have a horoscope dominated by planets and supposedly significant astrological points in zodiacal signs attributed to the Water triplicity.

In certain circumstances such a horoscope could appear very sinister indeed to someone applying to it the astrological rules that were in vogue at the time when Nostradamus was practising what was then still termed 'the celestial science' – widely regarded as second only to theology in its importance.

If, for example, both the sun and the planet Mars were on the ascendant in the Water sign of Scorpio in an individual's horoscope a competent 16th-century astrologer would have expected its subject to be brutal, bloody, liable to furious rages, highly sexed, clever and deceitful – in the jargon of our own times, a highly intelligent, extremely cunning and abnormally violent sociopath.

This raises an interesting possibility. It may be that Nostradamus did not clairvoyantly discern the horoscope of the individual concerned, but merely got an impression of his or her character and, on the basis of his knowledge of astrological rules, decided that the unpleasant ruler must inevitably have the sort of birth chart indicated.

CHEMICAL WARFARE

So far humanity has not experienced a war in which enormous numbers of people – either combatants or civilians – have died from the effects of chemical or nuclear warfare. While there were a large number of occasions on which chlorine, phosgene and mustard gas were used in World War I the fatal casualties inflicted by their use were surprisingly small; and while nuclear weapons were used in 1945 against Hiroshima and Nagasaki the number of civilians killed in these two cities was small compared to those who had already died elsewhere in Japan as a consequence of conventional bombing.

This situation is not destined to last – or so it would seem from the content of Century X Quatrain 72, one of that small minority of quatrains in which Nostradamus gave a specific date for a predicted future event. This quatrain reads:

> *In the year 1999* [and] *seven months,*
> *From the sky will come a great King of Terror,*
> *He will resurrect the great King of Angolmois,*
> *Before and afterwards Mars rules happily.*

As it stands, this Nostradamus quatrain is a great deal easier to interpret than many others. First, in the seventh month of 1999 (that is, July or perhaps early August), the King of Terror will come from the sky and bring back to life the

King of Angolmois. Secondly, both before and after the coming of the King of Terror 'Mars rules happily' – a fairly obvious piece of predictive symbolism meaning that in the months before and after the descent of the Terror King the world will be ravaged by armed conflict.

There are still some puzzles, however. Who is the King of Angolmois? And how will he be brought back to life by a King of Terror, and exactly who, or what, is the latter?

'Angolmois' can be read simply as a French province (as discussed earlier) or it can be taken as a good example of the sort of wordplay that recurs over and over again in the quatrains – the devising of a meaningless word or name which is either an anagram or, more usually, an imperfect anagram, of the actual word or name the seer had in mind. In this particular case 'Angolmois' can be read as an imperfect anagram of the Old French word Mongolois – Mongolians.

Now the greatest of all Mongolian rulers was Genghis Khan, who was reputed to have been monstrously cruel and destructive. Certainly he conquered a great kingdom for himself, and in so doing was directly or indirectly responsible for the deaths of millions of human beings. In other words, it seems very probable that by the phrase 'the great King of Angolmois' Nostradamus was indicating Genghis Khan. However, it does not seem likely that the seer was predicting that the mysterious King of Terror would literally restore the Mongol ruler to life; he was saying that the King of Terror would be another Genghis Khan in that he would kill as many or more as the Mongol king.

Who or what, then, could be the Terror King whose victims will equal or outnumber the millions killed by Genghis Khan? He could be a living being, quite literally a great ruler who inflicts terror on those subjected to his power. In that case, however, it is difficult to understand how he could come from the sky unless he were an alien being – a conqueror who comes from outer space. At least one student of the Centuries is convinced that the latter is the correct interpretation of Century X Quatrain 72 – that in July or August 1999 our planet will be invaded by beings from outer space who will destroy much of humanity and enslave the rest.

Perhaps – but it seems much more likely that Nostradamus was employing the phrase 'King of Terror' in a metaphorical sense pertaining to an inanimate object – much as a copywriter might refer to a product he or she was writing about as 'the car that is king of the road' or 'the queen of perfumes'. If so the meaning of the quatrain is clear and, considering the many examples of fulfilled Nostradamus predictions, extremely alarming: in July or August 1999, at a time when a war is in progress, a weapon of mass destruction will come from the sky which will be so powerful that it will be responsible for the deaths of more people than was Genghis Khan.

This immediately suggests the use of a fusion weapon by one of the warring powers; but even the largest of the present-day hydrogen bombs would be unlikely to destroy as many lives as did the Mongolian ruler. Perhaps

Nostradamus was using the word 'King' to symbolize a collective reality, tens or hundreds of fusion weapons – in other words, he may have been predicting the outbreak of a war in 1999 in which nuclear weapons would be employed on a very large scale.

Another possibility is that the King of Terror will not be a nuclear weapon of any type: it will instead be a chemical or bacteriological weapon which gets out of control and spreads either chemical poisons or disease spores throughout a continent or even the whole world, killing millions.

For reasons explained later, some present-day Nostradamians believe that it is likely to be the continent of Europe that is destined to be the victim of the mass murder of 1999.

WAVES OF ALIENS

Since 1947, UFO sightings seem to have come in waves – almost as though we have been 'investigated' by some alien civilization at regular intervals. The biggest wave of sightings was in 1952, when the astronomy consultant on the US government's UFO monitoring project was Professor Allen Hynek of the University of Ohio. After investigating no fewer than 1501 cases, of which 303 remained unexplained, his original scepticism was thoroughly shaken. Cases where radar confirmation tallied with visual evidence in the vicinity of Washington D.C. were particularly hard to ignore. Sightings by trained airline pilots were also common, and on one occasion military planes played tag with several UFOs while the whole thing was being watched on radar. UFOs seem to have been less frequently sighted recently, but this is not to say they won't come back in force in 1999!

ALCHEMY, MAGIC
AND CULTS

As was explained earlier, the so-called occult quatrains of the Centuries have always puzzled commentators. Their attempts to give answers which would provide a solution to the riddle of precisely why the seer thought fit to insert into his prophecies a number of verses which appear to pertain more to the techniques of alchemy and magic than to the future have invariably given rise to more heat than light; they have tended to receive little acceptance or response from others, save for dismissive reference to the oddly worded Century VI Quatrain 100 – to which Nostradamus uniquely gave a title: Legis cantio contra ineptos criticos, 'the Song of the Law Against Unintelligent Critics' (see below).

Yet it is possible that some of those who have gone beyond attempting to understand the meanings of just the purely predictive quatrains of the Centuries have a great deal of information to give concerning the details of what was prophesied by Nostradamus in some of his precise but infuriatingly incomplete prognostications – for example, Century X Quatrain 72, in which he wrote of the King of Terror whom he foresaw as descending from the skies in the summer of 1999. These interpreters have attempted to understand the innermost nature of those subjects that are dealt with in the occult quatrains – alchemy, magic and those strange paths to inner knowledge which some have termed 'cults of the shadow' – and, by applying them to the Centuries, have endeavoured to learn more of the nature of particular aspects of 'future history'.

Such interpreters risk attracting derision and making foolish mistakes, but they are probably following the path which Nostradamus referred to as being that of 'priests of the rite' (see below). One such experimenter, a person who in Nostradamian terms could be called 'a priestess of the rite' – that is, a woman who possesses a detailed theoretical and practical knowledge of both ceremonial divination and of those ancient techniques of consciousness-alteration which supposedly enable those who practise them to obtain a glimpse of the pattern of the future – has supplied the present writer with the result of an experiment which was aimed at re-experiencing the 'King of Terror' vision which Nostradamus recorded in Century X Quatrain 72. The techniques that were used to carry out this experiment are described later; here it suffices to summarize the content of the psychic vision which was the outcome of their employment.

According to this experimental psychic vision, by the beginning of 1999 the ruler of an expansionist central Asian state which was formerly a constituent republic of the Soviet Union will have within its control some sort of orbiting space vehicle. By this time, the whole of what was formerly the USSR will be riven by a turmoil of ethnic and religious foreign and civil wars. As a means of deterring both actual and potential enemies, this orbiting space vehicle will be equipped with some means of launching bacteriological and chemical weapons. As a consequence of what will be subsequently claimed an accident, these terrible weapons will be launched, hitting the southern part of France but spreading death and devastation over the entire European land mass.

If this modern prediction proves to be correct, Europe will have been subjected to a murderous attack from one of the states of the former USSR and World War III will have been unleashed in all its terror.

THE SEER'S SONG

Century VI Quatrain 100, the only quatrain to which Nostradamus gave a title (see below), is possessed of another singularity: it was printed (except for one word) in Latin, instead of the usual convoluted language of French, anagrams and neologisms to be found in other quatrains. The verse reads:

Let those who read this verse ponder its meaning,
Let the common crowd and the unlearned leave it alone:
All of them – Idiot Astrologers and Barbarians – keep off,
He who does the other thing, let him be a priest for [or to] the rite.

In this quatrain the seer was clearly indicating that the content of this verse was intended neither for the generality of men and women ('barbarians') nor even for 'idiot astrologers' – mere fortune-tellers as distinct from those who at the present day might be termed 'initiated diviners' – but for 'priests of the rite'.

However, the seer obviously intended to communicate more than this and it is likely he was saying one or both of two things: first, that there is – as some students of his writings assert – a hidden structure to the Centuries. Secondly, that those who were 'priests of the rite' – that is, those who were skilled in the predictive arts and not mere fortune tellers – should be able not only to interpret the quatrains but to expand and elucidate their meanings by the use of ritual divination.

WORLD WAR III

Nostradamus makes what can be interpreted as a prediction of World War III in at least 12 quatrains. The most famous, Century X Quatrain 72, has already been discussed, but it can be interpreted in another way which yields a bit more detail. Instead of interpreting Angolmois as an imperfect anagram of Mongolois (Mongolians) it could be taken to mean the French city of Angoulême. A recent French leader who comes from near here is François Mitterand, who was born in Charente. The quatrain now suggests that after the 'King of Terror' comes from the sky, Mitterand will be politically resurrected and brought back to power temporarily to deal with the situation. Mars could then either refer to war generally or a French leader whose horoscope is strongly martial, and whose rule is interrupted by the temporary reappointment of President Mitterand – or perhaps some other French leader from the same region.

In Century I Quatrain 16, Nostradamus uses astrological symbolism to date the impending war:

A scythe joined with a pond in Sagittarius
At its highest ascendant.
Plague, famine, death from military hands,
The century approaches its renewal.

The scythe in this astrological context represents the planet Saturn, while 'joined with a pond' refers to a watery zodiacal sign or planet. One commentator has translated 'pond' as Aquarius, and has interpreted the passage as 'when

Saturn and Aquarius are in conjunction with Sagittarius'. However, it is not possible for two zodiacal signs to be in conjunction and it is more correct to talk of two planets in conjunction rather than a planet (Saturn) joined to a sign (Aquarius). Obviously, the 'pond' may represent the Moon in conjunction with Saturn in Sagittarius. The fourth line strongly suggests that the events occur at the end of a century. The most recent time in which Saturn was in Sagittarius was 1988; from now until the end of this century, Saturn, being a very slow-moving planet, only passes through Aquarius, Pisces, Aries and Taurus. This suggests that the arrival of this particular plague, famine and death is not scheduled until well into the 21st century.

Century II Quatrain 46 gives us further insight into the possible advent of a third world war:

> *After great misery for mankind an even greater one approaches*
> *When the great cycle of the centuries is renewed*
> *It will rain blood, milk, famine, war and diseases*
> *In the sky will be seen a fire, dragging a tail of sparks.*

Again the time frame is specified as 'when the great cycle of the centuries is renewed'. Unlike Century II Quatrain 41, which talks of a Great Star boiling or burning, this quatrain specifies 'a fire, dragging a tail of sparks'. This would seem to be an even more likely reference to some great comet. As Halley's comet came and went in 1986 with very little visibility or astrological disturbance, Nostradamus's 'fire' is likely to be an unexpected meteorological phenomenon, perhaps the impact of a meteor on earth.

Whatever the exact timing, the phrase 'when the great cycle of the centuries is renewed' does suggest the end of this millennium. The war will bring with it a rain of blood, milk, famine, and disease. The odd word out is 'milk', so perhaps the original French word 'laict' would be better interpreted as laïcité, meaning an outbreak of secularity or anti-religious feeling.

Nostradamus refers to the advent of the comet yet again in Century II Quatrain 62:

> *Mabus will soon die and there will happen*
> *A dreadful destruction of people and animals:*
> *Suddenly, vengeance will appear,*
> *A hundred hands, thirst and hunger, when the comet shall pass.*

The key to the timing is the identity of Mabus – perhaps someone who has not yet come to prominence. In view of the reference to animals dying as well, the cause of this dreadful destruction is probably some kind of indiscriminate nuclear device. Erika Cheetham suggests that 'a hundred hands' refers to the many refugee camps springing up all over the world where there are wars or famine. The passing of a comet might, however, be Nostradamus's vision of a missile rather than a natural comet.

Another quatrain which is specifically relevant to the 20th century is Century I, Quatrain 63 where, amazingly, Nostradamus says very clearly that:

> *Pestilence is past, the world becomes smaller,*
> *For a long time the lands will be inhabited peacefully.*
> *People will travel safely through the sky [over] land and seas:*
> *Then wars will start up again.*

The world becoming smaller is a 20th-century phrase – it seems as if Nostradamus had even overheard a snippet of 20th-century conversation. He certainly would not have 'seen' the physical world shrink. It is an interesting aside on how Nostradamus received the quatrains, almost as if he had time-travelled at random (or so it appears from his ordering of the quatrains) and then both viewed and overheard events. Some of his visions are of things like the fighter pilots for which he could have had no frame of reference, so he describes them in terms of objects of his own time, often quite ingeniously.

The last line suggests that wars will start up after a period of peace. This phrase might refer to the world wars that have already taken place, or suggest a third erupting after an interval of 50 years of relative peace. From the end of World War II, an interval of 50 years brings us to 1995.

As the first two world wars of this century both started in the Balkans, that confused and ethnically very divided area which was until recently called Yugoslavia, it is very tempting to point to the present troubles in the Balkans as the potential touchpaper for the third world war which Nostradamus predicts.

THE FUTURE OF RUSSIA

The country of Russia existed for many centuries before the Revolution of 1917 which was to herald the formation of the Soviet Union – now, after 72 years, again broken down into its constituent parts. The alliance between the old Soviet Union and the US in early 1990 is predicted by Century VI Quatrain 21, where these countries are identified in the first line:

> *When those of the Northern Pole are united together,*
> *In the East will be great fear and dread:*
> *A new man elected supported by the great one ...*

The second line may refer to the reaction of China, now left alone as the only large Communist country. The 'new man elected' is obviously Boris Yeltsin, who, was supported by the 'great one' who brought it all about, Mikhael Gorbachev.

The break-up of the Soviet Union into its constituent republics, no longer governed by Moscow, has left a legacy of squabbling between these new countries who are trying to forge a Commonwealth of Independent States. Nostradamus has something to say about two of them – the Ukraine and Belorussia – in Century III, Quatrain 95:

The Moorish law will be seen to fail,
Followed by another that is more attractive:
The Boristhenes will be the first to give way,
To another more pleasing as a consequence of gifts and tongues.

The 'Moorish law' was actually a pun meaning the teachings of Marx and hence communism, which has been seen to have failed. The reference to the river Boristhenes (or Dneiper) clearly identifies the two states as the Ukraine and Belorussia (White Russia, as it used to be called), through which it flows. It is clear that the upsurge of Islamic fundamentalism in some of the previous republics of the Soviet Union will fail in these two states. The form of government which will finally take over in these countries is seen by Nostradamus as more pleasing than Islamic fundamentalism or even communism.

As these former Soviet satellites are the 'first to give way' to Western propaganda and perhaps bribery or the lure of consumer goods (gifts and tongues), the thought occurs that they will at some stage be involved in a conflict, presumably with their neighbour, Russia.

Further elaboration is to be had in Century IV Quatrain 95, where Nostradamus writes:

The rule left to two, they will hold it a very short time,
Three years and seven months having passed they will go to war.
The two vestals will rebel against them;
The victor then born on American soil.

The 'rule left to two' suggests two world powers, the old Soviet Union (now Russia) and the US. The dating of this event would seem to be very accurate – three years and seven months after the break-up of the Soviet Union, some time in 1994 or early 1995. At this time there will be a war, not between Russia and America but between Russia allied with the US and the two 'vestal' (virginal) or new states. The new states might well be the newly independent states Belorussia and the Ukraine, which used to form part of the old Soviet Union.

The war will be won by assistance from America, or by a commander or diplomat born there. Despite this help from America, the alliance between the two world powers will last no more than 13 years, according to Century V, Quatrain 78:

The two will not remain allied for long.
Within thirteen years they give into barbarian power.
There will be such a loss on both sides,
That one will bless the Barque and its leader.

The date when this alliance gives in to a barbarian power is some time early in the new millennium, about 2003. The only major non-Christian power likely to qualify is China, whose sheer population size dwarfs the two world powers combined.

The 'barque' is usually interpreted as the papacy or its leader the Pope – if you believe Malachy and other references made by Nostradamus, the last of the line of Popes. The quatrain may refer to the rapid rise of Christianity in the northern republics whose believers were so thoroughly repressed by communism and its doctrines over the period of its 72-year rule, or alternatively it may suggest the intervention of a Catholic president in the US.

Other quatrains suggest a growing Islamification of the southern ex-Soviet republics contrasting with Russia's newly revived Christianity, thereby causing friction amongst the southern republics.

THE PROPHECIES OF RASPUTIN

One of the most influential men in Russia before the Revolution broke out was the monk Grigory Rasputin, who was intimately connected with the Russian royal family. Before his violent death at the hands of Prince Yusupov, he wrote a letter to the Tsarina in which he made the prediction that he would die before the first day of 1917, the year of the Revolution. He added that if he was killed by a peasant then Russia would remain a prosperous monarchy for hundreds of years, but if he was killed by an aristocrat the Tsar and his family would die within two years, and no nobles would be left in Russia after 25 years.

All his predictions came true after he was murdered by an aristocrat on 29 December 1916. The Russian Revolution broke out the following year, and a year later Rasputin's second prediction came to pass with the murder of the royal family.

WORLD DROUGHT
AND FAMINE

One of the most unequivocal quatrains is Century I Quatrain 17. It states in very plain French that for 40 years Iris will not be seen. Iris means 'rainbow' in Greek, and from this statement the quatrain appears to mean that for 40 years there will be no rain, a drought even longer than those experienced in the very dry central parts of Australia.

The next line of this quatrain states that for 40 years Iris will be seen every day. This sounds like rain of deluge proportions, followed by flooding, but with at least the sun showing through long enough to create a rainbow. To confirm this interpretation, the quatrain continues:

> The dry earth will grow more parched,
> And there will be great floods when it is seen.

Although the Bible records a flood of 40 days and 40 nights, the world has not seen either a flood or a drought of these proportions, so the quatrain must refer to the future. The increasing occurrence of the 'greenhouse effect' and its alteration of the climatic patterns of the globe, including the spread of desert and semi-desert conditions into parts of Africa which were previously fertile, might be a beginning of the fulfilment of this terrible prophecy.

If we try to look beyond the fairly obvious literal meaning of the quatrain our only clue is Iris, who in Greek mythology was the daughter of Electra and the sister of the Harpies. In Homer's Iliad she is referred to as the messenger of the gods (particularly Hera and Zeus, the most senior Olympian gods of ancient Greece), so perhaps the drought and floods are to be construed as a serious warning of an ecological nature from the gods. Iris is also the wife of Zephyrus, the drying west wind and the cause of drought; by contrast, in her hand she holds a pitcher of water that symbolizes rain.

Drought brings famine, and in Century III Quatrain 42 Nostradamus speaks of famine in Tuscie, or Tuscany in Italy:

> The child will be born with two teeth in his throat,
> Stones will fall like rain in Tuscany.
> A few years later there will be neither wheat nor barley,
> To satisfy those who will weaken from hunger.

The reference to the person born with two teeth in his throat occurs again in Century II Quatrain 7, also in conjunction with famine:

> Among many people deported to the islands
> Will be a man born with two teeth in his throat.
> They will die of hunger having stripped the trees.

'People deported to the islands' was a common French method of dealing with criminals, who were sent to penal colonies such as the Ile du Diable in French Guiana. The key to both of these quatrains is the child born with two teeth in its throat.

The clearest reference to a great famine is made in Century I Quatrain 67, which is quoted earlier. The emphasis is upon local famines becoming world-wide, possibly as a response to the greenhouse effect and the consequent alteration of climatic conditions. The African famines are just a forerunner of a much more widespread global famine.

The timing of this great famine is expressly indicated in Century IV, Quatrain 67:

> *In the year that Saturn and Mars are equally fiery,*
> *The air is very dry [from a] long passage*
> *From the hidden fires a great place burns with heat.*
> *Little rain, a hot wind, wars and raids.*

The next dates when Saturn and Mars occur in the same fiery sign, Aries, are from 8 April to 2 May 1996, and from 5 March to 13 April 1998. Nostradamus' prediction of widespread famine in this century is most likely to come true in these two key date ranges. These two planets are also both in fire signs from 10 September to 30 October 1996 and again from 29 September to 9 November 1997. These dates will probably see an increased climatic hardship in African countries, for Nostradamus indicates that the drought will escalate at the time of the proximity of these two 'malefic planets', as they used to be known. Because of the excess heat and very drying air, this may well be the worst famine of the century, and the famine will be more widespread than just Somalia or Ethiopia.

A very specific reference that Nostradamus made in Century V Quatrain 90 to famine in Greece confirms that the famine will not be limited to Africa:

> *In the Cyclades, in Perinthus and Larissa,*
> *In Sparta and all of the Pelopennese:*
> *A very great famine, plague through false dust.*
> *It will last nine months throughout the whole peninsula.*

The 'false dust' may be either an agricultural spray, radioactive fall-out, or possibly some kind of southwards-drifting chemical weapon from wars in the Balkans.

HUMANITY AMIDST
THE STARS

Space exploration has only been a fact of life for the last three decades, yet Nostradamus appears to have foreseen even events occurring within this context – though, in an age when even basic flight had only been hinted at by

Leonardo da Vinci (1452–1519), the idea of leaving the surface of the earth like a bird would have been beyond the imagination of the average man. The clearest reference to flight is in Century II, Quatrain 29:

> The Eastern man shall come forth from his seat
> Passing the Apennine mountains to France:
> He will cross through the sky, the seas and the snow,
> And he will strike everyone with his rod.

The third line clearly indicates Nostradamus's vision of air travel over both seas and the snowy mountain peaks of the Italian Apennines on the Eastern man's way to France, suggesting a Middle Eastern origin. One can only speculate if he 'saw' the shape of aeroplanes to come. Probably he did: Century I Quatrain 64 refers to 'battle fought in the skies' where the early flying helmets seem to have been 'visible' to him. The same theme is picked up in Century II, Quatrain 45 where 'human blood is spilt near to heaven' – a very unambiguous image of human warfare in the heavens. The next quatrain describes a missile (or possibly a comet): 'in the sky will be seen a fire, dragging a tail of sparks'. A less ambiguous reference is supplied by Century IV, Quatrain 43, which clearly states that 'weapons will be heard fighting in the skies'.

It is but a short conceptual step from here to manned space flight. The key quatrain is Century IX Quatrain 65, which reads:

> He will be taken to the corner of Luna,
> Where he will be placed on foreign land.

If Luna is taken to be the physical moon, rather than some symbolic allusion, then this describes the landing of astronaut Neil Armstrong on lunar soil in a ship placed on the moon's surface by the controllers at NASA headquarters. Here he claimed the 'foreign land' for the US and made his giant step for mankind in 1969, more than 400 years after an astrologer in a small town in Provence gazed up at the moon and foretold this extraordinary event.

THE CHALLENGER DISASTER

The third and fourth lines of Century IX Quatrain 65 touch upon the events of 28 January 1986 when, 71 seconds after lift-off, the space shuttle Challenger exploded, killing its crew of seven:

> The unripe fruit will be the subject of great scandal.
> Great blame, to the others great praise.

The 'unripe fruit' is the malfunctioning space shuttle, whose explosion set back the whole US space programme by perhaps a decade. Great blame indeed, and unthinkable that such an expensive and complex operation could have gone so wrong before it even escaped the earth's atmosphere. Nostradamus's great praise goes instead to Neil Armstrong's team. At the same time the USSR space programme had been very successful in establishing the MIR orbiting space station, which is still in use.

Nostradamus refers to the Challenger disaster yet again in Century I, Quatrain 81, where he gives some intriguing clues:

> *Nine will be set apart from the human race,*
> *Separated from judgement and advice:*
> *Their fate is to be divided as they depart,*
> *Kappa, Theta, Lambda, banished and scattered.*

'Their fate to be divided as they depart' is an image of the crew being torn asunder in the explosion as the Challenger departed – beyond all help, without even the time to make a decision ('separated from judgement'). However, Nostradamus got the number of astronauts wrong, for he says nine rather than seven. The Greek letters, banished and scattered, sound like American fraternity letters, and may have corresponded to the fraternity allegiances of some of the crew, or alternatively spelt their initials, or even the code name for this particular launch. These are details which probably only NASA can confirm or deny.

DOOMSTERS AND PROPHETS

Many of Nostradamus's prophecies were of unpleasant events rather than joyful ones. Cynics have remarked that it is always wise for those who wish to gain a reputation for being able to see into the future to forecast plenty of disaster, doom and gloom – for catastrophe, like death and taxes, is always with us. The clairvoyant who tells us to expect calamities, will, so it is said, inevitably be admired for his or her psychic powers, for calamities there will surely be.

So many of Nostradamus's prophecies were negative that in 1562 no fewer than 20 English printers were fined for selling the Prognostications of Nostradamus. These fines are entered in the Stationer's Register for that year, alongside the titles and authors' names of a number of almanacs of the period. Political predictions were taken very seriously by the English government of the day and they made such an impact upon the citizens that, according to a pamphlet dating from 1561, 'the whole realm was so troubled and so moved with blind enigmatical and devilish prophecies of that heaven-gazer Nostradamus …

that even those which in their hearts could have wished the glory of God and his Word most flourishing to be established were brought into such an extreme coldness of faith that they doubted God'.

Such publications were big business, and perhaps the establishment was loath to see what may have been considered pro-French prognostications distributed in England. This gives us some idea of how popular Nostradamus's publications were even in England, as well as an insight into the official disapproval they provoked.

There has always been an ambiguous relationship between prophets and their rulers. No ruler likes to feel that his or her decisions will be brought to nought by a prophecy of failure, and besides it is bad for morale. Perhaps the most universally disliked and persecuted prophet was the Hebrew prophet Jeremiah: his first book of prophecies was first cut to pieces and then burnt. He was often imprisoned under very unpleasant conditions for his apparently unpatriotic prophecies, and had to ally himself with the Babylonian governor for safety before fleeing to Egypt, where he was finally stoned to death for his lugubrious insights.

Amongst the earliest of the Greek prophets were the Sibyls. Like the priestesses of Branchus, whose techniques of prophecy Nostradamus copied, they were also priestesses of Apollo. The most famous of the Sibyls was the Cumaean Sybil, who is reputed to have guided Aeneas to the underworld as reported in Virgil's Aeneid Book VI. This Sibyl, whose talents were obviously not appreciated, offered nine books of her prophecies to King Tarquin. When he refused to pay the apparently exorbitant price for these prophecies she threw three books into the flames of a brazier and then demanded the same price for the remaining six books. He refused and she repeated the same performance, burning a further three books. He finally gave in and paid the price asked for the whole nine books just for the remaining three. These books were preserved in the temple of Jupiter on the Capitol in Rome until it was burnt down in 83 bc.

Apart from books containing actual oracular pronouncements, many books which were not originally compiled for such interpretation were used for oracular purposes; they were literary or religious works which had come to be held in such veneration that they were looked upon as being endowed with a supernatural virtue. In both ancient Rome and Renaissance Europe, for example, Homer's Odyssey and Virgil's Aeneid were regarded with such respect that copies of the books were used in this manner.

The process of using the oracle was referred to as 'casting the lots'. The inquirer would carefully formulate the question and then open the book three times at random, each time letting a finger fall upon the page. A note would be made of the three lines upon which the seeker's finger had fallen, and an attempt would be made to apply these lines to the situation about which the question had been asked.

From the latter decades of the Roman Empire onwards, both the Old and

New Testaments were quite often employed in the same manner, the process being referred to as sortes Sanctorum, 'the lots of the Saints'. Even though the use of the Bible in this manner was specifically forbidden by many local ecclesiastical councils, the casting of the sortes Sanctorum was widespread.

In the History of the Franks, Saint Gregory of Tours (538-594) recorded that when the Frankish prince Merovechus was in terror of the wrath of the bellicose Queen Fredegond he cast the sortes Sanctorum in the Basilica of Saint Martin of Tours. The oracles he derived from these books were of a gloomy nature, especially one that read: 'The Lord our God has betrayed you into the hands of your enemies.' The oracle was to prove accurate enough, for Merovechus was eventually killed by henchmen of Queen Fredegond.

Such an accurate prediction would seem to have been by no means unique. It is small wonder, then, that prophets were often seen as doomsters and consequently persecuted.

SIBYLLINE ORACLES

The early Christian Sibylline oracles proclaimed the Em-peror Constantine as a messianic king. For them, of course, a Roman emperor who was also a Christian was a real godsend. One of these oracles (Tiburtina) spoke of the Emperor of the Last Days who fought against the Antichrist, for in those times the early Christian converts fully expected that the end of the world would follow closely upon the crucifixion of Christ. This Emperor of the Last Days was a wish-fulfilment figure for the early Christians, as he was expected to convert the pagans, destroy the temples of the false gods and baptize the converted, particularly the Jews. The prophecy concluded that when his work was finally done he would lay down his sword and retire to Golgotha, the hill upon which Christ was crucified.

LILLY AND THE FIRE OF LONDON

The Fire of London and Nostradamus's uncanny pinpointing of the year 1666 with his 'three times twenty and six' in Century II Quatrain 51 is discussed earlier. The famous diarist Samuel Pepys was aware of Nostradamus's prophecy, which had been reprinted in Booker's Almanack before the fire.

A number of other prophets seem to have come to the same conclusions about this seminal event. The astrologer William Lilly (1602-81), who was born just over a century after Nostradamus, published a pamphlet called 'Monarchy or no Monarchy' 14 years before the Great Fire of London. In it were 19 'heirogliphics' (sic) or enigmatic pictures designed to depict the future of the

'English Nation and Commonwealth for many hundreds of years yet to come'. Besides a number of plates that depict scenes which may be yet to come – for example, a strange animal like a weasel attacking a crown and Parliament lounging idly by while an invasion of England takes place – there are two particularly striking pictures printed on the same page.

The first shows bundles of corpses lying on the bare ground and two men busily digging graves for two coffins, while over a church in the background fly four birds of ill omen. This disturbing vision of the plague that preceded the Fire is linked by proximity with the picture of a city in flames by a large river – a city which is almost certain to be London. Nearby some men are pouring water on to a flaming bonfire, into which falls a pair of twins. The twins are symbolic of the zodiacal sign of Gemini, the sign most usually associated with London.

Although plague and fire were common hazards of the time, the striking aptness of these pictures was reinforced by a pamphlet that Lilly wrote in 1648, in which he pointed a further astrological indication of what was to come. 'In the year 1665 … when the absis … of Mars shall appear in Virgo who shall expect less than a strange catastrophe of human affairs in the … kingdom of England.' He goes on to say that 'it will be ominous to London, unto her merchants at sea, to her traffique on land, to her poor, to all sorts of people … by reason of sundry fires and a consuming plague'. The description of this twofold tragedy could hardly be more clearly expressed, seven years before its occurrence.

Lilly was astoundingly accurate, for in the aftermath of the Fire of London there was no lack of theories as to its cause, and the citizens of London were more than happy to pin the blame on any individual or conspiracy. Lilly noted in his diary that several persons including Colonel John Rathbone 'were then tried for their lives' for plotting to burn the City as a way of killing the King and overthrowing the government of the day. The conspirators had even used Lilly's Almanack to calculate a lucky day (3 September) for their evil deed. In the event, fate forestalled them and the Fire broke out one day before their planned attempt. Nevertheless, they were still hanged.

Lilly was duly summoned to the Speaker's Chamber in order to be cross-examined about his prediction. In some apprehension, he asked his friend the well-known antiquary Elias Ashmole to accompany him. Ashmole had been made a herald at Windsor by the King, and by his presence helped to protect the prophet from undue victimization. The Committee may have even suspected Lilly of setting fire to the city in order to vindicate his prophecy, but the presence of Ashmole helped to keep the discussion away from conjecture and firmly on the provable, and Lilly walked away a free man. He gave Ashmole a parcel of rare books by way of thanks for his aid. Such is the danger involved in making prophecies that turn out to be true during one's own lifetime!

Nostradamus must too have been worried when he was summoned to Paris in 1556 by the French Queen Catherine de' Medici. As a result of this meeting the Queen believed implicitly in Nostradamus's predictions for the rest of her life, but the meeting could so easily have gone the other way – especially as Nostradamus was charged with the delicate and difficult task of drawing up the horoscopes of the seven Valois children, whose tragic fates he had already revealed in the Centuries. It is no wonder that for his own safety Nostradamus deliberately obscured the dates and names in his quatrains.

THE FIRE FORESEEN

Francis Bernard, a physician and astrologer, attempted to establish a general astrological theory which would enable him to chart the course of all future fires that a city was likely to fall heir to by the astrological process of 'rectification'. This is a practice whereby the horoscope of a city (or, more usually, a person) is adjusted by reference to known events in the life of that person or city.

Others thought that in the Fire of London they recognized one of the many prophecies of Mother Shipton, the seer born in 1488 at Knaresborough, Yorkshire, who was reputed to have lived in a cave. This was first mooted in 1641, 21 years before the Fire, but as each successive edition of her prophecies seemed to contain new predictions that were suited to the season, little credence can be placed upon this.

It seems almost as if the gravity of the Fire of London was sufficient to stir a number of prophets to make the same prediction. Or was it that the Fire became inevitable after so many seers saw it?

NEW AGES OF CHAOS

In 1985 Dr Ravi Batra published a book called The Great Depression of 1990 in which he accurately predicted the onset of a terrible recession or depression in 1989, with a great increase in unemployment, a decrease in inflation, a rapid fall in property prices, a great increase in business failures, and a number of other economic events which have come very true in the western world. He even suggested that real estate investments should be sold at the end of 1989, and business indebtedness reduced – perfect timing, as it turns out. Yet he never claimed to be a prophet, merely a close observer of economic cycles.

By implying that 1990 paralleled the events of 1930, and by extrapolation that 1996 will herald the real end of this current recession, he has provided us with a prediction and unconsciously underlined two interesting key ideas. First, the period between events of the 1930s and those of the 1990s chosen by Dr Batra is exactly 60 years. This is exactly the time specified by the ancient Chinese to complete one 'Great Year', during which all possible combinations of events as described by the interaction of the 10 Celestial Stems and 12 Earthly Branches of Chinese metaphysics are supposed to happen. After 60 years, everyone comes back to exactly the same Chinese year combination of Branch and Stem as the year they were born in. Perhaps the Chinese Great Year has other implications which are relevant to prophecy and not obvious to the world at large: perhaps the very choice of the words 'Branch' and 'Stem' which echo the structure of the 'time tree' discussed later is not a coincidence.

Secondly, the use by Nostradamus of astrological dating of the quatrains suggests that a particular prediction may 'actualize' at any one of the times when a certain astrological conjunction occurs. This means that as the planets cycle at different rates round the sun, certain configurations come up very frequently, and others at long intervals. Those occurring at very long intervals – say every couple of centuries – can be seen as almost uniquely dated events, fated to happen once. Others that come round several times a century may happen at one or other of these conjuctions, or even in one form or another at several of these conjunctions. Likewise, the revolution of the earth around the sun enables calendarmakers to 'predict' the seasons.

Perhaps these astrological configurations mark points when the twigs of the 'time tree' brush against each other in some cosmic wind. Maybe they are points where events 'grow together' again, and a divergent twig is reunited with the main branch. An examination of the cyclical aspects caused by the revolution of the planets round the sun over unequal periods of time might reveal some of the patterns of futurity, for after all it is by the revolution of only one of these planets, the earth, around the sun that all human time is measured. An understanding of the workings of the whole cosmic clock might reveal the structure behind the sequence of events we call history, be they national or personal. In fact it is these very aspects in the natal horoscope of an individual which may predict some of the events in his or her life.

Perhaps Nostradamus was in reality a much greater astrologer than has ever been appreciated, but in a different way to that which is normally understood by the term. It may be that he comprehended some workings of the cosmic clock that enabled him to gain a vision of other times, not just those that are governed by the revolution of one planet – the earth – round the sun.

SIXTY-YEAR CYCLICAL PREDICTIONS

Ravi Batra draws a number of 60-year parallels:

1920 & 1980 Both years of high unemployment, high inflation and high interest rates, which is a very rare combination.

1921 & 1981 A large tax cut favouring the upper end of the pay scale, with unemployment rising sharply.

1922 & 1982 Both years see a sharp fall in inflation and interest rates, with a sharp rise in the UK stockmarket.

1923 & 1983 A strange parallel is that banks offered interest on cheque accounts for the first time in history in 1923 and reintroduced it after a long break in 1983. In both years there was a very sharp fall in unemployment (the largest in three decades in the latter year).

1924 & 1984 Inflation is lower and the UK stockmarket continues to rise.

1925 & 1985 A sharp rise in bank failures, with 120 failing worldwide in 1985 alone.

1926 & 1986 The UK stockmarket reaches record highs in both these years, while unemployment falls sharply. Energy prices fall steeply in both years.

THE WEB OF THE FUTURE

With all forms of prediction, the trickiest part for the seer is to get an exact date, a precise fix in the interconnected web of the various possible futures. The seer might 'see' an event with all sorts of detail but have trouble in identifying the exact date of an era into which he or she has arrived almost by accident, while with forms of divination like the I Ching, geomancy and the Tarot, there is virtually no way of getting an accurate date fix. Consequently, it is extraordinary that Nostradamus was able to pinpoint exact years and sometimes even exact months.

Despite the fact that Nostradamus claimed in a letter to César, his son, to know the dates of all his prophecies, he only actually specified precise dates in just a few of his quatrains. These include:

Century II Quatrain 51, which gives the Fire of London's date as 'three times twenty and six' or 1666.

Century III Quatrain 77, where he accurately predicts the peace between the Turks and the Persians in 1727.

Century X, Quatrain 72 is the gloomy prediction of the coming of the King of Terror in July 1999 – a prophecy yet to be confirmed.

In addition to specific dates, Nostradamus gives a number of astrological indications from which a range of possible dates can be derived. Century I Quatrain 52, for example, depicts the time of its fulfilment as a conjunction of Jupiter and Saturn in the zodiac sign of Aries (the head of the zodiac):

> *The head of Aries, Jupiter and Saturn,*
> *Eternal God what changes?*
> *Then after a long century the bad times will return,*
> *Great upheavals in France and Italy.*

This conjunction took place in December 1702 during the War of the Spanish Succession, with the events 'after a long century' being the French campaign in Italy in 1803 and the declaration of Napoleon as President of the

Italian Republic. It is not a future prediction as asserted by several commentators, and this conjunction does not again take place between now and the end of this century.

Another astrologically indicated dating occurs in Century I Quatrain 16. The interpretation of the astrological references in this quatrain has confused several commentators, one of whom even says 'this description is so general it could fit the 20th century as well as any other'. Not true – the key line is 'A scythe joined with a pond in Sagittarius'. The scythe is a symbol for the planet Saturn conjunct with only one possible planet, the Moon, both in the zodiacal sign of Sagittarius. This conjunction happens for a period of 2½ years every 29½ years, because Saturn is a very slow-moving planet. One such occurrence of this conjunction is in 1999 – a highly significant Nostradamian year. Nostradamus could not date events solely by using the fast-moving planets such as Mercury because these would have provided a very large and confusing range of dates to choose from.

Another astrological dating occurs in Century II Quatrain 48, which states that:

> The great army will pass over mountains
> When Saturn is in Sagittarius and Mars moving into Pisces.

This conjunction has occurred three times in this century, the last time in late November 1986. However, an appropriate event corresponding to it does not appear to have yet transpired, so it seems it is a future prediction for the next century.

Century VI Quatrain 24 is another clear astrological dating:

> Mars and the Sceptre will be in conjunction,
> A calamitous war under Cancer:
> A short time afterwards a new king will be anointed,
> Who will bring peace to the earth for a long time.

Clearly a ruler will be appointed after a war that may take place between 22 June and 23 July (under the sign of Cancer). The year will be determined by a conjunction between Mars and Jupiter (the sceptre) in Cancer. This conjunction has occurred six times since 1812, and will happen next on 21 June 2002. This is a possible time for this war, but not a certainty.

There is a specific dating in Century V Quatrain 91, in which Greece is threatened by attack from Albania:

> At the great market called that of the liars
> All of Torrent and the field of Athens:
> They will be surprised by the light armed horses,
> By the Albanois [when] Mars [is in] Leo, and Saturn [is] in Aquarius.

The last occurrence of this conjunction this century was from 28 April until 3 June 1993. Consequently, this prophecy will not be fulfilled until the next millenium.

Apart from these quatrains, most dating is recognizable only in retrospect. It is a pity that Nostradamus, if he did know the exact dates as he claimed to his son, chose to obfuscate them in most quatrains. It is, however, more likely he was unable to put precise dates to many of his predictions.

NOSTRADAMUS & THE RIVER OF TIME

The amazing accuracy of many fulfilled predictions of Nostradamus, such as those in which he gave actual dates for specific occurrences, makes his mistakes – for instance, the "predictive miss" – all the more puzzling. Is it possible to reconcile them?

The amazing accuracy of many of Nostradamus's predictions raises several important questions. Firstly, was he a natural clairvoyant – that is to say, a person born with an innate ability to see in vision events taking place far away in both time and space? And did he employ any methods other than astrology in order to help him prophesy? If so, what was the nature of these methods and were any of them connected with ritual magic or other techniques regarded by some as pertaining to 'forbidden knowledge'? And if Nostradamus truly saw events that did not take place until long after his death, does that mean that the idea of free will is illusory, that all of us are, in a sense, robots, biological machines destined to live out our lives to a predestined end?

In the pages that follow, an attempt is made to provide tentative answers to all these questions in relation to the prophecies of Nostradamus, both fulfilled and as yet unfulfilled – as well as those few which were unquestionably erroneous or, very oddly, would appear to have been fulfilled before they were made.

In this respect readers will have to consider what is meant by the word 'time', for some theories concerning prophecies in general and those of Nostradamus in particular involve looking at time in quite a different way from that in which we almost all tend to view it. We think of it as being like a great river, running from its source to its end. The 'Big Bang' – or the divine act of creation – is seen as the source of the river of time, the extinction of the universe – or the Last Judgment – as its end. Our own lives are, metaphorically speaking, short journeys along that river which are always downstream.

There are, however, many other hypotheses concerning the nature of time. One of them, looked upon with favour by some reputable physicists, regards the structure of time as suggestive not of a river but the above-ground form of an enormous forest tree, 'our time', which embraces the entire universe of matter and energy as we know it, being no more than a twig upon one of the branches of the tree. In this section, this idea and others will be considered in relationship to the Centuries.

IS THE FUTURE FIXED?

An acceptance of what seems to be the overwhelming evidence that Nostradamus knew the nature of events that were to take place hundreds of years after his death in 1566 has some very unpleasant implications for all of us – for it suggests that the future is fixed by forces utterly outside our control, that when we believe we are making any choice, however trivial it may be, we are in truth making no choice at all. Rather we are simply following the dictates of Fate, whose playthings we are.

Another way of regarding our future is to posit an 'alternate realities' hypothesis – the theory which, metaphorically speaking, looks upon time as a tree rather than as a river. From the base of this 'time tree' grows a trunk from which sprout numberless branches, each of them an alternate reality, a 'parallel universe', of which only one is our own.

The beginning of all time is the base of the metaphorical tree's trunk, while the earliest alternate realities (formed after time had begun) are the huge branches which extend from the trunk. Later alternate realities are the smaller branches which sprout from the great main boughs of the time tree – and from these extend a countless number of twigs.

Our reality – which virtually all of us assume is the sole reality that exists – is viewed as just one of the twigs sprouting from a small branch of the time tree. Our history is only unique back to that point at which the twig – the alternate world in which we live – budded from its branch. Before that, we share our history with other twigs that sprouted at the same time as our own.

What caused our particular twig, and other twigs – each a reality in its own right and with all its intelligent inhabitants convinced that they live in the only reality – to sprout off from the small branch on which they grow? And what caused all the small branches to sprout from the greater branches which grew from the main trunk millions or hundreds of millions of years ago?

According to some theorists – who include not only writers of highly imaginative science fiction but also mathematical physicists – the time tree shoots forth a new twiglet on each occasion that a conscious being makes a choice between two or more possible courses of action. In the words of the noted science-fiction writer Harry Harrison, that means that 'there must be an infinite number of futures … If, on the way to work in the morning, we decide to take the bus and are killed … if time is ever-branching then there are two futures – one in which we die … and another where we live on, having taken the tube'.

Some mathematical physicists – whose work is concerned with an area where physics, philosophy and mystical concepts seem to blend into one – take the possibility of the existence of alternate realities very seriously indeed. Take, for instance, the following passage from a paper that was published by the mathematical physicist Dr Martin Clutton-Brock in the journal Astrophysics and Space Science vol. 47 (1977): 'Imagine the universe branching into many worlds, only one of which we experience. There are closed worlds and open worlds; initially uniform worlds and initially chaotic worlds; high entropy worlds and low entropy worlds. In most worlds, life never evolves; in some worlds life evolves but is scarce; and in relatively few worlds, life is abundant.'

From a comparison of these two quotations it is apparent that there is a resemblance between the fantasies of science-fiction writers who have concerned themselves with alternate realities and the hypotheses of some astrophysicists and mathematicians.

If one accepts some variant of the alternative realities hypothesis as it is outlined by Harry Harrison and Dr Martin Clutton-Brock there is no great difficulty in reconciling the fulfilled predictions of Nostradamus with a belief in free will – nor in explaining a string of prophecies by one and the same person which prove to be a curious mixture of the completely accurate, the almost completely accurate, and the utterly wrong. For if Nostradamus and other prophets were not, in fact, genuinely seeing into the future of our world in its own separate reality but into parallel universes of which the time lines differ from our own, there is no reason at all why our alternate reality should not be a decade, a century or a millennium in advance of, or behind, any particular parallel universe. In other words, it is possible that sometimes the 'future' that Nostradamus predicted was, in fact, the present of another reality in which the course of history followed a different path from that which it was to do in our own world.

FANTASY AND REALITY

Sir Fred Hoyle, who occupied the Plumian Chair of Astronomy and Experimental Philosophy at Cambridge University, combines the astrophysicist and the writer of imaginative science fiction in one person, and has handled the theory of time in his book *October the First Is Too Late*. In the preface Sir Fred made it quite clear that while he had written it as imaginative fiction, the discussions of the significance of time and the meaning of consciousness were intended to be quite serious.

In the course of *October the First Is Too Late*, a variant of the alternate realities hypothesis is advanced in which the entire history of our planet, past and future, consists of a four-dimensional spiral moving around the sun. Everything that has taken place in the past and everything that will happen in the future is in reality happening in the present – in other words, past, present and future are all one and it is only the limitations of human consciousness that lead us into dividing the past from the future.

WILD TALENTS

Is there an explanation of the fact that many natural prophets such as Nostradamus can be so very right in some of their predictions and so very wrong in others? The sceptic would say that such alleged prophets have never in fact been anything but lucky guessers. However, convinced believers in the existence of psychic 'wild talents' – which are natural human abilities, albeit exercised by very few – would maintain that a seer's prophetic abilities and power to accurately decode messages from the future wax and wane like the transmission of an ill-tuned radio.

A belief that there are authentic prophets amongst us at the present day is supported by a good deal of strong evidence that such men and women have existed in even the recent past. Towards the end of 1891 a 25-year-old palmist and clairvoyant, a man who called himself 'Cheiro' and 'Count Louis Hamon', made an extremely unlikely prediction about the future of the second son of the future King Edward VII, the then Prince of Wales. In the course of time, he said, the second son, Prince George, would inherit the throne of the United Kingdom. At the time most people would have considered such an eventuality not in the least probable for, although Prince George was second in line to the throne, his elder brother 'Eddie', the Duke of Clarence, was generally thought to be in excellent health, had just become engaged to be married to Princess May of Teck, and was virtually certain to have sons and daughters of his own in a few years' time.

In reality, the health of the Duke of Clarence was not as good as was generally assumed – there is some evidence to suggest that at the time of the Duke's engagement he had long been suffering from incurable syphilis. In January 1892 he died from pneumonia – or, at any rate, so it was said in an official announcement from Buckingham Palace. After a discreet interval Prince George became first engaged, and then married, to Princess May of Teck and eventually succeeded to the throne as King George V.

It would seem that a very specific prediction of what was an improbable event – the early death of the Duke of Clarence and the eventual succession to the throne of the Duke's younger brother – had been proved correct by the course of history. Cheiro appeared to have triumphantly established his possession of a 'wild talent' which enabled him to discern the shape of things to come. Alas, there is no independent written evidence of his prediction, so sceptics might totally disregard it. However, it can be proved beyond any doubt that towards the end of his life Cheiro made even more surprising, and absolutely accurate, predictions about both the eldest son of King George V and the former's brother, the then Duke of York.

In a forecast of the future which was in print before the year 1930, Cheiro wrote: 'The portents are not favourable for the prosperity of England or for the royal family, with the exception of the Duke of York. In his case it is remarkable that the regal sign of Jupiter increases in power as the years advance, which … was also the case of his royal father before there was any likelihood of his coming to the throne.' Cheiro also made a further statement with regard to the royal family. Writing of the Duke's elder brother, the then Prince of Wales, he first of all referred to 'changes likely to take place greatly affecting the throne of England' and then predicted a royal crisis: 'Owing to the peculiar planetary influences to which he [the Prince of Wales] is subjected, he will fall a victim to a devastating love affair. If he does, I predict that the Prince will give up everything, even the chance of being crowned, rather than lose the object of his affection.'

That is exactly what happened. On the death of his father in 1936 the Prince of Wales came to the throne as Edward VIII but was never crowned, the planned Coronation being cancelled because he abdicated rather than give up the twice-divorced Mrs Wallis Simpson. At the time Cheiro published this prediction the Prince of Wales was not involved with Mrs Simpson in any way – indeed, it seems likely that he had not even met her.

Cheiro also prophesied the creation of the State of Israel, and, writing in 1930, a world war within 10 years or so: 'Italy and Germany [an unlikely alliance at the time Cheiro was writing] will be at war with France … The United States will be at war with Japan and not take part until later in the European carnage.' These predictions were correct, although Cheiro's prophecy that during the world war he foresaw there would be a renewed Irish civil war was not fulfilled.

Beside being a palmist and an astrologer, Cheiro seems also to have been a 'natural prophet'. One of the most puzzling things about such natural prophets as Cheiro and Nostradamus is that even those of them who have made startlingly accurate predictions have also made forecasts which have proved to be partially or even wholly incorrect. Maybe they are not seeing into the future of our world, but into parallel universes whose time lines differ slightly from our own; it is possible that the 'future' they predict is the present of another reality in which the course of history followed a different path from that which it was to do in our own world. This might explain why their 'wild talents' enable them to perceive something that did not happen with the same clarity as something that actually did transpire.

DRUGS, MAGIC AND
THE SEER

Some commentators on the Centuries have described Nostradamus as the greatest astrologer of all time. They are almost certainly wrong, misled by an assumption that all the accurate predictions outlined in the Centuries and the other writings of the seer were derived from his observations of the ever-changing positions of the sun, moon and planets in relation to both one another and the signs of the zodiac. Nostradamus certainly used astrology as a shorthand method of expressing dates, but not to derive the prognostications themselves.

Nostradamus could not possibly have relied upon astrology alone when he made his predictions. This is proved beyond doubt by one simple fact pointed out by the 19th-century Nostradamian commentator Charles Ward – that the seer 'mentions the birth of persons who were born after his death ... judicial astrology could give no help in such cases, since to commence casting a nativity presupposes birth'.

In other words, while Nostradamus was undoubtedly an astrologer – after all, he was the compiler of a number of almanacs – and while at least some of his successful predictions may have been partly made on the basis of astrology, he must also have been a talented clairvoyant. Indeed, suggestions have been made that he used psychedelic drugs to induce trances in which his clairvoyant capacities could operate more freely (see below).

However, the most controversial question as far as the clairvoyant faculties of Nostradamus are concerned is not whether or not these faculties were heightened by drugs; it is whether they were supplemented by the use of methods which pertained to ceremonial magic, ritual divination and other secret and forbidden arts.

The possibility of Nostradamus having been a participant in magical rites, perhaps of a pagan nature, has been indignantly rejected by some of those who have devoted years of intense study to the life and writings of the seer of Salon. This has particularly been the case amongst those authors who have inclined to the ultramontane Catholicism which has been associated with French royalism since 1870. Yet there have also long been those who have considered it possible that Nostradamus was in fact an adept magician, a man who, like the writer Eliphas Levi (1810-75), engaged in mental gymnastics which enabled him to combine a qualified loyalty to the Church with the employment of certain techniques derived from ancient secret traditions.

It seems likely that even in the seer's own lifetime there were those who suspected as much, for in a passage Nostradamus printed in the preface to the first edition of the Centuries he seems to have been attempting to avert any suspicion that he dabbled in dubious occult arts. In this passage he solemnly warns his son against the dangers of 'execrable magic' and purports to give an account of how he himself had actually destroyed printed or manuscript treatises devoted to ritual magic and, by implication, alchemy. However, as will be demonstrated on the next pages, there are good reasons to suspect that Nostradamus's denunciation of 'execrable magic' was more than somewhat insincere.

DRUGS, SUFIS AND

BIOELECTRICAL ENERGY

A number of modern students of the writings of Nostradamus have claimed that the seer owed his remarkable clairvoyant abilities to his use of hallucinogenic drugs. However, there appears to be no real evidence, even of the most tenuous variety, of the truth of this assertion and it is perhaps significant that some of those writers who have disseminated it have made other statements about the life of the seer which are inherently improbable.

For example, the author of one recent book has not only stated that Nostradamus resorted to drugs in order to heighten his clairvoyant abilities but that while in Sicily he made contact with Sufi mystics, and when engaged in prophesying was accustomed to sit on a brass tripod with legs 'angled at the same degree as the pyramids of Egypt in order to create a similar bioelectric force which it was believed would sharpen psychic powers'.

As historians are convinced that all Muslims, Sufi or otherwise, had been expelled from Sicily long before Nostradamus was born, and that the angles of the pyramids were not properly measured until over 300 years after the burial of the seer, it is a great pity that the sources of this fascinating and novel information have not been given to the world!

BRANCHUS AND HIS RITES

It seems likely that some of the strange occult quatrains to be found in the Centuries provide coded details of ancient, secret and forbidden predictive techniques used by Nostradamus in order to look far into the future. The most easily understood and significant of these quatrains are the first two verses of the Centuries – Century I Quatrains 1 and 2. In these, Nostradamus described himself – in language that would have been understood by all who had some acquaintance with late classical mysticism – as carrying out 'workings' pertaining to white magic. Cleverly, he couched his descriptions in terms which would have been quite meaningless to the general reader. The quatrains read:

Sitting alone at night in secret study,
Rested on a brazen tripod,
An exiguous flame comes from the solitude,
Making successful that worthy of belief.

The handheld wand is placed in the midst of the BRANCHES,
He moistens with water his foot and garment's hem,
Fear and a Voice make him quake in his sleeves,
Divine splendour, the divine sits nigh.

Throughout these two quatrains Nostradamus was describing a variant of a divinatory magical rite of great antiquity, but the third line in each quatrain is of major significance. By wording these lines as he did the seer was doing two things: first, he was making it apparent to students of occult philosophy that he was acquainted with the Chaldean Oracles, a collection of ancient Hermetic lore, by echoing a passage referring to a 'Formless Fire' from which comes a 'divine Voice of Fire' to which the sojourner with the gods must listen. Secondly, he was hinting that the 'exiguous flame' of which he wrote was of heavenly origin, an emanation from the solitude, which in this context could have meant 'Oneness'.

The two quatrains also contain several clues as to the nature of the divinatory rituals employed by Nostradamus. One of them is the use of the word 'branches'. It was rendered in capital letters in the original printing of the Centuries; a clear hint, of the sort given recurrently by Nostradamus, that it was intended to be understood in more than one way, or that some punning or allusive word play was involved.

In this particular case Nostradamus was almost certainly using the word in three senses, all pertaining to prophetic inspiration. The most important one was as a word resembling the name of the Greek demigod Branchus, the son of the sun god Apollo. According to Greek legend, when he was a youth Branchus had been given the gift of prophecy and the capability of endowing others with that same gift. As a consequence of this he was the centre of a cult which flourished until the triumph of Christianity. The cult was focused on revelations about the future received through the mediumship of inspired priestesses, and the techniques employed to obtain them were described by Iamblichus of Chalcis, who died about AD 335: 'The prophetess of Branchus either sits upon a pillar, or holds in her hand a rod bestowed by some deity, or moistens her feet or the hem of her garment with water ... and by these means ... she prophesies. By these practices she adapts herself to the god, whom she receives from without.' This passage, which describes a divinatory rite involving the wetting of a foot and the hem of a garment, was clearly being referred to by Nostradamus in the second line of the second quatrain of Century I. Another passage in the same ancient text mentions the use of a bronze tripodic stool in a rite of prophecy.

The work from which the above quotation has been taken was originally written in Greek; in the 15th century it was translated into Latin as De Mysteriis Aegyptorum – 'Of the Mysteries of the Egyptians'. It is very likely that Nostradamus became acquainted with this work early in his life, for there is reason to believe that copies of Italian printings of the Latin translation were circulating among French students of Neoplatonic mysticism as early as 1500. In any event, it is certain that De Mysteriis Aegyptorum was published in France in the 1540s, and it may be highly significant that Nostradamus began to issue his almanacs not long after that event. Certainly it can be inferred from these two quatrains that the seer employed similar methods to those described in Iamblichus's text as one way of obtaining his knowledge of the future.

THE PYTHIA

In ancient Greece, the women who acted as oracles were called Pythia, after the python reputedly slain by Apollo, to whom all oracles were sacred. The Pythia were always natives of the town of Delphi, and once they had entered the service of the god they were never allowed to leave it, nor were they allowed to marry. In early times they were always selected from the town's young girls but, after one of them was seduced by Eucrates the Thessalian, the people of Delphi altered the law to the effect that no one younger than 50 should be elected to the position of prophetess. However, the dress of the Pythia remained that of maidens rather than matrons.

When the oracle was flourishing there were always three Pythia ready to take their seat on the tripod. The effect of the smoke rising from below the tripod was so great that sometimes a prophetess would topple from the tripod in her prophetic delirium, fall into convulsions or even die.

MAGIC AND RITUAL DIVINATION

There is evidence to be found in the curious forty-second quatrain of Century I that makes it seem quite certain that Nostradamus had some knowledge of both the darker aspects of the occult arts and of modes of divination involving the use of basins. The quatrain reads:

> *The tenth day of the Gothic Calends of April*
> *Is resuscitated by a wicked race,*
> *The fire is extinguished and the Diabolical Assembly*
> *Seek the bones of the Demon of* [and?] *Psellus.*

When read in conjunction with Nostradamus' reference to a divinatory rite involving water this verse indicates the nature of one of the white magical techniques that were used by the seer of Salon to supplement his clairvoyant abilities and his astrological expertise.

That technique was described by the Neoplatonic philosopher Psellus as follows: 'There is a type of predictive power in the use of the basin, known and practised by the Assyrians ... Those about to prophesy take a basin of water, which attracts the spirits of the depths. The basin then seems to breathe as with sounds ... The water in the basin ... excels ... because of a power imparted to it by incantations which have rendered it capable of being imbued with the energies of spirits of prophecy ... a thin voice begins to utter predictions. A spirit of this sort journeys where it wills, and always speaks with a low voice.'

That it was this passage from Psellus to which Nostradamus was referring when he made his allusions to a divinatory rite involving water seems clear beyond any shadow of a doubt.

In the light of this we are now in a position to understand Century I Quatrain 42 – which, when it is examined in conjunction with Century I Quatrains 1 and 2, is the most important of all the verses of Nostradamus in relation to both his life and his probable involvement in ritual divination and other varieties of white magic.

On a Good Friday – in the words of Psellus, 'the time when we commemorate the redemptive Passion of Our Lord' and, according to him, the annual ecclesiastical festival on which 'Messalian' sorcerers (see panel below) were accustomed to hold an incestuous orgy which was a prelude to murder and cannibalism – Nostradamus began to make serious use of a mode of ritual divination in which a bowl of water was employed. It would seem likely that his technique had a general resemblance to that described, in what seems to have been a slightly muddled way, by Psellus – although there is no need to believe that the water actually spoke to him in a 'thin voice'. However, in the words of the late James Laver, writing of Psellus in 1942, while there is 'something slightly comic in the notion of a basin of water composing verses ... we seem to be on the track of a mode of divination approaching Nostradamus's own methods [of predicting the future] well known in antiquity and ... still practised among primitive people. The fakirs of India are said to be able to make water boil and bubble beneath their gaze. Is it all any more than a technique for going into a trance?'

In the opinion of the present writer, the use of a bowl of water can be (although by no means always is) something 'more than a technique for going into a trance'. However, it does seem likely that Nostradamus used a bowl of water as a focus when he wished to induce the sort of dissociation of consciousness which is an essential preliminary to authentic scrying. In other words, Nostradamus sought the predictive 'demon of Psellus'.

Among the first things discerned by him in his Good Friday vision was a 'Diabolical Assembly' engaged in a black magical rite, which may have taken place anywhere and at almost any time. This blasphemous ceremony seemed to Nostradamus to be a re-enactment of the one conducted by that 'wicked race' of supposed Messalians.

MURDEROUS ORGIES

The connection that Nostradamus discerned between his vision of a black magical rite conducted by a 'Diabolical Assembly' and black magic as described by the writer Psellus was based upon an account given by the latter of a heretical rite conducted by people he termed 'Messalians': 'In the evening ... at the time when we commemorate the redemptive Passion of Our Lord, they bring together ... young girls whom they have initiated into their rites. Then they extinguish the candles ... and throw themselves lasciviously upon the girls ... each one on whomsoever falls into his hands ... They believe that they are doing something greatly pleasing to the demons by transgressing God's laws forbidding incest ... After waiting nine months, when the time has come for the unnatural fruit of the unnatural unions to be born, they reassemble ... On the third day after the birth, they ... cut [the babies'] tender flesh with sharp knives and catch the spurting blood in bowls. They throw the babes ... upon a fire and burn their bodies to ashes. After which they mix these ashes with the blood in the bowls and in this way make an abominable drink ... They partake together of these foodstuffs.'

Whether such a rite was actually celebrated at the time Psellus wrote his description of it is uncertain. Certainly, however, if it was so celebrated in any part of the Byzantine Empire at any date during the lifetime of Michael Psellus it was not done so by Messalians, for that sect was already long extinct by then. This does not mean to say that murderous orgies of this sort never took place at all; there is some resemblance between the rite described by Psellus and well-authenticated accounts of sinister ceremonies conducted by the initiates of unorthodox death-oriented tantric cults.

THE FUTURE THAT DIDN'T HAPPEN

While most of the predictions to which Nostradamus attached specific dates have been verified by the course of history, this is not true of all of them. The seer of Salon made a few notable prophetic misses as well as many hits. For instance, in Century I Quatrain 49 he made a prediction specifically related to the year 1700:

A long time before these events,
The peoples of the East, by lunar influence,
In the year 1700 will cause many to be carried away,
And will almost subdue the northern corner [area].

The events referred to in the first line of this quatrain are obviously those described in the preceding verse, Century I Quatrain 48, which seems to refer to a cycle of time beginning about AD 3000 – but what of the remaining three lines of the quatrain, with the exact dating of 'many being carried away'?

Alas, there is no real trace of any event taking place in or around the year 1700 which really fits this prediction – although some Nostradamian devotees, anxious to find the right happening to fit the prophecy, have attempted to apply it to such things as the occupation of Iceland by the forces of Charles XII of Sweden and a campaign in northern India undertaken by one of the commanders of the armies of the 'Great Mughal', the Emperor Aurungzeb. However, most sensible students of Nostradamus – that is, those whose enthusiasm and credulity are not unbounded – admit that in this particular instance the seer was mistaken.

There is strong evidence that all the psychic abilities of any particular individual – whether those abilities be innate or acquired through the use of arcane training and disciplines – are subject to a periodic waxing and waning. It is as if what could be termed 'psychic athletes' can, like their physical equivalents, go completely off form for no easily perceptible reason. Thus, for instance, mediums who have in the past produced amazing phenomena become so psychically enervated that they lose their authentic abilities and resort to childish trickery that would deceive no one possessed of the most elementary powers of observation.

There is no reason to believe that Nostradamus was immune from the tendency of lesser psychics to have their off days – times when psychic energy is low and clairvoyant vision is distorted or, much worse, entirely absent and replaced by self-deception.

It is therefore perfectly possible that when Nostradamus made his seemingly quite mistaken prediction that the year 1700 would be marked by some outstanding event his psychic abilities were at a low point of their cyclic waxing and waning. If so, however, it seems surprising both that the prediction was so very specific in its dating and that such an experienced clairvoyant as Nostradamus did not realize that his abilities were so diminished that the prophecy should be suppressed as doubtful.

Perhaps a more plausible suggestion is that on the occasion that this prediction was made – as perhaps on many other occasions – Nostradamus was not looking into the future of our own reality but was seeing, as it were, what was then the present of an alternate reality in which some major world event took place in the year 1700.

KENNEDY AND THE SHAH

Nostradamus was only one of many psychics who have had a remarkable run of predictive successes but have then made prognostications which time has proved to be partially or wholly incorrect. Take, for example, prophecies made by Jeane Dixon, the best known of all the clairvoyants who have practised their art in 20th-century America.

Some were truly remarkable. She forecast the 1963 assassination of President Kennedy as early as 1956, when Parade magazine published an interview with her in which she described a vision she had experienced some four years earlier: 'A voice came out of nowhere, telling me softly that this young man, a Democrat, to be elected as President in 1960, would be assassinated while in office.'

In the early 1970s she correctly predicted that the Shah of Iran would be overthrown by a popular uprising. So far, so good; but she forecast that the event would take place in 1977, two years earlier than was actually to be the case. Furthermore, she stated that after living in secluded exile the Shah would again 'stride into the world spotlight'. In reality he died in exile of cancer.

Ms Dixon's Iranian predictions were at least partially correct; those she made in the 1970s in relation to Britain were utterly wrong. For example, she said that the Labour MP Eric Varley would 'leap into the spotlight'; he is largely forgotten. She also tipped Sir Geoffrey Howe as the next Conservative Prime Minister. He never held that office and, at the time of writing, is remembered chiefly for the speech he made following his resignation as Foreign Secretary.

THE FRONTIERS
OF FICTION

Another explanation of how Nostradamus was able to obtain glimpses of the future – and perhaps the most interesting – is concerned with the existence of alternate realities, as explained above. The idea that we live in, and are conscious of the existence of, only one of a number of realities was first expressed in an easily graspable form by a number of science-fiction writers. It is none the less believable for that, for it is worth remembering that the early science-fiction writers were writing stories concerning the exploitation of nuclear energy at a time when almost all physicists were convinced that such things were simply not possible.

The whole concept of alternate realities, each branching off from another time line as a consequence of some seemingly insignificant decision – and sometimes destroying the original reality in the process of branching off – has been a favourite of science-fiction and fantasy writers since the 1930s. One example of such destruction occurs in *Bring the Jubilee* (1976). The author, Ward Moore, depicts a time-travelling historian from the future of a world in which the Confederacy won the American Civil War journeying into the past and visiting the scene of one of the Confederacy's most significant victories. His activities at the scene are mistakenly interpreted by a Southern advance guard as an indication of the presence of Union troops. The Confederate troops retreat in panic. This causes the Southern triumph that the time traveller has come to see to be transformed into a Southern defeat. The Confederacy loses the war and the future from which the time traveller has come vanishes in an instant! He finds himself trapped in an utterly alien alternate world – our own, the one in which the North won the Civil War.

Ideas similar to these were also given literary expression in the late Philip K. Dick's *The Man in the High Castle* (1962), set in an alternate reality in which the decision that caused that particular twig of the time tree to branch off was a collective rather than an individual one – that of the voters in the USA election of November 1931 thinking fit to elect to office someone other than Franklin Delano Roosevelt. This resulted in the creation of a time line in which Germany and Japan won World War II and the North America of the early 1960s was divided into three separate political entities: the eastern States of the Union, under brutal Nazi domination; the western area, a virtual colony of Japan, which adopted a much more beneficent approach to its American subjects than did the Nazis in their American domain; and finally, all that remained of the once great United States – the economically backward central mountain states.

There are many complexities in the plot of *The Man in the High Castle*. For instance, the central character, the man in the 'High Castle' – this being a fortified retreat in which he has taken refuge from Nazi murder gangs – is in some way in subliminal contact with an alternate reality, or time line, in which Japan and Germany lost the war. However, it is not our own world of which he is aware – the other reality which he senses is yet another twig of the time tree, one in which no ships of the US Fleet suffered any damage as a consequence of the Japanese aerial attack on Pearl Harbor because they had all been sent out to sea by a wise and wary US President.

Other alternate reality novels which are relevant reading in the same context are Keith Roberts's *Pavane* (1968) and Kingsley Amis's *The Alteration* (1976). Both are set in an alternate world in which the 16th-century Protestant Reformation was crushed and a triumphalist Catholic Church dominates every aspect of European life and culture. Amis's book, which features two notably unpleasant heresy hunters named Foot and Redgrave, is readable and funny – but *Pavane*, set in an alternate Dorset in an England in which Queen Elizabeth I was assassinated in 1588, is certainly the more original of the two.

ANCIENT WISDOM, MODERN SCIENCE

The magician has always been able to see into realms beyond the physical. His world-view assumes that by insights into other worlds, planes or realities he is able to bring about surprising changes on the physical plane – 'surprising' because, without a knowledge of the elaborate and serpentine connections between the different realities, the effects caused by the magician are as surprising as the workings of radio would be to a Stone Age hunter. The theory of how a radio works is well understood today, but even so nobody can point to the radio waves in the air actually carrying the sound. So it is with magic; unless the theory of other realities, such as the astral plane, is understood then the effects of magic cannot be understood.

Magicians have always been given to explaining the universe in terms of complex cosmologies, and do in fact often employ the tree motif as a metaphor. A traditional example of this is the use for more than 1000 years of the tree of life by Jewish Cabbalists, and later by generations of European magicians who appropriated this complex diagram as their guide to the universe.

The image of the tree of life parallels the idea of time as an infinitely branching tree. Each branch and twig contains a reality that is different, albeit maybe only slightly, from that of its neighbour. This vision of alternate realities could explain the non-fulfilment of the prophecy by the clairvoyant Cheiro of a war in Palestine in which Russian troops were to be directly involved; it may well have happened in an alternate reality, though it did not happen in ours. Fantastic? Perhaps – but the alternate realities hypothesis would also explain some varieties of psychic phenomena that have puzzled researchers for more than a century.

The psychic phenomena in question are those associated with almost right, but not quite right, premonitions, precognitive dreams, and even actual visions of the future that are, and have been, reported as being sometimes experienced by quite ordinary people – men and women who make no claim to the possession of seership or supernormal abilities of any sort whatsoever.

By comparison, modern science is moving away from the solid building blocks of matter, the elements, and moving towards a universe where force (energy) and form (matter) convert one into the other. Stephen Hawking, in his classic book *A Brief History of Time*, takes the modern reader through the various stages of modern scientific thought from the Greek philosopher Aristotle through Newton and Einstein to the latest theories of space and time. At each point in the evolution of scientific thinking, more apparent 'certainty' is thrown away. Ptolemy, for example, was certain that the Earth was the centre of the universe, and that both the sun and the planets revolved around it. In 1514,

Nicholas Copernicus observed the changing shape of the moon, and theorized that the planets instead revolve round the sun, although this was not generally recognized until Galileo Galilei used a telescope to confirm this in 1609, almost a century later. The Earth had moved from the centre of the universe to being just another planet.

In 1687 Newton published his findings which defined gravity – an invisible force, not directly measurable, which appeared to cause all bodies in the universe to be attracted to every other body, as if by magic! Man became less important, and even the Earth became dependent (upon every other body in the universe). It took almost 130 years before someone started to think about the relationship between gravity and light. Even that certainty, light, might now be 'bent' by gravity.

In this century, Einstein extended science further to embrace the concept that matter and energy might be interchangeable, finally reaching the magician's point of view that the universe is generated from the interplay of force and form. It still seemed that time must be 'eternal' – but then Hawking revealed that 'the theory of relativity put an end to the idea of absolute time! … Each observer must have his own measure of time, as recorded by a clock carried with him, and identical clocks carried by different observers would not necessarily agree.' If different observers have different times because of their different points of view, a really different point of view could have you observing a time that was decades or centuries different from our own. Nostradamus had found the secret of this different point of observation.

Hawking gradually kicks away each successive scientific theory designed to explain the deficiencies in the last, until the scientific explanation of the universe looks much more mystical than the most complex magician's cosmology and time looks as mutable as anything else in the universe. We are definitely not travelling along a simple time river – we are living in something infinitely more complex.

THE TREE OF LIFE

The Tree of Life is a mystical diagram of the universe of great antiquity, much older than the diagram of the paths of the planets round the sun. It is also a map of the mystical make-up of man, because the mystical 'anatomy' of both the universe and man was supposed to be similar.

The Tree of Life consists of 10 circles or spheres (Sephiroth) which are interconnected by 22 Paths (marked with the 22 letters of the Hebrew alphabet). Each of the spheres is symbolically (but not physically) associated with one of the planets or the sun or the moon. The total of 32 spheres and paths is thought of as being duplicated throughout four 'Worlds' of varying degrees of solidity, making a total of 128 paths and spheres.

Of all these different spheres, only one actually corresponds to the physical world around us as we know it. The rest of the diagram enables the cabbalist or magician to describe the secret and mystical parts of the Universe: the source of dreams, the treasure-house of the archetypal images of the subconscious mind, the abode of angels and of demons, and a million other things from which our late-20th-century consciousness has cut us off, but which are real nevertheless.

These depths of description and delineation address many more concerns than just those of light, gravity and relativity, although no doubt the worlds of the cosmologist and the magician are but metaphors for the terrifying reality of the Universe itself – a reality we understand about as well as a newborn babe is able to understand the content of a set of encyclopedias.

OUR DESTINIES ARE FAN-SHAPED

The problem we are confronted with in dealing with Nostradamus and the Centuries is that we simply don't have a wide enough perspective on his predictions. We can only see a window of history from before his time to the present day, while he was able to range forward and backwards along the various branches taken by events. In Century 1 Quatrain 2 he speaks of 'au milieu des BRANCHES', a reference to the prophetess of Branchus, as well as to the branching paths of fate which have been written about by the Argentinian writer Jorge Luis Borges.

There is an implication in this quatrain that the events of history are not one long continuous line, a concept dear to the heart of the modern historian, but a subtle interweaving of events and people which might allow the time traveller to pop up in very disparate places and times, and view events which are separated by many decades or centuries but which appear to be almost side by side.

This approach to the work of Nostradamus goes some way to explaining why his quatrains apparently jump backwards or forwards in time without any apparent pattern. Perhaps the seer simply wrote what he saw in the order in which he saw it, and this order is in fact a reflection of the way the past and present intertwine rather than a cunning 'blind' deliberately inserted to make the task of decipherment more difficult. In fact, it may be that it was impossible for Nostradamus to disentangle the skeins of time without the benefit of hindsight which is partially granted to us. Perhaps here we have not a deliberate obscurantism but a real key to the structure of the 'branches of time'.

Finally, in many theories of time, or even in ordinary wish-fulfilment, it is recognized that if the earlier action had been different, the course of events precipitated would also have been very different. In fact, once a different fork in the garden of branching paths has been taken, the course of events will never be able to return to the original route. Time, events and the people involved have branched off in a different direction.

At every major (or even minor) decision point in one's life there are a certain number of choices and each decision takes you along a particular branch of each fan of options. Our destinies are like a succession of fan-shaped decisions, or a garden of branching paths. Perhaps the true nature of our collective destiny, history, is likewise fan-shaped – in which case it is no wonder that there have been only a few seers who, like Nostradamus, found their way through this garden of branching paths centuries before the decisions charting this route had been taken. Perhaps this explains why some quatrains don't quite fit – they are visions of an alternate reality at the end of a path which was not finally taken.

This seems to provide us with some solid conclusions. First, time is not linear but infinitely branching, constantly splitting like a living, growing tree. Secondly, some prophets, through a 'wild talent' or a knowledge of certain traditional techniques, can assume a viewpoint which allows them to see into alternate realities. Thirdly, these alternate realities may well be 'ahead' of our own reality, so the prophet can see what is for us a future event, but for that reality is the present. Fourthly, we do have the free will to make decisions which can alter the flow, and some alternate realities that have been glimpsed by otherwise very talented prophets will not ever happen in our reality.

The following pages look closely at certain techniques of prophecy which you, the reader, can try out for yourself.

THE ALEPH

The Argentinian writer, poet and scholar Jorge Luis Borges (1899–1986) wrote many apparent fictions about the relationship of time to space and how events relate to one another. In his book *The Aleph*, he describes a vision that was brought on by his concentrating on a single luminous spot he calls the Aleph, which acts in the manner of a crystal ball. It was 'a small iridescent sphere, of almost intolerable brilliance. At first I thought it rotary; then I understood that this movement was an illusion produced by the vertiginous sights it enclosed'. Staring into it, Borges could see other times, other spaces and infinite objects – a heavy-laden sea, a paving tile he had seen 30 years before at the entrance to a house, horses on a beach by the Caspian Sea and convex equatorial deserts and every grain of sand in them.

ALTERNATE REALITY
AND YOU

There is no reason why Nostradamus, Cheiro and a handful of other seers should be the only ones who can traverse the time tree; the techniques used to peep into either the personal or collective future are not just the preserve of a few gifted people.

Oracles used to form part of the ongoing religious life of ancient Greece; the worship of Apollo included the establishment and maintenance of places of prophecy by means of which the gods could communicate with mankind. The practice at Delphi was for the prophetess to seat herself upon a brass tripod placed over a vent in the floor of a cavern from which emanated narcotic fumes. This is a very close parallel to the description of Nostradamus's own method in Century I, Quatrain 1.

We cannot easily replicate these methods, but we can look forward less than a century from Nostradamus's time to a method of divination that we can use. In Elizabethan times Dr John Dee, mathematician and court adviser to Queen Elizabeth I, wanted to see into the future, not by consulting professional oracles, but by 'scrying' – having visions in a crystal or 'glass'. Dee went even further in his efforts to obtain divine knowledge: he attempted to converse with the angels through the crystal. His techniques, if not his angels, are available to us still.

The technique of scrying requires only a quiet, darkened room and a non-reflective surface upon which is laid the crystal, sometimes in a dark wooden frame; a beryl is a suitable stone to use. After suitable preparation to clear the mind of distracting thoughts, the seer gazes into the stone, which is normally a spherical lump of polished natural crystal – usually some variety of quartz. There should be no distracting reflections on the surface of the crystal.

The purpose of staring intently into the stone is to bore, as it were, the part of the mind which is concerned with everyday consciousness so that it is switched off and the vision is freed to explore other times or places, or sometimes other planes. The seer may be lucky within minutes or may have to wait several hours, depending upon conditions and natural aptitude. When you are attempting the technique, try not to look at the surface of the stone, but about halfway into it. Once the extrasensory perceptive processes are fully in operation the crystal gazer 'sees', as though with a psychic analogue of physical vision, things far off in time and/or space. In the case of certain advanced forms of crystal-gazing involving what are known as out of body experiences, the scryer actually has the sensation of being physically present at the scene of the vision. Scrying is often found to be an effective dissociative technique by those who wish to look into the future and bring their psychic abilities into play. Only a minority of scryers employ real crystal balls as they tend to be very costly, and an imitation made of moulded glass is more easily available, much cheaper and usually productive of equally satisfactory or unsatisfactory results. In fact, almost anything can serve as such a focus – a glass of water, a pool of ink or a semi-translucent stone.

The fact that a number of accurate scrying visions have been experienced in the past cannot reasonably be doubted by any person who looks at the evidence dispassionately. Some scryers are possessed of a 'wild talent' which is sometimes innate, sometimes deliberately cultivated.

THE FALL OF A QUEEN

One scryer in Elizabethan times accurately foretold the execution of Mary Queen of Scots and the sailing of the Spanish Armada on the basis of visions seen in a polished piece of hard 'cannel cole' – which in a 16th-century context probably means anthracite or jet.

The scryer in question, Edward Kelley (1555-95), was one of those talented but amoral people who were a combination of authentic seer and petty criminal. Dr John Dee employed Kelley to scry in his experiments with 'angelic revelations'. The vision that was interpreted at the time as a forecast of the execution of Mary and an attempt at a seaborne invasion of England was recorded in Dee's diaries on 5 May 1583. Through the mediumship of Kelley, Dee asked 'the angel Uriel': 'As concerning the vision wch [sic] yesterday was presented to the sight of E[dward] K[elley] as he sat at supper with me in my hall – I mean the appearing of the very great sea and many ships thereon and the cutting off the head of a woman by a tall, black man, what are we to imagine thereof?' To which Uriel replied: 'Provision of foreign powers against the welfare of this land: which they shall shortly put into practice. The other, the death of the Queen of Scots: it is not long unto it.'

So it transpired. In 1587 Mary Queen of Scots was executed for treason, and the next year the Armada sailed against England. Dee had already informed Elizabeth I of this prophecy, and Drake had more than enough time to prepare; Kelley's was a prophecy which may have changed history.

EXPLORING THE
TIME TREE

Precise instructions for using classical methods of oracular prophecy such as were employed by Nostradamus are nowhere recorded in any detail, and scrying requires a certain amount of natural ability. However, there are a number of other tried and tested methods of divination that will, with a bit of application, allow anyone to explore the time tree and see into the future.

For one of the most reliable of all methods for obtaining answers to specific questions we have to look to the *I Ching* or 'Book of Changes', the world's most ancient and best-known oracle book. This classic Chinese text is attributed to King Wen and his son the Duke of Chou, who, in the 12th century bc, arranged the book 'in order to release the wise administrator from dependence on unstable priestly types for interpreting the oracle', a clear indication that this oracle is for everyday use.

The technique involves the generation of one or two of 64 distinct hexagrams, each made up of its own unique combination of six whole or broken lines called Yang (whole and male) or Yin (broken and female) lines. This is followed by consultation of the text. In addition to this, the numerous commentaries the I Ching gives on the hexagrams should be referred to. The hexagram is derived by either manipulating 50 special yarrow stalks or, more recently, by tossing coins, which by their pattern of fall will accurately predict the conditions of the moment and hence the outcome of the question being asked.

To perform a divination, first still the mind and perhaps burn a little incense to invoke the right mood. Then formulate the question as unambiguously and carefully as possible, and write it down. Take three coins (ideally but not necessarily Chinese ones) with holes in the middle. Each side represents Yang (usually heads) or Yin (usually tails). The coins are to be thrown in the air six times, with each throw indicating the type of line. If the coins fall with two Yang (heads) and one Yin (tails) side, the line indicated is Yang. Likewise, if two Yin sides and one Yang side appear, the line is Yin. If all three sides are Yang then the line is considered to be a 'moving' Yang line – that is, Yang but with a tendency to convert to Yin in the future. Three Yin sides give a 'moving' Yin line.

Let us take a sample question and answer to illustrate the technique. Suppose the question is, 'What will be the outcome for me of this court case?' The three coins are thrown six times, giving the following six lines:

1   2 Yang + 1 Yin sides = YANG
2   1 Yang + 2 Yin sides = YIN
3   3 Yang sides = moving YANG
4   1 Yang + 2 Yin sides = YIN
5   1 Yang + 2 Yin sides = YIN
6   2 Yang + 1 Yin sides = YANG

When you have constructed the hexagram of six lines as above you need to look up the meaning in the I Ching, which gives an interpretation of the outcome of the question. In this case the hexagram is number 21, called Shi Ho, of which the text reads: 'Success in legal proceedings. You are not to blame for the present trouble. Separateness.'

This is a very unambiguous answer to the question, but its interpretation can be taken one step further by taking the so-called 'moving' line and changing it to its opposite, in this case from Yang to Yin. The resultant hexagram is number 27, called I, of which the text is 'Consistent effort brings good success.' This confirms the reading.

Practice makes perfect and the use of the *I Ching* on a regular basis leads to a greater facility. Although the *I Ching* is not very good on dating its predictions, it sometimes offers advice where appropriate. If just dipped into it reads almost as abstrusely as Nostradamus's quatrains, but when it is used properly the particular text chosen by the oracle is often blindingly clear and apposite to the question being asked.

DREAMS & ALTERNATE REALITIES

Carl Gustav Jung, one of the greatest psychologists of the 20th century and originally one of Freud's students, was very interested in the way in which the human mind related to the world, 'reality' and time. From 1920 onwards Jung frequently consulted the oracle of the *I Ching*, fascinated by its uncanny predictions. Uncertain how to reconcile its consistent accuracy with its apparently random and unscientific method, he evolved a theory of 'synchronicity' to help explain how internal events or thoughts sometimes appear to be related to, or even cause, apparently unrelated actions in the world around us (see below). He also hoped to account for parallels between dreams and actual events, or dream prophecy.

Given that there is a connection between the subjective mind and the external universe, it is only a short step to the conclusion that if internal events can precipitate external events then perhaps some wild-talented individuals can, by inward concentration and the application of the right techniques, actually foresee external events that have not yet happened. In his book Dreams, Jung writes, 'In the superstitions of all times and races the dream has been regarded as a truth-telling oracle ... The occurrence of prospective dreams cannot be denied'. Examples of synchronicity appear to happen at random; to be able to precipitate them at will would be an almost magical ability.

John William Dunne, an aeronautical engineer and the author of *An Experiment with Time* (1927) noticed that stray images that had entered his mind in reflective moments or during dreams later became part of experiences which he could not have foreseen. In an effort to discover if this type of precognition was common, he got 22 people to write down the content of their dreams immediately upon waking and then report if any of these dream images became part of reality within a short period of time. He was amazed to find 'how many persons there are who, while willing to concede that we habitually observe events before they occur, suppose that such prevision may be treated as a minor logical difficulty'.

In 1916 Dunne dreamt of an explosion in a London bomb factory. This explosion actually occurred in January 1917, when 73 workers were killed and more than 1000 were injured. Dunne felt that this and similar experiences provided proof that segments of experience can and do get displaced from their proper position in time.

Take the case of the Hon. John Godley, later Lord Kilbracken. On the night of 12 March 1946 he had the first of several precognitive dreams. In it he was reading the following Saturday's newspaper and on waking he could remember the horse-racing results and the names of two winners, Bindal and Juladin, both with starting prices of 7-1. The dream impressed him enough for him not only to tell several friends of it but to consult the morning paper on Saturday. Bindal and Juladin were both running. He backed Bindal to win. The horse did so and Godley then put his entire winnings on Juladin, which also won. Godley's precognitive dream was exactly in accordance with reality except for the starting prices of the two winners, respectively 5-4 and 5-2.

A month or so later Godley had another dream in which he was once again reading the racing results. The only name of a dream winner he could remember was Tubermore. No horse of that name was listed as a runner in any race meeting, but a horse called Tuberose was running at Aintree on the following Saturday. He backed it and Tuberose obliged him by coming home first.

The next time his dream consisted of making a telephone call to a bookmaker. 'Monumentor at five to four', said the dream bookie. No horse of that name was listed as a runner at any forthcoming meeting, but remembering the Tubermore/Tuberose success Godley backed Mentores, which duly romped home at a starting price of 6-4.

We see here a slow divergence from the early, precise predictions, as if the alternate reality which he had tapped into was 'growing away' from this reality: soon some of his dream tips were not coming home at all.

Nine years later Godley had another precognitive dream, this time of a horse named What Man? winning the 1958 Grand National at Aintree. There was no such horse, so the lucky dreamer backed Mr What, who duly won this gruelling and extremely uncertain race.

This is an interesting illustration of how Nostradamus's predictions often included names that were not quite correct but were similar in meaning or were anagrams. The difficulty for the seer was sometimes having to render words he may never have seen.

JUNG AND SYNCHRONICITY

Jung defines synchronicity as a meaningful coincidence, but there is also a strong flavour of some hidden connection between an inner and outer event. One example that Jung quotes concerns a young female analysand with whom he was having considerable difficulty because she always 'knew better about everything'. One day she was telling Jung about a particularly vivid dream of a scarab beetle of a type common in Egypt but not in Europe. As she spoke there was a tapping on the window which grew more and more insistent. Jung finally opened the window and in flew a gold-green scarab beetle of the rose-chafer variety. Jung caught it and handed it to his patient, saying, 'Here is your scarab.' This broke the ice of her rationalism and resistance, and her analysis was rapidly and successfully completed.

NOSTRADAMUS AND THE TAROT

The Tarot is an ancient set of cards used for games of chance, divination and esoteric exposition. It consists of 78 cards, of which 22 are picture cards called the Major Arcana. These have played a very important part in Western esoteric thinking in recent years. Since the early 1960s, when only a few Tarot card packs were easily available, there has been a huge increase in the number of packs to the point where even catalogues of the packs that are currently obtainable fill large volumes.

In addition to the Major Arcana, there are a further 56 cards divided into four different suits: Cups, Wands, Pentacles and Swords. These are similar to ordinary playing cards, being numbered one to 10 with four Court cards per suit – the Page, Prince, Queen and King. The numbered cards range in complexity from designs simply carrying the numerical 'pips' in the appropriate suit through to fairly elaborate picture cards, according to the taste of the artist. Here we are primarily concerned with the picture cards of the Major Arcana. These archetypal symbols are drawn from the images that were current in Europe in the centuries prior to Nostradamus's lifetime.

Although it used to be popular to ascribe the creation of the Tarot to the ancient Egyptians, the images are very much of a European mould, although the gypsies (often mistaken for Egyptians in that era) certainly would have played a part in their spread throughout Europe. The earliest unambiguous reference to the Tarot in Europe occurs in Berne in 1367, fixing their origin as probably medieval and European.

The Tarot soon appeared both in cheaply printed forms in taverns and in splendidly executed versions used by the rich. Even King Charles VI of France had three personal packs painted for him in 1392 by the artist Gringonneur, who used vellum, lapis lazuli and gold to produce them very lavishly. They were variously seen as the devil's picture book, as pagan relics, as a leisure diversion, or sometimes as keys to the future. Certainly Nostradamus must have handled a pack at some time in his life.

To use the Tarot for divination, it is necessary first for you to become familiar with each of the main cards by spending at least half an hour meditating on its meaning before reading the interpretation of that card given by one of the standard books on the subject. In this way you will have formed your own instinctive relationship with the card before having someone else's views overlaid on the image.

When you have worked through each of the Major Arcana, and read a little about the basic meaning of the Minor Arcana, then you are ready to start your own voyage of discovery into what the cards can tell you. First try a simple question that will later be easy to verify, but one that has not got a highly emotional content: it's too soon to ask the 'big' questions. You may find that in the beginning it is easier to read the cards for someone else rather than yourself.

The simplest divination you can use involves first formulating the question and then writing it down. With your mind as free from specific thoughts as you can make it, carefully shuffle the pack several times and then lay the top three cards face down on the table. Turn these up one at a time and verbalize what comes into your head. (Sometimes the answer will be given to the question that was in the enquirer's mind, rather than the one that was actually put.) The first card will show the past conditions, the second the present situation and the last card the future as it relates to that particular question.

If the cards are the Major Arcana a story should naturally form itself in your head. If you are using a full pack it is permissible to look up the meanings of the numbered or court cards, or indeed the meanings of the Major Arcana if nothing intuitive comes to you. Remember that the meaning of a card differs according to whether it is the right way up or inverted.

A more comprehensive method of divination is the 'Celtic Cross', which uses 10 cards dealt from the pack in a specific order, and which gives considerably more information about the question. Further details will be found in any book on the Tarot.

THE MAJOR ARCANA

The 22 traditional images used on the Major Arcana fall into several distinct categories:
1 Personages: the Fool, the Magician, the High Priestess, the Empress, the Emperor, the Pope, the Lovers, the Hermit, the Chariot (or Prince), the Hanged Man.
2 Virtues: Temperance, Justice, Strength (Fortitude).
3 Astrological: the Sun, the Moon, the Star.
4 Allegorical: the Wheel of Fortune, Death, the Devil, the Tower (of Babel), Judgment, the World.
These cards can be seen to be an incomplete series – a number of the virtues

such as Faith, Hope and Charity are missing, for example, as are five of the planets that are to be found in the traditional Tarot pack. Some early packs called 'naibi' and 'minchiate' included these extra cards, plus the full set of 12 zodiacal images. However, the above set of 22 cards is the form in which the Tarot has evolved into an unsurpassed divinatory tool over the last 600 years.

RITUAL PREDICTIVE METHODS

Another of the methods of divination which Nostradamus would have encountered is geomancy. This is a particularly useful technique for answering specific questions about the future which relate particularly to material affairs, that is, matters concerning business, finance, agriculture and property. There is much evidence that geomancy's reputation for predictive accuracy in these fields is well-justified.

Many detailed records of both successes and geomantic failures exist. Among the most interesting are those kept by an Elizabethan doctor, Simon Forman (1552-1611), who used this method for everything from medical diagnosis to political prediction. There is no reason why the same geomantic predictive techniques employed by Forman and many others should not work just as well for you. Geomancy is, however, best confined to material matters and not employed where subtler considerations, such as those relating to human emotions, are in question.

The technique of geomancy consists of interpreting a series of dots made in the earth or sand, or by pencil upon a piece of paper. Whichever medium is chosen, the question must first be carefully and accurately framed to allow for no ambiguity in the answer. Let us assume that the question is, 'Will my new venture bring me financial gain?' The diviner must then make 16 lines of dashes or dots with whatever instrument he or she has chosen, while requesting the aid of the earth spirits.

The dots on each line are then counted. The first row of dots is totalled and, depending on whether the resultant number is odd or even, one dot or two dots respectively are marked on the first line of a fresh piece of paper. The same observation is made for each of the subsequent 15 lines. The resultant page has 16 lines, each containing either one or two dots. These are broken vertically into four groups of four. The first group of four lines might look like this:

odd number of dots   ●
even number of dots   ●   ●
odd number of dots   ●
even number of dots   ●   ●

This is one geomantic figure, the first so-called 'Mother' figure. The subsequent Mother figures are derived in the same way from the remaining lines and the results placed beside the first figure. For example:

It can be seen that what is being generated is a set of four four-line binary figures and that there are 16 possible combinations of such figures. These 16 figures are usually referred to by their Latin names. The four shown above are called Amissio (meaning loss), Fortuna Major (great fortune), Puella (girl), and Fortuna Minor (lesser fortune).

Immediately you have a very rough answer to your question: there will be a major loss of fortune, but luck may come through a girl or woman connected with the proposed venture. The next step is to use a form of binary arithmetic to combine the four Mother figures into four Daughter figures, and from these are derived four Nephew figures, who in turn produce two Witness figures. The combination of these last two geomantic figures produces the Judge figure, by means of which you may judge the outcome of the question. Without going through all these steps, which can be looked up in any of the books on the subject of geomancy, the result of these manipulations is:

This is Albus, usually a good sign, but in this case it simply confirms that the venture will be mercurial and unstable, one best not embarked on. Although you should not ask the same question more than once, this divination was performed a second time. It came up with almost the same Mother figures but the Judge was Caput Draconis – an emphatic warning that does not bode well for the new venture, which, if embarked upon, will almost certainly lose money.

It seems that geomancy first became popular as 'raml' in the ninth century in the Arab world, probably in North Africa. From there it travelled south across the Sahara to Nigeria, Dahomey and Ghana, where it was practised under the name of Ifa divination and was subsequently exported to the New World as part of the divinatory techniques of the practitioners of Voodoo. Before that, however, it migrated with the Moors into Spain and hence into Southern France, where Nostradamus would have known it as Geomantiae. It is certain that the seer would have read writers such as Ramon Lull (1235-1315) who were experts in this form of divination.

THE GEOMANTIC FIGURES

Geomantic Figure	Meaning	Ruler
Puer	Boy, yellow, beardless, rash and inconsiderate, is rather good than bad.	Barzabel
Amissio	Loss, comprehended without, that which is taken away, a bad figure.	Kedemel
Albus	White, fair, wisdom, sagacity, clear thought, is a good figure.	Taphthar-tharath
Populus	People, congregation, an indifferent figure.	Chashmodai
Fortuna Major	Greater fortune, greater aid, safeguard entering, success, interior aid and protection, a very good sign.	Sorath
Conjunctio	Conjunction, assembling, union or coming together, rather good than bad.	Taphthar-tharath
Puella	A girl, beautiful, pretty face, pleasant, but not very fortunate.	Kedemel
Rubeus	Red, reddish, redhead, passion, vice, fiery temper, a bad figure.	Bartzabel
Acquisitio	Obtaining, comprehending without, success, absorbing, receiving, a good figure.	Hismael
Carcer	A prison, bound, is good or bad according to the nature of the question.	Zazel
Tristitia	Sadness, damned, cross, sorrow, grief, perversion, condemnation, is a bad figure.	Zazel
Laetitia	Joy, laughing, healthy, bearded, is a good figure.	Hismael

Cauda Draconis	The threshold lower, or going out, dragon's tail, exit, lower kingdom, is a bad figure.	Zazel & Bartzabel
Caput Draconis	The head, the threshold entering, the upper threshold, dragon's head, entrance, upper kingdom, is a good figure.	Hismael & Kedemel
Fortuna Minor	Lesser fortune, lesser aid, safeguard going out, external aid and protection, is not a very good figure.	Sorath
Via	Way, street, journey, neither good nor bad.	Chashmodai

THROUGH THE CURTAIN OF TIME

To derive answers to specific questions you can use any of the techniques outlined in the previous chapters: scrying, the Tarot cards, divinatory sortes, the I Ching or geomancy – each in its own way will provide answers.

But what if you want to be there, see the future, feel the future, or the past, and record direct impressions as did Nostradamus? There is a way to penetrate the curtain of time. The idea that each human being has an 'astral body' capable of separating itself from the physical body and engaging in 'astral journeying' is very old. The Neoplatonic philosophers of the early Christian era referred to Plato's doctrines when they called this 'dream body' after the Latin word for star, 'astrum'. Centuries later, Cornelius Agrippa confirmed the possibility of leaving the body consciously in dream as 'vacation of the body, when the spirit is enabled to transcend its bounds'.

Creative dreaming or astral projection is, after scrying, probably the most direct form of perception of other places or other times, but it does take considerable perseverance to accomplish. Although astral projection does not lead directly to prophecy or predictive powers, once it has been achieved the scope for first-hand experience of other times or other realities is considerable.

The purpose of the technique of astral projection is to do with your conscious mind what is carried out by your unconscious mind after you go to sleep. There is nothing at all unnatural in that, except that you will be consciously aware of your 'dream', and be able to direct it, just as Nostradamus could.

The body has many unconscious functions, such as breathing. Most of the time it conducts these operations without any disturbance from the conscious mind, but you can take over with the conscious mind the function of, for example, breathing. If you had to do this all the time it would be a bore, but breathing is a function which can be controlled by either the conscious or the unconscious mind. Dreaming is another such function. There are some well-known positive benefits in regularly taking over and deepening the breathing cycle. Likewise, there are definite benefits in taking over and consciously directing your 'dreaming'.

There are a number of techniques designed to project the astral body, These all share several basic prerequisites, the most important of which is confidence in what you are doing, and a lack of fear. If for a moment you begin to succeed with a projection, even the slightest touch of fear will instantly drive you firmly back to your body. Fear is a natural response to new sensations which in this particular case needs to be curbed, just as the breathing response needs to be overcome while you are diving underwater.

The second is concentration. If your will or visualization slackens, either your mind will wander, in the everyday meaning of that expression, or you will go to sleep – not a bad thing in itself, but inimical to success with this practice.

The steps involved in projecting the astral body are:

1   Make sure there is no possibility of disturbance by the phone (take it off the hook) or any impending callers. Remove any metal objects touching your skin. Sit in a very comfortable and fully supporting chair, or stretch out on a bed in a north–south orientation, head to the north. (Although the latter is not always desirable as it does encourage sleep.) Concentrate on each part of your body in turn, starting with your feet. Tense the muscles and then relax them, working up to the top of your head. Then mentally check each part of your body again to see it is fully relaxed. Close your eyes and attempt to hold for a few minutes that delicious feeling of verging on sleep, while staying very much alert.

2   Take a few deep breaths. Try to imagine yourself lying or sitting 15cm (6 inches) to the left of where you actually are. When you have successfully convinced yourself of this, try visualizing a new position 15cm (6 inches) to the right of your actual position. When you are sure of this, try for 15cm (6 inches) above your present position. When this slightly more difficult position has been convincingly established, try sinking into the bed, through the mattress, and coming to rest in your imagination 15cm (6 inches) below it. At this point the temptation simply to go to sleep should be fought. Repeat these exercises every night for a week.

3   When these visualizations are successful, but not before, visualize yourself in your original position but slowly raising yourself into a sitting position. Then, without even attempting to open your eyes, try to see what is in front of you. Repeat these exercises every night for a second week.

4 Spend every night of the next week repeating the above exercises, but adding a further practice. Try imagining yourself slowly swinging side to side from one position to the other, like a pendulum. Get to feel perfectly comfortable with this, then try moving backwards as if someone were pulling you out through your own head and shoulders. Move this newly visualized position further back from your body each time you try it. With some luck the time will come when you suddenly find yourself apparently able to stand up and move away from your body.

5 If this does not work, add an additional exercise. This involves sitting in front of a mirror, closing your eyes, then attempting to reverse the situation, so that instead of looking at your reflection you may be able for a few seconds to feel you are looking out of the mirror at yourself. Add this to the previous exercises for another week, trying the whole cycle of exercises.

Eventually the time will come when you will get a jerk-back feeling, as if you had just pulled back from falling: try to encourage this but let yourself go. Keep persisting until suddenly you will find yourself apparently standing in your room, slightly disorientated, having successfully transferred your consciousness outside your body. Then the interesting experiments which are outside the scope of this book begin. Suffice it to say that there is much to explore before you need to go looking for other times.

SEEING THE ASTRAL BODY

The astral body is a concept that is found in most civilizations and is even indirectly mentioned in the Bible. The Theosophists, a worldwide movement founded by H. P. Blavatsky, went to great lengths to try to 'see' the astral body clairvoyantly and books were produced with coloured paintings of different auras, which were considered to be an extension of the astral body. In the early 1960s a type of goggle called the Kilner goggle was produced which enabled even people who were not psychic to see the flow of the aura round living human beings. In the 1970s, claims were made that a form of photography called Kirlian photography could actually photograph the aura. More recently, direct photography of the whole astral body has been attempted.

NOSTRADAMUS
IN THE 1990S

What of Nostradamus's prophesies for the 1990s? He predicted in Century VI Quatrain 21 that there would be a US/USSR alliance in 1990. Certainly the closeness that originated between Reagan and Gorbachev in the late 1980s has now reached the point (unthinkable just 10 years ago) where President Clinton of the US has offered aid to Russia. In Century II Quatrain 89 the same prediction is rephrased:

One day the two great leaders will be friends,
Their great power will be seen to grow:
The New Land will be at the height of its power,
To the man of blood the number is reported.

The man with the blood mark (on his head) is obviously Gorbachev, who subsequently loses his power. Even at the time of his friendship with Reagan his number was almost up. The New Land is the New World or the US, probably at the height of its powers before succumbing to the current recession.

Nostradamus predicted a Middle Eastern war in 1991 in Century VIII Quatrain 70 with amazing detail:

He will enter, wicked, unpleasant, infamous
Tyrannizing over Mesopotamia.
All friends made by the adulterous woman.
The land dreadful and black of aspect.

Saddam Hussein certainly entered Kuwait in a wicked and infamously underhand manner. He still tyrannizes Mesopotamia, the ancient Greek name for Iraq. The 'adulterous woman' might be a 20th-century friend and ally of Hussein, but this is more likely to be a reference to the Biblical whore of Babylon. Babylon's position as capital of the region has been taken over by Baghdad, Saddam Hussein's capital. The last line is a perfect description of the huge black clouds hanging over Kuwait after Saddam Hussein set fire to the oil wells.

In Century VI Quatrain 59 Nostradamus speaks of another drama which hit the headlines in 1991:

The lady, furious in an adulterous rage,
Will conspire against her Prince, but not speak to him.
But the culprit will soon be known,
So that seventeen will be martyred.

The Duchess of York was upset by the newspaper reports of her alleged adultery with a Texan (the culprit who was soon discovered). She left on a trip to Indonesia without Prince Andrew, not speaking to him. It remains to be seen who the 17 persons are who will suffer.

By early 1991, Margaret Thatcher had been pushed from power, and later that year Princess Diana was rejected by Prince Charles. It is possible that one or other of those events is reflected in Century VI Quatrain 74:

> *She who was cast out will return to reign,*
> *Her enemies found among conspirators.*
> *More than ever will her reign be triumphant.*
> *At three and seventy death is very sure.*

Whoever is the main protagonist, it looks like a welcomed return, ended by death predicted very precisely at the age of 73.

In 1991 civil war broke out in the former Yugoslavia, and has been rumbling along ever since. Here is an interesting resurgence of the old quarrel between Muslim and Christian groups which has fuelled feuds in Eastern Europe since the Turkish occupation from the middle of the 15th century until the end of the 17th. Nostradamus obviously points to the current unrest in this area and in Romania in Century IV Quatrain 82:

> *A mass [of men] from Slavonia will draw near,*
> *The Destroyer will ruin the old city:*
> *He will see his Romania quite deserted.*
> *Then will not know how to extinguish the great flame.*

Certainly there has been much destruction of the old city of Dubrovnik, and it is doubtful if the UN knows how to extinguish the flames of religious and civil hatred. Romania, meanwhile, has been reduced to a shadow of its former self by its last Communist dictator.

The year of 1994 is designated by Nostradamus for the beginning of the drought of 40 years followed by floods of the same duration. Despite the use of the French word 'ans', perhaps this should be interpreted as months, as a 40-year drought is inconceivable in terms of the world's current climate.

In 1995 an unloved Pope is predicted to be chosen from French or Spanish candidates – the penultimate Pope, according to Malachy. This year will also see friction in Albania with a probable attack by this country on Greece.

In 1996 environmental disasters not entirely unconnected with the depletion of the ozone layer are predicted in Century IV Quatrain 67.

Late in the decade will come two Islamic expansionist invasions, one from Algeria and the other from Iran (Persia), according to Century VI, Quatrain 80, resulting in the burning of a city and many deaths by the sword. This may be a holy war, or jihad, with Muslim armies converging from North Africa and Iran against Christian Europe, just like the Muslim invasion of Spain 700 years ago:

> *From Fez the [Islamic] kingdom will stretch out to Europe,*
> *The city blazes, and the sword will slash:*
> *The great man of Asia with a great troop by land and sea,*
> *So that the blues, Persians, cross, to death is driven.*

The concluding events of the 1990s and the millennium itself are discussed in the next few pages.

DESCENT INTO DESPAIR

The overwhelming quantity of catastrophic prophecies in the quatrains make the future look very bleak indeed. In this Nostradamus is not alone: the Revelation of St John the Divine, with which he would have been familiar, predicts the arrival of the four Horsemen of the Apocalypse (Plague, Famine, War and Death) which will herald the rise of the Antichrist, the millennium, and the end of the world. Century X Quatrain 72 warns of the arrival from the skies of the King of Terror, five months before the year 2000. Variously interpreted as a giant nuclear bomb, or even a full-scale alien invasion from outer space, whatever it turns out to be will be very unpleasant indeed. As if to confirm this prophecy, Professor Hideo Itakawa, who pioneered Japan's rocket technology, predicts the end of the world one month later in August 1999. He suggests this will be due to a very rare astrological Grand Cross of the planets which forms in this month.

This Grand Cross is formed by an opposition of Venus (in Scorpio) to Saturn and Jupiter (in Taurus), square (at right angles) to Neptune and Uranus (in Aquarius) opposed to the Sun, Moon and Mercury (in Leo). The four zodiacal signs – Taurus the bull, Leo the lion, Scorpio the eagle and Aquarius the man – are the signs of the four beasts of the Apocalypse which are also shown on the very last Tarot card in the pack, the World.

Scientists are beginning to associate the incidence of sunspot, earthquake and volcanic activity more with planetary positions than with solely geological causes. Consequently, as a result of this configuration there may be a much higher incidence of natural disasters at this time than one would normally expect. By way of confirmation, the American seer Edgar Cayce has prophesied that a shift in the polar axis of the earth will cause many natural catastrophes, earthquakes and tidal waves, resulting in the destruction of much of mankind.

This is also the time of Armageddon, predicted by Biblical prophets as the 'battle of the great day of God', when the last fight will take place between the powers of good and evil. Its name is indubitably taken from the famous battle-field mentioned in Judges V 19 in the plain of Esdraelon, where the Israelites fought their major battles. Unfortunately, it is not scheduled to be quite as local-ized as these battles.

Others who are in complete agreement about late 1999 being the end of the world are the Jehovah's Witnesses and the Seventh Day Adventists. Obviously a lot of people will be holding their breath over the last five months of 1999, just as they did with equal justification in 999.

In his Preface to his son César, Nostradamus speaks more plainly of the events to come before the last conflagration: 'the worldwide conflagration which is to bring so many catastrophes and such revolutions that scarcely any lands will not be covered by water, and this will last until all has perished save history and geog-raphy themselves.' Before this occurs, Nostradamus avers that 'This is why, before and after these revolutions in various countries, the rains will be so diminished and such abundance of fire and fiery missiles shall fall from heaven that nothing shall escape the holocaust ... For before war ends the century and in its final stages it will hold the century under its sway'.

A grim vision indeed, and one that may come to pass within a very few years. Nostradamus predicts in Century V Quatrain 25 that as we reach the year 2000 a new Arab Empire, probably made up of the more extreme Arab countries which are geographically located around Israel, will attack Iran (Persia), Egypt and Turkey (Byzantium). This empire will be supported by ruthlessly anti-Christian and venomously anti-Western fanatics in Algeria, Tunisia, and possibly 'Greater Syria', which will include parts of the Lebanon:

> *The Arab Prince, Mars, the Sun, Venus, [in] Leo,*
> *The rule of the Church will succumb to the sea.*
> *Towards Persia very nearly a million [men]*
> *The true serpent will invade Egypt and Byzantium.*

The precise conjunctions as described here occur on 21–23 August 1998 and 2–6 August 2000. As the Church is referred to by Nostradamus as a ship, its suc-cumbing to the sea means the end of the Church, or at the very least the papa-cy. The standard of the attacking force will be the sign of the serpent or in some way related to it.

Two years later, in June 2002, Century VI Quatrain 24 predicts a dreadful war that will be followed by the anointment and reign of a new king. This will 'bring peace to the earth for a long time', of that Nostradamus is in no doubt.

If we survive all these terrible events, Nostradamus clearly states that we may then look forward to 1000 years of much greater peace.

MODERN PROPHETS

One present-day seer predicts that on 1 January 2000 the centre of London will be almost completely destroyed by a cosmic catastrophe – a direct hit from a meteorite, containing large amounts of uranium, thorium and other radioactive elements, of a size even greater than the meteor which is now known to have devastated a vast area of largely uninhabited Siberian forest in 1908. According to Dr David Hughes of Sheffield University, there are perhaps 100,000 'small' asteroids in the solar system that we cannot currently detect. By small, Dr Hughes means less than 6km (3½ miles) across – ample 'ammunition' to devastate London.

Many of these prophecies relating to the year 2000 indicate major climatic variations, which will render large areas of the earth virtually uninhabitable. Also predicted are earthquakes which will devastate densely populated areas as far apart as California and Portugal and atmospheric pollution of such intensity in New York, Los Angeles, Tokyo, and a major Australian city that those who can afford to do so will move to the suburbs and countryside.

NEW HOPE
FOR HUMANITY

Nostradamus appears to give us two possible but incompatible scenarios for the world from 1999 onwards. The first scenario of horror and war was explained earlier. Now we look at the reverse side of the coin, where a golden age of enlightenment takes us into the third millennium ad, or the seventh millennium counting from Nostradamus's dating for the beginning of the world. Maybe both futures exist already on the time tree and it is our reactions to the very crucial last years of this millennium that will determine which of these worlds or realities we shall in fact enter.

Jewish scholars view the year 2000 as the end of a Shemitah and the beginning of a period when Utopian peace will reign. The Shemitah cyclical theory of time is based upon the almost universal reverence for the number seven; in a time context this is recognized in the number of days in a week, in the importance of 50 (seven times seven plus one) to the Hebrew calendar makers, and the academic and agricultural habits of a sabbatical rest year. The Jubilee year is the fiftieth year after every cycle of seven times seven years, and the larger Jubilee cycle is of 7000 years. After the present Shemitah ends in AD 2000 the Torah will no longer contain prohibitions, evil will be curbed, and Utopia will be realized: the return to Israel of modern Judaism is in preparation for this transmission to the next Shemitah. Nostradamus was born into Judaism, even if his family later converted, and these time cycles would have been part of his upbringing.

Many thinkers and prophets point to the end of this millennium as also the end of the Age of Pisces and the beginning of the Age of Aquarius (see panel). The present writer's view is that with the ending of the Cold War threat and with an increasing desire worldwide to treat our planet in a more kindly and thoughtful fashion, the branch has already been made and we are currently on course for the second of the two alternate realities – that of a new and more civilized age. However, it will not be by any means an easy journey, as it will be marred by flashes of ethnic and religious rivalry and other squabbles. This journey will lead eventually to Nostradamus's final date of 3797. Who knows what will happen then?

KEY MILLENNIUM DATES

The year 2000 approximately marks the beginning of the Age of Aquarius – a time of fundamental change for all humanity. It is measured by the precession of the equinoxes, and as the millennium closes we are moving from the Age of Pisces (which is frequently associated with Christianity because of that religion's early use of the symbol of the fish) into the Age of Aquarius after about 2160 years. A complete circuit of all the 12 signs takes 25,290 years.

Because each zodiacal sign is not exactly 30 degrees in extent there is some controversy about the exact date that marks the transition. Here are a few of the more interesting from the many possible dates:

1904 The 20th-century magician Aleister Crowley's Aeon of Horus was for him the point of entry to the Aquarian Age, an era of the Crowned and Conquering Child of Horus. The latter half of this century has certainly been an age of the child, particularly in the year of 1964, when Flower Power raised its head.

1962 The American clairvoyant Jeane Dixon had a vision of the birth of the Antichrist in Jerusalem, an event whose significance was not lost on the makers of the Omen series of films. On the previous day there had been a solar eclipse with all seven traditional planets in the sign of Aquarius.

2000 Many prophets agree that this magic number will be the start of the Age of Aquarius, including Nostradamus, Edgar Cayce (the American 'sleeping' prophet), Saint Malachy (who forecast each of the Popes until the end of the Catholic Church in this year), Garabandal and the astrologer Margaret Hone.

2001 Some writers, for example Barbarin, and the Seventh Day Adventists see the first year of the new millennium as the key date. Of course there is an argument for saying that the 'zero year' (like the 'zero year' of a baby before he turns one year old), is the first year of the Aeon. If these predictions come about then the answer to this arithmetical puzzle will be quite important.

2010 Peter Lemesurier, author of The Gospel of the Stars, suggests this is the correct year, quoting as his authority the French Institut Geographique National.

2012 Basing his conclusions on cycles in the ancient Mayan calendar, Jose Arguelles, author of The Mayan Factor, suggests this date for the collapse of global civilization and a regeneration of the earth.

2020 Basing his theory on the first conjunction of Jupiter and Saturn in Aquarius since 1404, Adrian Duncan, author of Doing Time on Planet Earth, proposes 21 December 2020 for the astrological transition.

2160 A date of exactly 2160 years since the birth of Christ forms another religious (but not astrological) entry point for the New Age.

NOSTRADAMUS AND ETERNITY

Nostradamus's writings give a number of key dates which help us understand his quatrains. He published his first predictions in 1547 – a date which was quite significant in France, for it was the year when French instead of Latin was declared the official language of the French authorities. It is not therefore surprising to find the Curé de Louvicamp stating in 1710 that 'when France's oracle [Nostradamus] made his Gallic prophecies, he hardly ever departed from the Latins' usage, often writing Latin under the pretext of writing French ... Often he even employed a Latinate French, drawing attention and alluding to the Latin phraseology in word order and ... syntax'. Latin would of course still have been the main language for scholarly interchange in Europe, and Nostradamus often thought in Latin even if he wrote in French. It is precisely for this reason that some of his quatrains so zealously guard the secret of their meaning, unless they are approached with both the Latin and French languages in mind.

In his letter to his son César, Nostradamus confirmed that his Centuries comprise 'prophecies from today [1 March 1555] to the year 3797'. This date is either the limit of Nostradamus's exploration of the time tree, or a definite date for the end of the world as we know it, 'when all has perished save history and geography themselves', at least in one of the alternate realities which make up the time tree. Even Nostradamus thought this far-distant date 'may perturb some, when they see such a long timespan'. As the events come to pass more of Nostradamus's predictions become understandable, but it is perhaps not until this far-distant date that all of them will become clear.

Looked at from a wider perspective, why should the end of the world be exactly 2000 years from the birth of Christ, an event whose dating could be incorrect by anything up to a decade anyway?

At the time that Nostradamus was writing the accepted calendar was the Julian calendar, so called because it was first adopted by Julius Caesar in 46 bc. Interestingly, the Julian cycle consisted of 7980 years, commencing on 1 January 4713 bc. Archbishop James Ussher (1581–1665), who lived shortly after Nostradamus, calculated from Biblical chronology that the world began in 4004 bc, a date which has since been referred to as Anno Mundi. To understand Nostradamus's chronology we could use Anno Mundi as a base date, but as Nostradamus's family were originally Sephardic Jews it is reasonable to look also to the Jewish tradition of dating to discover the significance of the year AD 3797.

The Jewish calendar commences from Creation in 3760 bc. The year of Christ's birth, according to the Jewish calendar, is therefore 3760. As Christ's birth is now thought by scholars to have actually been 4 bc, we add four years to this date to give 3764 Anno Mundi. As Christ is reputed to have lived 33 years, the date of his crucifixion becomes 3797 Anno Mundi.

Suddenly it all makes sense: Nostradamus has placed the Crucifixion as the central point of the history of the world, with the Creation and the end of the world at an equal timespan on either side. It seems, therefore, that the Jewish calendar is a far more accurate guide to time in a Nostradamian context than either the Julian calendar (current in his day), Archbishop Ussher or the Gregorian calendar (current in our own time).

The validity of the above calculation may be questioned, but this (or a very similar course of reasoning) is likely to have been used by Nostradamus to generate the date AD 3797 – with the implication that, for Nostradamus, time (embraced by the Creation and the end of the world) pivoted around the death of Christ. Beyond this timespan was eternity. By this reasoning, the total span of time between Creation and the end of the world was just over seven and a half millennium.

Nostradamus did not believe, as many prophets do now, that the end of the world would happen in AD 2000. On the contrary, he seemed fairly sure that AD 2002 was to be the beginning of a new and peaceful golden age.

At the very least, we should rejoice that the year 2000 is only a step upon the way. We should not see that year as the end, as did those farmers who in the year AD 999 left their crops unharvested because they were encouraged by the Church to feel that they would not live beyond the end of the first millennium to see the fruits of their labours. Nostradamus reassures us that there will be at least another 1797 years of human history beyond the year 2000!

For the very reason that Nostradamus could, like other prophets, see another reality which did not always take place, so we have the collective free will to guide events in order that the year 2000 brings us to that twig on the time tree which embodies a new age of relative peace, rather than fulfilling the prophecies of millennial terror, war and doom. We have that choice – though it is doubtful if we know how to make it. The future is predictable but it is not fixed!

THE PROPHECIES OF CHRIST

Although many wars and famines are predicted by Nostradamus, there is nothing new in these cycles of nature and history. Even Christ made similar predictions (Matthew 24, verses 6-8): 'And ye shall hear of wars and rumours of wars; see that ye be not troubled: for all these things must come to pass, but the end is not yet. For nation shall rise against nation, and kingdom against kingdom; and there shall be famines, and pestilences, and earthquakes, in divers places'.

On the other hand, in line with the theory of alternate realities, even Christ's prophecies seem to have failed on occasion. He correctly predicted the Fall of the Temple of Jerusalem in AD 70, when the Romans sacked it. However, he also predicted incorrectly that the end of the world would come shortly after the destruction of the Temple.

MILLENNIUM PROPHECIES

What does the immediate future hold for us all? The end of the millennium is due in less than four years. Who can afford to ignore the momentous events promised for this time?

The end of the world has always had a grim fascination for prophets, and perhaps even more so for their readers or listeners. We envisage it in terms of either natural disaster afflicting us (like earthquake, famine, plague, flood, fire, freezing, cosmic collision, ecological catastrophe), or a divine being punishing us for wrongs committed.

Whichever of these may overtake us, it is inconceivable that the world will end: we, mankind, may come to a full-stop, but it, the Earth, will continue to hurtle round the sun just as it always has. But will it?

Huge cosmic collisions between earth and forces from outer space have been recorded in the sacred writings of every race. Some modern prophets, like Immanuel Velikovsky, have drawn on this ancient evidence to suggest that the time may be ripe for another such planetary collision. It would take only one meteorite of modest size to capsize the climate of the planet. At a stroke we Earth-dwellers could be wiped out as surely as the occupants of Atlantis were once allegedly destroyed.

For the prophet, whether a bearded high priest or a bearded hippy, the fascination of pinpointing the last apocalyptic day is overwhelming. To do this, the prophet looks at the wheels of the cosmic clock to understand the nature of time. He or she measures the ages, probes back to find the date of creation, and performs mental gymnastics on every single number mentioned in the Bible or other holy books, scans the skies, or tries to find a mighty enough planetary conjunction which could just trigger the fatal event.

All the worry about nihilation and eternal damnation might prove to be misplaced, however. The gaping jaws of the Apocalypse might not snap shut, ensnaring us all. Many might survive the ordeal, or it might never happen because there is no need for it. Even now the children of the Sixties, that time of hope and idealism, are taking up the reins of power. Guided by their vision for a better world, we might avoid the worst scenario. The New Age philosophers and their forerunners, like Aleister Crowley and Madame Blavatsky, have wedged open the doors of perception to a wider consciousness based on non-materialistic values. Their influence may just prevent mankind from self-destructing and lead him to a paradise on earth in the form of a theocratic kingdom which can look forward to a thousand years of peace.

Despite the fact that we are all still here, and many a deadline solemnly proclaimed has passed without so much as an apocalyptic tremor, we should not dismiss the positive effects of such seemingly negative predictions. There is nothing like a deadline to galvanize humanity to action, or greater piety – or even greater craziness. Prophets act as our collective conscience – they keep us on our toes. We may not always believe that the end is nigh, but perhaps it would be better for us sometimes if we acted as though it were.

Even if the world survives the magic 2000 years after the birth of Christ, or 2160 years since the beginning of the Piscean Age, or the next grand conjunction, or avoids the destruction of its protective atmosphere, or any of the other cyclical deadlines looming up thick and fast, one thing is certain – every person reading this book will in less than a century from now meet his or her own end of the world.

If this half of the book does nothing but stir its readers into making preparations for that day, by doing now what they might otherwise have put off, then its author will be satisfied with his handiwork.

THE ANCIENT WORLD

The Ancients knew much about the measurement of long periods of time. With Apollo's help the Greek prophetesses could look deep into the future. Unimaginably long periods of time have been measured between the birth and the destruction of the Universe: are we nearing the end of this period?

TIME AND CHRONOLOGY

We need to examine the concept and meaning of time in order to determine when to expect the Apocalypse.

Time is what distinguishes the present moment from the domain of prophecy and the domain of history. We can only truly experience that infinitesimal sliver of time that is called the present. The past we can experience only vicariously, through memory or history. A very few people – true prophets – do seem to be able to perceive glimpses of the future. To map what they discover, we need to understand chronology.

Chronology, the science of computing time both for daily and historical periods, differs from history in that it takes no account of the significance of events or their relationship to each other. Many early civilizations used as their timepiece the changes in the moon's shape over the lunar month. This was soon found to be unsatisfactory, however, because it could not be used to measure the seasons, especially the growing seasons on which lives and livelihoods depended. Seasons wax and wane depending upon the earth's revolution round the Sun –

not an easy phenomenon to measure with the naked eye.

More advanced civilizations used the solar year, and dated events from some arbitrary date of national importance, such as the beginning of a king's reign. The Greeks employed this "epochal" method of dating. They used the Olympic Games to break their chronology into groups of four years, dating events from the victory of Coroebus in the first Olympic Games of 776 BC. This system was first suggested by Timaeus around 260 BC. If the Greeks' Olympic system were still in use today, AD 1994 would be the year of the Greek Olympiad 2771, and AD 2000 would be the year of the Greek Olympiad 2777.

The Babylonians chose the date of the foundation of their kingdom, 26 February 747 BC, under Nabonasser as their base line for calculating dates. This in turn was used by the famous Alexandrian astronomer and "father of astrology", Ptolemy, who flourished in Egypt in the second century AD.

Similar thinking lay behind the dating system used by the Romans, which starts from the foundation of the city of Rome, somewhere between 747 BC and 753 BC. For the Romans, AD 2000 would be 2754 AUC, anno urbis conditae, meaning from the founding of the city.

Islam dates its epoch from the retreat of the prophet Mohammed from Mecca to Medina on 16 July AD 622. The year 1378 in the Islamic calendar is the equivalent of the Gregorian AD 2000.

The key date in Christian countries is, of course, the birth of Christ. Even this concept of BC (before Christ) and AD (anno domini, or after Christ's birth), was not actually put into practice until the monk Dionysius Exiguus suggested it in AD 533. Before his idea was adopted, Christian countries used a dating system based on the supposed beginning of the world, or anno mundi. The Irish Protestant prelate and scholar Archbishop Ussher (1581–1656) was responsible for the assumption that the world began and man was created in 4004 – some 5,502 or 5,508 or even 6,000 years (according to the Septuagint, the Greek version of the Bible) before Christ's birth.

Modern geological techniques have shown these dates to be ludicrously inaccurate. However, despite this shortcoming, they do at least deal with a time-scale in human history that we are able to relate to – just imagine trying to encompass a dating system that spanned 4,600,000,000 years to the present!

These notional dates of when the world began, or Christ was born, or Rome was founded are symptoms of man's need to mould reality to his own pattern of thinking. Days, lunar months and years do not, in fact, fit neatly together as exact multiples, but because we prefer a "tidy" chronology we have invented one that appears to fit together.

Epochs and even numbers hold enormous fascination for us. Hence 1000 years or 2000 years after the birth of Christ suddenly become important points in the history of mankind. This is why chronology is a key to prophecy; to find out what the future holds for us, you must first of all know where you stand in the procession of events that together make up human history. Certainly, the next seven years mark the culmination point of many key dates.

If you are guided by Archbishop Ussher's dating method, the key date will be 1995, exactly 6000 years on from the "beginning" of the world. Alternatively, perhaps 1999 is the key date, for if you count from 5502 (another world "birth date") this year marks the 7500th birthday of the world or indeed the universe.

For contemporary astrological speculator Richard W. Noone, the key date is 5 May 2000. For Christians, however, the key date is still Christmas 2000. I did not, you will note, state 25 December 2000, because it is doubtful whether this was indeed the day on which Christ was born.

THE SOLAR SYSTEM'S CLOCK

Time is recorded astronomically, by the great clock of the solar system and its setting in the universe. The most basic cosmic occurrence for man is the rotation of the earth on its own axis, which defines the length of a 24-hour day.

The rotation of the Earth round the Sun defines a year, and the rotation of the moon round the Earth a lunar month or, imperfectly, a calendar month. Unfortunately, the creator did not make these three basic natural cycles divisible one into another. There are not, for example, an even number of days in the year or in the lunar month. As a result, man has produced several systems of reckoning drawn from his imagination. Perhaps the neatest of these was the Egyptian year of 360 days made up of 12 months, each of 30 days, with five (or occasionally six) days dedicated to the gods as holy days.

When Julius Caesar reformed the Roman calendar in 46 BC, 1 January was chosen as the date to mark the beginning of the year. In England in AD 1155 this was changed to 25 March, to coincide roughly with the Spring Equinox, and in conformity with European custom. In 1582 Pope Gregory XIII reformed the Julian calendar; 1 January was again adopted as the first day of the year, but the practice of each centennial year counting as a leap year was dropped. England did not realign itself with Europe until 1752, by which time the Julian calendar was 11 days out of step with the seasons.

MEANING OF THE MILLENNIUM

'Millennium' is a Latin word which simply means a period of one thousand years. However, this timespan, equalling about forty generations, has come to have a special meaning in the religions of Judaism and Christianity.

One thousand years was the period for which Satan was supposed to be bound, and also the duration of Christ's absence from Earth. The early Christians thought that Christ's second coming would occur within their lifetime. The disappointment of this expectation led to a revision of the timescale and the belief in his return after 1000 years.

The year 999 saw extensive preparation across Europe for Christ's return. When He failed to materialize, hopes were then pinned on a succession of dates until the year 2000 was finally settled upon. Even in these relatively godless times, millions of people are awaiting with bated breath the second millennium after Christ's birth.

American fundamentalist Christians form the vanguard of the expectant. His arrival, they believe, will be heralded by specific "signs", notably devastating wars and natural disasters, followed by a period of rule by the Antichrist. After mankind has endured these trials Christ will return to judge both the living and the dead, set up his kingdom, and rule it for a further 1000 years. Sometimes the actual period of His rule, a time of perfect happiness for those who passed judgement, is referred to as the millennium.

The term Apocalypse is derived from Greek and literally means "to uncover". The term can also mean a revelation, as in something revealed by God to a chosen prophet; for example, the Apocalypse of St John the Divine, the last book of the Bible. There are also a number of other apocalypses, supposedly revelations of the end-time or future state of the world, written by Hellenized Jews and early Christians in the form of visions. The branch of theology concerned with beliefs about the end of time is called eschatology. The four most important events in this category for Christians are the second coming of Christ, the resurrection of the dead, the last judgement, and the final recompense.

Belief in the importance of the millennial year AD 2000 is grounded in the sacred Jewish and Christian texts. Visionary thought concerning the end of this millennium comes from books written and visions seen between the middle of the second century BC and the end of the first century AD. These may have derived some of their inspiration from other cultures; early Persian mysticism, for example, contains strong apocalyptic elements, and in the broadest sense of eschatological or end-time beliefs, so do Ugaritic, Akkadian, Babylonian, Egyptian, Cannoned, Greek and Latin works.

Hesiod, a Greek poet of the eighth century BC, saw history as a divinely ordered succession of periods, descending from the golden age, through the silver to the bronze and then the iron age, long before historians used these terms to date periods according to the types of metal tools in use. For Hesiod, the end-time would come with warfare and social upheavals which would lead Zeus to destroy mankind for its wickedness.

In many traditions, the day of judgement or the end of the world is often referred to as Doomsday, derived from the word "doom", which means "law" and by implication "punishment". The idea is that everybody gets their just deserts in the end. It does not seem to have occurred to the formulators of the systems of religious belief that the universe may not in fact be fair, and actually may have little regard for man's conceptions of doom or law.

Fixing the date for the millennium is not as easy as simply adding 2000 years to Christ's birth. For a start, no one knows when Christ was born, and the best guess is 4 BC. By this reckoning, the millennium is due to arrive in 1996.

There is a further complication in that we use one number to refer to a whole year. For example, "1996" refers not to a date but to a twelve-month period. So should we aim for the beginning, middle or end of the year?

WHEN WILL THE MILLENNIUM ARRIVE?

Calculating the start of the 21st century is not as simple as it may seem. The obvious starting point for the millennium is midnight on 31 December 1999. However, before the 21st century can be said to begin, a full 20 centuries must have ticked away since the birth of Christ. Take the year 20 AD – at the beginning of this year only 19 years had passed.

Similarly, at the beginning of the year 2000 only 1999 years will have passed. The true arithmetical millennium, therefore, will come on midnight 31 December 2000, one year after the date many people are pinning their hopes on. So the question is, do you follow the arithmetic strictly, or simply go for the first moment of that magic number, the year 2000? Further, if you are measuring from Christ's birth, do you take 4 BC or the first moment of AD 1? Do you use 25 December or one of the other proposed birthdays? Anyway, there is always the chance of the millennium coming late! In this book we have taken the simplistic view and assumed that the millennium will begin on 1 January AD 2000, but the reader is free to make the above adjustments as he or she sees fit.

FURNACES AND FIRE
WORSHIPPERS

The Book of Daniel is one of the most controversial books of

the Old Testament and probably the most important

book of Old Testament prophecy, filled with key numbers.

The Book of Daniel is reckoned to be the earliest canonical book of prophecy, compiled c. 580 BC. Some scholars prefer to date it from the second century BC, partly to account for the accuracy of its prophecies. The historical events it relates happened between 534 and 607 BC, during which time Daniel's vision also revealed things about the end of time.

It is obvious that the Book of Daniel has been compiled from a number of sources. Whole books have been cut out of Daniel because they were thought to be non-canonical, that is, not part of accepted scripture; among these "rogues" are The History of Susanna, about an attempted seduction, and Bel and the Dragon.

The Book of Daniel opens "in the third year of the reign of Jehoiakim king of Judah", after Nebuchadnezzar, King of Babylon, had conquered Jerusalem and taken the Jewish people into slavery. The best of their children were taken to Babylon to learn the Chaldean ways. Four children were selected and given Chaldean names to replace their Hebrew ones. Daniel was among those shown special favour and renamed Belteshazzar. For religious reasons, Daniel and his three companions asked for a water and vegetarian diet rather than the standard meat and wine rations.

At the end of three years Daniel "had understanding in all visions and dreams". Nebuchadnezzar called for the children and found that not only did they have "fairer countenances", due to the vegetarian diet, but they also had a greater skill, wisdom and understanding of magic than his own Chaldean astrologers. Daniel rapidly proves himself the equal of Nebuchadnezzar's magicians and sorcerers, just as Aaron had defeated Pharaoh's magicians. It seems that in every age the best prophets were also the best magicians, and Jewish.

In 8:14 Daniel is told that the sanctuary and the host will be trodden under foot "unto 2300 days" and "at the time of the end shall be the vision".

In 9:2 Daniel states that "the Lord ... would accomplish seventy years in the desolations of Jerusalem". Seventy years is, of course, 25,550 days, the approximate period (in years) of the precession of the Zodiac.

In 9:26 Daniel is told to "know therefore and understand that from the going forth of the commandment to restore and to build [again] Jerusalem unto the Messiah the Prince shall be seven weeks, and threescore and two weeks". This commandment was issued by Artaxerxes in 457 BC. Now, 7 + 62 weeks equals 483 "days", or the 483 years from 457 BC until the crucifixion of Christ in AD 30, taking into account the four-year calendar correction of 46 BC. So Daniel has correctly prophesied Christ's advent as the "Messiah the Prince".

The prophecy continues "after threescore and two weeks shall the Messiah be cut off [crucified], but not for himself: and [they shall be no more the Messiah's people]", implying the Jews' rejection of Jesus's claim to be the Messiah.

The destruction of the Temple of Jerusalem is then prophesied: "and the people of the prince that shall come shall destroy the city and the sanctuary" (9:26). This took place in 70 AD, which is suggested by the reference to one week seven days, in which "he shall confirm the covenant with many for one week: and in the midst of the week he shall cause the sacrifice and the oblation to cease".

In the last chapter Daniel asks "How long shall it be to the end of these wonders" (12:6). The inscrutable answer he receives is "it shall be for a time, times, and a half". Daniel, like us, complains "I heard, but I understand not". Two last numbers are supplied as boundary dates of the final apocalyptic events, "there shall be 1290 days. Blessed is he that waiteth, and cometh to the 1335 days. But go thy way till the end".

How should we reconcile these conflicting dates? It could be that after the destruction of the Temple in AD 70 there were 1290 "days" times one and a half ("time, and a half")? This would yield 1935 + 70, a beginning of apocalyptic events in 2005 AD.

Then "the end therefore shall be with a flood, and unto the end of the war desolations are determined." At this time the Archangel Michael, who protects Israel in time of trouble, will arise. The dead – "them that sleep in the dust of the earth" – shall awake; some, but not all, will be resurrected and granted immortality: they will shine like stars in the firmament. The less fortunate, for their part, will be condemned to everlasting shame and contempt.

Using the same logic on 1335, the final resurrection of the dead should take place halfway through the year AD 2072, when the blessed who have waited will ascend to the stars.

KEY NUMBERS IN THE BOOK OF DANIEL

The book of Daniel is a veritable mine of numbers with which to construct possible dates for the Apocalypse. General principles of such manipulation includes reading "year" for "day", a procedure endorsed by Ezekiel (4:6). The key numbers are: Time, times and half a time – either a factor of 1.5, or sometimes

3.5 years; this is also expressed as season, seasons and half a season. Two thousand three hundred evenings and mornings, possibly representing 2300 years. It is a key phrase for the Seventh Day Adventists . Seventy weeks, also 7 weeks, 62 weeks, and 1 week, making respectively 490, 49, 434 and 7 years. One thousand two hundred and ninety days and 1335 days times 1.5 for the dating of the Apocalypse. Daniel mourned for three whole weeks (10:2), by which a period of tribulations of 21 years may in fact be meant.

CHARIOTS OF FIRE

Did Ezekiel really see God's arrival in a chariot accompanied by cherubim, or was he simply tripping?

The date of the Book of the prophet Ezekiel is often put at 595–7 BC. The brief apocalypse incorporated in the Book dates from the same time of crisis in Jewish history as that depicted in the Book of Daniel. This crisis was precipitated by the attacks of the Babylonian king, Nebuchadnezzar. In the course of his war with the Egyptians, he captured Jerusalem and took back with him as hostages King Jehoiakim and his court. Ezekiel was a Jewish priest and prophet during this period of history.

The first chapter of Ezekiel, specifically verses 4 to 28, contains one of the most extraordinary descriptions of a vision ever written. What Ezekiel saw has been the subject of millions of words and many pictures, but in essence it was this:

A great whirlwind containing a very bright amber fire came from the north to the river Chebar, where Ezekiel was sitting. In the middle of this brightness were four creatures called cherubim. These beings had some of the physical characteristics of men (their hands, for example, were shaped like human hands), but only one of them had a human face – the others bore, respectively, the faces of a lion, ox and eagle, like the beasts of the Apocalypse of St John hundreds of years later. Each cherubim also had four long wings, two touching above their heads and two folded around their bodies, and above their heads were crystal halos like the night sky. Their feet were like a calf's and gleamed like brass. These beings looked more like the winged bulls of ancient Babylon than the Victorian conception of angels. Almost 700 years later St John, after he had swallowed the same substance, saw the same cherubim. Can we expect a similar visitation in the next few years?

The cherubim moved very rapidly backwards and forwards without moving their wings, making a sound like rushing water or a large crowd. They were accompanied by something resembling ball lightning and beryl-coloured wheels within wheels, like gyroscopes, which were full of bright eyes and did not turn as they moved. The cherubims flashed like lightning as they moved, and folded their wings downwards when they were still. Above the heads of the cherubim was a sapphire throne containing a fiery god who looked like an old man, surrounded by a multicoloured rainbow of splendour.

Without a doubt, such a detailed description is intended to make one believe that Ezekiel did actually witness this incredible scene. There is no attempt to describe the event in obscure, symbolic terms. Ezekiel really saw something fantastic. But was this extraordinary phenomenon one of the "chariots of the gods", a sort of early UFO, to use Erich von Daniken's phrase, or the arrival of some god, perhaps Jehovah himself?

Jehovah commands Ezekiel to get up from his prone position, and gives him instructions with regard to the Jews who were in exile. In true prophetic style, Jehovah outlines a number of punishments to be served out to Ezekiel's fellow countrymen for their hardheartedness and interest in idols. Ezekiel, however, is a reluctant bearer of bad tidings and much more at home as a visionary, so Jehovah has to provide some convincing arguments before he will agree to go back and threaten the people of Israel over their unacceptable conduct (3:17–22).

At the end of their conversation, the visitor takes off into the ether, or, as Ezekiel puts it: "I heard also the noise of the wings of the living creatures that touched one another, and the noise of the wheels over against them, and noise of a great rushing. So the spirit lifted me up, and took me away ..." (3:13-14). The temptation to ascribe these sounds to some advanced flying machine is almost overwhelming. It seems too palpable to have just been an internal vision.

If Christ returns to Earth at the millennium, for the second time, will He make a similarly spectacular entrance? Probably not is the answer. Jehovah was always much more of a showman than Christ. However, as next time Christ is due to arrive for the execution of the Last Judgement, perhaps He will adopt some of the fire and fury of His father, Jehovah.

PSYCHEDELIC VISIONS

Ezekiel's description of the arrival of Jehovah has the immediacy of a psychedelic vision, and even from our perspective, 2,500 years after the event, it is arresting. The idea that the prophet's vision may well have been drug-induced is not as outrageous as it seems. Consider these words by Ezekiel, "an hand was sent unto me; and lo, a roll of a book was therein ... moreover he said unto me ... eat this roll" (2:9–3:1). Ezekiel did as he was told, "so I opened my mouth, and ... did eat it". This substance was at once provided by his vision and helped to fuel it. It was a sort of sacrament, which was also a book with writing in it.

St John, as recorded in his Apocalypse almost 700 years later, was also told to eat a little book: "Give me the little book. And he said unto me, Take it, and eat it up; and it shall make thy belly bitter, but it shall be in thy mouth sweet as honey" (10:9).

If you think that in either of these instances a symbolic "eating" was meant, the words of Ezekiel refute the idea: he was to "cause thy belly to eat, and fill thy bowels with this roll that I give thee" (3:2–3). You can hardly get more anatomically specific than this!

Ezekiel and St John ingested something during the course of their visions which enabled them to see other dimensions, other times, and perhaps even the end of the world.

PERSECUTION AND PROPHECIES

Prophets were often less than welcome in their own countries.

Perhaps the most universally disliked and persecuted Hebrew

prophet was Jeremiah.

Jeremiah's first book of prophecies was cut to pieces and then burnt by his fellow-countrymen. He was often imprisoned under very unpleasant conditions for his apparently unpatriotic prophecies, and finished up attaching himself to the Babylonian governor for his own safety before fleeing to Egypt, where he was finally stoned to death for his lugubrious insights.

Many prophets seem to have had their vocation forced upon them rather than actively seeking it. Apart from the well-known prophets like Jeremiah there seem to have been bands of roving prophets as part of everyday life in ancient Israel, not necessarily all of them Jewish. Some in fact may have even been Philistine. For example, in Samuel 10:5 Saul is told:

"After that thou shalt come to the hill of God, where is the garrison of the Philistines: and it shall come to pass, when thou art come thither to the city, that thou shalt meet a company of prophets coming down from the high place with a psaltery, and a tabret, and a pipe, and a harp, before them; and they shall prophesy; and the Spirit of the Lord will come upon thee, and thou shalt prophesy with them, and shalt be turned into another man."

It seems as if Saul was incidentally initiated into the mysteries of prophecy in the company of these wandering Philistine prophets. The narrative continues with Saul's kinsmen being very surprised at his new-found prophetic talents.

One of the ongoing promises of the prophets has always been the arrival of a Messiah who will save the Jewish nation from whatever persecutors they happen to have at the time. The Jews looked forward, and still do, to the coming of a saviour, one born to the royal line of the house of David. Christ did not deliver them from the Romans, and was consequently dismissed by most Jews as a pseudo-Messiah.

For reasons which seem to be buried deep in the Jewish psyche, these periods of enslavement have always provoked the idea that they were a punishment for neglecting their god. This reaction is an extreme version of the almost universal religious idea that the world is ruled by a god or gods who dispense justice.

Having said this, the Jewish reaction, above that of all other religions, was to produce a series of prophets whose hallmarks were a warning against past misbehaviour as an explanation of present misfortune, and a promise of future bliss if their rules are adhered to. The repeated degradation and enslavement to pagan nations endured by the Jewish people and the resultant intense desire for the fulfilment of age-old prophecies of ultimate glory gave rise to a wealth of Jewish apocalyptic literature, and a strong expectation of the arrival or return of the Messiah.

The idea of a coming Messiah was a Christian inheritance from Judaism. Christianity, of course, maintained that the Messiah had arrived, and had shown Himself several times after the crucifixion to His disciples. The common belief was that He would soon return yet again, hence the concept of the Second Coming.

Many believed that He would return with an army, maybe even an army of angels, and triumph as a military saviour over their oppressors, the Romans. Early belief, before it was mythologized by Origen and St Augustine, was clearly in an earthly kingdom of God, not in some long-deferred heaven. But as the centuries rolled on the expectation was moved forward and hopes were pinned on years like AD 1000 or AD 2000.

From a purely military point of view, Egypt, then Babylon (the Persians) and, finally, the Romans were the main enemies of Israel and its smaller sister kingdom of Judah. Christian commentators have ceased to look at the historical perspective and often take the names of these countries as symbols of evil. Even the later Protestant view of Catholicism, with its headquarters in Rome, shares the feelings that the Jews of ancient Israel had for the conquering Roman armies, who eventually destroyed their Temple in AD 70.

The result of this is that apocalyptic writings, both Jewish and Christian, often speak of the destruction of Babylon (or in a more guarded way of the destruction of Rome), and the arrival of a saviour Messiah who, after a period of tribulations, will do physical battle with the enemies of the godly, often at Armageddon, before establishing a 1000-year kingdom here on earth. That, in a nutshell, is what is due to happen when the Apocalypse finally arrives.

JEWISH MYSTICAL AEONS

The Great Jubilee of 7000 years is a recurring theme in Jewish apocalyptic writings. (A full period of cosmic development is reckoned as seven times seven thousand years.) In the fifty-thousandth year the universe is expected to return to its source. This was first expounded in the book Temunah, written around AD 1250 and based on a new interpretation of the "Shemittah" or Aeon.

The current 7000-year period is one of judgement, with its attendant commandments and prohibitions, and opposition between pure and impure, holy and unholy.

In the Aeon due at the end of this century, the next Shemittah, the law or Torah will no longer contain prohibitions, the power of evil will be curbed and Utopia will be realized, like the 1000-year reign of the Messiah. This idea is very like that of the 12th-century Calabrian Christian visionary Joachim of Fiore, which outlined three cosmic periods – those of the Father, the Son and the Holy Spirit.

THE GREEK PROPHETESSES

Prophecy is not the exclusive province of Old Testament prophets. The Greek words for prophetic power are "manteia" and "propheteia".

The word "prophetes" means "a person who speaks for someone else", which is exactly what a prophet does in speaking for a god.

The ancient Greeks consulted the will of the gods on all important occasions of public and private life, such as the sale of slaves, cultivation of a field, marriages, voyages, loans and so on. The oracle was not merely a revelation to satisfy the curiosity of man, but a sanction or authorization by the deity for what was intended.

Cassandra, daughter of King Priam, was given the gift of prophecy by the god of the sun, Apollo. In vain she foretold the fall of Troy, in which she was captured and ravished by Ajax, but no one believed her until it was too late and the prophecy had come true.

Apart from those given the gift of prophecy by the gods themselves, there were also trained priestesses of Apollo, called Pythia or Sibyls. The most famous of the Sibyls was the Cumaean Sibyl, who is reputed to have guided Aeneas on his journey through the underworld. The entrance to this underworld was near

Baia on the Bay of Naples, in Italy (and still exists). An oracle book purporting to contain the sayings of these Sibyls, called The Sibylline Oracles, was very popular in the Middle Ages.

The most celebrated of all oracles was the oracle of Apollo at Delphi whose name was Pytho. The word Pytho means to consult as well as "to putrify", a reference to the fumes which arose from a cleft in the earth at Delphi and which were sometimes said to be the stench from the corpse of the dead serpent that once inhabited the chasm. These fumes intoxicated the priestess, who uttered the god's warnings in a trance. It is possible that the fumes acted as a hallucinogenic. In the inner sanctuary, the priestess sat on a high golden tripod (a three legged chair) above the cleft from which issued the conscious-altering fumes, in front of a golden statue of Apollo, the sun god. An eternal fire fed with resinous fir wood blazed in front of the statue. The inner roof of the temple was covered with laurel garlands and upon the altar laurel was burnt as an incense – a heady mixture indeed.

In response to a question put to her the priestess would rapidly enter a state of delirious intoxication, uttering a stream of words, moans, and sounds which one of the five priests or "prophetes" would write down and later interpret. These interpretations were often presented in verse in the form of hexameters. Sometimes the effect of the smoke upon the priestess was so great that she leapt or fell from the tripod, fell into convulsions, and sometimes died. For this reason, in later times three priestesses were kept on standby.

Those who consulted the oracle had to wear laurel-garlands tied with virgin wool, to pay a fee, and then sacrifice a goat, ox or sheep, which had to be a perfect, healthy specimen.

The divine agency in Pytho was first discovered by shepherds whose sheep fell into convulsions when they approached the chasm over which the temple was later built. People from all over the ancient world flocked to consult this oracle, not just from Greece. It did not lose its power until the sanctuary was done away with by the Christian Emperor Theodosius in the 4th century AD.

There were at least 20 other well- known oracles in the Greek world, of which the most interesting to us is the oracle of Apollo at Didyma, usually called the oracle of the Branchidae, in the territory of Miletus. This was the oracle usually consulted by the Ionians and Aeolians. The altar itself was said to have been constructed by Heracles, and the temple by Branchus, a son of Apollo, who had come as a priest from the oracle at Delphi.

The cult relied upon the mediumship of inspired priestesses, and the techniques employed to obtain their divine intoxication were described by the Greek Iamblichus of Chalcis, who died in about AD 335:

"The prophetess of Branchus either sits upon a pillar, or holds in her hand a rod bestowed by some deity, or moistens her feet or the hem of her garment with water ... and by these means ... she prophesies."

Another passage in the same ancient text mentions the use of a bronze tripod in a rite of prophecy. This oracle is of particular interest to us because it used the techniques of prophecy which were later borrowed by Nostradamus, who in 1555 used them to discover the darkest secrets of the millennium and the events leading up to the year 2000 (see previous chapters).

CLOCKS OF STONE

The reason for the construction of the Great Pyramid at Giza has been lost in the mists of history. For the Victorians it became the centre of enormous prophetic activity: they felt the world was about to pass through the last portal into the King's Chamber, heralding the end of time.

THE HOROSCOPE FOR AD 2000

Astrology can help us to take the pulse of the future. Among the pivotal dates looming on our horizon, that of 18 August 1999 is one of the most widely known.

This date was given prominence by Professor Hideo Itokawa, the pioneer of Japan's rocket technology, in his book and in a documentary made for television in 1980.

If we examine the astrological configuration for the first minute of this date, we find Sun, Mercury and Venus in the zodiacal sign Leo, the Lion with the Moon and Mars in Scorpio, the Eagle with Pluto closely alongside in Sagittarius,

Jupiter and Saturn in Taurus, the Bull with Uranus and Neptune in Aquarius, the Water Bearer. The four signs in which the planets are quartered are the four beasts of the Apocalypse of St John, the four heads of the cherubim of Ezekiel, and the four symbols on the last card of the tarot pack, the World. They are symbols for the so-called "four last things".

Professor Itokawa and his team of like-minded pessimistic futurologists were so fascinated by this so-called Grand Cross formed by the planets that he predicted widespread environmental devastation caused by conflict over energy and food resources. What the professor may have overlooked, however, is that very close to his Grand Cross – one week before it in fact, on 11 August 1999 – there will be an eclipse, the last eclipse of the 20th century. It is tempting to surmise that this eclipse will act as the catalyst and release the destructive energies of the Grand Cross.

In March 1993 we had a foretaste of what this Grand Cross holds in store for us with the conjunction of Neptune and Uranus, an extremely rare phenomenon which only occurs once in every 171 years. In the United States the conjunction was accompanied by "the single biggest blizzard storm this century", which swept from Florida to Maine, releasing more snow, hail, rain and sleet than any other similar phenomenon since 1888. It was followed by catastrophic flooding in the region of the Mississippi. The extraordinary weather that afflicted large parts of the States in 1993 may be put down to the imperfect motion of these planets.

It is not a coincidence that Neptune, or Poseidon, was the god of water, particularly rivers and seas. His wife, Amphitrite, held sway over the sea as well as winds and earthquakes – we may well hear from her again before the end of the century.

Another extremely rare configuration involving all the planets, and one which has been misrepresented as a Grand Cross by some writers, will be formed on 4 May 2000 at exactly 3.12am Greenwich Mean Time. On this day the Earth will find itself in opposition to the planets, at 13 degrees 58 minutes of Scorpio, with only distant Pluto, at 11 degrees 21 minutes of Sagittarius, providing any gravitational muscle against the rest.

This mighty conjunction of planets will not be observable to the naked eye, and becomes clear in the mind only when it is plotted on paper. At right angles to the Earth, forming a "square" aspect of 90 degrees, will be the two other outer planets, Uranus and Neptune; Uranus at 17 degrees 46 minutes of Aquarius, and Neptune at 4 degrees 40 minutes of Aquarius. The inner planets of the solar system will line up as follows: Venus at 19 degrees 23 minutes of Aries; Mercury at 20 degrees 8 minutes of Aries; Moon at 13 degrees 24 minutes of Taurus; Sun at 13 degrees 58 minutes of Taurus; Jupiter at 17 degrees 31 minutes of Taurus; Saturn at 20 degrees 12 minutes of Taurus; Venus at 10 degrees 56 minutes of Gemini.

Astrologers have a compelling term for this unique configuration: "opposition".

Who knows what natural disturbances might occur on Earth as a result of the gravitational pull of the entire inner solar system being pitted against us?

CHAOS THEORY – BUTTERFLY WINGS AND AXIAL WOBBLES

Although it could be said that the planets are too far away to have any effect on us here on Earth, you have only to examine the so-called chaos theory to realize that changes in the delicately balanced solar system may indeed be extremely significant. This theory holds that all forms of life on earth are interconnected; even the fluttering of a butterfly's wings in the Amazon can be indirectly associated with a typhoon in Hong Kong, or so the theory runs. Applying this logic, the combined gravitational pull of the other planets occupying the solar system – especially the two heaviest, Jupiter and Saturn – are not to be dismissed as irrelevant.

The line-up of such heavyweights with the Sun and the Moon could well activate sunspots, affect tides, and disturb the highly tuned crustal balance of the Earth to produce natural catastrophes such as tsunamis (tidal waves), flooding, volcanic activity and freak weather conditions.

The most extreme disaster scenario that might be produced by this configuration could involve a shift in the position of the Earth's axis. This has been demonstrated to move over time, so that the magnetic North Pole and the geographic north pole continue to drift further and further apart. Any shock to this already unstable system might cause a big "wobble".

ASTROLOGICAL PROPHECIES

A connection between astrology and the Apocalypse may seem improbable, but history shows that there has been much agreement between the casters of charts and the church authorities.

Through the ages prophets and astrologers alike have regarded the movements of the planets, particularly those of Saturn and Jupiter, as significant; Nostradamus, for example, used them to date future events.

The cyclical nature of the revolution of the planets led early astrologers to assume that all life, including man's life and history, was governed by cycles. These cycles might even be multiples of the time it took the outer planets to revolve round the Sun. In this period of history the two outer planets were Jupiter (taking 11.862 years) and Saturn (taking 29.458 years). It is no coincidence that the Roman god Saturn corresponds with the Greek Cronos, the god of Time and one-time ruler of the heavens.

The "Annus Magnus", or Great Year, was conceived as being the period of time it would take for the planets to return to their starting point on the first day of Creation. The return to this point would obviously be a very significant date, they reasoned. Greek philosophers like Zeno believed that the events of one age in history were repeated in another, just as human souls reincarnated.

Another Greek, the astronomer Aristarchus of Samos (c. 250 BC), who taught that the Earth moves round the Sun and who calculated the distance from the Sun to the Earth, believed that this Great Year was 2,484 ordinary years in length. Heraclitus (535–475 BC) calculated the Great Year at 10,800 years. A more valid time cycle, however, is the Precession of the Equinoxes (see below).

In medieval Europe attempts to date the Second Coming of Christ were based on both astrological and Biblical data. The famous astronomer Tycho Brahe interpreted a new star he discovered in 1572 as a herald of the Second Coming, a view later endorsed by King James I of England. Tycho linked the star to the appearance of a great northern ruler, also mentioned by Nostradamus. This new star played a part in the millennarian speculations of Sir Christopher Heydon in 1618. Heydon prophesied the seventh return of Jupiter and Saturn "to the fiery trigon" which would bring about the destruction of the papacy, the fall of the Turks, and the return of the Jews to the new "kingdom of Christ".

The Jewish astrologer "Master Salomon" drew on astrological evidence to predict that Charles V was about to defeat the Turks, leading to the conversion of the Jews and the second coming of Christ.

A certain symmetry of dating was expected of events directly involving God. As the Flood, for example, was estimated to have occurred in 1656 Anno Mundi (ie 2348 BC), so an equally momentous upheaval, perhaps the Second Coming, was assumed for AD 1656. An additional 10 years brought commentators to the highly significant "Beast's Millennium" of 1666 AD.

The German astrologer Mussemius decided that as Christ's birth had followed a conjunction of Saturn and Jupiter in the zodiacal sign of Virgo, the Antichrist would be born when these planets met each other again on the opposite side of the zodiac in Pisces, in 1544. A later attempt to use this conjunction was made by the Bohemian astrologer Cyprian Leowitz, who predicted the end of the world based on the conjunction of Saturn and Jupiter in 1583.

Richard Harvey predicted the world would end at noon on 28 April 1583, when Christ would appear.

Johannes Alsted, who derived some of his ideas from Tycho Brahe and the astronomer Johannes Kepler, regarded the Reformation as merely the prologue to the millennial reign of Christ. His "Speculum Mundi" is a large table on which he synchronized the three eras and seven ages of Elias with the four monarchies of Daniel and the revolutions of Saturn and Jupiter.

THE PRECESSION OF
THE EQUINOXES

The key astronomical concept lying behind the theory of the cycle of the ages, or aeons, is the Precession of the Equinoxes. This astronomical phenomenon was first discovered by the ancient Egyptians. Hipparchus (c. 120 BC) found that the longitude of the stars regularly increases by 50.2 seconds of longitude every year, or, to put it another way, the apparently "fixed" belt of zodiacal stars actually moves, albeit very slowly. This is caused by the axis of the Earth describing a very gradual backwards circle as the Earth spins, a bit like a wobbly toy top.

The axis makes a complete rotation in 25,725 years (which is usually approximated to 25,600 years, or even 25,000 years). This backwards movement through the zodiacal signs means that a particular date – that of the Equinox, for example – will gradually move from one sign to another at the rate of one sign every 2,143 years. The dawning of the Age of Aquarius occurs as the polar axis leaves the sign of Pisces, where it has been for over 2,000 years, and moves backwards into Aquarius.

THE PYRAMIDS AND
PROPHECY

In 1864 Professor Piazzi Smyth, Astronomer Royal for Scotland, spent four months at Giza in Egypt trying to work out the mathematical relationships between prophecy and the dimensions of the Great Pyramid.

Professor Smyth's most astonishing observation was the accuracy with which the ratio of height to circumference of the base represents ½ pi. He concluded that the "sacred cubit" used by the builders of this enormous monument was the same length (25.025 imperial inches) as the one used by Moses to construct the tabernacle. With this assumption the measurements took on a life of their own.

33The oppressive passageways of the Great Pyramid are extraordinary only for the sheer weight of stone encasing them. From these few passageways the enthusiastic Christian Robert Menzies and his followers devised, or decoded, a plan which spelt out the pyramid's wider and deeper significance. Every inch of the tunnels was measured, converted into years and then matched with Biblical chronology.

The outside entrance of the pyramid was taken to represent Creation (in 4004 BC) and the Fall of Adam, the entrance of the downward sloping tunnel the Flood, and its intersection with the upward sloping tunnel the Exodus from Egypt in 1615 BC. The point at which the upward-sloping tunnel broadened into the "Grand Gallery" represented the birth of Christ, while the doorstep at its mouth symbolized Christ's life and crucifixion in AD 33.

The Victorians' certainty in Christian progress was reflected in several areas. The Grand Gallery itself was seen as the upwards progress of Christianity over 2000 years, or the "Gospel Dispensation of Grace". The King's Chamber marked the "passage into heavenly bliss of the saved". The entrance to the King's Chamber and its antechamber are of most relevance to us today, for it is this part of the pyramid which is supposed to correlate with the period of history we are now entering upon.

Morton Edgar, one of Menzies' followers, believed that the millennial age of bliss would come about in 1874. He reached this figure by taking 4128 BC as the year of Creation. Working on the assumption that Edgar was 124 years too early, and taking instead Archbishop Ussher's date of 4004 BC, the millennial age, according to the Great Pyramid, should coincide with the year 1998. Edgar also dated the end of the millennial age and final test for humanity at AD 2914.

Davidson, co-author of The Great Pyramid: Its Divine Message, identified the low passage between the Antechamber and the King's Chamber as representing the period 1928 to 1936; in one sense the narrowing of this passage does reflect the conditions of the Depression following the Wall Street crash of 1929.

Max Toth's interpretation of the measurements highlights July 1992 as the end of the passageway and the beginning of what he terms as "end time". Toth predicts fierce storms and volcanic eruptions from 1995. He claims that a Kingdom of the Spirit (after Joachim of Fiore) will emerge after a period of tribulations ending in the collapse of civilization in AD 2025. The Messiah will appear in the sky in AD 2034 and six years later will assume a human appearance and live on Earth for 76 years.

Flinders Petrie dismissed the supposed correlation between human history and the passages of the Great Pyramid by re-surveying the Pyramid and correcting Smyth's errors of measurement. To add insult to injury, he showed that the end of the current dispensation should have come on 18 August 1882. To keep hopes alive, one Colonel J. Garnier shifted the date, gauged from the measurements marking the outer entrance to the antechamber of the King's Chamber, to 1913.

Their eagerness to fix the date of the Second Coming of Christ within their own lifetime led the Victorian millenarians to change the rule. The "inch to a year" rule gives the following interesting set of dates. Immediately after the entrance date of 1913, 51.95 inches bring us through the opening and into the Antechamber in late 1964. The other side of the Antechamber is reached in 116.26 inches, or 2082, which then enters another low passage running from 2082 to 2182. The entrance to the King's Chamber represents 2182, while its final wall and ending is reached in 2388. Only time will tell!

A NEW CHAMBER IN

THE GREAT PYRAMID

In early 1993 a German researcher, Rudolf Gantenbrink, discovered a new chamber in the Great Pyramid. Using a remote-controlled device, he probed to the end of a 45 degree sloping air duct 210 feet (65 metres) long and only 8 inches (20 centimetres) wide and high. At the end of this passage is a miniature stone door, possibly made of alabaster or yellow limestone with possibly grooves to slide it upwards. A scatter of fine black dust suggests the presence of organic material and a considerable chamber the other side of sufficient size to allow air currents to circulate.

It is inconceivable that tomb robbers have gained access to the passageway, so the contents of the chamber must be intact. The chamber is situated deep in the rock of the pyramid, some 65 feet (21.5 metres) above the floor of the King's Chamber and 80 feet (25 metres) from the outer facing of the pyramid, on an alignment possibly directly opposite the mysterious Dog Star Sirius, associated with the goddess Isis. Coincidentally (or perhaps not) the distance vertically between the Queen's Chamber and the King's Chamber is also precisely 65 feet (21.5 metres).

THE 60-YEAR CYCLE

In 1985 Dr Ravi Batra published a book in which he accurately predicted the onset of the recession in 1989.

According to Dr Batra, this recession would be characterized by a great increase in unemployment, a decrease in inflation, a rapid fall in property prices and a marked rise in business failures – all adverse economic events which came true in many countries around the world.

Dr Batra suggested that real estate investments should be sold at the end of 1989 and business indebtedness should be reduced – perfect timing, as it turns out. Yet he never claimed to be a prophet, merely a close observer of economic cycles. Dr. Batri has compared events of the 1990s with those of the 1930s. According to his reckoning, 1996 will mark the end of this recession, just as 1936 marked the end of the previous one. The study of cycles might well be a useful adjunct in determining the timing of prophecies.

Sixty years is a recurring timespan to be found in many cultures. It is, for example, the exact time specified by the ancient Chinese for the completion of one "Great Year', during which all possible combinations of events as described by the interaction of the 10 Celestial Stems and 12 Earthly Branches of Chinese metaphysics are supposed to happen. After 60 years, everyone comes back to exactly the same Chinese year combination of Branch and Stem as the year they were born in.

The sexagenary characters representing the Chinese 60-year period are called dragons. Each has one of the five Chinese elements – Wood, Fire, Earth, Metal and Water – ascribed to it with one of the 12 zodiacal animals.

The Egyptians associated the period of 60 years with Osiris, the god of (among other things) cycles, death and resurrection. The "henti" period of his cycle consisted of two periods, each of 60 years' duration.

The ancient Greeks pinpointed the reason for selecting a 60-year cycle. The Neoplatonist Olympiodorus, who lived in Alexandria, wrote:

"… the sphere of Saturn and the sphere of Jupiter are conjoined with each other in their revolutions, sixty years. For if the sphere of Jupiter comes from the same [place in the heavens] to the same in twelve years, but that of Saturn in thirty years, it is evident that when Jupiter has made five, Saturn will have made two revolutions: for twice thirty is sixty, and so likewise is twelve times five; so that their revolutions will be conjoined in sixty years."

Among the Babylonians, the priest Berossus (flourished 260 BC) mentions three extended periods of time, the "sossus" (60 years) and multiples of it, the "neros" of 600 years and the "sarus" of 3600 years, or 60 squared. Two of the last mentioned amount to just over seven millennia, or one week of God, a period used by the Jews to indicate the completion of a full cycle.

Josephus Flavius, who lived in Rome during the first century AD, tells us that ancient time was divided into periods of 600 years. In the manuscript of Liber Vaticinationem, 60 is a key period. Later Nostradamus would express the dating of some of his quatrains in terms of the 60-year conjunctions of Jupiter and Saturn.

All the above precedents indicate that, for the purposes of prediction, it may be more revealing to divide up the past and also the future in cyclical periods of 60 years rather than centuries.

THE SAROS CYCLE

One particularly interesting component of the 60-year cycle is the Saros cycle, which was first discovered by the Chaldeans. The cycle is 6585.32 days' long, or 18 years 10.7 days or the equivalent of 19 eclipse years.

The connection between this cycle and the 60-year cycle is made by dividing 60 by 18. If the answer, 3.333, is then multiplied by 60, we get exactly AD 2000, a further pointer to the prophetic and millennial significance of that year.

We have already seen how the 60-year cycle has been used to predict economic events. The Saros cycle would seem to have a similar potential. Coincidentally, one of the most successful financiers and currency speculators of the 1990s is called George Soros. In the autumn of 1992 his speculative activities against sterling caused the British Treasury to use millions of pounds in a futile support operation. On a bleak day for British self-esteem, "Black Wednesday", the pound was withdrawn from the European Monetary System and allowed to "float", effectively downwards to reflect its true value in the market. Thus, through a series of shrewd speculative gambles, Mr Soros added the pound to a list of devaluations of weak European currencies.

It is not known whether Soros relies on business instinct or a proper method of calculation. Some "bets" on currency markets are based on the use of charts revealing cyclical fluctuations. It is possible that the Soros cycle of just over 18 years was involved in George Soros' calculations. Certainly, the movements of the pound in 1974, 18 years earlier, make interesting reading.

SUNSPOTS – THE SUN'S CYCLE

A feature of the surface of the Sun which varies from day to day is its sunspots. These correspond with a clear cycle which matches the rotational cycle of Jupiter.

Sunspots are areas of lower temperature which appear as black spots by contrast with the rest of the Sun's surface. They have been known to man since ancient times, when enormous ones visible to the naked eye were supposed to herald important events. They were first recorded in Europe in 1610, but only in detail from the beginning of the 18th century. Samuel Schwabe was the first to discover their periodic rise and fall, in 1843. In China they have been observed since AD 188.

For the most part, sunspots occur just north or just south of the Sun's equator, between 10 and 30 degrees north or south; they are never seen near the Sun's poles. They have strong magnetic fields which change in polarity according to the cycle. The average spot lasts for a week before it "decays"; some last only a day and some for several months. A large sunspot may cover an area five times the width of the Earth.

For reasons nobody fully understands, sunspot activity seems to follow a pattern, occurring in regular cycles which are virtually identical to the 11.86 year Jupiter cycle. There was an extremely high peak from 1947 to 1950, and an even larger one in 1957. These peaks of activity seem to be accelerating as we reach the end of the millennium. It may be that large numbers of sunspots are indicative of some kind of basic change in the relationship of the Sun to the Earth and the rest of the solar system.

At one time science was baffled by sunspots and offered various explanations: for example, Kirchhoff identified them as solar clouds; Zollner, less imaginatively, as slag deposits; and Hale, appropriately perhaps, as electromagnetic storms. There is a definite connection between magnetic storms and large sunspots, and for 60 years or more it has been accepted that climatic changes on the Earth, such as exceptionally high rainfall and severe drought, have been connected with their cycle. Climatic aberrations are becoming more frequent as we approach the millennium and it may be that sunspots will play a part in the cyclical climax arriving around the year AD 2000. The planets are thought to affect sunspot activity, an idea that ties in with the expected changes predicted for May 2000 when the planets will line up against the Earth.

Each outbreak of sunspots is accompanied by an upsurge in the emission of every kind of solar energy, X-rays, ultraviolet, radio waves and visible light. This energy emission, called the solar wind, causes significant changes in the Earth's environment. It may well be that these changes will herald a cataclysmic event at the end of the century.

In recent years an enormous amount of computer time and effort has been expended on trying to correlate sunspot activity with a variety of other phenomena, ranging from stock market cycles to tree growth rings. Trees certainly show an 11-year cycle in their rings, but there is as yet little evidence to support the notion of a connection between sunspots and economic cycles.

An interesting correlation from which no satisfactory conclusions have yet been drawn is that between peak sunspot activity and periods of intensive UFO sighting, as well as periods of variation in the Earth's magnetic declination.

SUNSPOTS, WEATHER

AND THE PLANETS

Meteorologists recognize the effect of the 11.5-year sunspot cycle on the weather. A great increase in sunspot activity produces a heavily ionized solar wind which causes bad weather on Earth, resulting in poor harvests and higher crop prices. The correlation between a rash of sunspots and storms seems strongest in certain parts of the world, such as Siberia, Scandinavia, the West Indies, southeastern USA and possibly the South Pacific.

The sunspot cycle has also been shown to correlate with shifts in the jetstream. Wild weather is more likely to happen at both solar maxima and minima. The next minima which might well provoke more wild weather is 1999, just before the millennium.

The sunspot cycle has been used successfully to predict drought. In the 1950s it was prophesied that severe drought would occur in 1975/6; in Britain these years turned out to be the hottest and driest summers on record this century. According to the cycle, 1998 and 2021 will also be years of severe drought. The former date fits in with other prophecies of famine and drought leading up to the millennium.

Professor Wood of Colorado University has discovered a mega sunspot cycle of 179 years. Thus in 1778 the number of sunspots was very high, in fact a record. Exactly 179 years later, in 1957, a new peak for sunspot activity was recorded. A report written for NASA by Prescott Sleeper in 1972 suggested that this might have been due to Jupiter, Saturn and Uranus coming into a three-way conjunction, by their estimate every 178.9527 years, representing 6 revolutions of Saturn and 15 revolutions of Jupiter.

THE PLANETARY

CONJUNCTIONS

The significance of the conjunctions of Jupiter and Saturn has a history extending back to the Babylonians, when the planets were used as the time-keepers of the 60-year cycle.

More recently, a great deal of interest has been shown in the degree to which the movements of these two planets influence the Earth's climate.

The first to start the debate rolling were John Gribbin and Stephen Plagemann in a book called *The Jupiter Effect*, in which they tried to show how the configurations of the planets indirectly affect both climatic and geological events on Earth. The authors, one a NASA scientist and the other a former staff writer for the science journal Nature, examined sunspot activity, an increase in which they thought could be related to earthquakes. Sunspot activity was also, they believed, associated with the configuration of the planets in the solar system.

These connections might shed light on some ancient mysteries, and also be relevant to events at the end of the millennium. Their first point was that the movement of all the planets in the solar system can and does affect the Sun.

Of all the planets, the one with the greatest effect on the Sun is Jupiter. This influence is brought to bear by its huge mass, which is 318 times that of the Earth. Saturn, 95 times "heavier" than the Earth, is the second largest planet. Obviously, when both planets line up in the same part of the sky, their gravitational effect is reinforced. Astrology refers to this as conjunction, so we can safely say that astrological conjunctions, particularly those of the two heaviest planets Jupiter and Saturn, have a gravitational effect upon the Sun.

The work of Professor K. D. Wood of the University of Colorado has shown how gravitational pull can result in surface disturbances such as solar flares and increased sunspot activity. In 1973 he graphed sunspot activity against gravitational variations imposed by the heavier planets. Professor Wood's findings explain why the average sunspot cycle of about 11.5 years varies: the changing pattern of the planets increases or decreases sunspot activity.

So sunspots reflect major changes in the Sun's magnetic field, which affects every planet in the solar system. They can ruffle the usual calm of the ionosphere, a layer of atmosphere 200 miles (322 kilometres) above the surface of the Earth composed of ions and charged particles. It is the ionosphere which, when calm, acts as a reflector of radio waves which can be bounced back to Earth. Little wonder, then, that radio transmissions on Earth suffer interference in times of increased sunspot activity. The latter also signals a time of wild and unsettled weather worldwide.

The changes in the electromagnetic field of the Sun also affect the magma under the Earth's crust or lithosphere, producing additional stresses and strains which can only be released by earthquakes, sometimes volcanic activity, and slippage of one tectonic plate against another. Such events often need only a tiny trigger, for the stresses will have already built up to a point where a small additional stress will cause a major catastrophe, like the San Andreas fault slip in California of 18 April 1906, which, incidentally, occurred shortly after a conjunction of Jupiter and Pluto. Another recent example is the earthquake in Turkey of 22 May 1971, which occurred in the same month as a conjunction of

Jupiter and Neptune. The earthquake in the Liaoning province in Manchuria in February 1975 coincided with a conjunction of Jupiter and Venus.

The conjunction of Jupiter and Saturn causes not just sunspots but the type of events which the ancient prophets always associated with the apocalypse: turbulent weather, earthquakes and volcanic activity.

ANCIENT PREDICTIONS
OF NATURAL DISASTERS

One astrologer at the court of Ninevah was aware of the connections between astrological conjunctions and natural disasters. More than 2600 years ago, he wrote: "When Mars approaches Jupiter, there will be great devastation in the land." Ninevah lies in an area that is prone to earthquakes, so the priests and astrologers who kept records of such natural phenomena had a range of data on which to work. To be used for the purposes of making a prediction, however, conjunctions of the planets need to be supported by other astrological configurations.

The Babylonian priest Berossus writes: "All terrestrial things will be consumed when the planets, which now are traversing their different courses, shall all coincide [come into conjunction] in the sign of Cancer, and so be placed that a straight line could pass directly through all their orbs. But the inundation will take place when the same conjunction of the planets shall occur in Capricorn. In the first is the summer, in the last the winter of the year." [Seneca Nat. Quaest. III:29].

Censorinus goes further, stating that these are two separate events; the one in the northern hemisphere summer (when the Sun is in Cancer) will be a conflagration, or Ecpyrosis, while the other in winter (when the Sun is in Capricorn) will be a cataclysm or deluge. The Biblical deluge is seen as one example of this. One "Great Year" after Noah's deluge, Censorinus expected the planets to return to the same conjunction and precipitate another Flood.

CHRIST'S SECRETS

Some of the teachings imparted by Christ to his

disciples remain secrets to all but a few to this day.

Hostages to scholarship, and long lost to the Church,

the manuscripts which contain these secrets may

shed much needed light on what awaits us at

the millennium.

EARLY CHRISTIAN
PROPHECIES

In the New Testament, both John the Baptist and Jesus

are called prophets, men who continue the tradition of conveying the

will of God to His people.

Jesus was sometimes taken to be a reincarnation of one of the ancient prophets. In Mark 8:27, he asks "Whom do men say that I am?" The consensus of opinion seems to have been that he was a reincarnation of either John the Baptist, Elias, or one of the Old Testament prophets. It is hard to see how he could have been a reincarnation of the prophet by whom he was baptized, but that has not deterred the believers in this theory.

In the next chapter of Mark (9:1), Jesus makes a prophecy about the coming kingdom of God: "Verily I say unto you, that there be some of them that stand here, which shall not taste of death, till they have seen the kingdom of God come with power."

It is no wonder that many early Christians expected the end of the world and the coming of the kingdom of God within their lifetime. They would have been even more surprised to learn that after two millenniums it has still not arrived. Jesus may have been speaking in the personal sense of initiation into the mysteries of the kingdom of God before their death, but many must have read his words as a prediction of the end of the world.

This prospect of the arrival of the kingdom of God arose again after 1000 years, and again in the year 1033, one millennium after the death of Christ. Another favourite millennial year was 1666, 1000 years after the birth of Christ plus 666, the number of the Second Beast of the Apocalypse of St John. Now, the imminent arrival of the end of the second millennium is supported by astrological and indeed astronomically significant signs and "heavenly markers" which have led many observers to wonder if perhaps ours really is the time predicted so many generations ago.

In the time of the early Christian church, members who had the special gift of uttering words (sometimes in foreign languages) while in a trance were called prophets, thus expanding the pre-Christian idea of specially trained and "contacted" prophets. These people, sometimes also called "charismatics", were "inspired" by God with an intelligible message. They were very different from so-called "speakers in tongues", who babbled in a language that was unintelligible to their listeners.

After the death of its founder Christianity fought a long, hard struggle against the pagan cults. Many strange doctrines derived from the Greeks, many of whom were early literate converts to Christianity. It is not often realized that all the New Testament scriptures were written in Greek – a language that Jesus himself did not speak.

Much of the early, more direct, experience of religion, such as "travelling in the spirit" or visiting the third heaven while still alive, have been filtered out of official Christian doctrine. Other Gnostic ideas were squeezed out of mainstream Christian thought to resurface in 20th-century theosophy or occultism.

The wonderfully detailed images of the Apocalypse of St John have been drawn on ever since they were written, by people attempting to pierce the veil of the future and determine what the turn of the millennium may have in store for us.

WHAT IS ESCHATOLOGY?

Eschatology, a Greek word meaning "last discourse", is the doctrine of the four last things. It is concerned with the events destined to happen at the end of the world, according to Christian doctrines. There are two different aspects to eschatology.

Individual eschatology is concerned with what happens to man after death. Most people regard death as the end of their personal world. Some sects believe that man lies in the grave until the universal judgement at the end of the world.

The Seventh-Day Adventists, for example, believe that "the condition of man in death is one of unconsciousness. That all men, good and evil alike, remain in the grave from death to the resurrection" (Fundamental Beliefs, article 10).

General eschatology is concerned with what happens to the world at the end of time, which is the subject of the Apocalypses. The four "last things" supposed to happen at that time are:

- The return of Christ, or the Second Coming
- The resurrection of the dead from their graves
- The Last Judgement of the dead and those who are still living at that time (the "quick")
- The final recompense, or separation, into the saved and the damned.

RESURRECTION AND VAMPIRES

The early Christians believed in bodily resurrection. Their conviction was that human life is inseparable from bodily experience: if a man comes back to life from the dead, he must come back in physical form.

The early Christian fathers Irenaeus and Tertullian both emphasized the anticipation of bodily resurrection. The Gnostic Christians on the other hand, who ridiculed the concept of bodily resurrection, thought that spiritual resurrection was the norm and frequently devalued the body, considering its actions unimportant to the "spiritual body".

Christ's resurrection is a central tenet of Christianity. If he had not risen from the dead, he would be considered as just another spiritual teacher. Some religions celebrate cycles of life, death and rebirth in other forms, and only Christianity insists on the return to life of one individual, Jesus Christ. This new departure in religious thought represented a turning point in world history. Despite the specific statement in the Christian scriptures that Jesus of Nazareth was "crucified, dead, and buried" and rose "on the third day", many modern theologians seem to be uncomfortable with the idea of his physical resurrection. Christ, so the scriptures tell us, ate a piece of fish to demonstrate to his disciples that he was not a ghost, and even asked Thomas to feel the wound in his side.

Tertullian (c. AD 190) defined the orthodox viewpoint by stating that "as Christ rose bodily from the grave, so every believer should anticipate the resurrection of the flesh ... The salvation of the soul I believe needs no discussion. What is raised is this flesh, suffused with blood, built up with bones, interwoven with nerves, entwined with veins". Tertullian goes on to declare that anyone who denies the resurrection of the flesh is a heretic, which presumably means that many modern Christians are heretics.

The phrase "suffused with blood" has a familiar ring, for it has been used in almost every description of a vampire ever penned! A vampire is one who has risen from his grave some time before the general resurrection of the dead, and who troubles his neighbours by slaking his thirst for blood at their expense. If you believe, as did the early Christians, in a bodily resurrection, then a vampire is simply un-dead before his time.

There are many strange parallels between orthodox Christian belief and belief in vampires. The early Christians, for example, specifically used catacombs, underground charnel houses, as places of worship (see below). From time immemorial, particularly in eastern Europe, there has been a tradition of vampire resurrections from such tombs. Those who have become vampires have become so by having had their blood drunk by an existing vampire. Interestingly, the central sacrament of Christianity has been the drinking of the blood of Christ. This was first done on the night before his death and became, as a consequence, a part of Christian practice.

The communion consumption of Christ's blood is accompanied by a rubric suggesting that this blood offers life everlasting. Tradition has it that vampires also live forever, or at least for very long periods of time. The cure for vampires is said to be a stake in the heart. Eccarius pointed out that the centurion's lance thrust into the side of Christ was designed to save any further pain by killing the man on the cross, and should effectively have prevented a resurrection.

The story of St Peter denying his Lord three times before cock-crow receives an echo in vampire folklore, which holds that the vampire must return to his tomb before cock-crow.

As if to prove the generality of physical resurrection, in St Matthew it is recorded (27:50–53) that at the time of Christ's death upon the cross a number of other men who were dead rose from their graves and roamed the streets: "the earth did quake, and the rocks rent; and the graves were opened; and many bodies ... came out of the graves after his resurrection, and went into the holy city [Jerusalem], and appeared unto many."

CATACOMBS AND CHRISTIANS

Why were many early Christian ceremonies held in catacombs, the old Roman underground necropolises? This cannot have been entirely because of fear of persecution, as is often suggested. On the contrary, worshippers could easily have been trapped in such places by Roman soldiers. Nor is there any evidence to suggest that early Christians lived in the catacombs to facilitate worship. Even in those repressive times, believers managed to meet in houses.

The most plausible reason for using the catacombs for services is intimately connected with the belief in resurrection at the time of the Second Coming. In the minds of the early Christians there was a very close link between the life and death of their founder, Christ, and the bodies of their own dead, whom they confidently expected to undergo physical resurrection on the Day of Judgement, a day they expected at any time. It was appropriate, therefore, for the whole community of the "quick" and the dead to worship in the same place. Until fairly recently the illustrious dead were still buried inside churches, further evidence of the close relationship between the dead and the living in Christian thought.

THE APOCALYPSE OF ST JOHN

The Apocalypse of St John the Divine lies at the heart of this book, because it contains prophecies of what will happen if AD 2000 is indeed the year of the Apocalypse.

The Apocalypse of St John, written in AD 96 (see below), refers back to the Old Testament books of the prophets no less than 285 times, and is in substance a continuation of the apocalyptic works of Daniel and Ezekiel. Like Ezekiel, St John eats of a strange and obviously psychedelic little book (10:10) which enables him to see what the future holds. Interestingly, the writer George Bernard Shaw once flippantly dismissed the Apocalypse as the product of a drug addict's fevered imagination!

The Apocalypse of St John is highly structured and numerological in its approach. It has 22 chapters, like the 22 letters of the Hebrew alphabet, and groups many of its symbols and scenes into sevens. The 7th, 10th, half the 11th, and 14th chapters are written as asides from the main narrative and could be removed without much loss of coherency. The opening three chapters of the Apocalypse consist of St John's letters and warnings to the seven branches of the fledgling Christian Church in Asia Minor (modern Turkey).

During his vision St John has a conversation with the Spirit, described as "the first and the last . . . in his right hand seven stars: and out of his mouth went a sharp two-edged sword" (1:16). This Spirit, identified as the "Word of God" (19:13), variously threatens to "fight against them [the churches] with the sword in my mouth" (2:16) or "rule them with a rod of iron" (2:27) or blot out the name of their members from the book of life. Later in the book (19:11–15) he is shown as a crowned warrior on a white horse. None of the descriptions of this being remotely resemble the Christ figure as he is usually depicted.

The truly apocalyptic part of the book begins with the opening of a door in heaven (chapter 3) through which St John enters "in the spirit", just like the entry of St Paul into the third heaven. As he loses consciousness and leaves his body, the voice calling the prophet sounds distant and brassy, like a trumpet. St John immediately sees a figure seated upon a throne. The figure, which most commentators have taken to be Christ, looks as if it is made of "jasper and a sardine stone" (a sard or sardonyx), and is surrounded by a rainbow. Seven spirits of God are seated in front of the throne and around it are grouped 24 crowned elders. As in Ezekiel's vision of the flying throne of Jehovah, the throne flashes with lightning.

Also in evidence in St John's vision are the same four beasts, or cherubim, that Ezekiel saw around Jehovah, resembling a lion, a calf, a man, and an eagle, but all with six wings and studded with many eyes. "Thousands of thousands" of angels surround these strange beings. The Christ figure holds a mysterious book in one hand. A lamb which has been slain, symbolic of Christ, offers to open this book which no man is able to open. The lamb, which has seven horns and seven eyes, is related to one of the many-horned beasts that are encountered later in the Apocalypse.

The lamb opens the seven seals of the book, one by one. A portion of God's wrath is released upon humanity with the opening of each seal. Then John hears the seven trumpets, signalling the release of further horrors, namely several beasts and prophets. Next, seven vials are poured over long-suffering mankind.

Finally, the "Word of God" returns riding a white horse and wearing many crowns, in his mouth a sharp sword and accompanied by a company of heavenly troops. With these troops he vanquishes the Beast and the kings of the Earth. As John said, "the time is at hand" – words that are equally relevant at the present time, as we rapidly approach the Apocalypse that is expected at the end of the 20th century.

THE MYSTERY OF REVELATION

"Revelation", sometimes referred to as the Apocalypse of St John, contains one of the most extraordinary visions ever recorded. Through this vision St John was shown what will happen at the end of the world, at the time of the resurrection and judgement of the dead, and was given a premonition of the 1000 years of peaceful rule thereafter.

The authorship of "Revelation" is disputed, with some claiming that an individual called Cerinthus "borrowed" the name of St John the Apostle to add weight to his own writings. The one certainty that is connected with the work is the date it came into being, about AD 96.

"Revelation" is so rich in imagery that it could almost be a manual for one of the pagan initiatory religions of the period rather than a book of the New Testament.

Various legends have grown up around "Revelation". One is that St John experienced his vision on the Greek volcanic island of Patmos. In later life, St John is said to have chosen to be entombed at Ephesus, the final resting place of the Virgin Mary. After selecting his vault the Apostle allegedly closed the entrance upon himself and was never seen again. It was believed that he would sleep in this tomb until the Second Coming of Christ, when he would rise from the dead, presumably to confirm the truth of his vision. The Second Coming of Christ, therefore, is very likely to be accompanied by the second coming of St John.

UNHOLY BEASTS

Through the ages, various human bogeymen have been

associated with the terrible Antichrist. In the time of the

Romans, it was the emperors themselves who were linked with

him, and latterly churchmen and politicians.

Protestant antipathy for the Roman Catholic Church led to the Pope being identified as the Antichrist. In the 19th century, Napoleon was identified as the Antichrist and in the 20th century Hitler was Nostradamus's candidate for the second Antichrist. Strangely, the Antichrist is not even mentioned by name in the Apocalypse. The Greek word antichristos only occurs in the first and second gospels of St John.

The Beast is another perplexing figure in the Apocalypse. He has been identified with many historical figures, right down to Aleister Crowley in the present century. A number of beasts crop up in the Apocalypse and are often confused with each other. Two separate Greek words are used for the Beast, zoon and therion.

Zoon, or living creatures, is used for the four holy beasts, which have the heads of the lion, calf, man and the eagle. Similar to the cherubim of Ezekiel, they have six wings embedded with many eyes. They are the four beasts found on the last tarot card, and their job is to guard the throne of Jehovah or the entrance to the lower heavens. They may also be derived from the Assyrian astral gods Marduk (the winged bull), Nebo (with human features), Nergal (a winged lion) and Ninib (an eagle).

The Greek word therion, however, is used to describe altogether wilder beasts. The first of these is the "beast that ascendeth out of the bottomless pit" (11:7). This beast may possibly be the same as the first Beast, which will "rise up out of the sea, having seven heads and ten horns, and upon those horns ten crowns, and upon its heads the name of blasphemy ... like unto a leopard" (13:1-8). To this polymorphic beast, which has the feet of a bear and the mouth of a lion, "the dragon gave him his power, and his seat, and great authority".

In Daniel chapter 7, it is suggested that the three great Gentile empires are referred to here: the lion of Babylon, the bear of Persia and the leopard of Greece. Nowadays, the bear is of course equated with Russia. The ten horns are often equated with the Roman Empire, the horns being ten kings (Daniel 7:24).

Many commentators have suggested that the rise of a new pan-European power, the European Union, is a further sign of the immediacy of the apocalypse. Before this prophecy comes true, it is claimed, membership of the Union will rise in number to 13 states and then decline to 10. The theory has been put forward that the first Beast might even be a dictatorial leader of the EU (see below).

The first Beast will be put on his throne by the Dragon, usually identified as Satan. He will reign for 42 years. If the first Beast's reign starts in 1995, as has been suggested by some, then it will last until 2037. During this period, both the Dragon and the Beast will be worshipped.

The second Beast has "two horns like a lamb, and he spake as a dragon ... he maketh fire come down from heaven on the earth ... and his number is 666" (13:11–18). This Beast is the most infamous of all. His speaking as a dragon allies him with Satan. He inherits the power of the first Beast and performs miracles, including bringing fire from heaven, like Prometheus, in full view of witnesses.

This second Beast is the antithesis of the lamb that symbolizes Christ, and is often identified as being the Antichrist. The second Beast causes a statue to be put up for the worship of the first Beast, and enables the statue to speak, just as Simon Magus caused statues to speak and appear to live. The second Beast is mentioned again with the false prophet in Daniel 19:19–20, 20:4 and 20:10.

St John the Divine identifies this second Beast by the number 666. Many have taken this to mean that John was writing about Nero, a nebulous connection to say the very least. More significantly, St John prophesies that when the second Beast comes to power no one will be allowed to buy or sell without wearing his mark on either their right hand or on their forehead.

The second Beast will be finally overcome by the warrior on a white horse called "The Word of God" and be cast into a lake of fire and brimstone together with his false prophet. His supporters will be eaten by carrion birds specially called by an angel for this purpose.

THE SCARLET WHORE AND
THE EURO-BEAST

The first Beast is probably the same as that called "a scarlet coloured beast, full of names of blasphemy, having seven heads and ten horns" (17:3) and carrying the Whore on its back. The Whore was "arrayed in purple and scarlet colour, and decked with gold and precious stones and pearls, having a golden cup in her hand full of abominations and filthiness of her fornication", and on her head was a label proclaiming her "Mystery, Babylon the Great, the mother of harlots and abominations of the earth" (17:5). The Whore also drinks the blood of saints and martyrs, which her mount the Beast aims to destroy.

The seven heads of the first Beast are explained in 17:10 as seven kings, of whom "five are fallen, and one is, and the other is not yet come". The ten horns are interpreted as "ten kings, which have received no kingdom as yet". These ten horns or kings "shall hate the whore, and shall make her desolate and naked, and shall eat her flesh, and burn her with fire" (17:16). They treat the Beast somewhat better, giving their ten kingdoms to him. This passage has been interpreted as the surrendering of the sovereignty of 12 European countries to a central European parliament.

THE LAST JUDGEMENT

The idea of the judgement of the soul after death is ancient,

dating from before 2400 BC, and widespread.

The ancient Egyptians believed that the soul implored the heart not to give evidence against it at the time of judgement. Judaism did not originally include immediate personal judgement, which was conceived more as a trial of nations at the end of time. The 1st-century AD Nag Hammadi Gnostic Christian codexes suggest that the body can give evidence against the soul in the judgement process. The penalty for misdeeds was rejection from heaven and reincarnation in a new body.

Neoplatonism introduced the idea of initiation into a "Mystery" cult giving real benefits in the afterlife by admitting the initiate to heavens he might not otherwise reach. This represented a departure from Homeric thinking, which did not allow for life after death.

The early Christians assumed that Christ would return for the second time within their lifetime, usher them into a perfect world and administer punishments to their persecutors. When it became obvious that Christ might not return for 1000 years, a different idea was adopted, of the dead undergoing a preliminary judgement just after their death but then waiting in the grave, or perhaps in purgatory, for a final appraisal. At this so-called Last Judgement the dead will be resurrected to undergo examination of their moral worth. This judgement, however, will not happen until the events outlined in the earlier chapters of the Apocalypse of St John have taken place. Christ has to come again to take up the job of the awful judge, whereupon the dead will be summoned to his presence by the sound of the final trumpet blast.

In medieval England the Last Judgement came to be known as the Doom, when it was considered that individuals could expect either heavenly bliss or torment in the lake of fire. After this, time will cease and history give way to eternity in which there is no more death, sorrow or pain. Paintings of this period often depicted the scene as the Archangel Michael weighing the souls of the dead. Similarly, the ancient Egyptians showed the weighing of the heart against the feather of truth.

The pattern of judgement and resurrection had become quite complicated by the time St John put pen to paper. According to his writings, the first judgement will take place when Christ comes among mankind a second time. The souls of martyrs who have not worshipped the second Beast will be immediately reprieved and live in paradise with Christ during his 1000 years of rule. This is called the first resurrection.

The early martyrs certainly deserved God's favour, if the many gory paintings depicting their martyrdom are accurate. The dead who could not match their magnificent example of faith will be left in their graves until the end of Christ's 1000-year rule. At the end of this period, Satan, or the Dragon, will again be on the loose and making trouble by deceiving the living. Then the second and final judgement will take place. On this occasion, judgement will be made on the basis of what has been written of the dead man's deeds in the Book of Life. Woe betide anyone without an entry in this book, for he or she will be cast forever into the lake of fire, along with Death himself. Such a sentence is called "the second death".

ADVANCE RESERVATIONS IN HEAVEN

Those chosen to be saved from damnation will be pre-marked and belong to one of the tribes of Israel, according to chapter 7 of the Apocalypse. The passage dealing with this aspect of the Last Judgement has encouraged many Christian sects to believe that only 144,000 will be saved. In the Apocalypse an angel "seals" the foreheads of 12,000 members of each of the tribes of Israel with "the seal of the living God", hence the total of 144,000.

This seal is very similar to the mark imposed by the Beast upon his followers, and in both cases serves to show which "side" the individual is on. It is also the origin of Joanna Southcott's seal with which she made up "heavenly passes" for her followers. As ten of the tribes of Israel are currently "lost" or dispersed, it is easy to see how the concern to reunite them grew into a major millennial concern for 18th-century Christians.

The benefit of being sealed could be said to be the same as that of having secured an advanced booking for heaven.

FALSE SECOND COMINGS

In the second century AD one group of Christians believed

that the heavenly version of the city of Jerusalem was going to

materialize in the clouds and descend to Earth.

The group called the Montanists was founded in Phrygia around AD 156. Their leader, the prophet Montanus, practised ecstatic prophecy together with his priestesses, Prisca and Maximilla, who preached that the end of the world was at hand.

Asceticism and voluntary martyrdom were also part of the creed of Montanus. In fact, the sect was a throwback to the apocalyptic beliefs and desires of early Christianity which had almost been eradicated from the teachings of the ortho-dox church by this time. The best-known member of the Montanists was perhaps Tertullian.

Believing that Christ would reappear in the town of Pepuza in Syria, the followers of Montanus established a large community there to await him. Accusations of a number of vices were levelled at Montanist prophets, who were accused of dying their hair, painting their eyelids, gambling and staging sacred dances with virgins. The Montanists particularly venerated the rich imagery of the Apocalypse of St John and claimed to have the apostle's tomb, a distinction that was also claimed by the pagan city of Ephesus.

In AD 550 the Bishop of Ephesus dug up the corpses of Montanus and his prophetesses and ritually burnt them, thereby hoping to stamp out this trouble-some cult. Despite its best efforts, however, orthodox Christianity did not finally succeed in this aim until the 6th century AD.

The Montanists were not the only sect to claim knowledge of the second coming of Christ. Some sects have mixed the claim with promises of resurrec-tion and eternal life and in so doing have encouraged mass suicide. One exam-ple of this is provided by the 900 members of the so-called People's Temple in

Jonestown, Guyana, whose leader, Jim Jones, persuaded them to follow him to the grave.

Another, equally disturbing case occurred in the Ukrainian capital, Kiev, in November 1993, when 33-year-old Marina Tsvyguna, the leader of a sect called the Great White Brotherhood, declared herself to be the Messiah, Maria Devi Christos. Her mission, she claimed, was to save mankind from the approaching millennial doom. Like other prophets before her, Maria had claimed that only 144,000 of her elect would be saved.

In her role as the returned Christ, Maria dressed in white, wore a strange peaked hat, a shepherd's crook like that of the ancient Egyptian pharaohs, a crucifix and bead jewellery. Together with her second husband, Krivonogov, a former youth leader who had received training in psychological warfare, she expressed the wish that her followers would follow her to the grave and beyond. The couple used a combination of old-style religious exhortation and the latest brainwashing techniques to achieve their goal. Thousands of well-educated children from good homes who had joined the cult were persuaded to break all contact with their families and to slowly starve themselves to ensure their resurrection with Maria in heaven. Like other prophets before her, Maria claimed that only 144,000 of her elect would be saved. Post-hypnotic suggestions kept the children's attention fixed on a distant realm of light, reached only via the grave. Fortunately, the Ukrainian authorities intervened and jailed the "messiah" before any of her victims died.

The Russians have a long history of mass religious suicide in the expectation of better times to come. Maria's Great White Brotherhood had a ready-made precedent in the obscure Russian religious sect called the "Old Believers". During the late 17th and early 18th century at least 20,000 of them burned themselves to death rather than accept state religious orthodoxy. One extremist Russian Christian sect, called the Krasnye Krestinnye or Fire Baptists, would commit mass suicide by assembling with their family and friends in a house which they would then systematically set on fire, like the holocaust at the end of the Waco siege in April 1993. In one such Russian mass suicide, in the Paleostrovski monastery, over 2700 men, women and children burned themselves to death.

THE FIRST COMING OF CHRIST

St John also relates the secret history of the first coming of Christ, which was obviously part of the more extended war between God who wishes to incarnate his Son in a sinful world, and Satan (in the form of a Dragon) who wishes to avoid this at all costs.

The spiritual side of the action is played out in heaven. The Dragon (in Greek, drakon) and the Woman both appear as "a great wonder in heaven", and represent Satan and the Virgin Mary. The Dragon may also have astrological connections, for the dragon's tail covers a "third part of the stars of heaven" (12:4). The Dragon is introduced as the persecutor of the woman who is "clothed with the sun, and [has] the moon under her feet, and upon her head [wears] a crown of twelve stars" (12:1). She is pregnant and is suffering the pangs of childbirth. The Dragon, which is red in colour and has seven crowned heads and ten horns, waits for the child to be delivered so it can kill and eat him. God, however, intervenes and saves the child from the dragon's jaws, so that he may carry out his appointed role as saviour.

The Apocalypse then says that the woman flees into the wilderness, where God feeds her for 1260 days. The Dragon persecutes her, even causing floods in an attempt to engulf her. On the assumption that the woman is Mary, mother of Christ, and using the "year for a day" rule, the period of her stay in the wilderness is 1260 years after the birth of Christ. In an earlier verse (11:3), power is granted to two witnesses to prophesy for 1260 days before they are killed by the beast from the bottomless pit (11:7). These two witnesses are later resurrected, echoing Christ's resurrection.

THE SEVEN SEALS, SEVEN TRUMPETS

The Lamb, symbol of Christ, is due to open the seals of the secret book of the Apocalypse of St John at the end of the millennium and release all kinds of horrors onto the Earth.

The first four seals of the secret book of the Apocalypse of St John will release the legendary Four Horsemen of the Apocalypse (6:1–8) who will torment mankind (see panel).

The fifth seal will reveal something quite different – the souls of martyrs found underneath an altar, crying out for revenge against their murderers (6:9–11). The next two seals are purely concerned with natural disasters and ecological doom. The Apocalypse describes earthquakes, the removal of the ozone layer ("the heaven was removed as a scroll when it is rolled up"), meteorites ("the stars of heaven fell upon the earth") and many other natural disasters.

The opening of the seventh seal will initiate the next sequence of seven, the blowing of the seven trumpets by angels. These seven trumpet blasts will bring down disaster on the heads of those not favoured with God's seal. One angel will hurl the contents of a lighted incense burner onto Earth, causing thunder, lightning and earthquakes. These terrible disasters will destroy one-third of all sea creatures and one-third of all shipping.

One event of particular interest is the fall of a meteorite called "Wormwood", which will poison all the rivers and many people; it is also possible that "Wormwood" will turn out to be a man-made bomb. The fall of this meteorite, heralded by the fifth trumpet blast, will open the "bottomless pit" and release the armies of the angel Abaddon (in Greek Apollyon) to destroy mankind. His hideous soldiers are like locusts but with human faces and crowns. They are winged with powerful scorpion-like stings in their tails which produce lingering illness in victims. These were the creatures that Charles Manson and his "family" hoped to unleash on an undeserving world through a spate of killings.

The sixth trumpet will release four angels previously "bound in the Euphrates river". From this description they sound more like spirits, or jinn, who were often put in lead bottles by magicians and thrown into a river or the sea; King Solomon is reputed to have done this to the recalcitrant spirits he used to build his Temple. These four will be accompanied by 200,000,000 horsemen whose job it is to kill a third of what remains of mankind – for angels, they seem a remarkably bloodthirsty bunch.

The seventh and last trumpet blast will occur when the "kingdoms of this world are become the kingdoms of our Lord, and of his Christ". It will herald the resurrection of the dead and their judgement by God.

One final series of horrors is still to come, though. The seven angels, clothed in pure white linen with golden girdles, will appear bearing seven golden vials. Each of these vials contains a plague to be inflicted on mankind. The contents of the first vial will give sores to those with the Beast's mark; the second will kill every form of life in and on the seas; the third will turn the rivers to blood, further poisoning the water supplies; the fourth, taking its power from the sun, will scorch mankind; the fifth vial will darken the kingdom of the Beast; the sixth will dry up the Euphrates River to allow the kings of the East to invade Israel and perhaps Europe, as is also foretold by Nostradamus. The final vial will poison the atmosphere with previously unknown infections.

Thus the seven seals are opened, the seven trumpets blast out their individual messages of destruction and the seven vials are poured upon mankind. Only those protected with "the seal of God" will be spared these tribulations.

THE FOUR HORSEMEN

OF THE APOCALYPSE

The first horseman rides on a white horse, carries a bow, and wears a crown: he is usually called Conquest. The second rides on a blood-red horse, wields a great sword and is sometimes depicted dressed in black armour: he is usually called War.

Wars have always been associated with the end of the world.

The third horseman rides a black horse and holds a balance in his hand. Sometimes he is depicted as a monk. He symbolizes Famine; in the vision of St John this association is emphasized by a voice quoting the prices of wheat and barley, staple foods which were eight times what they should have been. The prophecy is that there will be severe shortages of these staples in the final days, as predicted by Nostradamus.

The fourth horseman, who rides a light-coloured horse, is Death. He is usually depicted as a skeleton, and is sometimes also called Plague or Pestilence. Behind him comes Hell, sometimes shown as the jaws of a disembodied head belching flames.

ST MARK'S APOCALYPSE

Chapter 13 of St Mark's Gospel is a mini-Apocalypse every bit as threatening as the Apocalypse of St John.

On the Mount of Olives Jesus explains to Peter, James, John and Andrew the conditions of his second coming, and the end of the world. The prophecy falls into three distinct phases.

First, Jesus warns of social and political changes to come on Earth. He predicts that there will be many false messiahs, who should be avoided. Before the millennium there will be many wars and rumours of wars, "nation shall rise against nation, and kingdom against kingdom", a prediction dated by Nostradamus for 1999. There will be an increase in earthquakes, famines and related troubles.

Then comes a passage that has puzzled many interpreters: there will be "the abomination of desolation, spoken of by Daniel the prophet, standing where it ought not" (St Mark 13:14). This is said to refer to the introduction by Antiochus Epiphanes (reigned 175–164 BC) of the statue of Zeus into the holy of holies, the Temple of Jerusalem, in an attempt to Hellenize the Jews. This passage is underscored by the parenthetical remark "let him that readeth understand", a very broad hint that the meaning is to be interpreted by one of the secret keys of the Qabalah.

The reference to the Old Testament prophet Daniel is also of interest, for it was he who provided numerical clues as to the arrival of the Apocalypse. Sects like the Jehovah's Witnesses and the Seventh-Day Adventists use the dating from Daniel.

Jesus then advises his followers to flee to the mountains, advice taken by the Essenes, who left Jerusalem for Qumran before the time of this Gospel; the

Millerites, who waited in 1843 on the hills for the Second Coming; the Mormons; Aetherius Society members, who made many such pilgrimages, and other groups anticipating the end of the world.

The period of great tribulations involving false prophets and messiahs will be followed by hardships of a different kind, when "the sun shall be darkened, and the moon shall not give her light" (13:24). From Jesus's description these cosmic happenings sound very much like the opening of the sixth seal of the Apocalypse of St John, or the interpretation that Immanuel Velikovsky put on the cosmic events of 1502 BC and 1450 BC, when a huge heavenly body came so close to Earth that it caused the revolution of the globe to falter. It looks as if this event is set to be repeated in the not too distant future: "And the stars of heaven shall fall", indicating perhaps a bombardment of the Earth by comets or meteorites.

These cosmic events will be followed by phenomena of a supernatural nature, and Christ himself will be seen "coming in the clouds with great power and glory". This century there have already been several well-documented appearances by the Virgin Mary, with strange effects marking her coming, like the sun moving in the sky in an unnatural way.

Christ and his angels will gather the "elect" from the four winds, presumably meaning from the four corners of the Earth. This passage has concentrated the thinking of those prophets who like to think that the "elect" will be drawn exclusively from their particular sects. In the Apocalypse it is suggested that the elect will number only 144,000. The passage concludes with an injunction to be watchful, in case the Second Coming of Christ occurs suddenly and catches the faithful off guard.

Finally, a most perplexing verse occurs in which Jesus says "Verily I say unto you, that this generation shall not pass, till all these things be done" (13:30). Does this mean that Christ's prophecy has failed, because certainly these events have not occurred in the sequence promised? Alternatively, perhaps the word "generation" is intended to refer to the seed and descendants of those who were with him on that day.

These prophecies made a deep impact upon the early Christians. They were repeated almost word for word in Matthew chapters 24–25 and also in Luke 21, and formed an important part of early belief.

JOEL PREDICTS WAR

The Old Testament prophet Joel also had visions of the end of the world, which he called the "day of the Lord". In Joel 2:30–32 he writes of the initial heavenly signs heralding the end of time: "And I will shew wonders in the heavens and in the earth, blood, and fire, and pillars of smoke. The sun shall be turned into darkness, and the moon into blood, before the great and the terrible day of the Lord come." In 3:15 he continues, "the sun and the moon shall be darkened, and the stars shall withdraw their shining."

These events mirror the descriptions of the end of time given elsewhere, except that Joel strikes a more optimistic note than many other prophets of these events: "whosoever shall call on the name of the Lord shall be delivered". Salvation, it seems, can be achieved quite simply, without great sacrifice.

On the down side, however, Joel is less generous to non-believers, threatening to sell the children of the gentile or heathen nations into slavery, and positively warlike. At the time of God's judgement, he plans to "gather all nations and ... bring them down into the valley of Jehoshaphat" (3:2). Then he calls on the people to prepare for war (3:9), "wake up the mighty men, let all the men of war draw near; let them come up: Beat your plowshares into swords, and your pruning hooks into spears."

SECRETS OF
THE GNOSTICS

If the garden of forking paths that is history had followed the Gnostics, Christianity might have depended upon knowledge and individual effort rather than faith and the intercession of the Church. Some of the mysteries of Gnosticism are very relevant to us now at the end of the millennium.

THE GNOSTIC APOCALYPSE

The early Christians were regarded by some as a new Jewish sect who believed they had finally found the long-awaited Messiah and not a new religion.

The initial Jewish disciples were joined by many Greek converts, who brought their philosophical heritage to the new religion of Christianity. The New Testament was in fact written in Greek, and the Old Testament used by the early Christians was the most ancient Greek translation, known as the Septuagint and made in Alexandria about 255 BC. Christianity may be seen as a Hellenized Jewish sect.

Centres of Greek-speaking Jews, such as at Alexandria, drew their religious inspiration from Hellenistic, Judaic and Egyptian sources. Gnosticism (literally meaning "knowledge") was intertwined with early Christianity, while emphasizing spiritual knowledge rather than merely faith as the road to salvation. Many Gnostics regarded themselves as Christian.

Philo of Alexandria (c. 20 BC–AD 50) was a typical Gnostic. A member of a distinguished family of that city, he was learned both in Jewish knowledge and in the ancient Greek philosophers such as Plato. He originated the doctrine of the "Logos", which was used by St John in his Gospel: "In the beginning was the Word ['Logos' in the original Greek], and the Word [Logos] was with God, and the Word was God."

Thus a basic Christian doctrine was derived from Gnosticism. Many of Philo's ideas appear in the Gospels, notably in the fourth Gospel and in the Pauline Epistle to the Hebrews.

Clement of Alexandria, an early Christian father, said "the Gnosis itself is that which has descended by transmission to a few, having been imparted unwritten by the Apostles" (*Miscell.* Book VI, chapter 7).

Many early Christians were Gnostics, including some of the Apostles. Christianity could well have grown up as a Gnostic religion, emphasizing knowledge above blind acceptance. So what happened?

As in any religion or movement, the successors of the founder decided which things to keep and which to throw out. They discarded the spiritual knowledge of Gnosticism as being too dangerous, and kept the concept of blind acceptance of Church doctrine. Then they declared Gnosticism a heresy. If this had not happened then maybe the Dark Ages would not have been quite so dark, and the classical texts that were destroyed by the thousand would have survived, to leaven civilization. The intolerance of the early church fathers decided to cover up the Gnostic origins of Christianity, plunging Europe into the Dark Ages.

Meanwhile, the classical texts of Greek philosophy and civilization either mouldered away or were partially saved in Arabic translations. With them Islam spread across the Middle East and Northern Africa. Eventually, as a result of the Moorish conquest of Spain, some of the classic texts of Greek civilization were translated into Latin again, and gradually ancient culture was reintro- duced into Europe from the 13th century.

Europe and Christianity had to wait more than a thousand years for this re- translation. The light of the Renaissance marked the birth of modern Europe when some of what had been lost during the early centuries of Christianity was rediscovered.

As J. A. Symonds put it, the "word Renaissance really means new birth to liberty – the spirit of mankind recovering consciousness … recognizing the beauty of the outer world … liberating the reason in science, and the con- science in religion".

With this rediscovery the gloomy doctrines of the end of the world, of Judgement and damnation were seen from a different perspective, as part of a much wider horizon of belief. Gradually people became aware of the vast lit- erature of the ancient world which supported myriad ideas and speculations about the place of man in the cosmos.

Much of the early Gnostic writings, however, did not become available until the 19th century (see below). Even when these texts were discovered, and were proved beyond a shadow of doubt to be genuine, they were reserved for study by scholars and did not become widely available to the general public. Christianity and the establishment continued the great cover-up, even though many of the texts discovered dated from closer to the time of Christ than those that are officially recognized as forming part of the Bible.

RECOVERING THE LOST
SECRETS OF THE GNOSTICS

Much of the Gnostic writing was suppressed by the early Christian Fathers. Once it was decided to brand Gnosticism as a heresy, its texts were ruthlessly destroyed. Although some texts came to light in Luxor in 1769, discovered by the Scottish traveller James Bruce, and in 1773 on a London bookstall, it was not until 1851 that one of the greatest Gnostic texts, the "Pistis Sophia" was actually published.

"The Apocalypse of Peter", the "Gospel of Peter" and one of the three "Books of Enoch" were unearthed in the tomb of Akhmim in upper Egypt in 1884. These were followed in 1896/7 by the "Gospel of Mary" and the "Gospel of Thomas".

In 1945 an Arab peasant, intent upon murdering an enemy, found the Nag Hammadi codexes, regarded as the single most important source of Gnostic writings ever to have been uncovered. It has taken scholars over 45 years to make these fully available to the general reading public in English.

SNAKE WORSHIP AND THE
FLYING MAGUS

As Christianity evolved it taught its followers that they could be saved by their belief in God, or by the intervention of a saint or Jesus Christ on their behalf.

Gnostic Christians thought that people are largely masters of their own destiny, spiritual or temporal. After death, the Gnostics believed, the soul rises from the body through various heavens. The point it reaches in this hierarchy depends on the dead person's level of spiritual knowledge and awareness. Although now denied, multiple heavens once formed a central part of Christian doctrine. In the second Corinthians 12:2, for example, Paul speaks of "such an one caught up to the third heaven".

The Gnostic Christian belief also encompassed the notion of man's soul travelling from his body during sleep, exploring even the heavens before returning to the body. In Corinthians again Paul writes, "I knew a man in Christ [i.e. a believing Christian] above fourteen years ago (whether in the body, I cannot tell; or whether out of the body, I cannot tell: God knoweth)".

Philo of Alexandria refers to a ladder of words or "Names stretching from Earth to Heaven" where the ultimate Word, the Logos, resides. At each level the soul is confronted by guardians who will not admit him to that particular heaven if he does not have the necessary purity or spiritual knowledge to gain admission. The Gnostic rises from one heaven to the next because he knows the secrets of the Spheres and their guardians.

By the late 2nd century such practices had been purged from the canon of "acceptable" Christianity. Irenaeus, Bishop of Lyons at this time, spoke disparagingly of Gnostic knowledge: "They [the Gnostic Christians] use magic and images and incantations and invocations, and after inventing certain names as if they belonged to angels, they proclaim that some are in the first heaven, others in the second, and then try to set forth the names, principalities, angels and powers of the . . . heavens."

Irenaeus perhaps was not aware of the fact that no less a person than St Paul had given similar instructions in his own Apocalypse.

The Samarian-born Simon Magus (15 BC–AD 53), son of a Jewish sorcerer, was educated in the cradle of Gnosticism, Alexandria. He was a disciple of Dositheus, who had been a follower of John the Baptist and contended with Jesus Christ for the title of Messiah. Simon travelled widely in Persia, Arabia, Egypt to learn all he could about magical lore. He was accompanied by a sorceress called Helena, whom Simon claimed was a reincarnation of Helen of Troy. In Samaria, even Christians spoke of Simon as "the great power of God", and Peter, fearing the competition, had refused to baptize him.

Simon Magus performed many miracles, including healing the sick, raising the dead, walking through fire, flying through the air, turning stones into bread, creating phantom banquets, making himself invisible, animating stone statues, changing his own shape and, of course, reputedly commanding elemental spirits or possibly demons to do his bidding.

Clement of Alexandria called Magus the "Standing One", perhaps a discreet reference to his phallic rites with Helen, which he used to generate the necesary power for his magic. He also used the resultant semen, and Helen's menstrual blood, in his rites. In Rome the old rivalry with the apostle Peter resulted in Simon challenging him to a demonstration of magical skill before the Roman emperor. Simon levitated and hovered while Peter kneeled and prayed hard. Peter's prayers must have been answered because Simon fell and broke his thigh, fairly conclusive proof that the Samarian had actually levitated.

SNAKE WORSHIPPERS

According to the Ophites, an early Gnostic sect, there were seven obstructive animal demons barring the soul's way to the Lesser Heavens. The names of the first four were Michael (a lion), Souriel (a bull), Raphael (a hissing snake) and Gabriel (an eagle).

Three of these are immediately recognizable as the beasts guarding the throne of God in the Apocalypse of St John: "and the first beast was like a lion, and the second beast like a calf, and the third beast had a face as a man, and the fourth beast was like a flying eagle" (5:7).

The odd one out between these two sets is, of course, the snake/man. The Ophites held the snake to be holy. This creature also represented a very special part of man. The Ophites (derived from "ophis", Greek for serpent) were in a way the predecessors of the mid-West American fundamentalist snake-handling congregations.

The three animal demons making up the seven are Thauthabaoth (a bear), Erathaoth (a dog or ape, like the Egyptian god Thoth) and Oneol or Thartharoath (an ass). There may also be a correspondence between these and the Beasts that rule the world close to the millennium. As the Beast whose number is 666 has the feet of a bear (13:2), and the Beast on which the Whore of Babylon rides (17:3) is related to the ass, this seems very likely.

NAG HAMMADI COVER-UP

In December 1945 books containing many secrets of the Christian religion came into the hands of Mohammed 'Ali al-Samman, an Arab peasant, near the town of Nag Hammadi in upper Egypt.

Undisturbed since their concealment almost two thousand years ago, the manuscripts that were found near Nag Hammadi rank in importance with the Dead Sea Scrolls. The relatively uncorrupted texts cover the periods immediately before and after the lifetime of Christ.

What is perhaps even more extraordinary is the time it has taken scholars to make both of these very important collections of documents available in English.

The first extensive translation into English did not appear until 1977. The managing editor in charge of the project said that "the publication of the tractates has encountered a number of obstacles of a political and scholarly sort. As a result, though it has been some thirty-two years since their discovery, the Nag Hammadi tractates have not previously been available in their entirety in ... any ... modern language".

Of the 13 codexes remaining, a total of 53 separate works have been identified, written on over 1000 sheets of papyrus – we can only guess at how much more material might have been made available had Mohammed's resourceful mother not used it as kindling (see panel).

Among these 53 works are some of the early Gospels, including secret Gospels which were not preserved in the New Testament, Greek writings and philosophy such as portions of Plato's "Republic", cosmology, poems, mystical exercises, sexual magical techniques, Jewish merkaba (chariot) mysticism, hermetic tracts and no less than five separate Apocalypses.

The Apocalypse of Paul is an account of the apostle's ascent into Heaven and what he found there, with instructions for other souls on how to conduct themselves during Judgement.

The First Apocalypse of James contains the secret teachings of Christ that were given to James the Just, his brother. In it James refers to Jesus as "Rabbi", or teacher, not God. Jesus warns James to leave Jerusalem, for the city is a dwelling place of a great number of archons (wicked or evil angels or aeons).

Jerusalem is tellingly stigmatized as the city which "always gives the cup of bitterness to the sons of light". Jesus coaches James on what to say when he is judged and challenged by the "toll collectors" of heaven in order to pass through the gates of heaven – remember, this was written before St Peter was given that job!

Less interesting are the Second Apocalypse of James and the Apocalypse of Adam, although both stress the secret knowledge of the Gnostics whose thinking made up the original Christian doctrine until the Church fathers decided to become the sole dispensers of grace and knowledge.

The Apocalypse of Peter is a record of the vision of St Peter, in which he speaks with Christ in the spirit. In this Peter is clearly seen as the true successor to Christ and the founder of the Gnostic community. In the vision, Peter first sees hostile priests who seem to be intent upon stoning him and Christ to death.

Next, Peter recalls the crucifixion during which Jesus stood nearby talking with him. Peter asks, "Who is this one glad and laughing on the tree [cross]? And is it another one whose feet and hands they are striking?" Christ replies, "He whom you saw on the tree [cross], glad and laughing, this is the living Jesus. But this one into whose hands and feet they drive the nails is his fleshy part, which is the substitute being put to shame, the one who came into being in his likeness. But look at him and me."

This version of the crucifixion is obviously rather discomforting to a Church whose doctrines about the central event of Christian faith have changed considerably during the intervening centuries. It is not so surprising therefore that even in this relatively free age some pressure was exerted to keep their secret a little longer.

Peter seemed to realize that it would be a long time before his book was read and understood, for he writes "These things, then, which you saw you shall present to those of another race who are not of this age." He seems to be right, as this Apocalypse has only just seen the light of day before we enter the new age.

THE DISCOVERY OF
THE MANUSCRIPTS

Shortly before Mohammed 'Ali al-Samman and his brothers avenged their father's murder in a blood feud, hacking off the limbs of their enemy, they went with their camels to the Jabal al-Tarif mountain near the village of Nag Hammadi to dig for "sabakh", a soft soil they used as fertilizer for their crops. The mountain was honeycombed with caves, some of which had been used as grave sites for over 4000 years. While they were digging round a massive boulder, they came across a red earthenware "Ali Baba"-type jar two or three feet high. It was carefully sealed.

At first they thought they had found one of those jars in which Solomon or some other magician used in past ages to imprison a jinn or genie. Their fear of releasing such a being was very real and was only overcome by the thought that the jar might contain gold. Taking his courage in both hands, Mohammed raised his pick and smashed the jar. Imagine their disappointment when out tumbled some 13 papyrus books bound in leather.

The brothers took the papyrus volumes home and dumped them next to the oven. Mohammed's mother burned much of the papyrus in the oven along with straw to warm the house. The family sold the surviving codexes (books) for a very small sum, not realizing that into their hands had fallen one of the largest arsenals of "spiritual dynamite" the world has seen since the establishment of Christianity.

NEOPLATONISM

After Christ's death Christianity began a long struggle against the

pagan cults. In AD 313 it became the official religion of the Empire.

In the course of the struggle to establish Christianity over paganism some strange doctrines emerged, many of them taken from the literate Greeks who swelled the ranks of Christianity in its infancy. The Neoplatonists are an interesting example of this Christian borrowing from Greek culture.

Plutarch (AD 46–120), one of the leading Neoplatonic philosophers, lamented the passing of the old oracles and explained why he thought these had declined both in number and quality. He knew that daemons (not the same as demons) and other spiritual beings inhabited the earth along with man and the animals, something that has long since been forgotten by the majority of people.

He explained that these spiritual beings think so intensely that they produce vibrations in the air which enable other spiritual beings as well as highly sensitive men and women to receive their thoughts. This is how Plutarch explained clairvoyance and prophecy. Magicians can similarly influence the thoughts of sensitive men and women.

In as much as the daemons were not gods the information that prophets picked up from daemons sometimes turned out to contain only a grain of truth. In his book On the Cessation of Oracles, Plutarch explained that, unlike the gods, who are immortal, daemons do grow old and eventually die, although perhaps only after many centuries. This is how he explained the fact that the great oracles of the ancient world were by this time declining; these daemons were then very old and dying. For centuries after the advent of their religion, Christians continued to believe in the power of pagan gods, who in those days were clearly differentiated from evil spirits.

The philosopher who is usually looked upon as the founding father or codifier of Neoplatonism was Plotinus (AD 204–270). He was looked upon by his followers as divinely inspired (see panel) and by some of his detractors as an enemy of astrology.

Porphyry (AD 233–305) was a pupil of Plotinus. His books include many on magic and some 15 books devoted to attacking Christian doctrine, including the Christian view of the second coming of Christ. One of his works, a criticism of the Book of Daniel, was publicly burned by the Emperor Theodosius.

From surviving quotations we know that Porphyry declared the Book of Daniel to be the work of a Palestinian Jew, written in Greek in the period 175–64 BC. According to Porphyry, the predictions in the book correspond too exactly to events and therefore must have been written in retrospect. This is the highest tribute anyone could pay to a work of prophecy, but does not satisfactorily explain the prophecies that came true after the date of composition.

An opposing view to that put forward by Porphyry is that the Book of Daniel was actually written during the Babylonian captivity, as the text states, a dating which corresponds to its inclusion in the canon which contains no work more recent than 400 BC. The Book of Daniel was written in both Hebrew and Aramaic, but not Greek. In addition, Jesus specifically recommended it as a work of true prophecy, and he should have been in a position to know.

The Syrian Iamblichus (d. AD 333), who shared some of Porphyry's views, transformed Neoplatonism from theoretical and religious speculation into a system of magic. He explained specific procedures handed down from the ancient Greeks which were in turn passed on to seers like Nostradamus, enabling them to see into the future centuries with clarity.

Neither Porphyry nor Iamblichus used the word "magic", but spoke instead about theurgy in terms that mystics usually reserve for worship. These Neoplatonists, like the Gnostics, went into considerable detail over the use of talismans, seals, spells, invocations (for angels and guardians of the gates of the lower heavens) and evocations (for demonic manifestations). They developed a religious approach to the techniques of the magicians which were so important to pseudo-messiahs like Simon Magus.

The idea of hierarchies of spiritual and demonic beings was also introduced into the theology of Christianity, although the magical techniques which were part and parcel of them were rigorously suppressed. This suppression sparked off a battle that would run for centuries, a war ostensibly between the forces of good and evil but in reality a continuation of the conflict between paganism and its usurper, Christianity.

INVOKING THE DAEMON

The Neoplatonist Plotinus maintained that only the physical and irrational side of man's nature was affected by either drugs or sorcery. The rational soul, he declared, may free itself from the influence of magic.

Nevertheless, an Egyptian priest had little difficulty in persuading Plotinus to allow him to demonstrate his magical powers by invoking his familiar daemon. Plotinus, who had by this time been living and teaching in Rome for 26 years, decided that the only pure place in the city for the priest to undertake his experiment was in the Temple of Isis.

One evening the two men went to the temple with some friends of Plotinus, and set about the invocation. Instead of a daemon or guardian spirit appearing, a god materialized. One can imagine the impact this made on the assembled group. Given the spiritual standing of Plotinus, however, perhaps a god was only to be expected.

SECRETS OF THE TEN HEAVENS

A large number of the books in the New Testament were written by the Apostle Paul. The manuscripts of several of these have only recently come to light.

"The Apocalypse of Paul" was discovered in December 1945, together with a number of other manuscripts, near the village of Nag Hammadi in Egypt. This work outlines the early Gnostic Christian idea of what happens after death, when the soul is judged.

According to Paul's Apocalypse, each soul has to rise as best it can through a hierarchy of heavens and face the increasingly difficult challenges posed by the guardian angels of each heaven. The book focuses on Paul's ascent to the tenth and highest heaven. The journey begins with Paul meeting a child on the mountain of Jericho, on the way to heaven (symbolized by Jerusalem). This child turns out to be the Holy Spirit, who takes Paul first to the third heaven.

The Holy Spirit warns Paul to keep his wits about him, for they are about to enter the realm of "principalities ... archangels and powers and the whole race of demons". The Holy Spirit also mentions that they will pass "one that reveals bodies to a soul-seed", that is, the being that takes souls and plants them in new bodies for reincarnation. For the soul who wished to ascend to the highest heaven, reincarnation was to be avoided. This was part of Christian doctrine until AD 553, when it was suppressed.

When Paul reaches the fourth heaven, the Holy Spirit encourages him to look down upon his body which he has left behind on the mountain of Jericho. As Paul ascends he witnesses in the fourth heaven the judgement and punishment of another soul. He says, "I saw the angels resembling gods ... bringing a soul out of the land of the dead". The soul has been resurrected so that it can be judged, one of the four events promised for the end of the world. The angels were whipping it, a scene which clashes with the sugar-sweet angels depicted by Victorian Christians!

The soul spoke, saying, "What sin was it that I committed in the world?" The "toll collector" of this heavenly gate accuses the soul. The soul replies, "Bring witnesses! Let them [show] you in what body I committed lawless deeds". Three bodies rise up as witnesses and accuse the soul of anger and envy, and finally murder. "When the soul heard these things, it gazed downwards in sorrow ... It was cast down."

At this point we expect the soul to be cast into hell, as in later Christian doctrine, but no: "the soul that had been cast down [went] to [a] body which had been prepared [for it]", and was reincarnated.

Paul, somewhat shaken by this experience, was beckoned forward by the Holy Spirit and allowed to pass through the gate of the fifth heaven. Here he saw his fellow apostles, and "a great angel in the fifth heaven holding an iron rod in his hand". This angel and three other angels, with whips in their hands, scourge the souls of the dead and drive them on to judgement. Paul remains with the Holy Spirit and the gates to the sixth heaven swing open effortlessly before him.

In the sixth heaven Paul sees a strong light shining down on him from the heaven above. He is motioned by the "toll collector" through the gates of the seventh heaven. Here, he sees "an old man [filled with] light [and whose garment] was white. [His throne], which is in the seventh heaven, [was] brighter than the sun by [seven] times." This old man bears a striking resemblance to Jehovah as he is described in the vision of Ezekiel.

The old man asks, "Where are you going, Paul?" Only reluctantly, after some encouragement from the Holy Spirit, does Paul speak with him and give the Gnostic sign he has learned. The eighth heaven then opens and Paul ascends. Here he embraces the twelve disciples, most of whom he has not met before, and together they rise to the ninth heaven. Finally, Paul reaches the tenth and highest heaven, where he is transformed.

SECRET SPIRITUAL KNOWLEDGE

It is not surprising that the early Christian fathers edited out the practical spiritual knowledge which was once an integral part of Christianity, and was known and practised by the Apostle Paul. For these men, it was far more convenient and gratifying for their egos to assert that spiritual grace could only be attained through them as Christ's representatives on Earth. In a move that is very unlikely to have met with the approval of Jesus Christ himself, the worldly aspirations of a few won out over the spiritual enlightenment of the many.

As we approach the end of the millennium, when some expect the Apocalypse to become a reality, it is only fitting that this early spiritual dimension should be fully recognized and understood. After 2000 years of silence, the essence of Paul's early teaching again became available to us just 23 years before the end of the millennium.

Ironically, the Second Coming, or reincarnation, awaited with such relish by some zealots may be viewed as proof of God's imperfection rather than of his omnipotence. According to Paul, reincarnation was the lot of anyone who failed to scale the heights of the ten heavens.

SORCERERS, SPIRITS & SCRYERS

History was seen as a progression through various ages, governed by angels, culminating in the end of the world and the rule of Christ on Earth. Scryers called upon the angels to divulge the secrets of the future, and the Pope elected to rule the Church on the last day of the millennium was a well known sorcerer.

GERBERT AND THE FIRST MILLENNIUM

Towards the close of the first millennium, in AD 999, many Christians in Europe thought that the world was coming to an end, and that Christ's Second Coming was at hand.

For a few short months in AD 999 people could talk of nothing else but the Second Coming. The Pope who reigned at the end of the first millennium was one of the most fascinating and mysterious personalities in papal history. After the death of Pope Gregory V at the tender age of 27 (by poison, according to rumour) a scholarly prelate called Gerbert was chosen to occupy the throne of St Peter as Pope Sylvester II.

Gerbert, the first Frenchman to become Pope, was from a humble home in Aurillac in the Auvergne region. Tradition has it that he was an advanced student of the black arts, which he first learnt during three years in residence at certain

Arabic schools in Spain. It was said that he regularly conversed with the Devil, and was even thought by some cardinals to be the cloven-hoofed Devil himself.

The official version of the background of the shepherd charged to usher the Catholic flock into the second millennium was, of course, slightly different. This emphasized his devotion to mathematics and the natural sciences which in those days were largely overlapping disciplines, particularly in the popular imagination. Gerbert taught grammar, dialectic, rhetoric, arithmetic, music, astronomy and geometry and supported the classics as an essential part of education. Like Friar Bacon, he was credited with possessing a "brazen head" which spoke to him and could prophesy future events.

As the first year of Gerbert's papacy approached the millennial hour, his parishioners in Germanic and Slav countries expected the world to end in fire. In the countries bordering on the Mediterranean, meanwhile, the most popular vision was of a great blast on Gabriel's trumpet summoning the dead from their graves to share in the Last Judgement with "the quick", those who had not yet died.

In Europe generally a sort of mass hysteria progressively took hold as the year end approached. This atmosphere led to some astonishing happenings. Some men forgave each other their debts; husbands and wives rashly confessed their infidelities; convicts were released from prison; poachers made a truce with their liege lords; fields were left fallow, and buildings went unrepaired by their owners. After all, their reasoning ran, why repair a building that will not be needed in a few months' time? In direct obedience to the Bible, some of the more pious rich gave their surplus vestments to the poor, although keeping their best for that all-important meeting with their divine maker. More mercenary souls went round snapping up property at knock-down prices. Many people were convinced by the argument that, in a world with no future, such possessions were worthless.

The confessionals did a roaring trade as people put their spiritual life in order to stake a claim in the afterlife as best they could. The demand for absolution almost outstripped the ability of the priests to physically give it, so great was the rush, and general absolutions were celebrated in special masses. Many who had lived in sin promptly got married. Huge bands of pilgrims set out for the Holy Land with the hope of arriving in time to meet Christ in Jerusalem. On the road they either whipped themselves as penitents, or sang hymns, while at night they scanned the heavens for the signs of His coming.

December saw fanaticism reach new heights as communities attempted to rid their area of the ungodly so that the Angel of Judgement would not need to call: bands of flagellants roamed the countryside; mobs called for the execution of suspected sorcerers or unpopular burghers, and even some farm animals were freed to roam through the towns, giving a slightly surrealistic air to the proceedings.

On the night of 31 December, Gerbert celebrated mass in the Basilica of St Peter's in Rome. The packed congregation believed this might be the last mass they would ever attend. When the mass had been said, a deathly silence fell over the congregation – but they waited in vain.

Life soon resumed its usual pace. Perhaps the only people not disappointed were those who knew they would never have made it through St Peter's gates, and those who had gained at the expense of the gullible.

WHAT GERBERT LEARNED FROM THE MOORS

According to the 12th-century historian William of Malmesbury, Gerbert fled by night from his monastery to Spain to study astrology and "the other arts with the Saracens". The Muslim invaders of Spain had at that time reached a higher level of civilization than Christian northern Europe. Under Muslim tuition, Gerbert learned "what the song and flight of birds portend [augury], to summon ghostly figures from the lower world [necromancy], and whatever human curiosity has encompassed whether harmful or salutary" [other arts and sciences].

Michael Scott, referring to him as Master Gilbertus, claims he was the best "nigromancer" (necromancer or magician) in France, "whom the demons obeyed in all that he required of them day and night, because of the great sacrifices which he offered, and his prayers and fastings and magic books and great diversity of rings and candles".

Given this background, it is not surprising that Gerbert was regarded by his contemporaries as the best man for the job of Pope at the end of the world.

THE APOCALYPSE OF JOACHIM

The classic apocalyptic prophecy of the 13th century was produced by Joachim of Fiore (1145–1202), abbot of Cortale in the Italian province of Calabria, who was asked by three Popes to write a work on the Apocalypse.

Joachim's response was *Expositio in Apocalypsin*. He divided history up into three periods, with each period prefaced by a time of incubation. Joachim's idea is very similar to that behind the Astrological Ages. Joachim describes how while meditating one Easter night he became aware of a stream of bright light pouring into his soul. The meaning of the Apocalypse was laid open to him. He prophesied the advent of the Antichrist, and informed Richard Coeur de Lion, when he came to consult him, that the Antichrist would soon occupy the Papal throne itself. Joachim said that the Papacy would be stripped of all temporal power, a prediction that was not to come true for another six centuries, in 1870.

Joachim's book provoked much speculation about the arrival of the millennium, a topic for discussion which St Augustine had desperately tried to discourage during his lifetime. The kingdom of God, Augustine said repeatedly, had already arrived. In the half-century after Joachim's death, *Expositio* was revered as a new eschatology beside that contained in the Book of Daniel, the Apocalypse of St John the Divine and the forged Sibylline Oracles. Let us now look at Joachim's three ages of history.

The first Age was the Age of the Father, the age of the Mosaic Law of the Old Testament. The second Age was the Age of the Son, during which the Gospel of the New Testament held sway. Both these Ages had already run their course, and Joachim claimed to be living in the incubation period of the third Age. This was to usher in the Age of the Paraclete or Holy Spirit, which was to begin at some time between 1200 and 1260, and would endure until the millennium and the Last Judgement.

The first Age was one of fear and servitude, the second one of faith and brotherly submission, and the third Age, Joachim predicted, would be one of love, joy and freedom, with spiritual knowledge revealed directly into the hearts of men.

Joachim expected that there would arise a new teacher, a new Elias or *novus dux* who, like Christ, would have 12 apostles who would form a new order of monks. Another figure expected before the end was the first Antichrist, who most authorities are agreed should be described as an ordinary ruler with extraordinary powers. His reign would last only three and a half years, but in that period he would overthrow the Church and expel the Pope. This parallels the vision of a 20th-century Pope who saw his successor being forced out of the Vatican.

After the overthrow of the Antichrist there would be a period of universal peace. This would precede the natural disasters and upheavals heralding the coming of a second Antichrist, followed soon after by the Last Judgement.

One ruler became an almost mythical figure thanks to Joachim. The Holy Roman Emperor Frederick II (1194–1250), who was excommunicated at least three times for perjury, blasphemy and heresy, was thought by his enemies to be the Antichrist. But his supporters saw him as the Emperor of the Last Days or the novus dux written about by Joachim.

During the Crusades, Frederick captured Jerusalem, Bethlehem and Nazareth from the Muslims, together with part of what is now Lebanon. He was crowned King of Jerusalem, and it was whispered that he had come to claim the city for Christ's impending descent to Earth. For his followers, Frederick's success in the

Crusades confirmed his status of near-divinity.

When Frederick died in 1250, his supporters fully expected him to rise from the grave and lead them once again. As Joachim's deadline for the unfurling of the Age of the Spirit, 1260, approached, so-called "armies of saints" took to flagellating themselves in public, with the aim of avoiding much greater punishments on the approaching Day of Judgement. The famine in 1258 and plague in 1259 lent credibility to 1260 as the correct millennial date, but the year came and went and life carried on as normal.

THE TABLES OF THE LAW

The Irish poet W. B. Yeats mentions in his Mythologies a little-known book of Joachim's entitled Liber Inducens in Evangelium Aeternum. Yeats wondered if the book was perhaps just "some mediaeval straw-splitting ... which is only useful today to show how many things are unimportant to us, which once shook the world".

After reading Joachim's book, Yeats wrote of his experience: "the dust shall fall for many years over this little box [the book was kept in a box made by the Renaissance goldsmith, Benvenuto Cellini]; and then I shall open it; and the tumults which are, perhaps, the flames of the Last Day shall come from under the lid". Yeats' poetic vision also looked to the end of this century for the Second Coming of Christ.

Another of Joachim's books, Adversus Judaeos ("Against the Jews") propounded the argument that while all Jews will be finally converted to Christianity in the last days, they will before then follow the Antichrist (in company with a large number of Christians) and bring great suffering upon themselves and the whole world.

To avoid this fate, Joachim urged the conversion of the Jews before the appearance of the Antichrist. His suggestion would later cause a lot of grief and hatred, although his intention had been well-meaning and anticipated a much purer millennial Age of joy and brotherly love.

THE ABBOT TRITHEMIUS

Prophecies of events and of the angelic rulers of the world

through to the year AD 2233 were made in 1508 by

Trithemius, a master of cryptography and magic.

The turn of the 16th century was a strange time. Columbus had just discovered America by accident while making his way to China and the East. The Pope was the corrupt and worldly Rodrigo Borgia (Alexander VI), who inhabited the Vatican between 1492 and 1503 with his mistress Venozza Catanei and his four children. It was no secret that he had secured his election by paying enormous bribes to the other cardinals. Borgia lived like a decadent pagan emperor, with all that entailed, including orgies, and was hardly plausible as the representative of Christ on earth.

At this time was born the mysterious Johannes Trithemius (1462–1516), a man who could speak with the angels and send messages long distances in the twinkling of an eye, almost four centuries before the invention of the telephone. A brilliant scholar and teacher of two of the greatest commentators on and practitioners of European magic of the period, Cornelius Agrippa and Paracelsus, Trithemius was appointed Abbot of Sponheim at the incredibly young age of 23. Trithemius was also interested in "magical alphabets" and was in a sense the father of cryptography, the science of writing secret messages in code. Some of his methods of code writing were used by John Dee, a spy for Queen Elizabeth I.

Prophecies made by Trithemius are recorded in a very strange little book entitled De Septem Secundeis, id est, Intelligentiis, sive Spiritibus Orbes post Deum moventibus, or "Of the Seven Spirits, or heavenly Intelligences governing the Orbs [of the Planets] under God's Rule". Despite the obscure title, the book clearly explains an elaborate system of cycles of time, and a succession of angels who govern these cycles.

Trithemius gives the whole history of the world from the Creation to the end of time. He divides this massive spectrum into Ages, each made up of chunks of 354 years and four months. Each Age is ruled over by an Angel. The first in the sequence is Orisiel (reporting to Saturn), who is followed by Anael (Venus), then Zachariel (Jupiter), Raphael (Mercury), Samael (Mars), Gabriel (the Moon) and, finally, Michael (the Sun).

The first Age, from the Creation, which according to Trithemius began on 15 March, is ruled over by Orisiel. During the period of his reign, Trithemius notes, "men were rude, and did cohabit together in desert and uncouth places, after the homely manner of Beasts".

From Anno Mundi 354 to Anno Mundi 708 (calculating from Creation), Anael, under the influence of Venus, encouraged men to build houses and erect cities, create clothes and develop the arts of spinning and weaving. The influence of Venus made man wanton, and as a consequence men "took unto themselves faire women for their wives, [and] neglected God".

Trithemius himself lived in the nineteenth Age when the world was ruled for the third time by Samael, representing Mars, the god of war. His rule extended from the year 6378, measured in years Anno Mundi (since the Creation, otherwise known as AD 1171) until 6732 Anno Mundi (AD 1525). One of the main happenings in this period of history was the so- called Hundred Years' War between England and France.

Samael's reign was followed by that of the Angel Gabriel, ruled by the Moon, from 6732 Anno Mundi (AD 1525) until 7086 Anno Mundi (November AD 1879). In the following Age, the reins were taken over by the Angel Michael, who will hold sway until the year AD 2233. Michael was the archangel who led the forces of light to victory against the Devil in the first war in heaven.

The events of the millennium will thus be under the control of this angel of the Sun, reflecting the idea of the Second Coming, as Christ is sometimes identified with the Sun and is indeed called Michael by some commentators. It is as if Christ is to return to complete the work he began when he was on earth. Interestingly, Communist stalwarts Joseph Stalin and Leon Trotsky were both born in 1879, the beginning of the Age of the Sun.

Under the dominion of the angel Michael, "Kings began first to be amongst Mortall men", but in this reign he is concerned with the removal of as many kings as possible, so we can be sure that by the year 2233 the institution of monarchy will no longer be alive in any country.

Michael also originally presided over "the worship of several Gods", and so a revival of paganism at the end of the century is on the cards. This angel was also in at the birth of the sciences of mathematics, astronomy and magic. Appropriately, Albert Einstein, the prize-winning physicist, was born in that key year, 1879, the opening year of Michael's Age.

Mathematics and astronomy have taken great strides in the first two thirds of Michael's reign. A revival in that third art, magic, is on the cards for the last third of his reign, starting in the year 2115.

By placing Michael last in the cycle of angels, Trithemius was indicating that this reign would see the end of the world. If you accept his prophecy, this will not arrive earlier than AD 2233.

TRITHEMIUS THE SORCERER

Trimethius' ability as a sorcerer is demonstrated by the feat he performed for the German Emperor Maximilian I in 1482. At this time Maximilian was greatly distressed by the death of his wife Maria, daughter of Charles the Bold, Duke of Burgundy. He asked Trithemius to call up her shade or spirit.

Trithemius did so, and although the Emperor was not permitted to speak with the vision that appeared before him, so complete was the materialization that the Emperor recognized a wart upon its neck, which convinced him that it was indeed the spirit of his Empress. This episode in Trithemius' life has become part of the legends that were later associated with Faust.

ST MALACHY

Time has proved wrong the many people who originally

dismissed the prophecies of St Malachy as a hoax.

The passage of time has proved doubters of St Malachy wrong, for his prophecies have turned out to be amazingly accurate. He even prophesied the precise date of his own death, and got it right. The prophecies concern the papacy, starting with Pope Celestine II in 1143. In all, 112 Popes and their characteristics are listed from 1143 "to the end of the world"!

Maelmhaedhoc O'Morgair (later Latinized to Malachy) was born in Armagh in 1094. He became Archbishop of Armagh in 1132, dying on All Souls' Day 1148 in the arms of his French biographer to be, St Bernard of Clairvaux.

When making his prophecies Malachy usually encapsulated the Pope's name, family background or coat of arms. The heraldic coat of arms was either of the Pope's family or that given to him when he ascended to the papacy. For example, Pope Alexander VII (1655–67) had a family coat of arms showing three hills with a star shining above them: Malachy calls him Montium Custos or "the Guardian of the Hills". That of Leo XIII (1878–1903) depicted a golden comet on an azure field, which Malachy foreshadowed with his tag Lumen in Coelo, or "a Light in the Sky".

Sometimes the personal history of the Pope plays a part in the motto given by Malachy. Clement XIII (1758–69), who had connections with the government of the Italian state of Umbria and whose emblem was a rose, was called by Malachy Rosa Umbriae, the "Rose of Umbria".

In our own century, Benedict XV (1914–22), who was indicated by Malachy as Religio Depopulata ("Religion Depopulated"), reigned in a time which saw the founding of Communism, an anti-religious movement if ever there was one, and the rapid reduction of intense religious belief. His successor, Pius XI (1922–39), truly lived up to his motto of Fides Intrepida ("Unshaken Faith"), speaking out against both Hitler and Mussolini and denouncing Communism. Pius Angelicus, the "Angelic Shepherd", was an apt description of Eugenio Pacelli, who wore the papal hat as Pope Pius XII.

The election of Pastor et Nauta ("Shepherd and Sailor") brought a touch of farce to the election process. It is said, on flimsy evidence, that while the conclave to elect the Pope was being held in Rome, Cardinal Spellman of New York attempted to fulfil Malachy's prophecy by hiring a boat filled with sheep and sailing it up and down the River Tiber. Giuseppe Roncalli was eventually appointed, his elevation from the See of Venice (symbolized by the sailor) to the papacy (symbolized by the shepherd) amply vindicating Malachy's motto.

This Pope was succeeded by Paul VI (1963–78), whose coat of arms was three fleurs-de-lys, Malachy's Flos Florum ("Flower of Flowers"). The next Pope was John Paul I, whose real name, Albino Luciani, means "pale light". His birthplace, Belluno (beautiful moon), was identified by Malachy as De Medietate Lunae, or "Of the Half [or middle of the] Moon".

The present incumbent, John Paul II, is the former Archbishop of Krakow, Karol Wojtyla. He was born on the day of a solar eclipse (18 May 1920) and once laboured in a quarry in his native Poland. In Malachy's prophecies he is referred to as "De Labore Solis".

According to Malachy, there are only two more Popes to come before the end of the world. Significantly, the last Pope will have the same name as the first shepherd of the Roman Catholic Church, the apostle Peter. Malachy refers to this second Peter as "Petrus Romanus" ("Peter of Rome"), and he has more to say about him than any of the other pontiffs. His prophecy is unequivocal. This Peter "will feed his flock among many tribulations; after which the seven-hilled city will be destroyed and the dreadful Judge will judge the people."

It is clear from this that Pope Peter will preside over the end of the Roman Catholic Church, which will suffer persecution, perhaps at the hands of the Antichrist. The word "tribulation" is commonly used to describe the immediate pre-millennium period. The seven-hilled city is obviously Rome itself. The "dreadful Judge" may well be a reference to Christ, who will come to sit at the right hand of God the Father to judge the living and the dead.

THE POPE IN A TRANCE

Further confirmation of the end of the Roman Catholic Church was given to Pope Pius X (1835–1914) in 1909 in a vision. During an audience with the General Chapter of the Franciscans, Pius fell into a semi-trance and sat with his head sunk upon his chest. After a few minutes he came to and opened his eyes, a look of horror etched on his face. He cried out:

"What I have seen was terrible ... Will it be myself? Will it be my successor? What is certain is that the Pope will quit Rome, and in fleeing from the Vatican he will have to walk over the dead bodies of his priests. Do not tell anyone while I am alive."

In times of trouble the Pope could leave the Vatican for the relative safety of the castle of St Angelo via a causeway high above street level. This was not part of the vision, so it is likely that the Pope Pius saw was fleeing from more than a temporary danger. In Pius's lifetime Communism was identified as the greatest enemy of Catholicism, and it was a takeover by such a secular force that Pius most feared. But who is to say that what he really saw was not the departure of the last Pope, as foretold by Malachy?

THE YEAR OF THE BEAST:
1666

A favourite for the accolade of Apocalypse year was 1666. It had been chosen because it represented the sum of the first millennium (1000) plus the number of the Beast recorded in the Apocalypse of St John (666).

In the mid 1660s the citizens of London must have thought they were indeed witnessing the end of the world: in 1665 they were ravaged by a plague which killed at least 68,000, and in the following year much of their city was destroyed by a great fire. In the 17th century traditional sources for prophetic calculations continued to be the Bible. The most widely read prophetic source of the period was Merlin Ambrosius, a sort of blend of the prophecies of King Arthur's magician Merlin, the nationalist Welsh bard Myrddin, those included by Geoffrey of Monmouth in the seventh book of his Historia Regium Britanniae and those of Ambrosius in the Historia Britonum of Nennius. Also well-known were the prophecies of "Mother Shipton".

The prophecies of Merlin had been reissued in the 14th century to support the English claim to the throne of France, and in the 15th to justify the aspirations of the rival houses of York and Lancaster. Some prophecies of the Welsh Merlin lent support to the rebellions of Owain Glyndwr against Henry IV, and by Rhys ap Gruffydd against Henry VIII. Prophecy became so intertwined with rebellion that laws were brought in by the Tudors to stifle its pernicious influence.

Many of the prophets prominent in the century before the English Civil War saw themselves as playing a part in the Last Judgement and the arrival of the Kingdom of God. There was no shortage of messiahs. In the late 16th and early 17th centuries the coming apocalypse was frequently cited in the conflict between the Roman Catholic Church and Protestantism. The Puritans called the Church of Rome "the Whore of Babylon" which, according to the Bible, would be destroyed. Ironically, it was during the reign of the anti-Puritan King James I that the Bible was made available in English in a standard edition. Suddenly, many people who could not have read it before in Latin were now able to find those wonderful, stirring passages in Daniel, Ezekiel and the Apocalypse of St John which had for centuries been providing fuel for prophetic interpreters, and still do.

Some people who believed that the end was near – known as millenarians – reported visitations by prophetic messengers. William Sedgwick, preacher at Ely Cathedral, believed that Christ himself had told him that "the world will be at an end within fourteen days" and went to London to inform the King. The most active millenarianism occurred in the turbulent years before the rule of the Puritan Oliver Cromwell. At this time a number of pseudo-messiahs attracted followings, among them two weavers, Richard Farnham and John Bull, who in 1636 proclaimed themselves "divine witnesses". They professed to have knowledge of things to come, and to be able to inflict plagues on their enemies if they so chose. They quoted the Apocalypse of St John 11:3: "and I will give power unto my two witnesses, and they shall prophesy a thousand two hundred and threescore days." Empowerment by the Lord did not prevent their imprisonment and subsequent executions in 1642.

Yet another messiah from this period was Edward Wightman, who claimed to be the Elias or Elijah foretold in Malachy 4:5. In 1612 he became the last Englishman to be burned for heresy. The Ranter John Robbins was deified by his followers who held his wife to be the Virgin Mary and his son Jesus: his divine mission was to carry out the conversion of the Jews and to reconnoitre Jerusalem!

From the mid 17th century prophecy and popular interest in the millennium were on the wane, certainly in England. In 1655 Meric Casuabon, in A Treatise Concerning Enthusiasm, declared that every case of religious ecstasy was no more than "a degree and species of epilepsy"; this from a man who had previously published the diaries of that arch seeker after divine knowledge and dealer in angelic prophecies, Dr John Dee.

In the later 17th century, when everyone had had a bellyful of millennium predictions, it became acceptable to declare that the books of Daniel and Revelation should be read metaphorically and not literally. Even the Quakers came to accept that prophecy was distinctly odd. Thanks to the Reformation, religion had lost its wonder-working qualities. Not until more than a century later would prophecy be taken seriously again.

OLD MOTHER SHIPTON AND

ARMAGEDDON

Mother Shipton was one of a number of prophets – Nostradamus and the astrologer William Lilly were others – who predicted that London would be ravaged by fire. Her prophecies were first published in 1641, some 25 years before the Great Fire.

The real name of "Mother Shipton" was Ursula Southiel (1488–1561). Born at Knaresborough, Yorkshire – the result of a union between her mother and a demon, so it was claimed – she was reputed to be extraordinarily ugly, and perhaps because of this she lived in a cave for part of her life. Her most interesting prediction concerns Armageddon:

"Then shall come the Son of Man [Christ], having a fierce beast in his arms, which kingdom lies in the Land of the Moon [perhaps the Middle East], which is dreadful throughout the whole world; with a number of people shall he pass many waters and shall come to the land of the Lyon [lion, hence England]; look for help of the Beast of his country, and an Eagle [USA] shall destroy castles of the Thames, and there shall be a battle among many kingdoms ... and therewith shall be crowned the Son of Man, and the ... Eagles shall be preferred [by the people] and there shall be peace over the world, and there shall be plenty."

THE BOOK OF PROPHECIES

Around AD 346 one of the most extraordinary books of prophecy, the **Liber Vaticinationem Quodam Instinctumentis,** *was born. Written by an unknown scholar, it is the only prophetic book to provide exact dates.*

This book was rigorously suppressed by the Vatican, and appears to have only survived in one or two manuscript copies. One copy found its way into the huge collection of esoteric books and manuscripts amassed by the Nazis during World War II, and was stored in a warehouse in Poznan in Poland.

This manuscript probably dates from around the second half of the 16th century, and may have been made from a much earlier original. The main text is written in Latin. The manuscript divides history into a series of overlapping periods. Each of these is called a *norma*, Latin for "a rule, precept, model, or pattern".

The normae cover fixed periods of time, usually 60 or 144 years, and the prophecies allocated to them are very precise indeed.

Liber Vaticinationem suggests that certain events cause other events to happen. If the first, precipitating, event is delayed, then the second event may not happen at all. The date at which each norma begins (its dies natalis) depends upon complex calculations centred on the dates of realized events in the previous normae.

Let us take a specific norma, the 63rd, and examine its prophecies. This norma is called *Nullus Modus Caedibus Fuit* which, roughly translated, means "there was no end to the slaughter". It reads:

63:1 *"This 'norma' will only be fresh born*
When none but the quarrelsome wolf
Has lifted up his arm against another
In the Empire for one hundred years."

I interpret this to cover the period 1915 to 2058. The word "Empire" indicates Europe, as defined by the Roman Empire. The prophecies predicted will take place (the norma will be born) only after a period of 100 years of relative peace in Europe. The "quarrelsome wolf" is Germany. Now, as there was a period of relative peace in Europe for 99 years from the defeat of Napoleon at Waterloo in 1815 until 1915 (with the exception of the Franco-Prussian War in 1870) this norma was due to begin in 1915:

63:4 *"There will be no end to the slaughter*
As the wolf from the North of Rome
Tears thrice at the body of the Empire.
Even the Eastern empire shall shake."

This seems to suggest a state of war and death caused by the wolf (Germany) attacking the rest of the Empire (Europe) three times. Even Russia (the Eastern empire) will be involved. There follows a description of each of these three wars:

63:5 *"For the first a noble is twice attacked*
In the streets of Illyria and dies.
The wolf lifts up its eyes to the moon,
And the Eastern empire loses its head."

The first war is obviously the 1914–18 conflict, with the "noble twice attacked", the Austrian Archduke Ferdinand whose assassination in Sarajevo on 28 June 1914 sparked hostilities. There were two separate attempts to kill Ferdinand on that day.

"The wolf lifts up its eyes to the moon" refers to Germany's alliance with

Turkey, represented by the crescent moon of Islam. Russia (the Eastern empire) was drawn into the war and in 1917 deposed its Tsar ("loses its head"). Verse 63:14 states "when two years of months has passed away", making an opening date for the second war at 1915 (when the norma started) plus 24 equals 1939.

63:6 *"For the second, Rome conspires with the wolf:*
Between them they eat the Empire.
Mighty sounds light up the nights
And countless multitudes trample."

The last two lines are a fairly accurate description of the fruits of World War II: aerial bombardment, forced migration, and millions of displaced persons.

63:7 *"For the third, the earth shakes*
The throat of the Gaul is ravaged
Many die fleeing from the awful winds
The sun halts in its path in the heaven."

World War III has not yet happened, but this prophecy tells us what to expect. In 63:16, we are told: "The norma will die or be completed [*vita decedere*] when the wolf is cut in two", which could refer only to the partition of Germany in 1945. This particularly violence-packed norma is succeeded by the 64th norma which, by this reckoning, covers the period 1945–2089

THE FUTURE ACCORDING TO

LIBER VATICINATIONEM

Trying to get to the bottom of the dating of the prophecies contained in the *Liber Vaticinationem* is a bit like tackling a very difficult IQ test. Having said this, when the calculations are made correctly the book appears to provide exact dates for major events which occurred centuries after the book was written. The amazing predictions of the 63rd chapter of the manuscript are good examples. But what of the future? It is time to lift the corner of the page and glimpse the predictions which the 64th norma makes for the years 1945–2089. See what you can make of these:

64:9 *"The gods of the ancients will return*
To the streets and the taverns of the Empire.
The trees will shrivel in the hot wind
And the waters of Florence will become dry.
In the land beyond the Pillars of Hercules
There will rise the ghost of an horned image

And the prophet [haruspex] will return to the table
While the waters retreat from the hives[?].
In lowing, the cattle will bring the tiger upon them
But the stave of the farmer stays his mouth
From the country of the Jews comes quickly
The man who is justified by the horn of plenty."

KINGDOM OF THE CULTS

Many Christian cults spawned their own messiahs.
Many disciples followed them only too willingly, from
the women of the Abode of Love who buried their dead
standing up, through cults with millions of followers
and powerful publishing empires, to the flaming
Apocalypse of Waco and the strange female messiah of
modern Russia.

PROPHECIES ON PLATES OF GOLD

There is probably no American religious group with a more
fascinating history than the Mormons, who were founded in
the 19th century by the New England prophet Joseph Smith.

Vermont-born Smith received his first revelation in spring 1820, when he was only 14. He was praying in the woods near his home when two figures suddenly appeared. One pointed to the other and said, "This is my beloved Son, hear Him!" Smith immediately assumed he was experiencing a visitation from God himself and lost no time in asking which was the correct sect or church for him to join in order to be saved. The figure replied that "all their creeds [were] an abomination".

His second vision occurred two years later when an angel, or "messenger from God", as he put it, visited his bedside and told him that he had work to do in spreading the true gospel.

From that moment on Smith had a burning compulsion to bring the real truth, whatever that might be, to his fellow men. This angel, Moroni, told Smith that a book written on golden plates, giving an account of the former inhabitants of North America and containing the "fullness of the everlasting Gospel" as delivered by the Saviour to the ancient inhabitants of North America, had been deposited on the hillside outside the town where Smith lived. With the plates were the Urim and Thummim, the two stones which were the prophetic oracle and interpreter of God's words and worn by the ancient Jewish High Priests.

As you can imagine, the next day Smith went straight to the location on Cumorah Hill indicated by the angel, where he promptly found the book of golden plates deposited in a stone box with the stones Urim and Thummim, and the High Priest's breastplate. The angel, who paid him a visit on the hill, too, told Smith not to take out the contents of the stone box, but to return to the same location every year for the next four years. Finally, on 22 September 1827, at the autumn Equinox, the angel entrusted the plates and other paraphernalia to Smith.

Smith married Emma Hale and moved in with her father, where he began the task of translating the text written on the golden plates. The text was not written in Hebrew or even Greek as one might have imagined, but in "Reformed Egyptian". To satisfy Martin Harris, a potential financier and publisher of the book, Smith provided examples of this unique language together with his translation of it. The financier took them to a Professor Charles Anthon who identified the characters as a mixture of "Egyptian, Chaldean, Assyriac and Arabic". How anyone untutored could translate such an esoteric mixture is hard to say, but apparently divine inspiration triumphed over mere book learning, and the translation progressed.

In 1929, Smith and a friend, Oliver Cowdery, met another heavenly messenger while praying in the woods. This messenger, who identified himself as John the Baptist, immediately initiated both Smith and Oliver into "the priesthood of Aaron". Aaron was the elder brother of Moses and the first in the long line of Jewish High Priests to come after the Israelites' escape from captivity in Egypt. It is unclear how John the Baptist was able to confer the Jewish priesthood upon these two, but according to Smith he did, and later the pair received an even higher accolade, that of the priesthood of Melchizedek (see panel).

Smith's translation of the book of the golden leaves was published on 26 March 1830, close to the spring Equinox, two and a half years after he had begun working on it. A few days later the "Church of Jesus Christ of Latter-day Saints", as the Mormons refer to their church, was officially constituted at Fayette in New York.

The Mormons eventually settled at Nauvoo. Here, Joseph Smith and his brother were killed when an anti-Mormon mob stormed the jail where they were being held for destroying a printworks. Brigham Young (1801–77), who succeeded the martyred Smith, moved the colony westwards to Salt Lake City, Utah, which is still the headquarters and home of the sect.

THE PRIESTHOOD OF MELCHIZEDEK

The original Melchizedek was called "Priest of the Most High God". He was a Caananite priest and possibly king of Jerusalem at the time of Abraham. By one sect of Gnostics (these were early Christians who claimed to have certain mystical knowledge denied to other people) he was held to be an earlier incarnation of Christ. This strange view, that God has reincarnated more than once, is supported in the Epistle of Paul to the Hebrews 7:3 where Melchizedek is referred to as "like unto the Son of God". In the same chapter St Paul even questions Christ's ancestry by suggesting that the tribe of Judah, from which Christ descended, was not renowned for producing great priests or prophets, as was the tribe of Levi or the descendants of Melchizedek.

All male Mormons of a certain age, good standing and good character may be received into one or other of these two priesthoods, Levi or Melchizedek. It is for this reason that the Mormons have a very large male priesthood and a predominantly female laity.

BAPTISM FOR
80 MILLION DEAD

"Celestial marriage" and "baptism for the dead" are among the ceremonies celebrated in Mormon temples. Ironically, their programme of "baptism for the dead" has resulted in the mass forced baptism of the faithful of other churches.

Mormons believe in the literal gathering of the Ten Tribes of Israel in America, before the return of Christ who will then reign over them personally. This will happen close to the millennium in three distinct stages:

1. The Gathering of Ephraim. The tribe of Ephraim from whom Joseph Smith claimed (presumably spiritual) descent is to gather first in Zion, the site of the New Jerusalem. The site of Zion was previously thought to be the city of Independence, Missouri, but is now designated as a site near the Rocky Mountains. This gathering is progressing at the moment.

2. The Gathering of the Jews. This gathering of the descendants of the Kingdom of Judah (not the descendants of the Kingdom of Israel) is currently taking place in Palestine, as also predicted by the Old Testament prophets. This prediction just recently got a boost from the signing of the PLO/Israeli peace accord in September 1993. The Temple, and possibly the city, of Jerusalem have yet to be rebuilt before the return of Christ.

3. The Gathering of the Ten Lost Tribes. Distinct from the previous gathering, there will be a gathering of the ten lost tribes of Israel, which are still hiding somewhere "in the lands of the north". They are to regroup and go to Zion where they will be received by the Ephraimites who have already arrived there. This has not yet happened, and may well be quite tricky to arrange, unless you believe the British Israelite doctrine that these lost tribes are, in fact, the British!

The Mormons believe that when these three gatherings are complete, Christ will return to earth. For them, the Millennium constitutes a period of 1000 years beginning at about the year AD 2000. There will be two resurrections, one at the beginning and one at the end of this millennial period. In the first resurrection the believing dead will be raised, and in rapture will literally rise through the air to meet the descending Christ, touching down again with him as he lands. Charitably, the Mormons include the "good heathen" in this resurrection. The wicked, on the other hand, will be "burned as stubble" without a second chance, and during the millennium their spirits will remain in some gigantic spirit prison.

Shortly after the beginning of the millennium, in the year AD 2000, the "City of Enoch" (or the New Jerusalem) will descend from heaven and materialize in the prepared site of Zion. Satan will be bound and his power to do evil severely limited. People living during this time will die if they are unrepentant, or alternatively become immortal at the age of 100 instead of facing death, an attractive prospect. After his return to Earth, Christ will rule in the flesh over two capital cities, Jerusalem in Palestine and "Zion" in the USA. After this the Earth will rest from wars for a further 1000 beatific years.

At the end of the millennial period in AD 3000 there will be a second round of resurrections, Satan will be released, and the very small number of those who follow him will become the "Sons of Perdition". These unfortunates are destined never to be redeemed, and to eternally reside in Hell. With his new converts, Satan will again attempt, albeit unsuccessfully, to storm heaven. After his defeat the Earth shall become "celestialized" and a fit home for the remaining spiritualized humans, who will receive varying degrees of immortality.

80 MILLION DEAD HELD

IN COMPUTERS

The Mormon crusade to "baptize the dead" has resulted in the sect accumulating vast quantities of genealogical information, including birth, baptism and marriage details, for over 80,000,000 dead people!

This data is stored in memory banks in Salt Lake City. Copies are kept in enormous tunnels bored into the mountains, in what must be one of the safest data storage facilities in the world today. It is a comforting thought that if the world were wiped out by some apocalyptic cataclysm, the details of all these people would be available for inspection at some remote time in the future.

The more than 80 million dead so documented are not necessarily Mormons, but are mostly of Anglo-Saxon descent, and seldom aware that their details are being added to and preserved by a sect they may never have heard of.

There are several non-religious by-products of this extraordinary endeavour. First, the records, once computerized, are supplied on microfiche cards at Mormon centres throughout the world, and are used extensively by ordinary genealogists and family historians.

Recently researchers into "genetic epidemiology" – research into the incidence, distribution and control or dissemination of a disease in the overall population – have been using this vast collection of records to trace back diseases to the parents, grandparents and great-grandparents of current patients. This enables researchers to then contact other branches of a family to trace genes which predispose to certain conditions. Maybe medical help will come to some of these potential patients, instead of the religious salvation originally intended.

JEHOVAH'S WITNESSES

Charles Taze Russell (1852–1916), the founding father of the Jehovah's Witnesses, calculated a date for the end of the world, Armageddon and the Second Coming of Christ. The year 1999 is the current expectation.

Russell first put forward 1874 as the date of the establishment of the Kingdom of God, and when this failed he settled upon 1 October 1914. He must have been one of the few people to be pleased by the start of World War I in the summer of that year. When Christ failed to materialize after this promising start, Russell said He was invisible, in fact merely a heavenly transaction in rulership. Armageddon was then comfortably predicted for 61 years later, in 1975, a date subsequently revised several times.

Armageddon will be Jehovah's decisive (though not final) battle against his enemies. The Witnesses regard this as a necessary battle to unseat Satan, the previous ruler of the world, before the ushering in of a glorious new world. The price will be high: over two billion dead, none of whom will be raised up to Heaven. One side will use bows, arrows, handstaves and spears, and the other cloudbursts, floods, earthquakes, hailstones, all-consuming fires and flesh-eating plagues. At the end of the battle Christ will cast Satan and his demonic associates into the abyss.

Cleansed by Armageddon, the Earth will become a temperate garden, an earthly paradise, replacing the paradise lost at the dawn of history. Beasts will be at peace one with another and man will have dominion over the "lower animals". The millennium will literally be a thousand-year period reigned over by Christ, with no ageing, no disease, no crime, no vice and no death. The earth will be populated by the survivors of Armageddon.

Russell arrived at these dates by plucking from the Bible whichever passages suited his purpose, regardless of context. This technique is still used by members of the movement today. From that old stalwart of all interpreters, the Book of Daniel, chapter 7:14, Russell deduced that Christ was to be given a kingdom which would never be destroyed, by God, "the Ancient of days".

Christ was supposed to receive this kingdom at the end of the "appointed times of the nations", calculated at 2520 days (see panel), for which read years. Prophets were often said to use "days" as a sort of shorthand for years, a practice supposedly supported in Ezekiel 4:6: "I have appointed thee each day for a year". To arrive at a date for the millennial year, you add 2520 to 607 (BC), when Israel lost its sovereignty and came under the rule of the armies of Babylon.

But to return to the beginnings of the Jehovah's Witnesses; in 1879 Russell first published a magazine called Zion's Watch Tower and Herald of Christ's Presence, which helped to publicize the new movement. Five years later Russell's society was legally incorporated.

The millennial bent of the organization was apparent from the beginning. In a series of books called "Millennial Dawn" Russell tantalized his disciples with promises of the kingdom near at hand. Over six million copies of the first book found homes.

In 1912 Russell began work on one of his most ambitious projects, the Photo-Drama of Creation. Through a mixture of slides and motion pictures with sound, years ahead of its time, Russell portrayed events from the Creation to the end of Christ's supposed 1000-year reign. Up to 35,000 people daily were seeing Russell's show when it opened in 1914. Just as the Jehovah's Witnesses had discovered the power of the printing presses, so they recognized the importance of cinema as a medium for spreading news of their cause.

Russell survived his 1914 prophecy by only two years. After his death the leadership of the organization was disputed, and further trouble followed in 1918 when the Canadian government forbade anyone to possess copies of the Watchtower. Also in 1918, eight leading members were found guilty of refusing to serve in the US military, an offence for which their leader was sentenced to 20 years' imprisonment, although a year later all the men were freed.

To get round this problem, which arose again during the Second World War, a number of members became 'ministers' full time, which helped to expand the movement.

The Church is now a huge organization with its own printing presses and sophisticated administration infrastructure. In New York alone, the Witnesses run seven factories and a large office complex.

The Jehovah's Witnesses deny any conscious existence after death. Man, according to them, will remain in the grave until the millennium, when the favoured few will be resurrected in a spiritual body. There are more than 3,750,00 Jehovah's Witnesses in the world today, but according to their own scriptures there is only room for 144,000 souls to reign as the elect with Christ in Heaven.

CALCULATING THE DATE OF
CHRIST'S RETURN

The starting point for the Jehovah's Witnesses is, as we have seen, 607 BC, the date the people of Israel were subjugated by Babylon. Nebuchadnezzar is told in Daniel 4:23 that he shall be reduced to the state of a beast of the field, "till seven times pass over him".

This is construed as seven years or seven times 360 (the number of days in a year, according to the usage then assumed current), which equals 2520. This last figure is interpreted as 2520 years, using the year for a day rule, which is then added to 607 BC. We then get the year AD 1914 as the date Christ was due to return to rule his Kingdom, invisibly.

Nebuchadnezzar's madness is seen as a sort of punishment for taking the Jews into captivity, and by extension becomes the calculator by which the date of the Saviour's reappearance is arrived at.

WILLIAM MILLER

Surprisingly, the story of the Seventh-Day Adventists does not begin with the observance of Saturday as the Lord's Day, but with a precise prophecy of the Second Coming, heralding the end of the world.

According to early Seventh-Day Adventist William Miller, Christ would return some time between 21 March 1843 and 21 March 1844.

Born in Pittsfield, Massachusetts in 1782, the young Miller underwent conversion, and after several years of intensive Bible study came to the conclusion that "in about twenty-five years from that time [1818] all the affairs of our present state would be wound up". Miller had found some interesting references to numbers in the Book of Daniel 9:24–27:

"24 Seventy weeks are determined upon thy people and upon thy holy city ... and to anoint the most Holy.

25 Know therefore ... that from the going forth of the commandment to restore and build [again] Jerusalem unto the Messiah the Prince shall be seven weeks, and three score and two weeks ...

26 And after three score and two weeks shall Messiah be cut off ... "

Miller took the starting date of this prophecy to be 457 BC, the year of the decree of Artaxerxes which permitted Ezra to return to Jerusalem and recommence worship in the Temple.

He understood one day in prophetic language to mean one year. Thus the 70 weeks mentioned in the text became 490 years. Miller promptly added 490 to 457 BC and was delighted when he got AD 33, the date of Christ's crucifixion. Now, he felt, he was definitely on the right track.

Miller then read Daniel 8:14:

"And he said unto me, Unto two thousand and three hundred days [literally 'evening morning']; then shall the sanctuary be cleansed [justified]."

Using the same formula as before, Miller established that the time period referred to was 2300 years. He added this number to 457 BC and got AD 1843. Reading further on, Daniel asks God for the meaning of this, and the Archangel Gabriel explains that "at the time of the end shall be the vision". Miller assumed then that, as AD 1843 was to be the end of the present order, the phrase "the sanctuary be cleansed" must indicate the return of Christ.

When the designated year arrived Christ did not return to reign on earth, and intense disappointment was felt among the Millerites, of whom there were by now many thousands. Miller himself was dumbfounded at the failure of his calculations. The year was moved forward to AD 1844 to take account of the BC/AD arithmetic anomaly (see panel). Again Christ failed to turn up. Then one of Miller's followers raised hopes again by suggesting that Christ's return would be not at the Equinox in 1844 but at the seventh month, specifically 22 October 1844, which corresponded to the Jewish Day of Atonement for that year. Miller accepted this new interpretation. Again they all waited, again in vain. The disappointment this time was overwhelming: 22 October is still referred to by Seventh-Day Adventists as "the Great Disappointment". Many people gave up the faith at this point, leaving only a small core of believers.

The movement was then rescued from oblivion by Hiram Edison. He claimed to have seen a vision which explained that the prophesied date was still valid, but that it represented the transference of the movement from one compartment of heaven to another! Joseph Bates, a retired sea captain, made a further contribution. In 1845 he became convinced that the seventh day of the week – when, according to Genesis, God rested – was Saturday. For centuries, he argued, Christians had been damning themselves by not observing the (correct) seventh day of rest. His reading of the Apocalypse of St John, chapter 7:4, was that only the 144,000 souls who correctly observed this Commandment would be saved at the end of the world.

But it is Ellen G. White (1827–1915) who can properly be credited with founding Seventh-Day Adventism as we recognize it today. She had roughly 200 visions, the contents of which were to do with both the Second Coming of Christ and the day-to-day theological problems of the new religion. White disseminated the ideas she received in these visions through the radio programme The Voice of Prophecy, the TV programme Faith for Today and a comprehensive list of publications.

Belief in the Second Coming of Christ is absolute among Adventists, although they no longer try to set a date for it. Some of their literature sets 1999 as the date for the end of the world, which will be brought about by the battle of Armageddon. All the wicked will perish in the battle, leaving the righteous, God's elect, to be transported to Heaven to rule with Christ for 1000 years, the new millennium.

At the end of this thousand years, Satan will be freed and the wicked dead allowed to rise from their graves and again overrun the earth. There will be yet another battle (not Armageddon) between Satan and his wicked hordes and Christ and his "camp of saints" in the newly descended New Jerusalem. Satan and his followers will eventually be annihilated.

WHAT MILLER'S CALCULATIONS
RESTED UPON

Miller made several assumptions, all of them possibly flawed: 1 That a "day" in prophetic writings always equals a year, but 2300 days might literally mean 6.3 years rather than 2300 years. 2 That the 70 "weeks" and the 2300 "days" began at the same time. If, for example, the 2300 "days" ran from AD 33, then the date of Christ's Second Coming becomes AD 2333, not AD 1843. 3 That the correct baseline date was 457 BC. A case could be made for picking 445 or 444 BC instead, when permission was granted for the rebuilding of the walls of Jerusalem. Artaxerxes simply allowed Nehemiah and Ezra to return to Jerusalem in 457 BC. 4 That the "cleansing of the sanctuary" actually refers to Christ's coming, rather than some other pre-apocalyptic event. 5 Lastly, there is a small matter of arithmetic which has proved a stumbling block for many date calculations that cross from BC to AD. Because there were two "year ones" (AD 1 and BC 1), you must always remember to subtract one year from the first total arrived at. For example, the timespan between the beginning of January 2 BC and January AD 3 is not five years but four years.

This last error will be found in a number of other predictions discussed in this book, such as Gerald Massey's calculations.

THE BURNING STAIRCASE

At noon on 19 April 1993, in Waco, Texas, David Koresh held

fast with oratory 85 of his followers before luring them to a

fiery grave with the promise of immortality.

The men, women and children who perished with their mad "messiah" on this day were victims of a system of beliefs devised 150 years ago by William Miller.

Following the chronology of Archbishop Ussher, and interpreting the 2300 days of Daniel as 2300 years, Miller predicted that the end of the world would arrive in AD 1843. After one failed prophecy, Miller chose the "Seventh month" for the Advent of Christ, and on 22 October 1844 solemnly led his disciples up into the hills to meet their maker. As we know, Christ did not arrive and his flock had to trudge back down again.

Some 90 years later, in 1931, a breakaway group from the mainstream of Seventh-Day Adventism, the self-styled Branch Davidian, established a centre at Waco. Since this time the sect has mainly recruited its members from the rank and file of Seventh-Day Adventists. The widow of the founder kept up his work until she died at the age of 85. In a frenzy of belief worthy of an Old Testament prophet the son dug up her body and declared that her successor was whoever could resurrect the body. David Koresh, a member of the cult, pragmatically reported the son to the authorities. His subsequent arrest for unlawful exhumation resulted in a long stay in an institution.

The way was then clear for Koresh to take over leadership of the cult. He introduced a number of doctrines with strong sexual overtones. For him the anointing oil of the Psalms was symbolic of the sexual secretions of his female followers upon the head of his erect penis. He practised what he preached and insisted that chosen wives from among his followers should have sex with him and not their husbands. He also "marked" children of his followers as future wives; one such was Rachel Sylvia, who was 13 at the time she died in the inferno.

He wanted his followers to be one big happy family: he had two children with disciple Nicole Gent, three with Michelle Jones, one with Lorraine Sylvia and a further two with his wife Rachel – not to mention the numerous affairs he had with other followers. Theological threats of damnation were reinforced by physical punishment and subtle peer pressure.

Koresh believed that 1993 would herald the second coming of Christ, exactly some 150 years after Miller's original date. He prepared to separate his followers from the outside world. The ranch was fortified, secret tunnels were built and large amounts of semiautomatic weapons were bought by mail order. It was precisely these extensive postal purchases which first drew the attention of the gun law enforcement agency (ATF) to the sect. A request to search the premises was met with a hail of bullets which killed several agents. This rash act brought the weight of the law against the community. On 28 February 1993 a siege began, with Koresh refusing to allow either the law enforcement agencies to enter or his followers to leave the stronghold. Koresh often spoke of glorifying the Lord by dying in the fire. The FBI bombarded the compound with loud music, lit it with searchlights, and towed away Koresh's favourite car, a black Chevrolet.

Children who had been allowed to leave Mount Carmel, as the stronghold was called, told harrowing tales of physical and sexual abuse. Girls, some as young as 11, were given a symbolic star of David which signified that they had been selected to have sex with Koresh and must not be deflowered by any other member of the cult. These children were then taught to refer to Koresh as "father", and their natural parents as "dogs".

On the final day, 51 days after the siege first began, the FBI employed a tank as a battering ram to punch holes in the outer walls of the ranch. Inside Koresh calmed his followers, who put on gas masks and read from the Bible while CS gas rained on the compound. Those who attempted to leave were shot. Five hours later the 24 children, many of them his own, were separated from their parents and systematically drugged. Koresh sat in a reclining chair and read the Bible to the adults. The Apocalypse was now, he said, and they would pass to heaven with him through the purifying fire.

Finally, at 12.06 pm, Koresh gave the order to torch the kerosene that had been poured around the buildings and the ranch was engulfed by flames.

THE SECOND COMING OF CYRUS

The name "Koresh" means "sun" and is the Hebrew spelling of Cyrus, conqueror of Babylon, king and founder of Persia who lived in the 6th century BC. Koresh even called his son Cyrus, in honour of this king.

The original Cyrus was a polytheist, and perhaps a Zoroastrian or fire worshipper. His favourite form of punishment was burning his prisoners alive. King Cyrus allowed the Jews to leave Babylon and return to Palestine to rebuild the Temple of Jerusalem. The very favourable reference made to him in the Old Testament was to capture David Koresh's imagination.

If the FBI had been a bit more aware of Biblical history, they might have been able to foresee the fiery inferno which this latter-day Cyrus had in store for his devoted followers.

PREGNANT WITH
THE MESSIAH

The prophet Joanna Southcott (1750–1814) experienced the

Second Coming of Christ in a unique way, claiming that she

was pregnant with the Messiah.

Born in Gittisham, Devon, into a tenant farming family, Joanna Southcott worked as a milkmaid and shopgirl before finding her real vocation as a prophet. An intensifying taste for religion and church-going made her reject carnal love and turn down suitors.

In 1792 she made her first prophecy, announcing during a Bible class that she was to be "the Lamb's wife". Then she had a fit and had to be carried out of the class. One day Joanna found a small seal with the initials "IC" and two stars on it. She adopted it as her own, interpreting the initials as those of Jesus Christ.

Joanna's big break came in January 1802 when she made the acquaintance of William Sharp, a wealthy engraver from Chiswick, west London, who became one of her disciples. Joanna moved to London, where she soon began to attract interest. The first Southcottian Chapel was opened in Duke Street, Southwark, by a dissenting West Country minister called William Tozer. Many in her growing audience "came to mock but remained to pray", according to one observer.

Eternal salvation would be granted to only 144,000 of her followers, Joanna declared. Furthermore, it was conditional upon them receiving the mark of the "IC" seal. A salvation document bearing the seal was accordingly offered to the faithful. This document stated that the recipient was "the sealed of the Lord ... [and was] to inherit the tree of life – to be made heirs of God and joint-heirs with Jesus Christ"; in short, he or she owned a share in paradise. Joanna issued at least 10,000 of these certificates, one of which was found in the possession of a murderess named Mary Bateman.

In late summer 1813, after a successful trip to northern England setting up new chapels, Joanna wrote letters to every bishop, peer, and Member of Parliament, as well as open letters to the London Times and other newspapers, announcing that she was soon to become the "mother of Shiloh". A short while later she withdrew from public life, presumably to get on with her messianic pregnancy.

In March 1814 her disciples called in nine eminent doctors to examine the 64-year-old prophet. They all agreed that she showed unmistakeable signs of pregnancy and they estimated that the child would be born on Christmas Day. The news caused a great stir, and gifts of money, jewellery and clothing poured in from donors eager to cultivate the goodwill of the incipient second Jesus Christ.

However, on Christmas Day, growing weaker and beginning to feel that rather than giving birth to Christ she was in fact dying, Joanna gave her last instructions. Her body was to be kept warm, and then opened up four days after her death. The presents for the new Messiah were to be returned. Two days later she was dead. The autopsy showed no organic disease or foetus.

Surprisingly few of her followers seemed in the least disconcerted by the non-arrival of the Messiah and 50 years after her death, donations received from her followers in just one city – Melbourne, Australia – enabled one of her disciples to build a mansion, Melbourne House, in Yorkshire.

This disciple was the bearded hunchback John Wroe. In 1823 he made two highly publicized attempts to walk on water, with predictable results. In the same year he had himself publicly circumcised. In the 1840s, after careful calculation, Wroe declared that the millennium would begin in 1863. His prophecy came true for him at least, as in that year he died.

THE MILLENNIAL PANDORA'S BOX

One of Joanna Southcott's legacies to the world is a locked and sealed box tied with cords and still kept with great reverence in southern England. In it, or so her followers believe, is the secret of world peace, happiness and the millennium foretold in the Apocalypse of St John.

This box first came to light after the death of the Southcottians' then leader Helen Exeter, who had formed the Panacea Society to promote Joanna's writings. Like Wroe, she died in her predicted millennium year; she met her death in 1914, on a torpedoed ship in the English Channel. The box may only be opened in the presence of the full complement of bishops of the Church of England, 24 of them in all, a stipulation that seems certain to keep it closed forever.

One man said to have opened the box was the famous psychical researcher Harry Price, in 1927. Among the strange assortment of items he discovered were an old nightcap, a flintlock pistol, some papers and a few odds and ends. The Panacea Society maintain that he cannot have opened Joanna's box.

In this last decade of the 20th century there are still groups of Southcottian believers dotted round the world who are awaiting the arrival of the millennium. This, they believe, will coincide with the opening of the mysterious box. Invoking Joanna's formula of "the fourth year after the first decade of the century", their estimated date of His arrival, and the millennium's, is 2014.

THE SHINING VIRGIN OF
FATIMA ·

If you want to know what is going to happen at the end of the

millennium from an impeccable source, then look no further

than the prophecies of the Virgin Mary.

On Sunday 13 May 1917, the Feast of the Ascension, Lucia, Francisco and Jacinta, children ranging in age from seven to ten, were tending sheep in a natural depression called Cova da Iria near the village of Fatima, about 80 miles (129 kilometres) north of Lisbon. Suddenly there was a startling flash of light in the clear sky. A second flash drew their eyes to a tree, in front of which stood a beautiful lady wearing a luminous white mantle and holding a coruscating rosary. She told the children not to be afraid and that she had come from Heaven. After asking them to return to the same spot at the same time on the thirteenth day of each of the next six months, the Lady rose into the sky and disappeared.

One month later the children went back to the same spot, this time accompanied by several incredulous villagers. At noon a small white cloud of light floated down from the sky and hovered above the same tree. Only the children saw the Lady, who prophesied that the eldest, Lucia Do Santos, would live to a ripe old age, whereas the other two would die soon, a prophecy which came true. The Lady departed, and the villagers present claimed to have heard a sound like a rocket as the small cloud vanished into the sky.

The news spread rapidly, and for the Lady's third appearance, on 13 July, there were some 5000 people present. This time Lucia asked the Lady who she was. The Lady did not answer directly, but promised that World War I would end soon (it did the following year) and that "another, more terrible one will break out" during the reign of Pope Pius XI, and would be heralded by an unknown light in the night sky.

This weird illumination of the sky occurred on 25 January 1938, when the skies of the northern hemisphere were filled with a crimson light, like "a reflection of the fires of hell". The New York Times devoted nearly a whole page to this strange occurrence. Pope Pius XI was put under tremendous pressure by the dictators of Italy and Germany and died just before the outbreak of World War II in 1939. The Lady said that the only way to prevent this second world war was for Russia to revert to Christianity, which as we know is just beginning to happen. After the reconversion and consecration of Russia, she went on, "the world will be granted a period of peace".

The next promised appearance of the Lady, on 13 August 1917, was spoilt by the authorities, who arrested the three children. Some 15,000 people gathered at the spot and saw the white cloud of light appear from the east, hover for a time over the tree and then leave.

The appearance of 13 October drew a huge crowd of 70,000 people, roughly 17 per cent of the then population of the whole country. The day was overcast and at 10am it started to pour with rain. At half past one a pillar of smoke rose above the heads of the three children and evaporated; this happened three times. The clouds then parted to reveal a disk (some said this was the sun) which shone like dull silver. This disk could be stared at without pain to the eyes or blinding. It began to whirl around and as it did so a succession of glowing colours passed over its surface. The atmosphere changed to a purple colour and then to "the colour of old yellow damask".

So what was this event – a miracle or a figment of the imagination? From the subsequent testimony of thousands, it is certain that something incredible did happen and that it cannot be explained as a "trick of the light", a hoax, or indeed a climatic aberration.

THE VIRGIN SPEAKS OUT

Great controversy surrounds the third of the prophecies of the Virgin. Lucia, it is said, turned white on hearing it and cried out in fear. She refused to disclose the contents of the prophecy, but eventually wrote it down and sent it to the Pope via the Bishop of Leiria.

Although part of the prophecy was released to the world in 1942 by Pope Pius XII, mainly that concerning the war, the rest of it has not been disclosed. There are fairly compelling reasons for believing that the rest of the prophecy predicts the persecution of the Pope and ultimate destruction of the Roman Catholic Church in about the year 2000. No wonder it is still suppressed by the Vatican, despite the Lady's instruction that it could, and should, be fully revealed to the public in 1960.

A Stuttgart newspaper, the Neues Europa, had no doubt that this was indeed the content of the third prophecy. On 15 October 1963, the newspaper printed what they claimed to be the text of the prophecy:

"For the Church too, the time of its greatest trial will come. Cardinals will oppose cardinals and bishops against bishops. Satan will march in their midst and there will be great changes at Rome. What is rotten will fall, never to rise again. The church will be darkened and the world will shake with terror. The time will come when no king, emperor, cardinal or bishop will await Him who will, however, come, but in order to punish according to the designs of my Father."

MR DONNELLY'S TRUTHS
HELD DEAR

Congressman Ignatius Donnelly did not succeed in convincing

many people with his strange, heretical theories of lost worlds,

but he certainly knew how to attract attention to them.

Born on 3 November 1831 to a middle-class migrant Irish family settled in Philadelphia, Donnelly trained as a lawyer before going into politics at the age of 24. By 1859 he was Lieutenant-Governor of Minnesota, despite an attempt to found a model city which had ended in bankruptcy. In public life he was a great orator and rabble-rouser, quick to denounce scandals, rackets and conspiracies.

Apart from his politicking, Donnelly is remembered for coming up with three improbable theories. The first concerns the destruction of the lost city of Atlantis, which is said by some to have sunk beneath the waves of the Atlantic. Not since the time of Plato had this myth held much interest for the rest of the world. After Donnelly's re-heating, it is doubtful if Plato would have recognized it. In his book Atlantis: the Antediluvian World, Donnelly tried to put right what he saw as the total corruption of history. The end-product was a model of how to make very flimsy evidence seem very substantial, and almost believable.

Donnelly identified Atlantis as the origin of such locations as the Garden of Eden, Garden of the Hesperides, Elysian Fields, Mount Olympus, Asgard, and virtually every other paradise dreamt about by man. After the deluge (which became the prototype of flood myths in many cultures) and destruction of this earthly paradise, Atlantean colonists were supposed to have initiated cultures in Egypt, America, and that of the Aryan and Semitic cultures. How else, Donnelly argued, can we explain the religious use of pyramids in both Central America, in the Inca culture, and in ancient Egyptian culture? These cultures must have sprung from the same, shared mid-Atlantic origin. In a word, Atlantis.

Donnelly's work was not simply disregarded as the ravings of a madman. No less a person than the British prime minister Gladstone tabled a motion in the House of Commons proposing that a Royal Navy task force be sent to the Atlantic to search for remnants of Atlantis. Harder heads in the Treasury vetoed this idea on the grounds of cost.

Not content to rest on these laurels, Donnelly then busied himself with theories concerning the destruction of the world, published in his book Ragnarok. The London Daily News referred to its author as "a stupendous speculator in cosmogony". Donnelly's visionary tone soon won many admirers for his grandiose notions. He theorized that a giant comet had almost, and indeed still could, bring death and destruction to Earth. Later, Immanuel Velikovsky was to expand these theories, giving them a scientific basis, and, amazingly, make scientific predictions from them which would later be proved correct.

Tiring perhaps of writing about the past, Donnelly made an attempt at predicting the events of the 1990s in a book he called Caesar's Column, published in 1890. He accurately predicted the supremacy of big business over morality and politics, but the notion that large cities would be powered by the earth's magnetic currents seems a long way from being realized. Restaurants would serve every imaginable dish from all over the world, cooked at the press of a button, which is a good guess at the technology of the microwave. News from any part of the globe would also be available at the press of a button and would be shown on individual screens, an amazingly accurate prophecy of current computer-based news technology.

Donnelly envisaged modern cities at the end of the 20th century relying heavily on slave labour. In Donnelly's book this under-class eventually revolts, destroying the state armies by aerial bombardment and massacring the ruling classes. The victims of the revolt are cemented into a huge pillar of concrete to commemorate the revolution, then the mob turns on its leaders and lynches them as well. The hero of the book escapes from New York in an airship and flies to Europe. From Europe he flees south, taking with him the people who will found a new civilization in, of all places, Uganda.

After being elected Vice-President of the People's Party in the United States, Donnelly took a second wife, who was 46 years younger than himself. He died peacefully in 1901.

SHAKESPEARE'S SECRETS

The crowning achievement of Donnelly's life, or so he felt, was his "deciphering"of Shakespeare. In this he followed an earlier American, Delia Bacon, who hoped to restore credit for William Shakespeare's plays to her namesake, Francis Bacon. This research involved incredibly tortuous manipulations of the text and its corresponding numerical values, which were designed to yield hidden messages from Bacon, the supposed secret author of Shakespeare's works.

Bacon's well-known penchant for ciphers made him a natural choice for the author of an immensely complex body of plays from which all kinds of messages could be extracted with the exercise of a little imagination. Donnelly, however, was not interested in applying a little imagination, and in the course of these intricate researches he claimed to have used up two tons of paper. His monumental work, The Great Cryptogram, runs to almost 1000 pages. Unfortunately, it amply demonstrates to what level a once great intellect can fall.

The second volume reduced Donnelly to a laughing stock in intellectual circles, from which a lesser man would never have recovered. Perhaps, though, he had the last laugh: the book sold out, was reprinted, and was soon followed by a sequel on the same subject.

THE CHRISTIAN ISRAELITES

Once it was thought that the most expedient way to bring forward the date of the millennium was to cause the appearance of the predicted signs of the Apocalyse.

One of the most important signs of the coming Apocalypse was the return of the dispersed Jews to Israel, and, according to some interpreters, their conversion to Christianity.

As early as the 4th century AD the Tibertine Oracle, the first of the forged medieval Sibylline Oracles, prophesied the Jews' eventual acceptance of Christ. In medieval Europe the persecution of Jews who refused conversion often went hand-in-hand with the Crusades for the recovery of the Holy Land. Pope Paul IV established Rome's Jewish ghetto in 1555 to facilitate originally well-intentioned conversion efforts.

The cult of Anglo-Israelitism emerged in England with Puritanism, which took literally the Bible's prophecies of the restoration of Israel, and now flourishes predominantly in the USA. Under the Puritan government of Oliver Cromwell in the 1650s the laws against Jewish immigration were relaxed, although not completely lifted. So curious were Cromwell's views of the Jewish people that the Jewish community in the Netherlands went so far as to send an investigator to check if Cromwell's roots were actually Jewish.

In recognition of their religious roots, one particularly fanatical Puritan, Praisegod Barebone, was in the forefront of moves by the Little Parliament (1653) to abolish the English constitution and replace it with the Jewish laws of Moses.

This was taken to a crazy extreme in the late 18th century by Richard Brothers (1757–1824), a retired naval officer who proclaimed himself the King of the Jews. He believed that he and his followers had been chosen to lead the Jews back to the Holy Land and lodge them in a splendid New Jerusalem before converting them to Christianity in preparation for the second coming of the Messiah.

Brothers told of visionary, and highly improbable, experiences, such as seeing the Devil walking down a London street and receiving two angels at his lodging house. Eventually the authorities tired of his rantings and had him committed to a lunatic asylum.

Before the Jews could be returned to Israel, there was the small problem of locating the ten so-called lost tribes of Israel. These tribes were captured by the Assyrians and dispersed from Palestine in the 8th century BC, leaving just the two tribes of the kingdom of Judaea. Several scholars, including Edward Hine (1801–85), "discovered" that, after long wanderings, these ten tribes had ended their journey in England.

Isaiah himself lent some credence to this idea when he said that "the Lord shall ... recover the remnant of his people, which shall be left, from Assyria, and from Egypt ... and from the islands of the sea" (11:11). Hine concluded that these islands were certainly the British Isles. Hine's idea drew support from Professor Piazzi Smyth, Astronomer Royal for Scotland, who had a few odd theories of his own regarding the Great Pyramid.

Anthony Cooper, the seventh Earl of Shaftesbury (1801–85), President of the Society for Promoting Christianity among the Jews, strove to bring about the Second Coming by converting the Jews. Described as the "prince of do-gooders", Cooper was famous for his reformation of the working conditions of Victorian chimneysweeps. He even arranged an emigration service for London's leading thieves. Cooper had less success with his conversion plan: his best year saw only three conversions. Strangely, most of his converts were rabbis!

Successive British governments were committed to the principle of a new Jewish homeland by the Balfour Declaration of 1917. Finally, in May 1948, this intention was translated into the establishment of the state of Israel. Interestingly, the sum total of the numbers in this date (1+9+4+8) comes to 22, the number of letters in the Hebrew alphabet and a mystical number in the Jewish qabalah.

BRITISH ISRAELITES IN
AMERICA

The Puritan settlers took their identification with the Jews to America with them. In the 19th century Edward Hine was among those who tried to keep the message alive there, in 1884 undertaking an extended speaking tour of the States. After several years of itinerant prophesying he fell on hard times and had to be repatriated to his homeland by his British followers.

The promised restoration of the Jews to Palestine loomed large in US prophecy conferences held between 1878 and 1918. When the state of Israel was founded a teacher at the Bible Institute of Los Angeles announced on radio that this was "the greatest piece of prophetic news that we have had in the 20th century". Jesus was expected to come at any moment.

A similar reaction greeted Israel's capture of the Old City of Jerusalem during the Six Day War in 1967, which seemed to confirm centuries of prophetic speculation. Hal Lindsey's Late Great Planet Earth, which came out three years later, sold in vast numbers on the back of a fresh resurgence of interest in millennial prophecies.

Of the post-War American proponents of Anglo-Israelism, James Lovell (of Kingdon Digest), Howard Rand (of Destiny Publishers) and Herbert W. Armstrong are perhaps the best known. Armstrong, founder of the Radio Church of God, editor of The Plain Truth magazine and veteran of religious programmes on television, concerned himself particularly with Anglo-Israelism and millennial prophecy.

SISTER MARIE GABRIEL'S WARNING

On Monday 19 July 1993, Sister Marie Gabriel Paprocski,

a "secular plain clothes religious Sister" with an interest in

astronomy, let it be known that a gigantic comet was on a

collision course with Jupiter.

According to this Polish nun's calculations, a comet would collide with Jupiter before 25 July 1994. Her prediction contradicted Velikovsky's notion of a massive body having been torn out of Jupiter 3500 years ago.

Sister Marie Gabriel's warning came in a letter addressed to all world leaders, including Pope John Paul II, President Bill Clinton and President Yeltsin of the CIS. Press releases were sent to the major television companies and full-page adverts were taken in the major international newspapers. The good Sister certainly went to some trouble to promote her prophecy.

Sister Marie Gabriel, who claims to be the "astronomer Sophia", first made known her prediction in July 1986. The collision between Jupiter and the comet would, she said, produce the "biggest cosmic explosion in the history of mankind". Although at the time her description of the comet as "a fireball asteroid" persuaded many astronomers to dismiss her pronouncement as the ravings of a publicity seeking crackpot, subsequently scientists themselves predicted that a collision between Jupiter and a comet was indeed on the cards, albeit with no catastrophic fallout for mankind.

Sister Marie Gabriel's Biblical precedent for her prophecy is Isaiah 24:1, where the prophet says "behold, the Lord maketh the earth empty, and maketh it waste, and turneth it upside down, and scattereth abroad the inhabitants thereof". Again, in Isaiah 24:18 there is a strange passage predicting natural upheavals of an unpleasant sort: "the windows from on high are open, and the foundations of the earth do shake", which sounds very much as if something loosed from the heavens has shaken the earth from its orbit, or at the very least caused earthquakes.

Finally, Isaiah 24:19–20 depicts the scene after the catastrophe, when "the earth is utterly broken down, the earth is clean dissolved, the earth is moved exceedingly. The earth shall reel to and fro like a drunkard". Presented here is a clear picture of the Earth being thrown off its normal path by the impact of the comet hitting Jupiter.

In the time-honoured fashion of prophets, Sister Marie Gabriel explained this cosmic event as a warning from God to all governments, to do His bidding swiftly and adopt the following eight measures:

1 Drastically reduce crime rates by copying Saudi Arabia's system of law and order.
2 Destroy all pornographic material.
3 Ban crime and indecency from TV.
4 The UK government was specifically enjoined to prevent the National Health Service killing off older patients in order to make room for more patients in its hospitals.
5 Ban all alcohol.
6 Compel women to observe an almost Muslim dress code.
7 Ban all animal cruelty, specifically the shooting of birds in Italy and Spain, trapping, bullfighting, etc.
8 End all wars.

However, Sister Marie Gabriel did not make clear the connection between changes in human morals and astronomical movements.

Asteroids as well as comets do pose a threat to our planet if they are large enough to survive the plunge through the Earth's atmosphere and reach the surface. Sister Marie might have been thinking of one such recent visitor to the Earth's atmosphere which changed its mind and left again just two months before she publicized her prediction.

This asteroid, estimated as measuring about 30 feet (9.2 metres) in diameter and weighing the equivalent of a navy destroyer, passed within 90,000 miles (140,000 kilometres) of Earth on 20 May 1993. The asteroid was reckoned to be travelling at about 48,000 mph (77,000 km/hr) so this distance, which represents less than half the distance between the Earth and the Moon, would soon have been gobbled up if it had survived the fiery plunge through the atmosphere. This near-miss went unnoticed until the asteroid was detected as it whizzed away from the Earth's atmosphere. It would have made a very large crater indeed if it had reached our planet.

1066 AND ALL THAT

The appearance of a comet was long believed to indicate the arrival of some cataclysmic event. Of all the heavenly phenomena, comets were perhaps the easiest to observe after eclipses, which were also meant to have significance for mankind. A comet was seen before William the Conqueror's invasion of England in 1066, a fact commemorated in the Bayeux Tapestry, where it is depicted as a star on a stick connected to what appear to be flames.

It is no wonder that the writer Erich von Daniken used this type of image to boost his flying saucer theory, as the depiction in the Tapestry gives a clearer idea of a comet than is afforded by looking through a telescope. The comet seen in 1066 could be said to have heralded the birth of England as a nation. Sister Marie Gabriel's comet seemed to signal the nation's demise.

Before the 18th century and the age of reason, events like the eclipse of the Sun or Moon were widely thought to presage important events in life. The precise nature of these events was open to interpretation. Not surprisingly, the paranoid drew little comfort from them. Pope Urban VIII, for example, was on tenterhooks from about the time of the eclipse of the Moon in January 1628 through the eclipse of the Sun in December 1628 and June 1630, such was his conviction that any of these events might be forewarnings of his death. He even engaged the services of a heretic and sorcerer, Tommasso Campanella, to help him avert the perceived danger.

Campanella had been condemned to life imprisonment after attempting to establish a Utopia and "provoke" the millennium. To secure the safety of his prestigious client, Campanella performed elaborate black arts rituals during the periods of eclipse. It is quite amusing to think of a Pope so desperate to cling to the mortal coil that he would employ for his own ends the same ungodly practices that he was trying to stamp out in the general populace.

SELF-MADE MESSIAHS

Some relatively modern-day prophets of the Apocalypse have

crossed the thin line dividing prophecy from theophany, and

have claimed to actually be the Messiah.

Prophets declaring themselves to be the Messiah is not an unusual phenomenon, and in the Middle Ages there was no shortage of Christian, Jewish and
even Muslim claims to the title.

Two extraordinary messiahs of the 19th century were Henry James Prince
(1811–99) and John Hugh Smyth-Pigott (d. 1927). Prince was an Anglican priest
with a gift for great oratory and for attracting women. He became convinced that
his sermons owed their force to the Holy Spirit. Prince took to preaching in the
open, and soon announced that he was, in fact, the prophet Elijah reincarnated.
He established his own chapel in the English south-coast resort of Brighton.

Enough people of means believed in Prince to buy him a large house with
some 200 acres (81 hectares) of land at Spraxton in Somerset. There, in 1846, he
established the "Abode of Love", or Agapemone. The group soon became known
as the Agapemonites (from the Greek word for love). Prince took the title of "the
Beloved One" and, eventually, "the Messiah".

As he was the will of God on earth, Prince suffered no questions from his
disciples about the luxurious lifestyle he enjoyed at their expense. On at least one
occasion he drove in his carriage through the Somerset town of Bridgewater
with his footman sounding a trumpet and proclaiming him as the Messiah. Soon
he began taking successive disciples as his "bride of the Lamb", a feature of his
"church" which other cult leaders, like David Koresh of Waco for example,
would later emulate.

Prince was "above sin" and so free to live as he pleased. Not so his followers,
who were expected to lead chaste lives. This double standard did not deter believers and even when funds ran low the needs of the Messiah were met. One wealthy
merchant contributed all his worldly goods, amounting to £10,000 ($15,000), a
large sum in those days, and came to work in the Abode of Love as a butler.

The facts of the ex-Anglican priest's defrocking and several lawsuits – brought
by families keen to prevent relatives handing over money and possessions – did
not harm his cause, and the Abode of Love flourished. It even raised the funds
to build a Church of the Ark of the Covenant in Clapton, London. Believing the
end of the world to be nigh, Prince granted his followers immortality. Those
who died had "lapsed into sin", and were buried standing up under the lawn, a

fate which awaited Prince himself in 1899.

Three years later the spiritual vacuum left by Prince's death was filled by John Smyth-Pigott, who declared himself "the Son of Man", the new Messiah, at the Clapton church. He continued Prince's practice of selecting "soul brides", who also bore his children. This eventually led to his defrocking as an Anglican clergyman. At any one time, there were as many as 100 women at the Abode of Love.

Prince and Smyth-Pigott had comfortable lives in comparison with some other "Messiahs", perhaps because comparatively few people took them seriously. The Chinese prophet and military leader Hung Hsui-chaun, on the other hand, stirred up a hornet's nest when he claimed to be the younger brother of Christ. His declaration inspired the Taiping rebellion, which began in southern China in 1851 and lasted until 1864. His followers thought they were the children of Israel and sought to overthrow the Manchu dynasty in order to establish China as the promised land. The British General Gordon suppressed the revolution; in Sudan in the 1880s he would also oppose the Mahdi, a Muslim claimant to the title of Messiah.

THE LION OF JUDAH IN AFRICA

One of the most extraordinary messianic movements of the present day is Rastafarianism, which has spread from Jamaica to the US and UK. The involuntary candidate for the messiahship was the Emperor of Ethiopia, Haile Selassie (1891–1975).

Rastafarianism took its cue from the rhetoric of the militant pro-Negro Marcus Garvey during World War I. Garvey, a Jamaican emigrant to the USA, wanted to be the political saviour of all black people, and was strongly anti-white. He maintained that Negroes should look to Africa "when a black king shall be crowned, for deliverance is near". Soon afterwards, in 1930, Ras Tafari became the Emperor of Ethiopia, Haile Selassie, the fulfilment of Garvey's prophecy. Haile Selassie, who assumed the title "Lion of Judah", became the last in what he claimed to be the longest unbroken monarchy in the world.

Some of the more extreme Rastafarians, such as the Niyamen, advocated the use of marijuana (ganja), grew 'dreadlocks', and promoted a militantly anti-white stance. A sort of cargo cult grew up around their expectation of a wholesale migration to a new kingdom in Africa, and fortunes were made on the sale of worthless tickets and passports.

Rastafarians have survived this disappointment and the death of Haile Selassie in 1975. Like the Jews of past generations, they have a homeland which is not recognized as theirs. Visions of the return of either Haile Selassie or another black Messiah coupled with the possibility of an Armageddon which might also entail a race war continues to feed Rastafarian expectations. This vision of a racial Armageddon was later to fuel Manson's murderous campaign in California.

THE AQUARIAN AGE

Has the dawning of this Age sounded the death knell for Christianity, and are we going forward into a strange New Age based on peace, love and the exploration of the drug–accessed depths of our inner space? Embracing the philosophy of the New Age may be our only defence against the Apocalypse.

MADAME BLAVATSKY

In 1888, Helena Petrovna Blavatsky (1831–91), the founder of theosophy, claimed that Lemuria was the home of the "third root race".

HPB, as she was known by her disciples, was born in the Ukraine as Helena Petrovna von Hahn, the daughter of a Russian army officer of German extraction. In 1849 she married General Blavatsky, the vice-governor of Erivan, but soon afterwards took to wandering the world.

Lemuria was a lost continent believed by some to have existed in the Indian or Pacific Oceans until it was destroyed by a volcanic eruption. According to Theosophists, the human species evolved through a number of root races. Among these were the Lemurians, who came before the Atlanteans and the current human species (the "fifth root race").

The name Lemuria was originally taken from the monkey-like lemur, which is found in Africa, south India and Malaysia. The wide distribution of these habitats caused scientists as distinguished as Thomas Huxley and Ernst Haeckel to believe that a continent must have once linked them. This conjecture by 19th-century naturalists looking for an Asian-African land bridge was soon hijacked by a group of people intent on finding a likely location for a rather less plausible theory.

Their Lemuria was the cradle of human civilization – the Garden of Eden, no less. The original inhabitants of Lemuria were, according to Madame Blavatsky, hermaphroditic, egg-laying, four-armed and three-eyed (like some Hindu gods) ape-like giants. Fortunately for us, beings from Venus offered to replace them and interbred with the local apes, a Darwinian touch. The irony is that scientists no longer believe that there was a bridging continent called Lemuria.

Madame Blavatsky said that the third root race of Lemuria was swept away more than 40 million years ago, although their descendants survive as Australian Aborigines, Papuans and Hottentots – a theory that it would be hard to persuade a modern anthropologist to accept. Perhaps stories of the Lemurians' incredible height were borrowed from descriptions of the supposedly very tall Tasmanian Aborigines, who were safely extinct by the time Blavatsky was writing. This height myth derived from the distances between step-cuts made by Tasmanian Aborigines when climbing trees.

After the death of Madame Blavatsky in 1891, the cause was taken up by her successor, Annie Besant, a tireless fighter for social justice. Together with W. Scott-Elliot, she elaborated on the history of Lemuria, and even provided detailed maps showing critical stages of the world's evolution. These bear more than a passing resemblance to the current maps of "Pangaea", a modern myth with which modern science attempts to document continental drift.

The fourth root race were supposed to live in Atlantis, where they developed a technology that was propelled by concentrated willpower. Finally Atlantis was destroyed, according to Plato's commentary on this civilization, possibly by the eruption of the volcano Santorini.

The fifth root race, the Aryans, evolved from Atlantis and settled in Egypt, India, Persia and Europe. From there they spread, as history records, in the last four centuries to most corners of the earth.

The sixth root race are said to be just beginning to develop in California, following on from the arrival of the new World Teacher or Messiah (see below). This race will develop steadily over many thousands of years and eventually displace the present race.

Life on earth will end with the seventh root race, at which point, according to Madame Blavatsky's Masters, it will begin again on the planet Mercury. This idea of life transferring to another planet was a theme also dear to the hearts of the Aetherians.

KRISHNAMURTI: MESSIAH

OF A NEW AGE

Theosophists subscribed to the Hindu doctrine of avatars which held that God incarnated himself as a man when it was necessary to advance evolution. The Society felt the time was ripe for a new incarnation, and started actively looking for one. In 1908 members of the Theosophical Society noticed a local boy watching them swimming in the Adyar river. Two members, Ernest Wood and the Reverend C. W. Leadbeater, noticed that this 13-year-old was possessed of an exceptional aura. After looking into his past lives, as they put it, they suggested to the boy's father that the Theosophical Society should take charge of his education.

The boy's name was Jiddu Krishnamurti. After several legal tussles with Krishnamurti senior, who was an orthodox Hindu, the Theosophical Society started to promote Krishnamurti as a new World Teacher, almost a new Messiah.

In 1911 the Society proclaimed that Krishnamurti was the channel for the wisdom of the Lord Maitreya, or the fifth and last incarnation of the Buddha, and decided that 1911 signalled the initiation of the Age of Aquarius.

Krishnamurti was then taken on a world tour in order to meet the faithful. In Sydney, Australia, Theosophists even went to the trouble and expense of building a huge amphitheatre by the Harbour from which they could greet the new Messiah, or, as they preferred to call him, the World Teacher.

In 1927 Krishnamurti underwent a profound experience which changed his relationship with the Theosophical Society. He felt he had been admitted to the ranks of "the Beloved" and accepted his dharma as a teacher, and this awareness prompted him to break away from the Society. In 1929 Krishnamurti rejected his role as a Theosophical guru, renounced his title of Messiah and made a new base at Ojai in California. His lectures on philosophy and the spiritual life were instrumental in developing the consciousness which would lead to the new Age of Aquarius proclaimed by the hippies in the early 1960s. Maybe they are the progenitors of Madame Blavatsky's sixth root race.

THE PROPHET
OF THE NEW AGE

The reputation of the prophet Aleister Crowley was made by the publication of his seminal **The Book of the Law,** *the contents of which had been given to him by one of the old Egyptian daemons.*

The entity which called on Crowley and his wife Rose in their Cairo apartment in the spring of 1904 was named Aiwass. It foretold the end of Christianity and the birth of a new age, a transition that would be marked by violence, force, fire and destruction.

The Book of the Law, or "Liber Al vel Legis", appeared as a short prose poem in three chapters. On its publication Crowley was heralded as the prophet of a new age, "the Aeon of the Crowned and Conquering Child" of Horus, the Egyptian hawk-god of war.

The rule of this new Aeon was similar to that of Rabelais' dictum, "There is no law beyond do what thou wilt". This was not meant as a licence to behave as you pleased. (He was rediscovered 20 years later by the hippie movement who found in his philosophy many parallels with their own attitudes and beliefs.) Crowley meant that each individual should try to find purpose in his or her life: in short, to discover what was their True Will. They should then strive to do only this, and not be bound by the fetters of conventional morality, or go through the time-wasting motions of "acceptable" but false behaviour.

When Crowley died in 1947 he was mourned by only a small band of disciples. Twenty years later publishers were reprinting all his books and his image was used prominently on the cover of the Beatles' album *Sergeant Pepper's Lonely Hearts Club Band*.

But what of Crowley's prophecies? Crowley was later to claim that not only did *The Book of the Law* prophesy the coming of war and bloodshed, but that it actually precipitated it. With each authorized edition of the book, the transition to the new Aeon was brought one step closer.

In the 46th verse of the third chapter are the prophetic words "I am the warrior Lord of the Forties". Crowley recorded that he did not understand this phrase when he wrote it, but read in the light of knowledge of World War II it seems shockingly clear.

If this still strikes you as pure coincidence, then consider one of Crowley's experiments with ritual magic. In 1910, while staying at the home of his friend and pupil Commander Marston, a former officer in the Royal Navy, Crowley agreed to invoke Bartzabel, the spirit of Mars, the god of war.

Victor Neuberg acted as medium; this means that he allowed Bartzabel to speak through him to prophesy and answer questions. The invocation was duly performed, using a ritual written by Crowley, and Victor began to speak the words of the Spirit of Mars. Commander Marston asked Bartzabel about the possibilities of an outbreak of war in Europe.

The spirit replied that within five years [from 1910] there would be two conflicts; the storm centre of the first would be Turkey and the second would be the German Empire. The result of these wars would be the destruction of the Turkish and German empires. Both these prophecies were fulfilled to the letter by the Balkan War of 1912 and World War I.

Crowley's book points to war in Europe in the year 1997; several of its coded passages refer to the 93 years to be added to its date of origination, 1904, giving April 1997 as a commencement (or completion) date of war. This conflict will spread through Eastern Europe or the newly independent states of the former Soviet Union. For the end of this century we must "expect the direful judgements of Ra-Hoor-Khuit! This shall regenerate the world". Ra-Hoor-Khuit, another Egyptian god of war, will help in the changeover from one Aeon to another at the end of the century.

The Book of the Law then foretells: "Hrumachis shall arise and the double-wanded one assume my throne and place. Another prophet shall arise, and bring fresh fever from the skies ... another sacrifice shall stain the tomb; another king shall reign". (Hrumachis is the Dawning Sun of the new Aeon. The "double-wanded one" is the Egyptian god from whom the Greeks derived Themis, goddess of justice.)

"Invoke me under my stars! Love is the law, love under wil ... take wine and strange drugs ... & be drunk thereof! They shall not harm ye at all" – a passage summing up the psychedelic love-ins of the 1960s, which it would have been hard to imagine in 1904! Crowley's book is certainly a powerful piece of prophetic literature, filled with love, and hate.

THE SECRET KEY

Book 2:76 of *The Book of the Law* contains a series of apparently disconnected letters and numbers. Crowley explained the purpose of these: "This passage following appears to be a Qabalistic test ... of any person who may claim to be the Magical Heir of The Beast". Crowley had adopted the title of "Beast 666" from his favourite Biblical book, the Apocalypse of St John.

So far, despite many attempts, nobody has publicly come up with really clear and convincing proof that they can untangle this "key", thereby proving themselves to be Crowley's spiritual successors. Charles Stansfield Jones claimed to have sorted it out, but Crowley later decided that his explanation had not got to the bottom of the puzzle. The puzzle is this:

4 6 3 8 A B K 2 4 a L G M O R 3 Y X 24 89 R P S T O V A L

At first glance this is so much nonsense, but by the application of the word to letter equivalency of the Qabalah, it begins to make some sense. It is worth noting that the "G" above is not really a "G" but symbolizes something else. Maybe the prophet who succeeds in cracking this will also come up with some explanations for the rest of the prophecies in Crowley's strange book.

THE SLEEPING PROPHET

Edgar Cayce (1877–1945), the so-called "sleeping prophet",

made a number of remarkably accurate predictions and an

almost equal number of wildly inaccurate ones.

Cayce realized at an early age that he had psychic powers, but it was only later in life that he would specialize in the trance diagnosis for which he became famous. What sets Cayce apart from most prophets is that his readings were carefully transcribed and kept in an archive which still survives.

During consultation with his patients he would lie down on a couch, make himself comfortable, and then allow his inner light to connect him with his "channel" of communication. He would then "read" off the diagnosis and solution to the condition or problem. When he awoke he claimed to remember nothing of what had been spoken through him.

Although poorly educated in the traditional sense, in trance Cayce often diagnosed illnesses, described conditions accurately, and prescribed detailed treatments and medicines in terms which suggested formal training as a doctor. He was not always right, and handed back his fee to anyone who was not happy with his "readings".

Once Cayce prescribed a remedy prepared from the plant clary, but no one could trace it. Eventually the patient, James Andrews, discovered that a doctor in Paris had marketed such a remedy 60 years previously. Cynics could argue that Cayce had been reading old medical manuals, but for the following case.

On this occasion he recommended the use of a drug called "Codiron", giving the name and address of the manufacturing chemists who could supply it. When the patient telephoned the firm in Chicago he found that the formula for the medicine had only just been established and its actual name chosen barely an hour before his call!

Cayce's "channel of communication" would later save the sight of his eight-year-old son, who had damaged his eyes while playing with matches. The specialist wanted to remove one eye. Cayce forbade the operation and sought his own counsel. Bandages steeped in tannic acid – the remedy given to Cayce during one of his trances – were placed on his son's eyes. In a fortnight the boy could see again.

In everyday life Cayce ran a photographer's shop in Virginia Beach, Virginia. As well as helping people with medical problems, Cayce was also able to use his psychic talents to give business advice. These forecasts were highly regarded by those who came to see him and profited from them. One man who sought his advice on 5 March 1929 was told not to invest in stocks and shares. Cayce gave similar advice on 6 April and described "a downward movement of long duration", just before the Wall Street crash of 1929.

Cayce predicted the end of Communism, and that Russia would be born again. He also saw a strong religious movement coming out of Russia. A less plausible prediction was that China will become the new "cradle of Christianity".

In 1934 Cayce made a series of pronouncements about major geological and climatic changes (see below). An eruption of Mount Etna was predicted – it last erupted destructively in 1991, destroying the village of Fornazzo, and again the following year. He also predicted an eruption on Vesuvius (near Naples in Italy) or Mount Pelee in Martinique, the last mentioned triggering earthquake activity in southern California. In 1999 the shift in the earth's axis, which began in 1936 according to Cayce, will cause a number of catastrophes. The year 2000 is scheduled to arrive with a bang, with major earthquakes in Turkey and the Balkans, causing areas of the land to disappear under the sea. The only positive occurrence would seem to be a climatic change for the better in Scandinavia and Britain as a result of an alteration to the Gulf Stream!

Like many Christian prophets, Cayce maintained that "the day of reckoning" was at hand. He predicted the arrival of World War III in 1999, followed by the New Age and the Second Coming of Christ. Cayce saw himself reincarnating in Nebraska in AD 2100 – he may then be able to check on his various predictions.

MAJOR UPHEAVALS DUE AT THE END

OF THE CENTURY

In 1934 Cayce gave a trance "reading" which described a number of quite unimaginable natural catastrophes that would occur at the end of the 20th century. These included:

• A shift in the world's axis around the year 2000, leading to:

• Inundations of many coastal regions, caused by a drop in the landmass of about 30 feet (9.1 metres) combined with a melting of both polar ice caps, including :

• Southern England, leaving London as a coastal town

• The loss of much of Japan

• Flooding of northern Europe, which will happen very rapidly

• Open waters appearing where Greenland used to be

• New land appearing off the east coast of North America

• Widespread destruction in Los Angeles, San Francisco and the destruction of Manhattan and disappearance of New York

• Upheavals in both polar regions

• Volcanic eruptions in tropical regions and an increase in Pacific rim volcanic activity, especially affecting Japan (severe damage), China, parts of South East Asia, Eastern Australia, and the Pacific coast of South America

• A land bridge between South America and the Antarctic (as it used to be shown on the extraordinary old Piri Re'is maps).

• A general warming of currently cool areas, and cooling of warm areas.

LEO TAXIL: THE GREAT HOAXER

In 1890s Paris, Gabriel Jogand-Pages, who also went under the pseudonym Leo Taxil, joined forces with a band of fellow "free thinkers" to indulge in a giant leg-pull against the Roman Catholic Church.

Jogand-Pages looked to the black arts to offend against the strong Catholic tradition of their country. This consummate confidence trickster was born in Provence in the mid 19th century, and educated in a Jesuit College. It was during his time here that he encountered Freemasonry, a forbidden subject in a Catholic boys' school.

Jogand-Poges became a Freemason, but then performed an apparent ideological about-turn by writing a denunciation of Freemasonry. In truth, Taxi's writings were little more than skilful hoaxes. He went on to guild the lily by inventing an ex-Satanist called Diana Vaughan, allegedly a descendant of English alchemist Thomas Vaughan, whom he dangled before a fascinated Catholic hierarchy as a potential convert. Diana, Taxil said, was a member of an organization called the Palladium, a worldwide Satanic cult reputedly run by Masons, acting under a man called Albert Pike, from Charleston in the USA. To give Diana some credibility, and a dash of devilish colour, Taxil even provided a pedigree for her and her fellow Satanists.

Part of this pedigree, and one of Taxil's greatest hoaxes, was the prediction of the birth and ancestry of the Antichrist (as mentioned in The Apocalypse of St John). One of the Palladium's priestesses, Sophia Walder, was presented as a literal "child of Satan", fathered by Lucifer. According to Taxil's prediction, Sophia would go to Jerusalem where in the summer of 1896 she would have intercourse with the Demon Bitru (or Sytry) and give birth to a daughter. Thirty-three years later this daughter would have a daughter by the demon Decarabia, who after a further 33 years, in 1962, would give birth to the Antichrist.

The prophecy goes on to say that the Antichrist will make his mission public at the age of 33 in 1995. He will then bring about the Pope's conversion from Catholicism. This will be followed by a year of war which will result in the destruction of the Catholic Church and the conversion of many souls to the Antichrist.

Although the whole affair has been characterized as a hoax, there were a number of real elements. For example, Albert Pike was a very senior American Freemason who wrote a classic book on the subject (Morals and Dogma of Freemasonry), although there is no evidence that he was in anyway connected with Taxil's Satanic conspiracy.

The prediction also influenced the contemporary American psychic Jeane Dixon, who had a vision of the birth of the Antichrist somewhere in the Middle East on 6 February in the same year as Taxil had stated, 1962. In her vision, the parents of the child were the ancient Egyptian Queen Nefertiti and Pharaoh Akhnaton.

For symbolic reasons the Antichrist should be born in either Galilee or Jerusalem to balance the birth of the Christ. Nicholas Campion, who decided to draw up a nativity of the Antichrist, discovered that the day before there had been a solar eclipse.

Campion chose this time to draw up the Horoscope of the Antichrist, at 0:10am Greenwich Mean Time on   5 February 1962 in Jerusalem. At this time, in addition to the eclipse, all seven traditional planets – Mercury, Venus, Sun, Moon, Mars, Jupiter and Saturn – were in the sign of Aquarius, a rare astrological conjunction.

The vision of a child being born as Antichrist was taken up in 1976 by David Seltzer in his novel The Omen. Damien, obviously the Antichrist, grows up in the family of an American career diplomat. Several very popular films have been based on this premise.

Aleister Crowley, the 20th century's most notorious magician, includes a child character with specific magical abilities in his novel Moonchild. Although the novel does not mention the Antichrist, Crowley had obviously toyed with the idea of deliberately breeding a future Antichrist to complement his own self-assumed title of "The Great Beast 666".

THE ANTICHRIST

The Antichrist, when he arrives, will claim to be a god and will work miracles, such as raising the dead, walking on water, healing the sick, and possibly even flying like Simon Magus. The Jewish tradition has the incarnation of an evil power in a bald person with one eye bigger than the other and who is deaf in the right ear. Early Christians adopted the Jewish notion of a war between God and his adversary.

One historical person identified as the adversary was the Syrian king Antiochus IV Epiphanes (ruled 175–164 BC), who captured Jerusalem in 171 BC and used the Temple for sacrifices to pagan gods. He later ordered the persecution of the Jews recorded in the second Book of Maccabees.

The most famous Biblical reference to the Antichrist is in the Apocalypse of St John, chapter 13, although John does not use the actual term Antichrist, referring instead to a Beast.

Other identifications of the Antichrist have been Mohammed the prophet and both the Napoleonic emperors of France, a convenient term of abuse at a time of hostilities! Often the term Antichrist is applied by Protestants to the Pope (particularly Boniface VIII and John XXII), but this is a perversion of the original meaning. This is to be the opponent of, or false claimant of the throne of, the true Christ. The Antichrist is not to be confused with Satan: he is Satan's human representative on earth.

THE DAWNING OF AQUARIUS

Of all the dates and predictions examined in this book, the following timetable of dates is the most significant for the dawning of the Age of Aquarius.

The following are the main contenders for the date of the dawning of the Age of Aquarius. These dates do not necessarily correspond with the arrival of the millennium, the Second Coming of Christ, or the Battle of Armageddon. They are an altogether gentler date with destiny, an ushering in of a period of earthly peace, not of Judgement, war in heaven, salvation and damnation.

1904 The beginning of the Aeon of Horus, as received by Aleister Crowley in April 1904 in Cairo. The arrival of this age was announced in The Book of the Law, the text of which was dictated to Crowley by the discarnate voice of Aiwass. This so-called "Aeon of the Crowned and Conquering Child" is often identified with the Age of Aquarius. For Crowley the new age spelled the end of the Christian period and its slave mentality.

1905 Entry to the Aquarian Age was identified by Gerald Massey as 2160 years after 255 BC. In fact, arithmetically it should have been calculated as 1906. The rationale for choosing 255 BC is also a bit doubtful, it being the date of the writing of the Septuagint, the Old Testament translated into Greek.

1911 Helena Petrovna Blavatsky's Theosophical Society chose this date on the basis of the words of the Lord Maitreya, as dictated to Krishnamurti, then Society's "World Teacher".

1914 Beginning of World War I.

1931 Messages received by Alice Bailey from Djwhal Khul, the discarnate Tibetan, indicated that the Age of Aquarius had begun.

1936 The beginning of the earth's axial shift as predicted by the American psychic Edgar Cayce.

1939 Beginning of World War II.

1943 Edgar Cayce stated that a new spiritual age would begin on this date.

1962 Birth of the Antichrist, according to both Leo Taxil (in the 1880s) and American clairvoyant Jeane Dixon (she reckoned the date as 6 February). Nicolas Campion chose 5 February, when all seven planets would be aligned in Aquarius. The Peruvian spiritual messenger Willaru Huayta, of the Quechua nation, also chose February 1962 as the commencement of the Age of Aquarius.

1963 Possible arrival of the Age of Aquarius, according to the author of Liber Vaticinationem. The beginning of the Hippie era, preaching the New Age of love.

1975 Arrival date for the Avatar of the New Age, according to the astrologer Dane Rudhyar.

1989 The break-up of Communism.

1995 Max Toth declares the arrival of the Kingdom of Spirit. The year in which Leo Taxil's Antichrist converts the Pope.

1997 The psychologist Carl Jung's date for the arrival of a New Age.

1999 Nostradamus predicts the arrival of the "King of Terror" in September, possibly followed by Armageddon – not really a candidate for the beginning of the New Age, but useful as a "marker". On 11 August 1999, there will occur the last eclipse of the 20th century, and a Grand Cross astrological formation.

2000 Chosen by many Christian and non-Christian prophets as the key date, including Nostradamus (the Second Coming), St Malachy (by inference), Edgar Cayce, the Virgin Mary at Fatima (by inference) and many Christian, particularly fundamentalist, writers and preachers; 4 or 5 May 2000 brings a significant astronomical formation which, according to Richard Kieninger and the Stelle group, will bring cataclysmic destruction.

2001 Arithmetically a more sound choice than the previous year, with support from the Seventh-Day Adventists, Hebrew chronology and Nostradamus. But both dates are more closely associated with the Apocalypse and Second Coming of Christ than the dawn of the Aquarian Age.

2010 A date favoured by a number of writers on esoteric subjects, including Nicholas Tereshchenko and Peter Lemesurier, the latter giving the French Institut Geographique Nationale as his authority.

2012 Jose Arguelles suggests that this year marks the end of a 396-year age, according to the ancient Mayan calendar. Terrence and Dennis McKenna regard the date as the culmination of many timescales.

2013 The end of the Inca calendar. According to Willaru Huayta, the New Age will be ushered in by the close passage to Earth of a huge asteroid.

2020 On 21 December this year Jupiter and Saturn will be in conjunction in Aquarius for the first time since AD 1404, according to Adrian Duncan. The ancient Jews certainly prized that particular conjunction as a portent of major changes.

2023 Woldben pinpoints this date as the beginning of the Age of Aquarius.

2060 Dane Rudhyar suggested that the Age of Pisces began in 100 BC, hence after the standard precessional period of 2160 years the Age of Aquarius will begin in either this or the following year.

2143 Christ's birth plus the precessional period of 2134 years, plus or minus a few years for inaccuracy about that particular birth date.

2160 Christ's birth plus the standard precessional period of 2160 years, also plus or minus a few years for the same inaccuracy; a date suggested by Woldben and Gordon Strachan.

2233 The earliest date for the Day of Judgement, according to the 15th-century monk Johannes Trithemius, and a possible time for the dawning of the New Age.

WHICH DATE IS RIGHT?

Everyone who has given an opinion on the likely date for the dawning of Aquarius seems to agree that it will be around the year 2000. This probably seems a bit vague, so let us see if we can narrow it down a bit.

It is reasonable to assume that the Age of Pisces started before Christ's birth, at the earliest around 200 BC. If we adopt the standard precessional period of 2160 years, the Age of Aquarius is likely to begin no earlier than 200 BC plus 2160 years or AD 1961. If we choose Christ's birth as the latest possible start to the Age of Pisces, then we get AD 2161 as the latest possible date for the dawning of the Age of Aquarius.

It is possible that the Age of Aquarius has already begun, in 1962 or 1963, and that the shackles of the old Age will now be completely thrown off until about 2001 or 2010.

HIPPIES AND THE AGE OF AQUARIUS

Most people did not realize that there was such a thing as the

Age of Aquarius until the hit musical Hair. The astrologers

had known about it long before.

First staged some 25 years ago, at the height of the hippie era, Hair celebrated in words and music the philosophy of turning on, tuning in and dropping out. The hippie movement popularized the notion of the Age of Aquarius, and perhaps saved humankind by doing so.

The world has still to catch up with this non-competitive, non-materialistic, non-violent view of life, although there are signs of a reawakening of interest in it. To many people the pace of life has quickened considerably since those lazy, hazy days of the 1960s when the new message was "make love not war". Let us look at what has happened since those days of the acid culture.

The Vietnam War has largely been forgotten; the Cold War and Communism have faded away; the threat of the atomic bomb (so much part of hippie rhetoric) has receded; China is increasingly opening up to "market" values; and the sexual revolution, having swung so far, is poised to crash back in the opposite direction. The LSD guru and ex-Harvard professor Timothy Leary, one of the leaders of the hippie movement, has, since his release from jail, made it up with Gordon Liddy (the agent who originally arrested him) and discovered the microcomputer. This device was originally assembled by two hippies on their kitchen table and programmed by Bill Gates, founder and owner of the Microsoft corporation and the richest dropout in the world.

Considering that their high point only lasted about five years, the hippies have had a great influence on the world. This has interesting implications for the Apocalypse. By tuning in to other "frequencies", be they drug-accessed or reached by mystical means, the hippies have helped to bring about a change in consciousness which may well have averted a different, darker destiny. This change may be seen in our present-day political leaders who generally have a more liberal attitude than many of their predecessors. It is possible, as is outlined in Liber Vaticinionem, that certain key events force destiny to switch rails, as it were. The hippie movement may well have been one such event, averting a looming catastrophe.

THE AGE OF AQUARIUS

There are many contenders for the date on which the Age of Aquarius started or is due to start, but everybody agrees that it is approximately the year AD 2000. (For the full astronomical background to the cycle of the Equinox through the Signs of the Zodiac, known as the precession of the Equinoxes.) All we need to know here is that the full cycle takes 25,725 years. Each sign takes one twelfth of this, or 2,143 years, although the figure has usually been taken as 2,160 years.

The sequence works backwards, almost as if the metaphorical "clutch" which controls the machinery of the universe has been "slipping" since the beginning of time. We are in the process of "slipping" from the Age of Pisces to the Age of Aquarius.

As we know the duration of the Age of Pisces, all we need is a start date to calculate its likely end. Most commentators have used the standard precessional period of 2160 years, but we can also apply the more accurate calculation of 2143 years.

Gerald Massey uses 255 BC as his starting point, and by adding 2160 years gets AD 1905, although it should have been AD 1906, because there are two year ones (1 BC and AD 1). A more obvious choice might have been Christ's birth, which would yield AD 2160 by the standard period, or perhaps AD 2143 as the date.

There is a second way of fixing the dawning of the Age of Aquarius, by choosing a date corresponding to some reputedly significant event, or to the reception of a particular revelation, the option taken by the majority of non-biblical end-time commentators. Aleister Crowley, for example, received The Book of the Law in Cairo in April 1904, and so for him the New Age began at that date.

The common thread that runs through most of these predictions is the arrival of an avatar, a reincarnation of a god, prophet or guru to guide humanity through the difficult transitional stage. There will certainly be a large number of false prophets appearing during the changeover period – in fact, that has been specified as being one of the signs of the times.

THE THREE AGES

Christianity is associated with Pisces, the sign of the fish, in a number of ways. For the first five to six hundred years of the Christian religion the sign most often associated with it was not the cross but the fish. The earliest disciples were fishermen. The symbol has taken on a whole new meaning with more recent and less orthodox practitioners of Christianity. The cult leader Moses David Begg, for example, used to encourage his female disciples to go "flirty-fishing", by which he meant securing converts to his cult by sexual means and seduction!

Before the Age of Pisces, from 2000 BC (in round terms) to Christ's birth, the sign of Aries, the Ram, prevailed. During this period many ram cults existed in the Middle East and elsewhere, and nomadic pastoral communities were common. Prior to this, from 4000 to 2000 BC, Taurus the Bull held sway, and bull cults such as that of the Egyptian god Apis were prominent. Before the time coinciding with the sign of Taurus, civilization is lost to view, but the influence would have been from the sign of Gemini, symbolized by the Twins.

THE AETHERIUS SOCIETY

One cold spring morning in 1954, after he had been experimenting with yoga trance states, George King heard a voice which told him to prepare himself to become the spokesman of the "Interplanetary Parliament".

In 1954, eight days after he had heard a mysterious voice telling him he had been chosen as the spokesman of the "Interplanetary Parliament", George King was "shaken to the core" by the miraculous appearance of a figure dressed in white robes and looking like an eastern saint. The apparition told him that he had been selected to act as the servant of the "Cosmic Masters". Thus the Aetherius Society was born, although King would not formally constitute it until 1960.

Soon King was holding public meetings. At these he would put on a pair of dark glasses and go into a trance to make contact with the communicating entity, often from Mars or Venus. Typically, the information passed through King would include movements of flying saucer fleets and also the advent of such terrestrial disasters as hurricanes and earthquakes. These upheavals in the natural world were thought to herald the new spiritual order which beings like the Master Aetherius are attempting to bring to earth, very much in the manner of the Second Coming of Christ. (The Latin word Aetherius means "relating to the ether, or to the abodes of the gods".)

During one or two of the early public meetings held by King in 1955 the Master Aetherius mentioned that Jesus Christ was living on Venus, along with other religious leaders such as Buddha and Rama-Krishna. The Star of Bethlehem was said to be a flying saucer which had brought Jesus to earth for his first incarnation. Press ridicule ensured sell-out performances.

On 23 July 1958 King claimed to have met with the avatar of Jesus Christ on Holdstone Down, in the west of England. As a result of this meeting, King made a practice of visiting the "high places" of the world and charging them with spiritual energy.

Courses offered by the Society, which is also incorporated as a church, include spiritual healing and yoga. Its rationale centres on the continuing mental transmissions from extraterrestrial sources to the Society's founder, and the concept of being able to store spiritual energy for later release.

George King believes that we have missed the Apocalypse by a hair's breadth several times recently, and have been saved by the spiritual battle he and others like him are waging on our behalf. During these battles, members of the Aetherius Society bear arms in the form of spiritual energy, which they generate through, among other things, prayer. King, who holds degrees from the Theological Seminary at Van Nuys in California, has invented a spiritual accumulator based on crystals and gold, into which he claims he can store the energy of thousands of hours of prayer, to be released during times of spiritual crisis.

Venus, with its overtones of love, holds a special place in the cosmology of the Aetherians. It is from the spiritual counterpart of this planet that they expect the imminent arrival of an avatar, perhaps a returning Jesus Christ or the Buddha as Maitreya.

OTHER FLYING-SAUCER MESSAGES

The 1950s saw a change in the type of communication experienced by mediums. Long used solely (or so it seemed in the public imagination) as conduits for messages from the dead, mediums began to receive information from flying saucers or UFOs (unidentified flying objects). These messages are in the main no less banal and sketchy than those received from the spirit world.

The "School of Universal Philosophy and Healing", run by Gladys Spearman-Cook in London, used regularly to deliver hints of an impending "Interplanetary Brotherhood". Also in London, the White Eagle Lodge, a spiritualist group in South Kensington, devoted most of its energies to making contact with flying saucers, although reporting little of interest to the average uncommitted spectator. UFOs became a vogue in the world of spiritualism and even the movement's official magazine, *Psychic News*, began to devote a lot of space to reporting major saucer sightings.

In America, too, contact with beings from space tended to eclipse for a while spiritualism's principal concern of reaching the spirits of the dead. "Summerland", the name given to the realm inhabited by spirit life, was even relocated by some to another planet in our galaxy. Even major Christian cults were bitten by the UFO bug – the Mormons, for example, allocated other planets as post-Apocalypse repositories for unredeemed souls. Into their post-Judgement Day "Telestial Kingdom" will go all people who have been "unclean", such as liars, adulterers, sorcerers, and those who have broken the covenants.

MANSON'S APOCALYPSE

Charles Manson, once described as a "hippie car-thief cult-leader sex-maniac bastard butcher", and his "family" of some 20 girl members (called Satan's slaves) plus sundry hangers-on established a headquarters at a ranch near Death Valley in California in the late 1960s. Manson had once been a member of the Scientology cult, whose techniques, he thought, would enable him to do, or be, anything he wanted.

From early 1961, Manson began to prepare for the end of Western civilization which, he was convinced, was about to be destroyed by some sort of Armageddon. He became obsessed with the idea of hastening the arrival of this catastrophe. One way of lending it a hand, he thought, would be to provoke a race war. He talked a great deal about the blacks he had met in prison who had secret arms caches, to be used at some future time against their white neighbours. One of Manson's strategies for starting a race war owed a lot to the occult: the beaming of "hate vibes" into the troubled black ghetto of Watts.

Another way of undermining American society would be to begin a campaign of murder. It is these murders, especially that of actress Sharon Tate, wife of director Roman Polanski, for which he is remembered. Manson's aim was to kill the famous, but the not so famous were also caught up in his plan. How many were murdered by "the family" is still not known.

Manson's hate-fear-sex-death commune was governed by a collage of myths drawn from Scientology, the Process Church of the Final Judgement, the Solar Lodge of Aleister Crowley's OTO and Beatlemania. For his "theology" he drew on obscure interpretations of the lyrics of the Beatles' songs (see below), and the Apocalypse of St John.

Manson derived some of his key ideas from the Process, whose publications included Satan on War, Jehovah on War, Lucifer on War and a magazine devoted to peddling ideas of fear and death. The leader of that cult, Robert Sylvester DeGrimston Moor, claimed to be a reincarnation of Christ (as did Manson at a later date), while his wife, Mary MacLean, said she was a reincarnation of Hecate, goddess of magic, ghosts and witchcraft. In March 1974 the publishers of Ed Sanders' book on Manson, The Family, fought a court case over the extent to which the Process had influenced Manson: the Process lost.

Manson's followers were encouraged to drink animal blood, hate blacks and believe in the idea of "race war Armageddon". This would erupt in 1969 after Manson and the "family" had lit the touchpaper by committing murders which would be blamed on blacks. Once wholesale slaughter had got underway, his group would slip away to an underground paradise. (Manson borrowed this concept from the American Cyrus "Koresh" Teed, whose ideas inspired the hollow-earth theory of the Nazis.) According to Manson, this paradise would be available at the right time, when the "seven holes on seven planes" came into alignment. The "family" would then "squirt through to the other side of the universe" via the "Hole" which would open up near their desert hideaway.

Charles Manson was an avid reader of the Bible, that vast repository of hidden apocalyptic messages. He annotated his copy of the Apocalypse of St John, drawing parallels between it and his life with the "family". The dune buggies they used were the horses of Helter Skelter with "breastplates of fire". One of Manson's favourite passages from 9:21 was "neither repent they of their murders, nor of their sorceries, nor of their fornication, nor of their thefts". What better justification for his way of life?

He saw himself as the angel of the bottomless pit who will at the appointed time pass with his family through the Hole to his kingdom, and from there emerge every so often, like locusts, to ravage and harry mankind. The angel with whom Manson identified was called Abaddon in Hebrew, Apollyon in Greek (meaning "destroyer"), and in Latin Exterminans, the Exterminating Angel.

Armageddon did not arrive on cue: instead, on 15 October 1969, police rounded up the remnants of his "band of nude and long-haired thieves" and put them on trial. Manson, together with his main disciples, Patricia Krenwinkel, Susan Atkins and Leslie Van Houten, was convicted of the Tate-LaBianca murders and jailed for life.

Manson said: "I am not the King of the Jews nor am I a hippie cult leader. I am what you have made of me … In my mind's eye my thoughts light fires in your cities." If he had his way, the Apocalypse would arrive tomorrow.

WHAT THE BEATLES
NEVER INTENDED

Manson read personal messages into the Beatles' song lyrics. Even an innocuous detail like the all-white cover of one of their albums was interpreted as a sign of an impending race war. One of the Beatles's songs, Helter Skelter, he took to signify his mission and the rush towards Armageddon. For the English Beatles, helter-skelter meant simply a children's slide in an amusement park! Manson saw the Beatles as four of the angels of the Apocalypse (8:7–12). Blackbird, he took, of course, to be a racial reference. The song Sexie Sadie thrilled one of his "slaves", Susan Atkins, who was also known as Sadie Mae Glutz.

For Manson, Revolution 9 was both revolution and the ninth chapter of "Revelation", in which St John says "in those days shall men seek death, and shall not find it; and shall desire to die, and death shall flee them". Generous-hearted as ever, Manson proposed to help such people. More obvious song titles, like Happiness is a Warm Gun, were taken literally. The song Piggies may well have inspired the murder of a plump middle-aged couple with a carving knife and fork. On several occasions Manson tried to telephone the Beatles to discuss his paranoid fantasies. Mercifully for them, he never got through.

THE GREAT WARS

Wars have been the subject of many prophecies down through the ages. The French Revolution was predicted by many prophets, at least 20 of them from the 15th and 16th centuries, including Nostradamus.

During the early 20th century many prophets foretold World War I as the "war to end all wars", although most of them settled on 1913 rather than 1914 as the date it would start. In Germany the years 1911 to 1913 were referred to in popular parlance as glutjahr, flutjahr and blutjahr; that is to say, the year of fire or heat (1911), the year of flood (1912) and the year of blood (1913).

The last of these was perhaps selected for cyclical reasons, because it was exactly a century since Prussia declared war on France, Napoleon was victorious at Lützen, Austria declared war on France, Wellington defeated the French at Vitoria, and Napoleon was defeated at the "Battle of Nations" at Leipzig: 1813 was a good "blood year", indeed.

One little-known prophet, Rudolf Mewes, a physicist, published in 1896 a book in which he predicted conflict between Eurasian and Asiatic countries, beginning in 1904, which corresponds neatly to the war between Russia and Japan (1904–5). The complicated system he devised for making his predictions was based on meteorological fluctuations. Although fallible, this system is of interest today because of the light it might shed on the increasingly wild fluctuations in climate we face in the last decade of this century.

From his observations of fluctuations in the earth's magnetic field, of sunspots and of the intensity of the aurora, or northern lights, Mewes developed the idea of a cycle of 111.3 years. Each cycle, he deduced from his investigations of the time span 2400 BC to AD 2100, experiences two periods of war and two periods of advances in the sciences and the arts. Each of these periods, or sub-cycles, lasts about 27.8 years.

Mewes' efforts were, by and large, way off target, but they did encourage others to try to develop a theory along similar lines. A system of prophecy that could predict just about everything, from the quality of harvests to the cyclical fluctuations of economies and the stock markets and the timing of the

Apocalypse, would be no mean achievement.

Perhaps the oldest theory of cycles applied to the timing of the First World War is the Egyptian Sirius cycle of 1461 years. If we count back 1461 years from the dates of the First World War (1914–18), we get 453–457, a time when imperial Rome was under attack by the Germanic tribes. If we use the same cycle to count back from World War II, we fall only a little short of AD 476, a date widely given for the ending of the Western Roman Empire, when the emperor Romulus Augustus was deposed by the Goths under Odoacer.

The Sirius cycle is too long to be of use in predicting future wars. The historian Arnold Toynbee (1889–1975) tried to work out a shorter peace-war cycle by analysing history back to 1495. He came up with four "regular cycles", each of which had a "prelude" (sometimes with a premonitory war), a "general war" (for which read pan-European war), a "breathing space", a "supplementary war" and, finally, a "general peace".

The four cycles were 1568–1672, 1672–1792, 1792–1914, and 1914 until 2118 or 2036. According to this system, we are currently in a period of "general peace". Unfortunately, Toynbee's four cycles are of uneven length and so will not work as an adequate prophetic dating system, but the principle of alternating periods of peace and war might well tie up with some underlying cycle. If we could discover this underlying cycle, then perhaps we should know the date of the last of all wars, Armageddon.

THE WORLD'S HEARTBEAT OR
BIOLOGICAL CYCLES

Known biological cycles like heartbeat, menstruation, tides, sunspots and the orbits of planets have always suggested that there may be other as yet unknown cycles. Astrology has since time immemorial tried to relate one set of known cycles, the planetary movements, to the affairs of men. Such horoscopes are still thought by some to be able to plot recurrent events in an individual's life, as well as personality tendencies. The study of the three biorhythms is almost as popular as horoscopes.

One well-known cycle is the Metonic cycle, which demonstrates that every 19 years the phases of the moon coincide exactly with the calendar date. The Metonic cycle was discovered by the Greek astronomer Meton in around 432 BC.

Edward Dewey has catalogued almost every known phenomena with the potential for varying cyclically over time. He has discovered, for example, that the breeding cycles of several species of wild animals, such as foxes and wolves in Canada, increases to a maximum every 9.6 years. This in turn is explained by a similar cycle to be found in the fluctuation of rabbit-fever, and hence of food supplies for the predators concerned. Dewey has also tried to find other connecting cycles upon which to base useful conclusions.

Weather cycles are partially dependent upon the differential heating of the earth's surface, but so far meteorologists do not seem to be able to come up with an reliable set of predictive relationships.

THE EARTH STRIKES BACK

Will the long suffering Earth finally grow tired of having her riches plundered and precipitate the prophecies of the Apocalypse in a way that the original prophet could not even have guessed at?

EARTHQUAKES IN DIVERS PLACES

When St Mark asked Christ (13:8) by what signs His Second Coming would be signalled, the Lord said "There shall be earthquakes in divers places, and there shall be famines and troubles."

Earthquakes, famines and troubles have always been with us, but there has certainly been an increase in earthquake activity over the last decade.

In the Old Testament the earthquake was one of Jehovah's traditional means of showing disapproval. Isaiah (29:6) records that the doomed city of Ariel "shalt be visited of the Lord of hosts with thunder, and with earthquake, and great noise ... and the flame of devouring fire".

The earthquake is a basic natural phenomenon against which man has little defence, except perhaps prediction. Earthquake belts are so extensive that a concerted upheaval could destroy most of the Pacific rim, southern Europe, the Near East and Southeast Asia. Even Britain is not immune, having had an earthquake registering 5.2 on the Richter scale as recently as 1990.

In recent years earthquakes have been occurring in previously stable areas. Liaoning province in Manchuria, for example, had not had a major earthquake for 100 years before 4 February 1975. The quake registered 4.8 on the Richter scale – a logarithmic measure of energy, which means that each step up the scale represents a ten-fold increase.

Shortly before the earthquake, animals in the Liaoning area began to behave strangely. Andrew Robinson describes it: "Snakes awoke from hibernation prematurely and lay frozen in the snow; rats appeared in groups so agitated that they did not fear human beings; small pigs chewed off their tails and ate them".

When the earthquake struck, sheets of light flashed in the sky, jets of water and sand shot into the air, bridges buckled, and the majority of buildings in the main towns of the province were wrecked. Only 300 people died because the populace received plenty of warning.

The greatest chronicled loss of life due to an earthquake occurred in July 1201 in the Near East and the Mediterranean. Almost every city in the area was affected and the human toll was estimated at 1,100,000. The highest death toll from an earthquake in modern times occurred at T'ang-shan in China (7.9 on the Richter scale) on 28 July 1976, when between 500,000 and 750,000 people perished.

The world's most destructive earthquake in material terms occurred on the Kanto Plain, Japan, on 1 September 1923 (Richter scale 8.2). This annihilated two-thirds of Tokyo and four-fifths of Yokohama and caused the sea floor of the adjoining bay area to drop an amazing 1300 feet (400 metres).

A major earthquake in Tokyo now would have other serious consequences, as it would provoke worldwide Japanese disinvestment, causing a worldwide financial crisis as Japanese insurance companies and businesses strove to rebuild the country.

The increase in earthquake activity observed over the last two decades may indicate that our time-ride to the end of the millennium is set to become even bumpier. Recent quakes of 6.7 on the Richter scale on the India/Nepalese border have been eclipsed by the more recent 8.5 Richter scale quake in Hokkaido in Japan, which resulted in massive tidal waves.

Some observers are convinced that the number of earthquakes has roughly doubled in each of the decades since 1950. The side effects of future earthquakes might include nuclear spillage, as some Eastern European reactors have been built along fault lines.

Conventional wisdom has it that earthquakes are caused by friction between the vast "tectonic plates" supporting the continents. An alternative view is that their incidence is related to sunspot activity, and sunspots might well have some bearing on the configuration of the planets in the solar system.

CALIFORNIA PREDICTIONS

The famous 1906 earthquake in San Francisco demolished almost five square miles (13 sq km) of the city and was accompanied by a huge rupture 270 miles (430 km) long. The San Andreas fault system – 60 miles (96 km) wide and 800 miles (1280 km) long – and its associated systems continues to generate tremors, and the whole shifts on average about 1–11/2 inches (2.5–3 cm) a year.

In October 1989 there was another serious earthquake along the San Andreas fault (6.9 on the Richter scale), which, in addition to killing nearly 300 people and damaging many buildings, caused a freeway and a section of the Bay Bridge linking San Francisco with Oakland to collapse. The quake was followed by a massive fire in the Oakland hills, and another quake in January 1994.

Such devastation must have reminded Californians of the predictions of Edgar Cayce. He had predicted destruction and minor earth disturbances from 1980 to 1990 as a preliminary to much greater destruction that will occur in Los Angeles and San Francisco in the last decade of the millennium.

Nostradamus appears to have prophesied earthquakes for Nice, Monaco, Rheims, Pisa, Genoa, Savona, Siena, Capua, Modena and Malta (X:60). A very specific earthquake for "Mortara" and the sinking of part of England is quite specifically prophesied in IX:31. Nostradamus's reference to an earthquake in California is not clear, except that it will occur in May.

COMETS IN COLLISION

The Russian scientist Immanuel Velikovsky (1895–1979) was born in the small town of Vitebsk in 1895. The son of a Hebrew scholar and publisher, he was vividly aware of the disaster and catastrophe stories in the Old Testament.

Velikovksy was a physician and psychologist who had studied at both the Medvednikov Gymnasium in Moscow, where he graduated with distinction, and at the universities of Moscow and Edinburgh. He then went to work in Berlin, where he became one of the founders of Scripta Universitatis. Here he met Albert Einstein, who was in charge of the organization's physics publishing programme.

In the 1930s Velikovsky went to Vienna to study psychoanalysis and the ideas of Sigmund Freud. It was at this time that he first became interested in ancient civilizations. The idea for his first and probably greatest book, *Worlds in Collision*, was born here. In this he wrote about the momentous natural phenomenon which had once devastated the world. The major ancient civilizations, including the Greeks, Samoans, American Indians, Chinese, Egyptians and Hebrews had left accounts of this cataclysmic event, which Velikovsky believed had been caused by a comet. He started putting together the pieces of evidence offered by the ancient scribes, and eventually reached the conclusion that it must have happened 3500 years ago.

The Bible gives one of the symptoms of the event as the Sun standing still in the sky. This Velikovsky dated to 1450 BC. Other cultures, on the other side of the world, recorded an enormously long night, the obverse of the experience noted in the Middle East – the same event seen from different sides of the earth. Velikovsky interpreted this as the approach of a huge comet, which had the effect of temporarily slowing down the Earth's axial rotation.

Velikovsky maintained that during a 52-year period from around 1502 BC to 1450 BC the Earth had been struck twice by the tail of this enormous comet, which had erupted from Jupiter, the largest planet in the solar system. These collisions had caused tidal waves, earthquakes and volcanic eruptions which radically altered the geography of the planet.

As a result, maybe whole continents like Atlantis sank into the ocean while new landmasses were raised from the sea bed. The sky rained fire, noxious gases, and millions of white-hot rock and tektite fragments. The two poles may even have reversed or at least fluctuated in position.

The comet, declared Velikovsky, threatened the stability of Mars as it passed before finally becoming the planet we know today as Venus. Venus would be extremely hot, he said, owing to its recent life as a comet, and it would have high concentrations of hydrocarbons in its atmosphere and a disturbed rotation. These notions were to be verified by space probes decades after Velikovsky's pronouncements.

Velikovsky predicted correctly that the Moon would have strong magnetic activity, that its surface would have a carbide and aromatic hydrocarbon content, and that Jupiter would be found to give out strong radio emissions.

You can imagine the furore his ideas caused in scientific circles. How could this be, they all cried. The establishment tried to block the publication of his work, but Velikovsky outsmarted his critics by allowing mass-market publications like Readers Digest and Harpers to publish his findings in America, thus assuring widespread awareness of his theories.

Some scientists still do not fully accept his ideas, despite the accuracy of many of his predictions. If we were visited by a huge comet in 1500 BC and again in

1450 BC, as has been recorded in many holy books, and as Velikovsky believed, what is to prevent a similar "second coming" by a destructive natural phenomenon from space in 2000 AD?

THE BIRTH OF VENUS

The ancients described the planet Venus as an intensely bright body, and ranked it second only in importance to the Sun and the Moon. Today it is just a small speck in the sky. Velikovsky believed that Venus erupted into life with spectacular results, an event recorded by many ancient civilizations.

The Aztecs called Venus "the star that smoked" and Quetzalcoatl ("the Feathered Serpent"). Their holy books record how at one time "the sun refused to show itself and during four days the world was deprived of light. Then a great star appeared; it was given the name Quetzalcoatl ... [and] a great number of people ... died of famine and pestilence."

The Greeks tell of how Phaeton (the "blazing star") nearly destroyed the world by fire, and then was transformed into Venus. The Jewish Talmud describes its comet-like appearance as "fire hanging down from the planet Venus", while the Midrash describes the "brilliant light of Venus blazing from one end of the cosmos to the other". The Assyrians called Venus "the fearful dragon ... who is clothed in fire".

In China, at the time of the Emperor Yao, "the sun during a span of ten days did not set" and "a brilliant star issued from the constellation Yin", demonstrating gravitational effect on the Earth during the birth of Venus.

CHANGING MAGNETIC FIELDS

Our view of the solar system is gradually progressing away from the unchanging perfect rotating sphere studded with stars envisaged by the ancients to one of an altogether more dynamic and less stable system.

The planet's orbits and axes can, it seems, be affected by a whole range of other bodies moving randomly through the solar system.

Changes in climate have been observed to coincide with changes in the Earth's magnetic field. The nature of the relationship is not known, but the sudden extinction of whole species of animals – dinosaurs are a good example – may have coincided with abrupt changes in the Earth's magnetic field. These changes have now been proved (see below).

Now, if these magnetic changes sound comfortably far away in time, think again. Researchers have found compelling evidence in the ashes from Australian Aboriginal camp fires that the North and South poles were in very different positions from where they are today. Indeed, a complete reversal of the poles is indicated. The changes of magnetic direction and their associated upheavals have taken place relatively recently.

A sudden reversal of magnetic poles, as has happened in the past, would cause both serious earthquakes along existing tectonic fault lines and huge tidal waves, generated by movements of the ocean floor. It would then be easy to imagine sinking islands, flooded coastal areas and low-lying inland areas, and even some ocean floors rising clear of the waterline. Many areas would experience flooding every bit as total as the one that taxed Noah's ingenuity. Predictions of such events by prophets like Edgar Cayce have been dismissed, but in view of this new evidence they should perhaps be reconsidered.

If the Earth were to tilt suddenly the planet would be swept by hurricanes and tidal waves. There is evidence to support the notion that such cataclysmic changes have occurred in the past. The extensive coal deposits in Britain are a good indication that in the Carboniferous era when the deposits formed the region was tropical, with extensive fern forests and swamps. Large areas of North America were similarly covered in rainforest. By contrast, western parts of Australia and southern Africa were buried under tons of ice.

One possible explanation, offered by Alfred Wegener in the 1920s, is of continental drift, but this presupposes that large land masses have "drifted" thousands of miles from their original positions. With the "axis flip" scenario it seems plausible that herds of mammoths were happily grazing in a warm Siberia until one fateful day the climate changed. The freeze was so rapid as to render the meat of the mammoths trapped in the ice still edible and even palatable after long periods of time. One mammoth was found to have undigested flowers in its stomach. A contrary view is that mammoths were always Arctic dwellers, but this seems unlikely. Such a harsh environment would surely not have provided enough vegetation for them to grow so large.

Experiments with gyroscopes (fast-spinning flywheels mounted on spindles) show that, given the right impetus, they will flip over and then quickly resume a new stable rotational position. The Earth could be viewed as a gyroscopic-type system, which requires the impetus of a large passing body – such as Venus or an asteroid – to give it the necessary gravitational impetus to tilt over.

An electrical engineer called Hugh Brown suggested in 1967 that the Earth's axis tilted through 90 degrees as recently as 7000 years ago. Brown's idea of regular polar shifts seems improbable, but the occasional cataclysmic axial flip is very much in the realm of the possible.

One advocate of Brown's theory, Adam Barber, predicted in a pamphlet – optimistically entitled The Coming Disaster Worse than the H-Bomb – that a 135-degree flip would occur in the next 50 years, at least before 2005. Fortunately, this prediction can be taken with a rather large grain of salt, but writings on the subject by Peter Warlow, published in the Journal of Physics in 1978, deserve to be taken more seriously.

Warlow puts the sudden axial flip at 180 degrees; that is, the North and South poles actually swap places. He successfully demonstrated this with a model, and backed it up with sound calculations. The flip occurs once roughly every 2000 years, he thinks.

Like Velikovsky, Warlow takes the evidence of myths very seriously. He claims that the Egyptians recorded four separate such swaps, during which the Sun appeared to reverse its motion across the sky. The most recent of them occurred, so he says, in 700 BC and again in 1500 BC, the latter corresponding to Velikovsky's dating and to the destruction of the Minoan civilization in Crete.

THE MAGNETIC PROOF

The geological record shows that the Earth's magnetic field has periodically reversed, with disastrous consequences for most living things, including man.

The geological record of these total polarity reverses is preserved in molten rock which has cooled at different periods in geological time. Every time such a rock solidifies it preserves a weak magnetic field induced by the Earth's gravitational field. Active volcanoes producing newly cooled lava and even man-made objects, like cooling pig iron, will take up the same weak field.

Even fireplaces will, in the course of heating and cooling, gather to themselves this weak field. Work has been done on both Australian Aboriginal and pre-Roman English fireplaces to catalogue the condition of the Earth's magnetic field at specified historic times.

Geologists have studied the ocean floor around the spreading mid-ocean ridges and have discovered a series of bands of rock which have solidified at different times, the furthest from the ridge being the oldest in geological time. Reading these bands, geologists discovered that the Earth's field has reversed more than 20 times in the strata so far sampled. The last flip, or reversal, apparently lasted only for 2000 years.

Even over a short period in recent history a degree of wandering of the north magnetic pole has been identified. In the early 17th century magnets pointed 11 degrees east of north. By 1643 they pointed 4 degrees east of north, and by the 1650s they had temporarily returned to due north.

PLAGUES AND THE BLACK DEATH

A virulent new strain of cholera emerges in India, and an outbreak of diphtheria breaks out in ex-Soviet Russia.

Recent outbreaks of deadly diseases confirm a growing trend that has been worrying scientists for the last decade. It is slowly dawning that the triumph of medical science over disease is no longer as inevitable as it seemed back in the 1950s. The bugs are fighting back, most worryingly by becoming drug-resistant.

Evolution works for bugs, too: the hardiest specimens are the ones that survive. Tuberculosis, which kills 3 million people a year worldwide, is beginning to acquire antibiotic resistance. In the USA a dangerous alliance has been formed between AIDS and tuberculosis. Another former scourge, malaria, is now making a comeback, claiming 2 million deaths per year worldwide. The fight against it is being hampered by both the drug-resistance of the microscopic parasite that causes the disease and by pesticide-resistance in the mosquitoes that carry it.

This has been partly countered by an acceleration in drug research and the production of even stronger drugs to deal with each new threat. But drugs are not winning the race, and even in industrialized countries thousands of people are dying every year from antibiotic-resistant infections which they pick up in hospital while receiving treatment for less serious conditions.

Man's intrusion into the tropical rainforests has exposed him to new reservoirs of infection from animals and insects which are further taxing the ingenuity of the scientists. Several of these apparently "new" diseases are probably caused by old monkey viruses, including AIDS, Ebola and Marburg fever. However, if you thought that you were only at risk from such diseases in tropical regions, think again. In the eastern USA the rapid increase of Lyme disease is due primarily to new housing developments being built close to wooded areas, as the bacteria responsible are carried by mice and deer, their normal hosts.

New farming and food processing procedures also put us at risk from bacteria and viruses. While often hygienic in the accepted sense of the word, these processes provide exotic mixing vessels for new infections. Recent salmonella and listeria scares in the UK, Europe and North America have arisen from intensive breeding of hens in batteries, a procedure which did not exist on a large scale until the 1960s.

The food industry's practice of using every last piece of slaughtered animal has meant that unwholesome remains now re-enter the food chain as food for another animal. Recent outbreaks of "mad cow disease" have been caused by this practice, the brains of infected animals being recycled and fed to cattle. This would never normally occur in nature; left to their own devices, cows would not eat meat. The only parallel may be found in New Guinea, where the transmission of Creutzfeld-Jakob's Disease was traced to the cannibalistic practice of one person eating the infected brains of another.

Genetic mutation by bacteria and viruses can produce new "super" germs. Dangerous strains of influenza have been found in south China, where integrated pig and duck farming is practised. The food interdependence of these two types of animals has produced a "genetic mixing vessel" which is recombining different flu viruses to form new and more virulent types.

Many viruses can undergo genetic change at frightening speed in response to environmental conditions. As a result of this "genetic forcing house", some very unpleasant new viruses and bacteria have come into existence. The coincidence of a few factors favourable to them could lead to an epidemic of appalling proportions. Consider AIDS: suppose that instead of transmission by body fluids this disease passed from one person to another via aerial infection, in the same way as influenza. The arrival of something as transmissible as influenza and as virulent as some of the viruses introduced from new "gene pools" or from animals could make the Black Death or the 1918 flu pandemic, which claimed millions of lives in Europe, seem mild.

It would be natural justice if the Apocalypse arrived not from the heavens but from the soil and forests that man has been systematically destroying: a case of the Earth striking back!

THE BLACK DEATH

The Black Death, or bubonic plague, has still not been completely eradicated, although outbreaks are now rare and deaths few. It first appeared in Europe during the reign of the Roman emperor Justinian, in AD 542, and in the Middle Ages accounted for millions of deaths as it ravaged the continent repeatedly. With each successive epidemic it lessened in severity as people built up immunity to it, so that by the 20th century it became almost confined to warmer climates.

One of the few recorded outbreaks of the disease in Western Europe in the 20th century occurred in the 1920s in England. Workmen engaged upon building a railway cutting near Lewes, in Sussex, unwittingly dug into an old plague pit, undisturbed for centuries. Before long the men began to succumb to an illness which was initially diagnosed as pneumonia. Several of the workmen died before the authorities realized that they were dealing with something a great deal more sinister and hastily quarantined everyone in danger. Eventually the crisis was brought under control, but it is sobering to realize that the seeds of death in the form of plague bacteria can survive in the soil for centuries.

NATURE MEETS THE SUPERNATURAL

An ancient apocalyptic theme is assuming new prominence as

the 20th century winds down to its end: the accelerating

destruction of the environment.

Nuclear accidents, oil spills, global warming, vanishing forests, rapid desertification of vast areas of Africa, the greenhouse effect, damage to the ozone layer, the sighting of comets and meteors, the arrival of new plagues and the distortion of usual climatic patterns – all these bring to mind similar environmental happenings and motifs written about in the Bible.

The Apocalypse of St John speaks of the breaking of the seven seals. The first four seals released the well-known four Horsemen of the Apocalypse, plague, famine, war and death (6:1–8). The fifth seal revealed saints and martyrs. The sixth seal revealed natural and ecological disasters (6:12–9:2): "And, lo, there was a great earthquake; and the sun became black as sackcloth of hair, and the moon became as blood". The sky and sun sometimes show strange lighting effects before an earthquake, and the moon taking a bloody cast has always been considered an omen as well as being a symptom of natural disaster.

Possibly a fall of great comets or meteors is indicated in "the stars of heaven fell unto the earth, even as a fig tree casteth her untimely figs, when she is shaken of a mighty wind" (6:13). The shaking might refer to a wobbling of the Earth's axis, which is likely to accompany the arrival of these destructive heavenly bodies.

With the destruction of the ozone layer which "departed as a scroll when it is rolled together" humankind will be forced to seek shelter wherever it can find it. The next verse (6:15) tells how at that awful time everyone, from kings and rich men down to ordinary free men, will hide "themselves in the dens and in the rocks of the mountains". In the recent past this verse was interpreted as the population escaping nuclear fallout in underground shelters. With such a possibility receding, it might be more appropriate to read this as some ecological disaster.

In the next chapter St John sees in his vision "four angels standing on the four corners of the earth, holding the four winds of the earth, that the wind should not blow on the earth, nor on the sea, nor on any tree". This verse conjures up an eerie vision of a silent land with not a breath of wind, that pregnant pause before disaster strikes.

Before the full horrific forces of destruction are released, a voice commands that the servants of God be identified by a mark on their foreheads so that they can escape harm. Interestingly, the same marking is carried out by the Beast, so that he, like God, will be able to recognize his own.

Until this is done, the avenging angels are instructed to "hurt not the earth, neither the sea, nor the trees" (7:3). It is almost a direct plea to our age to cease raping the earth, polluting the sea, and cutting down the once great forests of the Amazon.

Finally, after the seventh seal has been opened, there is a period of silence before "there were voices, and thunderings, and lightnings, and an earthquake" (8:5). The earthquake precedes widespread volcanic eruptions from which fire, hail and blood rain down on the vegetation. Then a "great mountain burning with fire" (8:8) turns the sea to a blood colour, poisoning one-third of the fish in the ocean.

The third trumpet brings yet greater destruction, "and there fell a great star from heaven, burning as it were a lamp, and it fell upon the third part of the rivers, and upon the fountains of waters". The star is named Wormwood, which does not appear in any catalogue of stars. The word is used as a pun on the bitter herb which went into the making of the drink absinthe, "and the third part of the waters became wormwood; and many men died of the waters, because they were made bitter" (9:10–11) or poisonous.

This might indicate a poisoning of water supplies, perhaps by some new plague from outer space. Another ambiguous passage concerns a type of poisonous locust which is sent to plague mankind (see panel).

When the fourth trumpet sounds more cosmic changes occur, reminiscent of Velikovsky's theories of cosmic cataclysm: "the third part of the sun was smitten, and the third part of the moon, and the third part of the stars; so as the third part of them was darkened, and the day shone not for a third part, and the night likewise" (8:12).

This ends the passages in the Apocalypse of St John which can be read as having ecological significance.

SUPERNATURAL LOCUSTS

The fifth trumpet provokes a strange race of creatures to emerge from the fires of the volcanoes, "there came out of the smoke locusts upon the earth"(9:3). These locusts were commanded to kill men who were not protected by the seal of God upon their foreheads. They were to kill with stinging tails like scorpions, but their victims were to die slowly over five months. These locusts sound more like demons than animals. They are described as being like horses decked with armour; they had the faces of man, and wore, or looked as if they wore, iron breastplates, with gold crowns on their heads. They could be looked upon as demons from the bowels of the earth, perhaps even from Hell itself.

It is not impossible, though, that they were as natural as the volcanoes from which they sprang, being some kind of creature whose bite provokes illness and finally death after five months of suffering. As locusts were very familiar creatures to the authors of the Bible, it seems strange to use the word for anything other than some kind of flying insect.

APOCALYPTIC WEATHER

In the first three years of the 1990s world weather has been distinctly weird. In one 12-month period alone the three most damaging climatic disasters in US history occurred.

In September 1992, Hurricane Andrew devastated Florida. Then, in March 1993, a giant blizzard swept from Florida to Maine. The US National Weather Service called it "the single biggest storm of the century", because it released more snow, hail, rain and sleet than any other US storm since 1888. The relentless rain brought floods to the American Midwest, wreaking damage that may, in dollar terms, make it the costliest weather disaster of all time.

The director of the Weather Service, Albert Friday, wondered if these events actually indicated not just a shift in the weather, but a more dramatic shift in the climate. There have always been natural disasters, but the number witnessed in recent years is verging on the apocalyptic. Even storms in southeastern Spain, which did not make the world news, turned the sky a sombre green, flushed the bats from their normal habitat, and resulted in the region of Murcia being declared a disaster zone.

Tropical cyclones, variously called typhoons (in the East) or hurricanes (in the West), are among the most powerful and destructive earthly phenomena known to man, capable of travelling at terrific speeds (up to 200mph/316km/h) and covering vast areas (up to 580 sq miles/1500 sq km). Fortunately, as hurricanes form over the sea, meteorologists usually have time to forecast their moves, and quite often they blow themselves out before reaching land.

In September 1989 Hurricane Hugo crossed the eastern seaboard of the USA at a breath-taking maximum speed of 160mph (260km/h), killing 71 people and causing $10 billion worth of damage. At peak strength such a wind can release energy that is equivalent to 25 Hiroshima-type hydrogen bombs.

In August 1992 Hurricane Andrew swept across Florida, causing $16 billion worth of damage in and around Miami. It was one of the most expensive natural disasters in recorded history. Every year as many as 50 cyclones rage through the tropics, but seldom do they hit such heavily populated areas. Thunderstorms kill more people in the USA than any other natural phenomenon.

On the other side of the Atlantic, on 16 October 1987, the south of Britain awoke to find a landscape devastated by a freak storm, which disrupted lines of communication and blocked many routes into the capital. The London Stock Exchange was forced to close down early as a result of the difficulties. Winds were stronger than any experienced in southern Britain in the previous 200 years, with gusts exceeding 80mph (130km/h). More than 19 million trees were uprooted in just a few hours, some falling on iron railings with such force that the spikes were driven deep into the timber.

All this took place despite a forecast of mild weather issued by the Meteorological Office only hours before the storm hit southern Britain (see panel). The total financial cost of this natural disaster was £1.5 billion ($2.2 billion).

On the next day of financial trading, Monday 19 October 1987, a crisis of another sort struck when almost all of the world's stock markets went into virtual free-fall. More value was wiped off stock prices in that week than had been lost in the stock market crash of 1929 during the same period of time. Were the two events connected? Had some mysterious, unknown cycle reached its crescendo, both on the physical plane and in that vast psychological arena which determines the prices of stocks and shares?

An even stronger, but not so widely publicized, wind hit Britain in January 1990, on Burns' Day (named after the Scottish poet Robert Burns), when daytime winds reached a furious 107mph (173km/h) and claimed a toll of at least 47 lives.

These and other disasters have piled one on top of another in such a short period of time that the world's main insurance market, Lloyds, has been brought to its financial knees by the sheer weight of claims. In the coming decade we may have to face increasingly vicious and destructive natural phenomena as the climatic system continues to destabilize.

MODERN WEATHER PROPHETS

Modern-day meteorologists, though they are equipped with the most up-to-date information technology, seem to be no more accurate in their predictions than their entrail-reading predecessors.

Meteorologists and astrologers have a great deal in common. Both have a long history of using precise observations and tables as the basic tools of interpretation, and in both professions that added bit of intuitive flair is still required to interpret the chart and draw the right and relevant conclusions from the mass of confusing data thrown up.

British meteorologists certainly drew the wrong conclusions from the chart for the night of 16 October 1987. Likewise, modern astrologers, even with the aid of computer-produced charts, can be way off target with their predictions. By contrast, the Elizabethan astrologer Simon Foreman could predict the day of his death without so much as a pocket calculator to help him.

For many centuries, meteorology was in fact the step-child of astrology. The greatest thinkers of antiquity regarded it as self-evident that weather conditions were governed by the stars. Thinking in this area may yet come full circle when the relationship linking conditions active in the solar system, such as sunspots, and atmospheric conditions are better understood.

HELL ON EARTH: VOLCANOES

Volcanoes are perhaps the natural phenomena which bear the closest resemblance to Hell in man's imagination. A computer file of active volcanoes compiled between 1950 and 1975 listed no fewer than 700.

By 1981, the computer file of potentially active volcanoes listed over 1300 of them. Volcanoes are destructive enough in themselves, but there is an even more insidious side to them.

On 27 August 1883, the Indonesian island of Krakatoa literally blew itself up as a result of volcanic activity, killing more than 36,000 people and spewing tons of pumice into the atmosphere. So much of this material was released that the heat from the Sun was not able to reach the Earth's surface, and temperatures around the world were significantly lowered for many months.

That was the effect of just one volcano! A succession of such explosions could rapidly precipitate a chain reaction. Minute rock particles with glassy fragments, pumice, superheated steam and sulphuric acid drops can spread amazingly quickly over large areas. (In 1982, El Chichon in Mexico spread a veil of 20 million tonnes of sulphuric acid droplets around the world in less than a month.)

It may take months for the dust and rock particles to finally settle out of the atmosphere, but the sulphuric acid droplets can ride the winds for years. The resultant "dust-veils" cause beautiful sunsets and strange optical effects, like the blue moon reminiscent of St Mark's words about the Apocalypse: "the sun shall be darkened, and the moon shall not give her light" (13:24).

Reduced temperatures on Earth might trigger other apocalyptic effects. The extra gases, sulphuric acid and dust particles belched out into the atmosphere by these eruptions would reduce the atmospheric temperature sufficiently to give the CFCs (chlorofluorocarbons) the catalyst they have been waiting for, enabling them to commence a wholesale "slaughter" of the ozone layer.

If this scenario comes to pass, then Armageddon will look tame by comparison. The Earth's ecosystem is delicately balanced. The onset of excessive volcanic activity would greatly increase the depletion of the ozone layer, leading to a fall in crop yields and a horrendous rise in skin cancers and burns.

The Apocalypse of St John does not use the word volcano, but nevertheless has some pretty accurate descriptions of phenomena that we would recognize as volcanoes. These are called upon by the angels in the last days to help destroy mankind. The angels are commanded to sound seven trumpets, the first of which ushers in a firestorm, "hail and fire mingled with blood, and they were cast upon the earth: and the third part of trees was burnt up, and all green grass was burnt up" (8:7). Such a firestorm has got to be the fruit of widespread volcanic eruptions.

The destruction continues with the second trumpet, "and as it were a great mountain burning with fire was cast into the sea: and the third part of the sea became blood; and the third part of the creatures which were in the sea, and had life, died; and the third part of the ships were destroyed" (8:8–9). This passage is reminiscent of the eruption of Vesuvius in AD 79, when those who were rowing away from the quay at Herculaneum were destroyed.

The fifth trumpet provokes a strange mixture of natural and supernatural disasters for man, "and there arose a smoke out of the pit, as the smoke of a great furnace; and the sun and the air were darkened by reason of the smoke of the pit." (9:3). From this fiery pit there emerges a strange locust-type creature.

St John would seem to have been under no illusions that volcanoes would be called upon by God's angels to destroy mankind.

DESTRUCTION OF ATLANTIS

Probably the most violent volcanic explosion in ancient times occurred on the Aegean island of Santorini (or Thera), 70 miles (113 km) north of Crete, in c. 1645 BC. It was probably the largest volcanic explosion known to man. Santorini today consists of three islands. These lie round a great expanse of water marking the huge caldera, or crater, where Santorini used to be before the volcanic explosion. Two volcanic islets are now at the centre of the water. The younger of these is still intermittently active.

The eruption began with an explosion which shot a column of debris 20 miles (30 km) high and scattered it over the whole of the eastern Mediterranean. When sea water finally entered the huge crater, it quickly turned to steam, exploding with unimaginable force and sending thousands of cubic miles of steam and fragmented lava into the air.

The crater measures about 7 miles (11 km) from north to south and close to 5 miles (8 km) from east to west, an area of 35 square miles (90 sq km) and reaching a depth of up to half a mile. The volume of rock displaced is estimated at about 14–16 cubic miles (60–65 cu km), an unimaginably enormous quantity which would have been pulverised, melted and even vaporized by the force of the blast.

It has been suggested that this monumental blast destroyed the civilization of "Atlantis" in nearby Minoan Crete. If such a place had indeed existed, it would have been covered with ash and pumice within a few hours. The tidal wave generated by the massive explosion would have wrecked the coastline of Crete and even reached up to Knossus, "sinking" Atlantis. If this is so, then it ended an entire civilization of considerable complexity. Such an explosion could also wipe out a modern civilization.

BOMBS FROM HEAVEN: METEORS

A meteor may strike at any moment – the miracle is that it has not happened many times before. The solar system contains many bodies that could wreak havoc on Earth.

An apocalyptic event took place in Siberia in the early morning of 30 June 1908. An eye witness of the terrifying occurrence recounts:

"When I sat down to have my breakfast beside my plough, I heard sudden bangs, as if from gunfire. My horse fell to its knees. From the north side above the forest a flame shot up. Then I saw that the fir forest had been bent over by the wind, and I thought of a hurricane. I seized hold of my plough with both hands so that it would not be carried away. The wind was so strong it carried soil from the surface of the ground, and then the hurricane drove a wall of water up the Angora [River]."

The farmer and his horse were more than 125 miles (201 km) from where the disaster struck. The farmer had felt the effects of a great natural phenomenon: a meteorite hitting the Earth. A rock the size of four or five supertankers ploughing into the Earth at a speed some 40 times faster than a bullet, and white hot from passing through the atmosphere, can cause as much damage as a huge nuclear bomb.

If this meteor had hit a large city rather than the Siberian wilderness, it would have destroyed it along with all life. One late-20th-century seer has actually predicted this very fate for London in the year 1999 – a chilling thought indeed.

Let us consider another "if". What if the meteor were the size of one of the larger asteroids (over 400 miles/650 km wide) which travel in very erratic orbits through our solar system? Might not such a mammoth meteor wipe out most of civilization as we know it? Far fetched? Certainly not to that farmer whose breakfast was so rudely interrupted, nor to the souls who were in its path, and so did not survive to give their testimony.

Scientists from Dartmouth College, New Hampshire, writing in Nature magazine, claim that Chixculub in Mexico is the impact point of a meteor which exterminated the dinosaurs. Whether this is true or not, a massive crater more than 120 miles (190 km) wide can be caused by a meteorite only several miles wide.

The impact at Chixculub threw up dust and debris with such force that particles have been found 1000 miles (1600 km) away in Haiti. Scientists reckon that the resulting worldwide cooling caused by the screen of dust and debris in the atmosphere might well have wiped out the dinosaurs. Man, despite technology, is probably less resilient than the dinosaurs were, and would succumb rapidly to the major climatic shift that would be caused by such a phenomenon.

According to Willaru Huayta, a Peruvian descendant of the Quechua nation, 2013 will mark the end of the current Inca calendar. In this year he predicts that a huge asteroid will pass close to the Earth's orbit, and will cause by its gravitational field a number of catastrophes. He states that the meteor will be three times larger than Jupiter. Interestingly, Jupiter is often implicated in terrestrial disasters, possibly because of its size. When this asteroid has spun away from the Earth's orbit and the resultant cataclysms have subsided, what remains of mankind will, according to Huayta, become a "seed" people, in the same way that Noah's children allegedly repopulated the Earth. These people will be the new Adam and Eve and the basis of the "sixth generation" as defined by the Incas. This event is well within the bounds of possibility, and would give a concrete meaning to the idea of a New Age.

Even a concentrated shower of much smaller meteorites striking a heavily populated area could cause more immediate damage than a concerted nuclear strike. Just imagine the damage if our protective atmospheric skin were to be thinned out as a result of this, with its concomitant temperature drop plus increase in ultraviolet and cosmic radiation.

Apart from a few well-known exceptions, like Halley's Comet, no one knows how to predict the paths of a fraction of the meteors passing through the solar system. Even Halley's Comet did not show up quite as brightly as predicted the last time it passed Earth in the 1980s. So who can say what is hurtling towards us?

WARNINGS FROM THE ASTEROID BELT

The asteroid belt is a group of fragments (some larger than 40 miles/ 644 km across) which orbits the Sun between the paths of Jupiter and Mars. Some of these monsters, which can exceed 400 miles (650 km) in width, have very irregular paths. Astronomers have yet to work out these out, but they known not to follow regular ellipses round the Sun.

Asteroids are thought to be the remains of a tenth planet which exploded at some time in the past. According to Dr David Hughes of Sheffield, England, there are perhaps 100,000 "small" asteroids floating around in the solar system that we cannot detect because of their size. He defines "small" as about 33/4 miles (6 km) across. They are important because a glancing blow by an asteroid this size would produce a crater large enough to swallow two average-size cities.

GLOSSARY

Antichrist St John the Divine predicted in the Book of Revelation that a false Messiah – the Antichrist – will appear shortly before the end of the world. Some commentators maintain that Nostradamus predicted three Antichrists, of which Napoleon and Hitler were the first two, but the traditional view is that there is only one Antichrist, yet to come. The Antichrist is also mentioned in the Epistles of St John.

Apocalypse A revelation concerned with the state of the end of the world, usually applied to the last book of the New Testament, the Revelation of St John the Divine.

Ascendant The exact zodiacal degrees of the horizon at any particular time, most usually the time of a birth.

Astral projection The ability of projecting consciousness out of the body to a distant place or time, or another plane of reality.

Astrology The art or science of charting the position of the planets, zodiac and other heavenly bodies at a specific time and place, often a specific birth, and drawing conclusions therefrom.

Branchus The Oracle of Apollo at Didyma in ancient Greece. Branchus was a son of Apollo, and his oracle can be traced back to the seventh century BC. It is upon the methods of this oracle that Nostradamus based his methods as explained in Century I, Quatrain 2.

Cabbala Ancient Jewish metaphysical system used by modern-day European magicians as a 'map' of the other planes and worlds of the universe.

Capet Name of an earlier French dynasty than the Bourbon family of which Louis XVI was the head. However, the word was often used in a looser sense by Nostradamus to mean any French ruler, or indeed any reigning king.

Caput and Cauda Draconis Ancient Latin phrases meaning 'the Dragon's Head' and 'the Dragon's Tail' – the highest and lowest points of the moon's 'wobble' on its orbit around our planet.

Century By this Nostradamus meant a group of 100 quatrains rather than a period of a hundred years. He did not complete every Century.

Cosmology   Theoretical account of the nature of the universe, particularly with reference to space-time relationships.

Divination   The art of obtaining the knowledge of future events through specific techniques – not necessarily divinely inspired, as prophecy is supposed to be.

Elementals   The spirits of the four classical elements Fire, Air, Water and Earth.

Feng-shui   The Chinese art of selecting the best positioning for houses or tombs in order to maximize the owner's luck. Feng-shui is not directly related to European geomancy.

Geomancy   A technique of divination which uses 16 four-line figures generated from dots made at random on paper or the earth, which are often related to gnomes, or the elemental spirits of the earth. (Not to be confused with Feng-shui or Chinese geomancy.)

Gregorian Calendar   The Calendar that replaced the Julian Calendar and corrected the calculation of leap years.

Hieroglyph   A form of symbolic writing practised by the ancient Egyptians. In the 16th century the word applied simply to any symbolic picture or sign.

I Ching   Chinese book of divination based on 64 hexagrams or figures made up of six lines, one on top of the other, either broken (Yin) or whole (Yang).

Ifa   An African form of divination which is based on Arabic geomancy.

Judicial astrology   Astrology that is largely concerned with the judgment of the horoscope of a particular individual in order to diagnose that same individual's character and to predict his or her destiny.

Julian Calendar   The calendar first adopted by Julius Caesar in 46 BC and used in Europe until the late 16th century in Catholic countries and even later in Protestant and Orthodox countries.

Malachy   A saint who was the supposed author of a list of Latin mottoes, one for each pope through to the end of the papacy. After the motto of the current pope there are only two more mottoes and thus only two more popes before the demise of the papacy.

Metaplasmic Pertaining to the process of altering a word by the addition, removal, transposition or substitution of a letter or letters.

Midheaven The exact zodiacal degrees of the maximum elevation above the horizon at any particular time, most usually the time of a birth.

Millennium A period of 1000 years, usually measured since the birth of Christ, at the end of which a new age is to be ushered in.

Monophysitism A heresy which arose in the fifth century, denying the humanity of Christ. In 451 the Council of Chalcedon outlawed it, but nearly all Egyptian Christians refused to accept this ruling.

Mundane astrology The branch of judicial astrology which is concerned with the horoscopes and fate of cities and nations rather than those of individuals.

Necromancy The raising and questioning of the spirits of the dead.

Neoplatonists A school of philosophers, including Iamblichus, Proclus and Plotinus, centred around Alexandria in Egypt. Contemporaries of the early Christian Fathers, they founded their doctrines on the works of Plato.

Occult Relating to hidden or magical knowledge.

Precession of the Equinoxes A slow westward movement of the position of the Equinoxes on the plane of the celestial Equator. The effect of this is that the signs of the zodiac no longer agree with the constellations with which they were first identified. In practical terms it means that the beginning of the first sign of the Zodiac (Aries) is now entering the constellation corresponding to Aquarius, hence the dawning of the Age of Aquarius.

Prophet A person who speaks or writes divinely inspired revelations of future events.

Quatrain A four-line rhyming verse used by Nostradamus to express his predictions. All are totally self-contained, and seldom relate to the adjoining quatrain.

Seer One who practises divination or who through natural talent sees revelations of the future which may not necessarily be divinely inspired.

Sortes Divination by lots, or by opening a sacred book at random and alighting upon a specific phrase which is construed as answering the question asked.

Tarot A pack of 78 cards used since the 13th century for play and also for divination.

Yang The male principle in Chinese cosmology, represented in the *I Ching* by an unbroken line.

Yin The female principle in Chinese cosmology, represented in the *I Ching* by a broken line.

Notes

Notes